HERMANN HESSE

His Mind and Art

Hermann Hesse

»«

HERMANN HESSE
His Mind and Art

»«

MARK BOULBY
Western Reserve University

Cornell University Press

ITHACA, NEW YORK

COPYRIGHT © 1967 BY CORNELL UNIVERSITY

CORNELL UNIVERSITY PRESS

First published 1967

Library of Congress Catalog Card Number: 67–13547

PRINTED IN THE UNITED STATES OF AMERICA
BY KINGSPORT PRESS, INC.

Preface

THIS study deals in detail with what are, beyond much possibility of dispute, the major novels of Hermann Hesse. Underlying the analysis is the assumption that these novels, and not his extensive and in some ways admirable contributions as a lyric poet, constitute this writer's essential and lasting achievement.

The argument of the book proceeds from two premises: first, that there is in Hesse's work a more complex, and more coherent, set of structural patterns than has yet been shown; and, second, that a satisfactory insight into these symbolic structures is possible only if the early writings, especially *Peter Camenzind* and *Beneath the Wheel*, are taken fully into account. Hesse's work, because of its eclectic nature, reflects much of the literary and intellectual history of Germany and indeed of western Europe in the first few decades of this century. Springing from deep Swabian roots, it has many points of contact, both conscious and unconscious, not only with the Neo-Romanticism and decadence of the nineties and beyond that with the Romantic movement itself, but also with Expressionism, with the years of literary turmoil and experiment after 1918, with the psychoanalytic movement and the new orientalism; and it responds poignantly and at times bitterly to the political changes of the last fifty years. But its real merit and its survival value do not lie so much in these contacts as in the considerable feat of art by which a personal conflict is universalized—the ironic technique, a good deal subtler than has generally been appreciated, by which the growth of an exceptionally searching self-insight is given imaginative form.

The deceptive simplicity of much of Hesse's prose disguises the fact that at its best it is untranslatable. While I have done my utmost in the translations offered (which are my own throughout) to convey his essential meaning, the strong tonal and associative qualities of the writing and its gentle but ubiquitous wordplay have inevitably been largely lost. In view of the publication, in the course of the last few years, of the fundamental Mileck, Waibler, and Bareiss bibliographies, it would appear superfluous to append to this book more than a bibliography of critical works cited. The literature about Hesse is now so vast that no one could satisfactorily survey it all, unless he were prepared to devote very many years to the task; but this would be unprofitable, since a good deal of it proves on inspection to be little more than uncritical eulogy or inflated marginalia. The voluminous character of this secondary literature is possibly partly accounted for by the eclectic nature of Hesse's writings and by the consequent variety of viable lines of approach; Hesse's work has long been a rich source of doctoral theses in various languages, a cornucopia which at the moment shows little sign of running dry; and there has inevitably been much unwitting repetition. The notes give some indication of those contributions to Hesse research, among so many other interesting and stimulating ones, to which the book is especially indebted. References in the text and—where appropriate—in the notes are to Hermann Hesse, *Gesammelte Schriften*, 7 volumes (Frankfort: Suhrkamp Verlag, 1957); titles of works which are included in this selection are given in English, whereas titles of books and essays by Hesse which have not been reprinted and must be sought elsewhere have been given in German to facilitate their location; the German title of individual lyric poems has been retained.

I wish to thank the Suhrkamp Verlag for permission to quote extensively from their edition of Hesse's collected works. I am grateful also to the director of the Schiller Nationalmuseum, Marbach, for allowing me to work in the Hesse archives in 1960, when the groundwork of this book was laid; to the university libraries of Leeds, Hull, and Oxford, and of New York City College and

Western Reserve University, and to the Wiener Library (London),
for their assistance at various times; to the *Neue Zürcher Zeitung*
for providing material from its files; to the editors at Cornell University Press for their patient work on the manuscript; to my
colleague, Mrs. Ruth Angress, for assistance with the proofs; and
finally to the many persons with whom I have discussed Hesse over
the years in Britain, Germany, and the United States.

Cleveland, Ohio   MARK BOULBY
January 1967

Contents

Biographical Note

HERMANN HESSE was born in the small town of Calw, Württemberg, in 1877. At this time his father, Johannes Hesse, worked for a local publishing house, the Calwer Verlagsverein, which was under the direction of the indologist Hermann Gundert, Hesse's maternal grandfather. Both these men, as well as Hesse's mother Marie Gundert, had seen service as missionaries with the Basel Mission in the East Indies. After a childhood spent partly in Calw and partly in Basel, Hermann Hesse became in 1891 a seminarian at the Protestant Theological Seminary at Maulbronn, intending to proceed in due course to the celebrated Tübinger Stift and possibly to enter the church. In 1892 he ran away from the seminary, and his education there was shortly thereafter terminated. After some time at a high school in Bad Cannstatt and then as an apprentice at Perrot's machine shop in Calw, Hesse entered the book trade, working as a bookshop assistant, first in Tübingen (from 1895 to 1899) and subsequently in Basel. In 1899 his first volume of poetry was published. The success of the novel *Peter Camenzind* (1904) made his name and enabled him to establish himself as a free-lance writer. He married Maria Bernoulli, and they settled down in the village of Gaienhofen on Lake Constance. They had three sons. In 1911 Hesse made a five months' journey to the East Indies and Ceylon. From 1912 to 1919 he lived in Bern, working throughout the war for the Deutsche Gefangenenfürsorge and editing a newspaper for German prisoners of war. His wife's mental illness contributed to the breakup of his marriage and the end of his family life. In 1916–1917 he underwent a course of psychoanalysis. The novel *Demian* (1919) created a sensation and re-established him in the forefront of German letters. In this same year he took up residence in the village of Montagnola, near Lugano, where he continued to live and write for the rest of his life—a number of major novels and novellas, much poetry, and a good deal of criticism. He became a Swiss citizen in 1923. He was married twice more, to Ruth Wenger (in 1924) and to Ninon Dolbin (in 1931). He was awarded the Nobel Prize for Literature in 1946 and the Goethe Prize in the same year. He died in 1962.

HERMANN HESSE

His Mind and Art

"Dies 'Deuten' ist ein Spiel des Intellekts, ein oft ganz hübsches Spiel, gut für kluge, aber kunstfremde Leute, . . . die . . . nie ins Innere eines Kunstwerkes Zugang finden, weil sie am Tor stehen, mit hundert Schlüsseln daran herumprobieren und gar nicht sehen, dass das Tor ja offen ist."

HESSE, *Betrachtungen* (VII, 471)

CHAPTER 1

Peter Camenzind

RETURNING home from the atelier of the paintress with whom he has just had the misfortune to fall in love, Peter Camenzind is suddenly overcome by a storm of emotion:

And just as the wind caressed the branches of the fruit trees and the black tops of the chestnuts, rushed at them and bent them so that they groaned and laughed and trembled, so did passion play with me. On the crest of the hill I knelt down, lay down on the ground, leapt up and groaned, stamped the earth, threw away my hat, burrowed with my face in the grass, shook at the tree-trunks, wept, laughed, sobbed, raged, felt ashamed, felt ecstatic and then hopelessly depressed. After an hour everything in me was exhausted and suffocated in a sultry gloom. I thought nothing, decided nothing, felt nothing; like a sleep-walker I descended the hill, wandered through half the town, noticed a late little bar open in an out-of-the-way street, went helplessly in, drank a couple of liters of Waadtländer and got home horribly drunk in the early hours of the morning [I, 271].

The experience recounted is an almost uncontrollable outburst of the feelings, an explosion of the subconscious, quite characteristic of the psychological type to which Peter Camenzind belongs. It has the directness of intense personal reminiscence, totally unreflective in its activity, its profusion of verbs. Yet the passage begins reflectively, with one of the more conventional similes of Romantic poetic diction. It may be compared fruitfully with another excerpt, which illustrates Hesse's more usual technique:

Near Rapallo for the first time I contested swimming with the sea, tasted the harsh salt water and felt the force of the swell. All around blue, clear waves, browny yellow rocks on the beach, a deep still sky and the endless vast murmur. Again and again I was gripped by the sight of the ships gliding afar off, the black masts and the white sails or the little smoke wisp of a steamer going by in the distance. After my favorites, the restless clouds, I know of no more beautiful, no graver image of longing and wandering than such a ship, sailing a great way off, then growing smaller and vanishing into the open horizon [I, 289].

Here the unaccustomed violence has gone. This is primarily a visual memory, with its color and clarity, though there is an admixture of the tactile. There are of course also many clichés—"the harsh salt water," "the force of the swell," "deep still sky"; and the passage terminates in an almost wholly reflective piece of discourse, the conventional symbol of the ship vanishing over the horizon, the figurative meaning of which is explicitly elucidated. In fact, in *Peter Camenzind* we have an essentially reflective work; the hero, in recounting his experiences, distances himself from them, mulls them over, extracts lessons from them with which he does not fail to instruct the reader, and uses them as a starting point for a generalizing, rather sententious commentary upon life. To assist in this, the technique is essentially one of retrospect, and the wisdom is one of hindsight: "At that time of course I wasn't aware of all this," he tells us from his author's vantage point. He reiterates his earlier ignorance, since overcome: "I thought I was standing at the start of a road which led upward. I didn't know that everything I had so far experienced was just accident and that my nature and my life still lacked their own deep keynote. I didn't know that I was suffering from a longing which knows no bounds and no fulfillment in love or rest" (I, 281). His self-knowledge, when he painfully achieves it, acquires for him the quality of dogma. Armed with such dogma, he frequently addresses the reader in his didactic style: "If you do not want to listen to me and my poor words, then go unto those in whom suffering has been overcome and transfigured by a love free of all desire" (I, 311). And this movement, from the direct communication of recalled experience to detachment from it and eventually to didactic commentary upon it, is one of the most essential features of Hermann Hesse's writing;

memory and reflection are aspects of that duality which is the framework of his art.

This characteristic predates *Peter Camenzind*, of course. Thus when Hesse calls the papers of Hermann Lauscher "documents of the curious soul of a modern aesthete and eccentric" (I, 93), he is evidently already distancing himself, both by the nature of the definition and the device of the fictional biographer, from this unhappy scapegoat of his own adolescence. The journal of Lauscher, the acolyte *poète maudit*, is supposed to be a penetrating psychological document, revealing "harsh, self-tormenting love of truth" (I, 93) and largely devoid (we are told with evident irony) of the industriously polished formal perfection which Lauscher's poetic works themselves possess; and since these latter were published pseudonymously, literary detectives might have hard work establishing their connection with the journal.[1] *Hermann Lauscher* (1901) comprises a collection of stories, sketches, and poems; the little work is characterized in the preface of the fifth edition, seven years later, as the beginning of the "dangerous path of self-observation and confession";[2] it contains, therefore, the two fundamental elements of critical self-observation and lyrical self-disclosure. Hermann Lauscher, naturally, is a decadent poet caught in the Romantic agony, a poseur conscious of his pose, for whom naïve experience seems no longer possible. The style was already prefigured in *An Hour beyond Midnight*, a volume of tales and vignettes which owed something to Maurice Maeterlinck, of whose "rather sickly, self-adoring form of introversion," however, the author pleads he was even then suspicious. In the same place we are told that at this time he had not read Stefan George;[3] when he did, he took strong exception to that poet's particular species of aestheticism, "a presumptuous clique-esotericism." It is interesting that in a later comparison of George's poetry with his own Hesse remarks that for the former what counted was "a selection dictated and controlled by the will";[4] his attitude toward George, his

---

[1] Hesse is playing with the reader here, referring of course to his own *Romantic Songs* and *An Hour beyond Midnight* (both 1899).
[2] Düsseldorf, 1908, p. 5.
[3] Preface to the 1941 edition (Zurich), p. 10.
[4] *Letters* (VII, 570).

revulsion from the astounding though repressive act with which
George mastered decadence, is revelatory of certain ambiguities
inherent in Hesse's whole conception of will and will to form.

In fact also, as a true decadent and *enfant du siècle*, Hermann
Lauscher has no will at all; he does, however, have irony, although
about this too he is ironical. "Irony? We have little of that. And yet,
strangely, I often long for it. To dissolve my whole deliberate style
and blow it away into the blue like a pretty soap bubble. To transform everything into surface, to reserve for oneself all the unspoken things with sophisticated awareness as a mystery revealed.
That, I know very well, is Romanticism" (I, 199). Romanticism this
process may be—it also perhaps provides something of a key to
Hesse's style, and even to his later novels. As a late decadent
Romantic, Hermann Lauscher suffers from the obsessive intellectualization of a mode of experiencing which is inherited from
countless literary forbears; his Pre-Raphaelite posing is conducted
in the full daylight of inescapable self-observation, and the mask is
consciously though compulsively worn. He complains to his
student friends in Tübingen that he has studied more than is good
for an artist and that the best part of his creative talent has been left
behind with the naïveté of his early youth: "Now we stretch out
our arms toward the sunken islands of innocence; but we no longer
even do this with the total, unconsidered movement of an intense
pain. On the contrary, there is already an element of the conscious,
of pose and deliberateness in it" (I, 144). And Ripplein tells the
Hoffmannesque philosopher Drehdichum that the Romantic dream
of the poet as prophet is "a happily surmounted disease of poets"
(I, 146). While the desirable Lulu sees the world of these young
aesthetes for what it is, *fin de siècle*, "colorful stage-walls of words
. . . while the entire astringent [*herb*] truth of life was foreign to
them and passed them by" (I, 156). In *Hermann Lauscher*, then,
not only Romanticism but Romantic irony itself is ironized.

Hesse's chief biographer, the percipient Hugo Ball, perhaps
rather prematurely called him the last knight of Romanticism, its
rear guard. For Hesse, Otto Basler thinks,[5] Romanticism meant not
an era or a movement but an innate attitude of mind. His contacts

---

[5] In Hugo Ball, *Hermann Hesse: Sein Leben und Werk* (Zurich, 1947), p. 281,

with Romantic writers, in fact, rarely served to modify his outlook, they merely confirmed it. But he was very much a child of his age, and was above all very much a Romantic in his lifelong struggle with his own Romanticism. On Hesse's own account, *Hermann Lauscher* represents an effort "to conquer a piece of world and reality for myself and to escape the perils of a partly retiring, partly arrogant isolation." [6] The irony, the depersonalization, the attempt at times to depoetize and hence to humanize Lauscher, and above all the technique of the literary double—Lauscher relates: "I had a long talk with Hesse, who of course nagged and teased me again till I became rude" (I, 214)—all these devices represent a rather pathetic attempt to find a way beyond the impasse of the decadent literature of the day, to which Hesse's young mind had been particularly subordinated. Equally, however, they must be said to reveal the fundamental structure of that mind, the split in the personality, the unmistakable introversion.[7] *An Hour beyond Midnight* has on its first page a narcissus image which is to run throughout this author's work: "In the dark green, still water of the inlet my mirror image lay" (I, 9). The wanderer then finds a pool, in which were once reflected the first dreams of his youth, and staring into it he strives to recall his own features of yesteryear: "I looked for traits in it to remind me of that face which had gazed up at me in those days out of the same depths" (I, 23). Thus also Goldmund, thirty years further on, is to contemplate the transience of the self— and there will be several intermediaries who will do the same. One might say that Hesse eventually found his way to some degree of serenity by going inward through the door of his dichotomized self, but at the time of *Lauscher* he was far from ready to turn in this direction; the impulse was rather to flee the innate situation altogether by a turning outward. *Peter Camenzind* was to be the next, the decisive, step on this way to escape toward the external world, "a step which almost overemphasized the healthy, the

[6] Preface (1941), p. 11.
[7] The Jungian term is used here purely descriptively; it does not represent an ultimate diagnosis, still less a value judgment. As Franz Baumer points out in "Das magische Denken in der Dichtung Hermann Hesses" (diss., Munich, 1951), pp. 51–52, the introverted pattern need not be regarded at all as a negative one, a view of the matter which both Jung and Hesse would certainly have endorsed (cf., e.g., VII, 122).

natural, and the naïve . . . and in which I actually found a kind of liberation." [8]

An Hour beyond Midnight and *Hermann Lauscher*, like Hesse's first collection of poems, *Romantic Songs* (1899), are inevitably rich in Neo-Romantic cliché. In the journal the first piece, "My Childhood," which dates from as early as 1896, has all the conventional elements in the first paragraph alone: flowers, melodies, melancholy, longing, prayers, and tears, while later there is a discourse on butterflies and occasional sarcastic or sententious remarks. Throughout all these works the language is careful, elegant, often, however, merely precious; oxymorons ("blissful-wretched," "laughing-suffering," and so on) are greatly in evidence, while negatives like "indescribable" and "inexpressible," so common in the writing of a principal model, Novalis, abound.[9] Here, in the wake of the French Symbolists, language is still almost as significant for how it sounds as for what it means. The word *"herb"* ("austere," "harsh"), it is worth noticing, occurs with surprising frequency—truth is *"herb,"* knowledge is *"herb"*—as it still is in *Peter Camenzind*, where we also have the word *"herbschön"* and where the Tuscan landscape, death, and the crotchety Peter himself bear the same epithet. Perhaps austerity and astringency were experienced as a necessary corrective to the honeyed sweetness of decadent art. Of course, this overconscious art, or artistry, of the poets of "La Décadence" rarely failed to distill some dram of beauty or to make the occasional fine point; for the aesthete of the nineties the justification demanded of life was often a modest one, "a little beauty" and even *Hermann Lauscher* and *An Hour beyond Midnight*, impossibly stylized though they are, are not without merits of this kind.

Not only their fundamental psychological situation, however, but also a good deal of their incidental material is of significance for a fuller understanding of Hesse's maturer works. In his room in Tübingen in 1895 there hung a large portrait of Chopin, for characteristically it was Chopin, rather than Wagner, who was the

[8] Preface (1941), p. 12.

[9] The phenomenon of such negatives has been aptly characterized by R. Wasserscheid as "Entgrenzung" ("Die Gestaltung der Landschaft in Hermann Hesses Prosadichtung" [Staatsexamensarbeit, Cologne, 1951], p. 21).

great musical love of his youth. Hesse's first real contact with music may possibly have come through his mother (who gave him a violin on his ninth birthday), although the passionate love of the art which Ball ascribes to her is unconfirmed by her letters and diaries.[10] In the two early works under special discussion Chopin is ubiquitous, one of the most vital ingredients of the mood, and the key is naturally most often minor. In music Hesse was a conservative, and in his youth in love with the great Romantic composers. This was the period too of his initial Italianism—his first Italian journey took place in 1901. There are many allusions to Dante here, and Botticelli is admired.

But Hesse's love and enthusiasm were above all else directed to memories of his own childhood, which Lauscher already sees as being at an insufferable distance, a lost world of innocence. "There is nothing," he tells us, "more wonderful and more incomprehensible and nothing that becomes more foreign to us and that we lose more completely than the soul of the child at play" (I, 100). The passion is muted with pose and reflection, but it remains strong, and here an intense sincerity is detectable; while the intuitive sense of the significance of "play" as an expression of "soul" is no mere arid allusion to Schillerian aesthetics. Childhood, Lauscher says, "is like a treasure which slips out of playing hands and falls over the rim of a deep well" (I, 98). The call of childhood sounds through memory, which in Hesse's work has an intense and active function to perform. In "Island Dream" we hear: "It is the gift of poets that they recall their earliest years more than other people do" (I, 25); while the well into which the treasure of childhood falls is also that from which dreams are drawn. The image of the well (like that of the pool) is recurrent in Hesse's works; in the fragment "Mutter" [11] he tells of his mother's death: "I felt obscurely that with her the best part of home and childhood had been torn from me and had fallen into the deep magic well (*Märchenbrunnen*) of memory."

---

[10] Cf. K. Matthias, "Die Musik bei Thomas Mann und Hermann Hesse" (diss., Kiel, 1956), p. 197. Cf. also, however, the picture we get of Frau Marie Hesse in the fragment "Julius Abderegg."

[11] "Mutter" (Nach den Aufzeichnungen eines Neunzigjährigen, mitgeteilt von Hermann Hesse) (Kunstverein für die Rheinlande und Westfalen, Sondergabe 1911).

The magic world of memory and old longings is a lost home in the depths of the self, forgotten childhood, the source of all dreaming; thus later in "A Fragment of Diary" (1918) Hesse considers the value of "bending listening over the edge of the streams and the gorges which one has within one," [12] a direction of mind which in due course had helped to make him receptive to the doctrines and techniques of psychoanalysis.

The poet's complaint that he has sacrificed his life to his muse, and that he is old before his time, is commonplace enough. In *An Hour beyond Midnight* the image of shipwreck recurs; and with this pose of deprivation and ruin is enmeshed the genuine frustration of adolescent yearning. Like all who suffer this particular corruption of the vital instincts (one may think, for instance, of Hugo von Hofmannsthal's Claudio) Hermann Lauscher longs in vain for his great passion; like Peter Camenzind after him, he makes the mistake of constantly waiting for life to begin. Talkative as he is despite his name, his passivity is organic; he is aware that his deepest yearnings are themselves tainted with cult, the product of too much art. The sense of the transience of youth is without freshness here and may be contrasted with that felt in the later story "The Cyclone" (1913), where the experience is puzzlingly real. This theme, however, is very much Hesse's own; even in *Lauscher*, it is not a mere borrowing from the German Romantics. And there are other motifs and allusions in these early works which are the germs of vaster things. The references to Hermes Trismegistus and Jakob Böhme were no doubt fashionable; but this is not just a façade of occultism: it discloses a real interest which goes back, at the very least, to Hesse's boyhood encounter with the "theosophist" Herr Claassen. "Incipit vita nova" (in *An Hour beyond Midnight*) already touches on a question later to become fundamental to this writer, that of fate. And connections are made here, which were to prove seminal, between the aesthetic life and the religious. Hermann Lauscher confesses proudly to the religion of the aesthete: the cult of beauty can provide experiences as lofty as those of the martyrs and saints. There are many parallels—

---

[12] VII, 144. Sixteen years later, Hesse was again preoccupied with the image of the well in both versions of the so-called "Fourth Autobiography" of *The Glass Bead Game*, where Joseph Knecht's father appears as a wellmaker.

sacrifice and struggle, original sin, fall and redemption—between the novitiate of beauty and the Christian life: "These truly pious men are indeed the only worthy enemies we aesthetes have" (I, 197). Indeed, they were to turn out to be even more than this as time went on. At this stage, however, it would not do if the respected enemy were excessively contemptuous or denunciatory; hence Lauscher reads Tolstoy with reluctance. The latter's heavy, gloomy Russian way is repellent, especially in contrast to the "*dolce stil nuovo*," and the manner in which St. Martin and St. Francis preach a basically similar doctrine; in Hesse's early work St. Francis of Assisi moves as an incarnation of half-formulated ideals, blending the aesthetic and the religious in an ardent union.

When *Hermann Lauscher* was finished and published, Hesse was pleased to imagine that in this work he had left behind him forever his poetry and his youth. Then, in the preface to the uncompleted tale, "Julius Abderegg's First and Second Childhood",[13] he tells his friend, Ludwig Finckh, that this pose was evidently absurd. Indeed, toward the end of his journal, Hermann Lauscher himself seemed to feel the stirrings of repressed life within him; his subconscious revolts, and in his congenital detachment he sees that its face is but one of his own faces, that of his dearest memories and of his childhood. Like Goethe's Werther, Lauscher has to die to free his author for more and, one hopes, for better things. But he leaves behind him a gene which dictates the structure of all the rest of Hesse's work—a divided self, dark and light, passionate and ironical, confessional and observing, dreaming and analytical, listening to the subterranean dreams of childhood with the ear of the critical mind. Indeed, for this reason he may well have been christened "Lauscher" (listener). So that when his creator turns his back upon him—or only half turns it, for in the edition of 1908 he tells us that he sees no reason "to deny a part of my youth, and since I am still ready today to defend Lauscher's style" [14] —he takes this inheritance with him willy-nilly into what was planned as the novel of escape, *Peter Camenzind*.

This best seller, which was already partly written when the publisher Samuel Fischer read *Hermann Lauscher* and asked to see

---

[13] In *Prosa aus dem Nachlass* (Frankfort, 1965); written in 1902.
[14] Preface to the edition of 1908, p. 4.

further examples of its author's work, germinated while the journal was being composed.[15] The outward movement, the search for firmer ground in art and feeling, to which it owes its life, is already observable in the "Abderegg" fragment; the frailty of the new extraversion, its quivering instability, discloses itself in its language, in such coinages as *"grobschön"* (coarse-beautiful). Julius Abderegg's childhood is idyllic, close to nature, incapsulated in a sphere which no longer has the character of decadent phantasmagoria, but still remains a dream. This work—the only one in which a substantial fictional portrait, close to life, of Hesse's mother is to be found—culminates in a collision between the maternal world and that of the school, pointing beyond *Camenzind* altogether to *Beneath the Wheel* (1905), with touches which suggest that here, as later in *Beneath the Wheel*, Hesse was in part portraying his younger brother Hans. The parents are clearly Marie and Johannes Hesse (the physical description of the father is photographically precise)—an autobiographical identification which the more emancipated *Peter Camenzind* discards. If the poetic core of the major novel is already found in "Abderegg," some part of its subject matter—notably the motifs of the *Handwerker*[16] and of *Wanderschaft*—may be discovered in the contemporary fragment "Peter Bastian's Youth" (1902), meant as a laudation of the vanishing life of the wandering journeyman, and the earliest version of *Knulp* (1915). "Peter Bastian" and *Peter Camenzind* were in (perhaps superficial) competition: "Only when I finally gave up "Peter Bastian" was it possible for me to finish *Camenzind*."[17] The motif of friendship, on the basis of ardent feeling, which dominates the novel is important too in "Peter Bastian's Youth"; the hero (with his physical vigor and rustic

---

[15] Cf. "Rigi-Diary" (IV, 814).

[16] It was an ambition of Hesse's to immortalize the life of the wandering journeyman, and a note to "Peter Bastian's Youth"—which apparently refers to an aborted attempt to bring out this fragment in 1927—observes: "If I publish this fragment now I do so particularly because it describes an aspect of German folk culture, crafts and the life of the journeyman, which in my boyhood and youth still lived on in more or less the same forms and with the same customs as for centuries, while since then it has disappeared" (*Prosa aus dem Nachlass*, p. 46).

[17] *Ibid.*

origins) is a close relative of Peter Camenzind, while the tramp Quorm is the direct precursor of Knulp. That Peter Bastian–Camenzind and Quorm-Knulp were originally linked in the same tale is of some significance, for it suggests that in freeing himself from his decadent reverie the Hesse hero takes on the role of the wanderer; in essence the Romantic epigone merely puts on more workaday clothes.

Peter Camenzind remains even today a very readable book. It establishes the prototype of the characteristic lyrical, monologic style of novel, but gives little indication of the torment and profundity to be found in later works. Its opening is portentous: "In the beginning was myth.[18] As the great God wrote poems and sought expression in the souls of the Indians, the Greeks, and the Germans, so he writes again each day in the soul of every child" (I, 219).[19] This is an overture to the glorification of nature, specifically the splendor of the Bernese Oberland, for this novel is in conception a return to nature, a fact which partly explains its success. The German Naturalists, poor novelists that they were, had written about town life, especially that of Berlin, and much of the impressionism which developed from their work in the nineties was similarly confined. A return to nature, not primarily as a Romantic, neo-Rousseauistic pose, but in the spirit of a fresh, healthy and self-confident ruralism—such a thing had been missing from the bookstalls since the age of the Biedermeier. This refreshment *Peter Camenzind* supplied—hence its success with jaded palates, with those who overlooked its ambiguities.

Its author, his disturbed adolescence now behind him, sought to put his new ideals into practice. This novel is, as Ball says, a vehement attempt on the part of the writer to find himself a home, and in 1904, the year of its publication, Hesse married Maria Bernoulli ("Mia"), a sensitive, introverted girl much older than himself who was also a devoted musician. In September of that year they settled

[18] Cf. J. J. Bachofen, *Mutterrecht und Urreligion: Eine Auswahl* (Stuttgart, 1954), p. 83: "Der Anfang aller Entwicklung . . . liegt in dem Mythus" (The beginning of all evolution lies in myth).

[19] The word *"Seele"* corresponds ill to the English word "soul," especially in Hesse's usage (it is one of his favorite words). Its meaning is neither constant nor precise, but in general it must be regarded as referring to the affective self and the unconscious, and as possessing little transcendental implication.

in the village of Gaienhofen on Lake Constance, living for the first
three years in a decrepit farmhouse: "The notions and ideals which
influenced us in this were just as close to those of Ruskin and
Morris as they were to those of Tolstoy." [20] The outlook of Jeremias
Gotthelf had also made its impression on Hesse, and the fact was
that in the first years of this century in Germany there seemed to
be a pretty wide desire for escape from the cities to the simple
rustic life—"with a moral and artistic basis." No doubt the influence of Hesse's wife was predominant in this decision. But the
years at Gaienhofen subsequently revealed themselves as a vain
attempt at an idealized form of *embourgeoisement*, a long and painful failure; in *Peter Camenzind* is enshrined the initial impulse
which led to them, in the attempt to create a vigorous figure beyond the thrall of decadence, rooted in nature and in its myths.

In an essay dated 1928, Hesse tells us something of the imaginative processes of his writing. The starting point for his novels is
always the moment when a figure (*Figur*) appears spontaneously
in his imagination, which for a while can become the "symbol and
the vehicle" of his experience, his ideas, his problems:

The materialization of this mythical individual . . . is the creative
moment from which everything springs. Almost all the prose works I
have written are biographies of the soul, they are none of them
concerned with stories, intrigues, and conflicts, but they are fundamentally monologues, in which a single individual, precisely that
mythical figure, is observed in his relation to the world and to his own
ego.[21]

Such monologic narratives, Hesse confesses, are not really novels
at all, "just as little as their great prototypes, sacred to me from my
youth, such as Novalis' *Heinrich von Ofterdingen* and Hölderlin's
Hyperion, are novels."

Out of creative myth emerge not only the figures of the poetic
but also the structures of the material universe, those of nature. The
novel now moves into an evocation of the mountain world of the
eponymous hero's childhood and youth. The spirits of the mountains and the lake inscribe their "beautiful bold deeds" (I, 219)

---

[20] "On Moving into a New House" (1931; IV, 620).
[21] "An Evening of Work" (VII, 303).

upon the waiting soul of the child. "Soul," a word of immeasurable resonance in Hesse's work, refers here already to the receptive, responsive, feminine element in the psyche, upon which the "great god" and the spirits of the mountains perform their creative act. The language seeks to personify the mountains and to evoke the agony of parturition from which they sprang: "The rigid walls and cliffs spoke defiantly and with awe of ages whose sons they are and whose scars they bear. They spoke of the time when the earth burst and writhed and expelled peaks and cols from her tortured body in the groaning distress of birth" (I, 219). And now they contest, as warriors, with the foehn and with all the elements; their harmless colorful children are the flowers and the mosses, and also the trees. Like the mountains, the trees are fighters, wounded but resolute contestants for life upon the harsh high slopes, locked with the rocks in a tenacious embrace. The passage which describes them is ruminating and reflective rather than evocative of mood. The trees are more masculine, perhaps, than the mosses and the flowers and a symbol of strength and inner-directedness. "Nothing," we are told many years later, "is more holy, nothing is a better model than a beautiful strong tree"; trees strive with all their might toward one goal alone, "to fulfill their own law which dwells within them." They teach the "primeval law of life," stated thus: "I live out the secret of my seed, nothing else is my concern." [22] An esoteric symbol, then, of the striving for self-perfection, and hence androgynous, trees also come naturally to denote the mother, the source of the self. They are never described objectively, but always acquire human characteristics or else are seen as explicitly or tacitly symbolic of the universal features of evolving being. And *Peter Camenzind* adds: "Our men and women resembled them" (I, 221). In this sentence the novel makes the transition, the narrow leap, from subhuman nature to man.

"Thus I learned to look at people as though they were trees or rocks, to formulate thoughts about them" (I, 221). This phrase is typical of the author in its insistence on the reflective process. It completes the link, and we are led into the Swiss village of Nimikon, which is then described. Changelessly the generations

---

[22] "The Hiking Trip" ("Wanderung") (1920; III, 406).

follow one another, the society is firm. From the outside little blood comes in, and a good three-quarters of the villagers are called Camenzind.[23] This microcosm is not without its eccentrics, and there is room, in this intimate little world, for conflicts revelatory of "the profundity and comedy of the human condition" (I, 222). The circumstances of existence, especially the sense of dependence hereabouts upon natural forces, are said to lead to the presence of a melancholic strain, "an inclination to melancholia" (I, 223), and with this comment the novel takes a significant further step and penetrates within, toward the psyche. Hesse proceeds with deliberation from nature to man, to show man as at the outset rooted in nature, so that later the unhappy sports of decadence may stand revealed as genuine *déracinés*. This introduction is a slow, organic narrative development which evokes the desired mood, the all-embracing dominance of nature, with considerable success.

From this background Peter Camenzind is gradually detached and, as the novel proceeds, the peregrinations and vicissitudes of his uprooted existence in the wide world are steadily unfolded. Peter's dour peasant father and his eccentric Uncle Conrad stand out in his memories of childhood; his mother is oddly colorless and attains some quality of vividness only in the description of her death. He tells us that his "education" as a young child came first and foremost through nature, from his friends the mountains and the lake, the storms and the sun, the clouds; and later on there comes the grandiose awakening, the Eichendorffian revelation when he climbs the Sennalpstock to be astounded by the limitless vista from this vantage point. This is a day, he tells us, which breaks some ice in his life and seems to set all in motion. Some *patres* at the local monastery arrange for his formal education, of which the reader learns precious little, except a few largely hostile recollections. Desiring to make his way in the great wide world, Peter Camenzind studies on scholarships, makes one great friend, travels a little and falls once or twice unhappily in love. He establishes himself as a journalist and as a writer of short stories for magazines. He spends some time in Paris in dissipations, then in Basel, and then in Italy. Finally he finds peace of mind, first in caring for a helpless

---

[23] For the name "Camenzind" see "At the St. Gotthard" (1905; III, 917).

cripple, Boppi, in the Swiss city, and then after Boppi's death in a return home to Nimikon, where he apparently proposes to spend the rest of his days.

This straightforward story of the countryman who tries to make good in city life, and even among the intelligentsia, but who in the end is driven to return home, is of course the reverse print of the longing, so obsessive in German literature since Heinrich von Kleist, of the tormented Romantic striving to break out from the entanglements of his own decadence. Its movement, from within a narrow circle out into the great Without, culminating in the return within, is in various disguises, right through to *The Glass Bead Game*, the characteristic movement of Hesse's novels. Its themes are really a transliteration of those of *Hermann Lauscher*, though it ends, by a tour de force, in a half-realized wish-dream. Superficially the resemblances between these two works might appear somewhat thin, since Hermann Lauscher, to use Maurice Barrès' term again, is *déraciné*, and it seems to be Peter Camenzind's salvation that his root has never wholly parted, his contact is never completely lost. And this contact is with nature and with myth. To Peter nature at first means far more than do men. As Hesse recalled in 1917: "In my youth I had closer and more intimate relationships with landscapes and works of art than with people; indeed, I dreamed for years of a poem in which only air, earth, water, trees, mountains, and animals appeared and no people." [24] Peter Camenzind dreams of just such a universal nature poem and hopes one day "as a poet to speak the language of the forests and the rivers," aspires "in a great poem to bring close to contemporary people the generous, mute life of nature and to make it dear to them" (I, 328), to make people sense, as he does, that they are all rooted in the earth and are fragments of a cosmic whole. An expression of Peter's deepest preferences, this work was nevertheless planned with didactic intent: "However I also wanted to teach people to find springs of joy and streams of life in the fraternal love of nature" (I, 329). The absurdity of such a poetic production, in which no human being was to appear at all, eventually dawned on the poet, and, as his misanthropism was gradu-

[24] "On the Soul" (VII, 70).

ally overcome, the dream of it faded. Peter himself, a fine and healthy physical specimen, sometimes feels innately closer to an animal existence. As a child his experience of the natural forces at work all around him had been intimate and intense. The foehn, for instance, which he first hated and feared and later was able to love as "the rebel, the eternally young, the audacious warrior and bringer of spring" came in the end to denote "the sweet, lovely, all too opulent south" (I, 226), which Peter and his successors, a long procession of characters in Hesse's novels, were to yearn for and sometimes attain. Such experience, we are told, is enough for a childhood, indeed for a life: "For all these things speak . . . the language of God" (I, 227).

Peter Camenzind's adoration of nature goes through several stages. It is only quite late in the book, in the countryside around Basel, that he eventually discovers what such a love really can mean, a passionate preoccupation in which a man's whole being becomes, and must become, absorbed. His longing "to get closer to the heart of existence" (I, 317) pursues its satisfaction: "So I peered more and more eagerly into the abyss of things existing" (I, 308). The sound of the wind in the treetops, the rushing of the mountain streams, the soft coursing of great rivers—all this, he knows, is the language of God, and to understand it is to find one's way back again to paradise. It is not surprising that St. Francis of Assisi is remembered in this connection: "St. Francis expressed this more maturely, more beautifully and yet in a much more childlike way. This was when I understood him completely for the first time. . . . He calls all the forces and phenomena of nature his beloved brothers and sisters" (I, 310). In the same year as *Peter Camenzind* there appeared Hesse's highly stylized life of the saint; [25] such a life as St. Francis lived, the author tells us, "is nothing less than a return to the beginnings of creation." [26]

The nature mysticism that Hesse ascribes to St. Francis, his embracing of the whole external world in the universality of his

---

[25] *Franz von Assisi* (Berlin, 1904). Analogies to this Franciscan attitude to nature may be found frequently in Hesse's works of this period, for instance in the story called "Sor Acqua" (1907).

[26] *Franz von Assisi*, p. 9.

love, finds its reflection in Peter's own visions. Although the novel mentions a God of independent identity, the feeling throughout is essentially pantheistic, and the fundamental experience is that of the confrontation of the divine in nature with the divine in man, with the soul. Without and Within, nature and the soul—these pairs are the same and the individual terms in each pair are even interchangeable. The essence of Romantic mysticism, the entire tradition of German Romantic subjectivism, is actually enshrined, many years after *Peter Camenzind*, in Emil Sinclair's words: "for mountain and stream, tree and leaf, root and flower, all the forms of nature lie prefigured within us, derive from the soul" (III, 198–99). In Peter's relationship with nature his repressed soul finds its obverse and thus some sort of expression; in some respects love of nature is a surrogate for love of man, and it discloses also the desire to express a love which cannot possibly be rejected, not a love for any particular or even finite object, but for the infinite. So Peter finds that art has striven in all ages "to provide a language for the silent yearning after the divine in us" (I, 310). Love of God is love of nature, love of nature is love of soul, love of soul is love of self —all these are one; thus what might appear at first sight a moving outward is, at least equally, a narcissistic turning inward, or a kind of maternal regression.

Peter Camenzind's nature mysticism is the groundwork of a novel which is, in its other aspect, a sharp attack upon the alleged corruption of civilization. In coming eventually, perhaps somewhat reluctantly, to the study of men, Peter struggles to understand what it is which separates them from nature. It is above all else their hypocrisy, their pose, their love of masks, ultimately their lying, the barrier is "a slippery jelly of lies" (I, 331), and the source of the production of this objectionable substance is the need each man has to act a role without first knowing his own real nature. The jelly, then, is a false personality, already acquired by young children "who always, consciously or unconsciously, prefer to act a role than to disclose themselves in a wholly instinctive and undisguised way" (I, 331). In the sketch "An Autumn Hike," in which the feeling for nature has much in common with that in *Peter Camenzind*, occurs the remark: "The changeable and mask-wearing human being is shocked . . . at the gaze of all natural-grown things." [27] Unlike trees, men are no longer natural growths; they do not, as they should, live out the secret of their seed.

Another story from the same period, "Harvest Moon" (1905) makes heavy weather of the failure of the young intellectual, Homburger, even to glance at the beauties of nature which lie beyond his windowpane, and because the writing is weak the moral itself seems an affectation. But in *Peter Camenzind* the wish to escape the charmed circle of decadence, to break out into green pastures, is not at all affected; it is evidently sincere and very strong. At this time Hesse saw man "distracted from the path of the soul, so dominated by will, so coarse and frenzied in his pursuit of animal, simian, primitive goals, so obsessed with rubbish and trash," [28] that for a while the "grave error" could take hold of him that perhaps man, as a way to the emergence of the soul, was already rejected and in decline. Will, then, in the sense of the entranced pursuit of worldly goals, is clearly seen to be opposed to the life of the soul; men are corrupted by their own wilfullness and thus do permanent damage to their innermost nature. Hesse never changed this view, which anticipates in some degree his acquaintance with the doctrines of the Tao; he merely came to see that it was indeed in man, and not in some new creature, that the way to the soul must be rediscovered and reopened. Peter Camenzind, as a would-be teacher, wanted to show men what they had lost:

I wanted to bring it about that you should be ashamed to know more of foreign wars, fashion, gossip, literature and the arts than of spring which unfolds its unbridled activity outside your towns, and of the river which flows beneath your bridges, and of the forests and splendid meadows through which your railroad runs [I, 329].

The implied aspersion on the railroad is itself enough to situate this outburst in the tradition of the Romantic epigones.

The self-exclusion of "other people" from the experience of natural things, contrasted with Peter's essential integration in nature and myth, is the central arch of the book's satire. It is far from

---

[27] I, 626. This story stands out for its sharply defined succession of descriptive and reflective passages.
[28] "On the Soul" (VII, 70).

providing, however, a full explanation of the problematics of Peter Camenzind the outsider, even on the author's own terms. Hesse knows well enough that the source of a neurosis never lies in others. Indeed, since the whole novel was conceived as a flight from decadence and a harking after mental health—Peter feels constantly distinct from the species of nervous aesthete with whom he associates, and he aspires himself to create "something deep and good" (I, 301)—one might therefore expect the work to deal in detail with the issues of "outsiderdom," in the hope of offering at least a partial cure. And this, of course, it does. While in rural Nimikon there are eccentrics and there is the comedy of humankind, an experience when in Florence of the reflection of the life of the quattrocento provides for Peter a much harsher contrast with the ways of the cultivated world, it shows him "the whole shabby absurdity of modern culture" (I, 290). For even Nimikon was in essence "a small reflection of the great world" (I, 222) and no utopia. Zurich, where Peter studies, and Basel come in for a great deal of criticism. Zurich, it is true, is at first a delight, the rich variety of its life contrasts so vividly with all he has been used to until then, and at the outset Peter is even confident that he will be able to find his place in this world. But soon he begins to find difficulties of adaptation, for instance to the life of the cosmopolitan intellectual set, who feel no need "to work on themselves without external purpose and to clarify their personal relationship to time and eternity" (I, 261). This sin of omission, it must be said (and he constates its presence also in himself), seems here to reflect a humanistic personalism without the esoteric or religious meaning which the notion of self-development was later to acquire for Hesse.

The aesthetic life in general comes in for a more direct attack than is to be found in *Hermann Lauscher*. Peter observes the various substitutes for the God whose disappearance secretly worries all these people: "They would have been ashamed of bowing before God, but they lay on their knees before the Zeus of Otrikoli" (I, 282). Aesthetes who practiced continence and failed to wash, artists who pursued a cult of music, wine, and perfumes, one talented young man who went insane on a surfeit of Pre-Raphaelitism and Chopin—such commonplace targets suffer their inevitable demolition with the words: "Fundamentally the whole

convulsive comedy was amusing and absurd" (I, 282). As satire
all this lacks both particularity and originality, and as descriptive
writing it also lacks the cacaphonic realism with which the demi-
monde later jumps to life in *The Steppenwolf*. Hesse's experience
itself is inadequate for the appointed task and there is much in this
novel that is conspicuously secondhand. Peter refuses to describe
his life in Paris, as he refuses later to give us an account of his
cultural studies, and the reason is of course the same—Hesse's
imagination has failed him. Of life in Basel, which Hesse knew well,
we learn of course a good deal, especially after Peter begins to visit
the academician's house and becomes acquainted with members of
the then very fashionable temperance societies. This acquaintance
merely shows him the human weaknesses, the conflicts, and corruption which dog all idealistic, reformist movements. "Look," he
thinks, returning one night—already clearly a forerunner of Harry
Haller, the wolf—from his tippling, "We wild ones are better
people after all" (I, 298). Social reform means nothing to him; he
does not care if his new-found friends achieve their multiple
variety of purposes. Basically, in any case, they are all bourgeois,
"the same stereotyped form of *homo socialis*" (I, 302); the few
significant individuals there are among them are for him as unapproachable as all the others, for he lacks the necessary cocktail-
party *sang-froid*, and he finds the hypocrisy of the conversation
about literature and art desolatingly painful: "I much preferred,
for instance, to hear a woman speak of her children or to talk myself about traveling, little events of the day and other real things"
(I, 303). But one may feel that Peter Camenzind is scarcely a good
judge of what is real and what is not, for he is a melancholic.

   This point is conceded from the beginning, and it is really the
axis upon which the psychological development of the hero turns.
Nimikon is shrouded in "an eternal veil of concealed or unconscious depression. . . . The dependence on the forces of nature and
the deprivations of a hard-working life had in the course of time
instilled a tendency to melancholia in our in any case aging clan"
(I, 222). This tendency to gloomy brooding is one of the reasons
that the local eccentrics, and especially Uncle Conrad, are so welcome. Peter feels that he has inherited from his father "a fear of
firm decisions, the incapacity for handling money, and the art of

practiced heavy drinking. . . . I certainly inherited a sly peasant intelligence, but also the gloomy disposition and the tendency to baseless melancholia which went with it" (I, 235). Hesse's own parents are still in part mirrored in Peter's; the puritanical Johannes Hesse did not drink and was certainly no peasant, but he did have the melancholic temperament, just as Marie Hesse perhaps gave her son something like the gift Peter received from his mother: "a modest practical common sense, a touch of faith in God and a quiet, taciturn nature" (I, 235). Through his adolescent melancholia Peter was drawn to literature, first of all to Heine, then Lenau, Schiller, Goethe, and Shakespeare. But his disease pursues him into his maturer life. When, in Zurich, he feels that he is going to establish himself as a journalist and small-time littérateur, his optimism is tempered by touches of a darker, though sweeter, mood; he is attacked at nights by the thought that nature, the black lake, the silhouettes of the mountains on the pale sky and the stars above (those perpetual judges of Hesse's protagonists), regard him with reproach, for he is failing in his duty as an artist, evading the task for which he was born, "to help mute nature to find expression in poetry" (I, 268). Later, in the Bois de Boulogne, Peter sits and contemplates suicide, till reminiscences of his mother's death dispel that notion. Back in Basel the affliction makes its presence felt more strongly than ever before: "I had the sense of a terrible loneliness. Between me and the people and life of the town, the squares, houses and streets, was a permanent wide gulf" (I, 295). The clinical observation is exact enough; also the dumb, plaintive trapped longing of the natural world of the countryside, the meadows and the trees, reflects the condition of the observing mind: "But there they were and could say nothing, and I understood their suffering and suffered with them, for I could not redeem them" (I, 295).

So Peter Camenzind goes to a physician and receives a warning. His mental condition, though as yet not exactly menacing, needs therapy, and this is to come from the direct effort to mingle more with humankind. It is this effort which leads him to the academician's and to his great love, Elisabeth. It is of course inevitably in his love life that the sick strain in Peter's psyche finds both nourishment and expression. The second chapter of the novel begins with the words: "To talk of love—in this all my life I have remained a boy" (I, 242). A study of Peter Camenzind's whole career forces us to agree with this diagnosis. Love of woman, he tells us, has for him something austere, reverential, its symbol is "prayerful hands stretched up to blue heavens" (I, 242). Under the influence of his mother and of his own instincts he reveres woman as "a strange, beautiful, and baffling sex, which is superior to us through the innate beauty and harmony of its nature, and which we must regard as sacred, because just like stars and blue mountaintops it is far from us and seems to be nearer to God" (I, 242). The goddess figure symbolic of this attitude of perpetual genuflection appears as early as "Island Dream" in *An Hour beyond Midnight*. Such a view of women, evidently in essence a mother-fixation, leads, as Peter is prepared to admit, to a number of difficulties. Though, as the years passed, women stayed upon their lofty pedestal unchanged, "my role, the solemn one of the worshiping priest, turned all too easily into the painfully comic one of the fooled fool" (I, 242).

His first real passion is for Rösi Girtanner, a quiet beauty seventeen years old; he gathers a bouquet for her in the mountains at the hazard of his life, carries it with him on a long journey to the city and leaves it at her house, but never knows whether she sees it or not. The whole cumbersome gallantry is a kind of oxymoron in life; it seems to him to have something about it both sad and happy, even poetic, but the affair is finally summed up as quixotic. Much later comes the first visit to the paintress Emilia Aglietti, the color of whose face reminds him of gorgonzola; he sits for her, and falls hotly in love with her, but of course her attachment is to another. The violent impact of his feelings for her has been illustrated; something in the subconscious is aroused, for which view there is further evidence in the way Peter, after falling asleep at one of the sittings, recounts his dream to her: "And in telling the dream I penetrated deep into my forgotten childhood . . . had told her and myself its entire story" (I, 272).

Confession, in this confessional novel, is already itself a motif; later this motif reveals itself as being of structural as well as psychological significance for Hesse's writings. At the academician's house Peter meets the dark-haired Elisabeth, who chats with him over a sketch of the valley of San Clemente, near Fiesole, which he knows well. He notices the childlike naturalness with which she listens to him; again he cannot help himself and he reveals to her, to his subsequent shame and annoyance, "intimate memories and a whole section of my inner life" (I, 306–307). In the art gallery he sees her as she stands, oblivious of him, and admires a Segantini, [29] in particular the solitary cloud. Contemplation of the work of art brings Elisabeth's soul, the most feminine quality of her psyche, to the surface, as it responds softly, serenely, displacing for one sensitive moment the sophisticated, the intellectual, the austere (*herb*) masculine traces in her face.[30]

Peter's love for Elisabeth leads, in him also, to a response of the soul, a blossoming of his pinched emotional life; the newly deepened love of nature, in the countryside around Basel, which now arises does not, it is true, entirely cure his melancholy, but it does "ennoble and purify" it. His senses sharpen, an intensified wish to penetrate nearer to the very heart of existence is combined with a simpler reverence for the surface of things. For Hesse, we shall find, this antinomy of surface and center is an essential tension; indeed upon it is eventually constructed the Glass Bead Game itself. Peter even dreams of Elisabeth as a possible wife and of finding in her a bridge to take him back to other human beings. His condition he describes with ironic distancing as a comical transformation: "I, the lonely eccentric, had turned overnight into a love-sick swain, dreaming of married happiness and the establishment of my own home" (I, 314). The irony is consciously double, for at the time of writing the author already holds this goal within his grasp. Elisabeth Laroche (as was probably her name in real

[29] It is a curious coincidence that C. A. Bernoulli, whose study of Bachofen (*Johann Jakob Bachofen und das Natursymbol* [Basel, 1924]) has a section on the figure of Frau Eva in *Demian*, should also deal in the same book with Giovanni Segantini: he observes that Segantini lost his mother at the age of five and that his whole work was a cult of her memory (p. 499).

[30] A comparison might be drawn with an aphorism of Novalis: "Der Sitz der Seele ist da, wo sich Innenwelt und Aussenwelt berühren. Wo sie sich durchdringen, ist er in jedem Punkte der Durchdringung" (The seat of the soul is at that point at which the world outside and the world within touch. Where they interpenetrate it is present at every point of the interpenetration) (Novalis, *Schriften*, eds. Paul Kluckhohn and Richard Samuel [Leipzig, 1929], II, 17).

life)[31] married another and so did Hermann Hesse; but these words nonetheless ring strangely and with *unconscious* irony too, written as they were at the beginning of the Gaienhofen years.

But as for the lover Peter Camenzind, that perpetual boy,[32] he is thrown back again and again upon himself, upon the uneasy sense of his own inadequacy. Love-sickness pursues him even toward the novel's end, when the experience with Boppi has already brought so great a change. The persistence of his feelings for Elisabeth— with whom, after her marriage, he maintains a social relationship— arouses his self-criticism and shame, beneath which, however, there lies concealed "a secret, warm feeling of pleasure, just as in my boyhood days whenever I thought of pretty Rösi and the warm [*lau*] dark shiver ran through me" (I, 365). We recall that he used to dream of Rösi in school, close his eyes, and feel himself glide "into a warm [*lau*] abyss" (I, 242), until the teacher or one of his comrades woke him up sharply. The epithets and images have their undertone of sensuality; and we remember also the passage in which Peter's friend Richard sits naked on a rock in a stream and mimes the Lorelei.

In all Hesse's major novels, with but one exception, the friend-ship theme is an introit—or else is played in counterpoint—to the theme of heterosexual love.[33] In school there is a brown-haired, serious youth, Kaspar Hauri, whom Peter venerates from a distance. To Peter he is inaccessible, and well he may be, for even down to the color of his hair he foreshadows Max Demian. Then, of course, there is Richard himself, whom Peter hears playing the piano— "and felt for the first time something of the spell of music, the most feminine and the sweetest of the arts" (I, 256). Richard plays Wagner,[34] and the music "flowed around me like a warm [*lau*] ex-

[31] Cf., e.g., Ball, *op. cit.*, p. 98.

[32] One may compare another early work, "The Preparatory School Boy" ("Der Lateinschüler") (1906), for further easily accumulated evidence that in the love relationships presented by Hesse the woman is nearly always in some sense the maturer party.

[33] True even of *The Steppenwolf*. The exception is *The Glass Bead Game*, from which heterosexual love is more or less excluded.

[34] The *Meistersinger* is evidently held to be "healthier" than Chopin. That Richard is a musician points to what was perhaps the literary prototype of this relationship, Walt and Vult in Jean Paul's *Die Flegeljahre*.

citing bath" (I, 257). The word *"lau"* usually signals something, and it is no surprise that the passage goes on: "Simultaneously I watched the slim neck and back of the player and his white pianist's hands with secret pleasure" (I, 257–258), and this sensual stimulus blends with a veneration like that which he felt for Kaspar Hauri years before (we may compare the various elements in Emil Sinclair's worship of Demian). Richard, of course, is much more sophisticated than the Oberländer Peter Camenzind, but his wit often goes no further than quotations from Wilhelm Busch, and he is liked by everyone not for his sophistication but for "the unconquerable serenity of his light, childlike nature" (I, 260). Peter tries to make his relationship with his friend an exclusive one, he attempts to keep him away from women (who find him agreeable), he shows his jealousy and quarrels with him, and then they make it up by rubbing noses "according to the oriental love-custom" (I, 262). Richard's friendship is of immense value for Peter, if only because it is a remedy for his melancholia. After the nearly disastrous aspiring after Emilia Aglietti's hand there is a new bond between them and Richard is "beautiful and serene in body and soul" (I, 284). An elegant billiard player, he introduces Peter to the world of music too, is amazed by Peter's ignorance of contemporary fashions, for instance of "Nietzsche and all that rubbish" (I, 259), and takes his peasant-friend with him, at his own expense, on a tour of northern Italy, now that his semesters are up and they must part. The parting is permanent, since Richard is drowned shortly afterward in a small south German river. Peter blasphemes and curses: all is finished, the universe is desolate. He admits that he should at this point have taken a grip on himself and his life, but he preferred passively to endure and to wait. From the hindsight of later years, however, he was able to see that Providence guided him even then: "Wise, thrifty life . . . let me play my comedy of pride and knowing better, ignored it and waited, until the errant child should find his mother once more" (I, 293).

But Peter Camenzind never really finds his mother, whatever Hesse may have been imagining in 1904, the year of his marriage. However, his desolation, his Romantic cosmos-hatred, are not wholly convincing; they do not have the emotional charge to be found, for instance, in *The Steppenwolf*. This is because Harry

Haller's despair is nearer the true dark night of the soul, and is scarcely adolescent melancholia; though it is clear that a similar ironic detachment, a similar dichotomy of the personality, is to be found in both novels, and it is perhaps in *The Steppenwolf* that the source of the old trouble first becomes wholly manifest and conscious. Peter is as incapable, almost, of naïve experience as was his predecessor Lauscher or as his successor Haller is; he goes, for instance, to an artists' party by the lake, where, illuminated by paper lanterns, "Some rotten young painter or other played the Romantic, wore a daring biretta, stretched on his back at the railing and fooled with a long-necked guitar" (I, 274). This is scarcely kind. And in this parodied Romantic atmosphere, in a boat with Emilia, Peter can think abstractly of "the beauty and poetry of all the evening scenery" (I, 275), which makes him nervous, for he feels that it is "a beautiful stage decoration, in the middle of which I have to act out a sentimental scene"—reminiscent of the "colorful stage-walls" of *Hermann Lauscher*. The entire atmosphere is later disposed of with Steppenwolfian iconoclasm as "stupid and absurd . . . childish" (I, 277). Indeed, to recover from it all the noble savage sleeps out that night and spends three days in the sunshine and fresh air, but to no avail. He has learned by now the bitter truth that there is some stumbling block in his relations with society, one which he has perforce to carry around with him all the time. He is, in the last resort, an "awkward fellow from the Oberland" (I, 245); he is a child of the mountains and is really afraid of the Flatland. He feels his peasant incapacity, that he can never achieve the polished self-confidence of these lowlanders, and is constantly dogged by his own gaucheries—at Emilia's tea party he consumes all the ham while the others are still prattling and thus creates an embarrassing void. His awkwardness in society, however, is not compensated for in the least by his extreme laziness and by a certain braggadocio. In the great outside world—not, he tells us, in Nimikon, through we may not believe him—he is an outsider, there is in him the spirit of the nomad, the tramp, the "fahrende Gesell"—"with dusty boots . . . on the road after dreams not one of which has yet come true" (I, 295). In this he is at one with his author, who declares of himself: "I am a nomad, not a peasant. I

venerate infidelity, change, imagination." [35] Peter is even a potential
suicide, not merely in the Bois de Boulogne but also on the cliffs at
Genoa—"the old, saddening longing . . . to hurl myself into the
arms of God and to unite my small existence with the infinite and
the eternal" (I, 289).

In the later story, "The Steep Road", mystical union is con-
summated by just such a leap. Death by water also attracts Peter,
on the lake at Nimikon, in the despair of his frustrated love. But
"Green Peter" (I, 256), as he calls himself with a self-conscious
allusion to Keller, finds his true release in wine, and his becoming
a drinker he regards as more important than anything he has up to
that time related. Chapter Four begins with a whimsical, and
knowledgeable, eulogy of the wine god, in a precious Neo-
Romantic style. Wine drinking is an arcanum, like other valuable
gifts and arts. It requires special study and application; and wine
destroys those who do not know how to learn. Wine is a way to
paradise, back to origins, to myth and the roots of being: "It transforms the confusion of life into great myths and on a mighty harp
it plays the song of creation" (I, 278). Moreover, in Peter this
divinity serves a double purpose: not only does wine, the androgynous—"the sweet god . . . with his womanly soft hand" (I, 300)—
restore him to his beginnings, to states of ecstasy and paradise, to a
receptive condition in which the wine itself begins "to conjure, to
create, itself to write poetry" (I, 279), but it also seems, when other
people are present, to have the diametrically opposite effect, to
accentuate the critical, masculine element in him. Then Peter experiences "a cool, strange fever" (I, 280), "a sharp, cool spirit"
takes possession of him and makes him "assured, superior, critical
and witty," and hostile toward others. In the dual effect of the
hermaphroditic wine god upon Peter Camenzind we find a pointer
to the ambivalence of his own psyche, to the conflict of male and
female, mother and father, in him; while the repetition of the
epithet "cool" speaks of Harry Haller, the Steppenwolf, and his
excoriating, hypermental world.

The Boppi episode is the culmination of the novel. It is the mis-

---

[35] "The Hiking Trip" (III, 388).

anthropist's cure. On a windy night Peter will go out into the
storm to visit a solitary tree, his bosom friend, to see how it is faring,
but yet he has no love for his own kind: "But how was I to find
the way from here to love of men?" (I, 312). Perhaps, he thinks,
through being a poet, a communicator of the experience of nature
to men. But Peter Camenzind's great works are of that class which
never get written, for the moment for them is never fully ripe.
He knows that he has only one way of salvation—through love of
men, and he determines to experiment with loving his father. Although this is a "difficult and sweet art" (I, 318), he tells us little
about it, and its results are inevitably minimal; such a love, indeed,
rather goes against the grain in the psychological world of Hesse's
works. So Peter turns to Italy again. Italy, the trip with Richard,
Florence and Fiesole—all this had been "the crown and beautiful
sunset of my youth" (I, 290). When still a schoolboy he had studied
Italian and the masters of the old *novelle;* their world (along with
that of the medieval *Märchen*) had become a kind of poetic refuge
for him. On the streets where his idol, St. Francis, himself had
walked, Peter feels at home. It had been in Florence that it dawned
upon him for the first time that he might have been *born* an outsider, and there arose the desire to pass his life outside the walls of
this society, if possible in the south. On his second visit, Peter goes
to live in Assisi, where at last he makes contact with the people,
the common people, not the intellectual parasites of Zurich and
Basel—to such an extent, indeed, that his landlady, Signora Nardini,
one of the most living characters in the book, seeks him for a husband. And he might have been tempted, for financial reasons, but
of course his longings still lie elsewhere, and he returns to Switzer-
land, his mind full of Elisabeth and his literary dreams. But naturally,
Assisi is not primarily the city of Annunziata Nardini. The St.
Francis experience, gently introduced before, now begins to take
over the novel and to bring about the hero's spiritual transformation.

As a student in Zurich, Peter's first love had been for history,
especially that of the late Middle Ages in Italy and France:
"Through this for the first time I learned more about my favorite
among men, Francis of Assisi, the most blessed and divine of all

saints" (I, 262). The saint's most outstanding quality for Peter was his childlikeness. In his own *Franz von Assisi*, of course, Hesse's approach as biographer is still essentially that of the aesthete; St. Francis is seen there as a poet, as an inspirer of the art of Giotto, and only almost as an afterthought is he a direct symbol of the transcendental spiritual aspirations of man.

But in *Peter Camenzind* another note is struck, and the antithesis between aestheticism and religion, as Lauscher formulated it, is freshly evaluated. Indeed, the idea of spiritual search is central to the novel, the wish to fulfill the function not merely of the poet but of the seer, to penetrate to the world of the spirit which lies behind phenomena, to tear away "the veil of the accidental and ordinary" (I, 241). Peter Camenzind is a homeless creature seeking a haven "in the kingdom of the spirit" (I, 252). He is constantly sensitive to the hesitant motion, the blockages, the false starts, the retrogressions of the inward flow of his life; like Lauscher he bends constantly over the well and listens. Sometimes he feels he is without question on the right path toward his goal—that is, "a wordless, constant love free of passion" (I, 310),[36] which is possible only for those who are "God's favorites, the good and the children among men. Many have learned this through severe sufferings— have you never seen, amongst cripples and unfortunates, some with superior, tranquil, shining eyes?" (I, 311). Here the Boppi theme sounds strongly; it is the Franciscan doctrine of all-embracing love for all the creatures of the earth, through which comes peace. After his return from Assisi, Peter comes more and more to perceive that happiness has little to do with the fulfillment of external desires and that the sufferings of love-sick youths are normally devoid of all tragedy. He learns to believe in Providence, and that the purpose of pain, disappointment, and melancholy is precisely "to mature and transfigure us" (I, 294). In a significant passage he discovers the link between the reconciling power of humor and the acceptance of fate: "Now gradually I began to notice the humor of life, and it seemed to me ever easier and more possible to recon-

[36] This may of course be seen in more than one light. H. R. Schmid regards it as the detachment of the libido from its object and thus, following Freud, as a form of narcissistic regression (*Hermann Hesse* [Leipzig, 1928], p. 156).

cile myself with my stars" (I, 314). But there are many levels of acceptance, and of rejection, as the author of *Peter Camenzind* was subsequently to understand; and some transcend such clichés.

The decision to seek "the warming proximity of human life . . . among the ordinary people" (I, 319) originated in Italy. Back in Basel, Peter is able to strike up an acquaintance with the carpenter who comes to fit his bookshelves, because he has lived so much among wandering journeymen and he knows their patois. The mood of this attempt to contact the "lower classes" is a striking reversion to the feeling of pre-Naturalist literature in Germany. The carpenter and his family are seen entirely sentimentally, and not with the eye of the social novelist, still less with that of the social scientist; they are seen as naïve human beings, honest and close to nature, in a vague emotional glow embarrassingly reminiscent of Heyse. The reader can scarcely fail to share the carpenter's own fear that Peter Camenzind is being condescending and even to go on fearing this longer than the carpenter does. "Besides," Peter remarks, "the little people (*Leutlein*) soon felt that I was only in externals a gentleman" (I, 334); but the diminutive "*Leutlein*" betrays the degree of self-deception involved. The satire which springs from all this sentiment is rather more blatant than before; among these simple people we find "instead of drawing room talk, realities" (I, 335); although their life is harsh (*herb*) and impoverished, they find satisfaction in it and have no time or inclination to deck it out with fancy, sophistication, and pose. For Peter their true attraction is maybe that he finds here "something of my childhood preserved for me" (I, 334), something of that life which the *patres* in the monastery near Nimikon had broken off when they sent him to school.

The illness of the carpenter's little girl, Agi, her death and funeral, all this leads, after a short interlude in Zurich, to the Boppi episode. Boppi, the younger brother of the carpenter's wife and a hopeless cripple, is left to the family's unwilling care. Peter's reaction to his appearance is at first like theirs, also adverse: why should he allow his, at the moment, relatively serene existence to be darkened with such shadows? The memory of St. Francis comes then like a blinding light of conscience, St. Francis of whom he had boasted to his friends in Assisi, "He had taught me to love all men"

(I, 344). It is as if God speaks to him, as if in the person of Boppi God had entered the carpenter's home. Peter Camenzind, confronted with this mirror to his own nature, sees himself for what he is, a braggart and a liar. He now becomes "the astonished and grateful pupil of a wretched cripple" (I, 347); for Boppi has serenity, inner beauty, a deep humanity, and has also learned how to accept his own weakness and to submit to the will of God. The Boppi story, in fact—the *Duzbruderschaft*, the inevitable confession (Peter tells Boppi of his failures in love), the visits to the zoo and the sense of community with the animals, the reading of literature together (mainly Keller; Peter keeps C. F. Meyer's stories away from Boppi, for fear they may disturb his serenity), the encounter between Boppi and Elisabeth, Peter's devoted care of Boppi and the cripple's worsening and death—the whole of this Hesse portrays with sincerity and conviction as the overwhelming experience which transforms Peter Camenzind and all but cures him. It is touching, and for the most part tasteful, although the imaginary animal dialogue is a disaster of false sentiment. During Boppi's last illness he falls into semidelirium and talks about his mother for two days. Of Peter he observes: "He's an unlucky fellow, that's true, but it hasn't done him any harm. His mother died too soon" (I, 361). This is percipient of Boppi; and a generation later the dying Goldmund was to speak in this way to Narziss.

Through Boppi, Peter Camenzind learns how to love men. He returns to Nimikon, with the intention of going on to Assisi when the winter is over. Spring and the foehn, however, bring an intolerable renewal of his nervous love-sickness, and they bring also storms and natural catastrophe to the village. So Peter stays, to represent a local distress committee at Canton level and to publicize the emergency through his newspaper connections—some useful work at last. Nimikon has changed far less than he in all these years. He takes up manual labor, wears down his soft hands on the harsh wood, and shakes off the corruptions of civilization. Looking back over his life, he arrives at a naïvely conservative moral: "that fish belong in the water and peasants belong on the land" (I, 369) and that no degree of art can make a man of the world out of a Camenzind from Nimikon. He attributes his failures of adaption to "the Nimikon spirit in me" (I, 370) and thus evades the recogni-

tion of his own personal inadequacy. He dresses and lives as
a peasant again, and no one takes him for an eccentric here. After so
many apparently wasted years he is left with a few angels who will
intercede for him in Heaven—his mother, Richard, Agi, and above
all Boppi—and he has experienced to the full the self-renewing life
of the village community. He thinks of finally settling down, of
taking over the village inn that it may not fall into the hands of city
brewers. He has found a simple union between love of nature,
rootedness in nature, and the service of man in the spirit of St.
Francis. Self-love and love of men have coalesced. It would appear
as if the ironic detachment with which he, when already under
Boppi's spell, still sought to combat his "Wertherish feelings"
(I, 353), has now solidified into an integrated view of life. The ideal
of service points forward as far as *The Glass Bead Game*, and the
novel has sought to take the step which should repair the torn
roots of the soul and lead to inner tranquillity.

But it remains a fair question: is this work, which was to be a
turning outward, away from introversion and toward health,
ultimately anything of the kind? To return to Nimikon is no doubt
to return to one's origins, but it is also to flee from the outside
world. The struggle to escape the Romantic situation leads in the
end only to yet another Romantic situation, a truth as material for
a full understanding of Hesse's last novel as it is of his first. It is of
course valid that Hesse throws off with this book the dominant influence of Novalis, only to succumb to that of Gottfried Keller.
The broad narrative flow, the attempt at objectivity and at establishing a sovereign superior standpoint for the narrator, are Kelleresque.
It was indeed a first reading of Keller that taught Peter "how far
my immature reveries had been from genuine, austere (*herb*), true
art" (I, 241)—and here the allusion to the Lauscher style is an
obvious one. Yet Ball sees little influence of Keller in this novel and
notes the total absence of the political viewpoint.[37] Still more
significant is the fact that the book is ultimately devoid of that
genuine serenity which Keller's works all possess. The emotional-
ism of the Boppi solution would have repelled Keller, who would

[37] *Op. cit.*, p. 117.

without doubt have seen through it. It is an attempt to stop the clock with the pendulum in an extreme position.

In any case, *Peter Camenzind* is the product of a temperament more meditative and less original and vitally creative than Keller's. Its apostrophe of the clouds has always been regarded as a sign of the book's overt Romantic feeling, and this of course it is. Clouds are the particular object of the young Peter's nature worship.[38] The figures pile up: "blessing and gift of God . . . anger and night of death . . . tender, soft and peaceful like the souls of the new-born . . . beautiful, rich, and beneficent like good angels . . . dark, inescapable and merciless like the messengers of death" (I, 230). Their movement across the sky may suggest "murderers," or "charging riders," or "melancholy hermits." Their shapes are those of "happy isles," "blessing angels," "threatening hands," "fluttering sails," "wandering cranes." These metaphors and similes (frequently from the sphere of religious language) do not, for the most part, assist the visual impression, but project mood. The clouds are the objective correlative of almost every kind of Romantic emotion that Peter Camenzind is able to experience. The language is intensely reflective, and preciosity is sometimes not far away. Direct description is usually avoided, and the figurative meaning is extracted with what might be regarded as overobvious precision: "They are the eternal symbols of all wandering, all searching, longing, and yearning for home" (I, 230). Later in the book we have the cloud in Segantini's painting, the association with Elisabeth, and finally Elisabeth herself apostrophized in the verses: "Like a white cloud." The poetry of all this first helped to make the novel famous, but it is in fact its abstracting, reflective quality which is its most revealing characteristic. Peter Camenzind's reveries are never naïve, they are the sophisticated constructions of a very conscious artist, of a Romantic, a passive, melancholic dreamer, hostile to society and inclined to alcoholism, full of fantasies about poetic genius and contemptuous of the professions of literature and journalism, whose supposed respect for the surface of things conflicts with his longing to burst through to the Infinite, whose

---

[38] Cf. also "At the End of the Year" (1904; VII, 7).

suicidal impulses stand in an odd relationship to his cult of health alfresco, who can experience nothing without pondering it, communicate nothing without commentary, and who stands outside all his successive selves except the last one, where the self-insight fails—he is, in fact, for all his protesting, a wolf in sheep's clothing, a rustic Hermann Lauscher.

Fundamentally, therefore, beyond all question, the language of *Peter Camenzind* reveals that the book, and equally the hero, are prisoners of the Romantic tradition. Yet Ball finds a "decided realism" and boyish freshness in the novel.[39] It is true enough that there are attempts to have done with this Romantic allegiance, not merely in the chosen theme but also in the style. Hesse's biographical essay *Boccaccio* (1904), in its musical, mannered prose, compares Boccaccio's writings to a delicate garden, in which however those who wish may find "a witticism, a buffoonery, a lusty anecdote." [40] As in Boccaccio himself, so in Hesse an ultrarefined style is married with a love of humor, of farce, of the popular (*das Völkische*), the virile anecdote, and more widely with a vigorous paganism, an aspiration after earthiness and health. Thus, in advancing from *Hermann Lauscher* to *Peter Camenzind*, Hesse consciously toughened his style by the introduction of more virile elements. The very rawness and potential violence of the landscape of the Oberland is in any case inimical to the mellifluous qualities predominant (though not universal) in Hesse's earlier prose. We now have "defiant, insolently crenelated Alpine peaks" (I, 258), and the verb plays a much greater part in the descriptions—"Rocky mountains bore up roaring and crashing" (I, 219). The introduction of touches of dialect is a concession to the contemporary fashion of *Heimatkunst* (regional art), by which the big city literature of the Naturalists had been largely superseded—it is noteworthy that none of the various cities used as locales in *Peter Camenzind* are themselves described at all. These modifications remain, however, on the surface of the novel, they do not touch the core of the book. A factor of much more far-reaching significance comes to light through a consideration of Hesse's interest in hagiography. That this was an early, a serious, and a meaningful interest is attested by

[39] Ball, *op. cit.*, p. 29.
[40] *Boccaccio* (Berlin, 1904), p. 10.

his reading,[41] by his own monograph on St. Francis, and by the recurrence of hagiographical material elsewhere, for instance in *Fabulierbuch*.[42] The monograph, *Franz von Assisi*, is characteristic of its genre in that it makes no real pretence to historicity, but it merely recounts the principal moments of change, for instance the conversion itself, by which St. Francis eventually attains to enlightenment. These moments taken together constitute the saint's *vita*. Of his conversion we read: "For his untutored poet's mind rediscovered with delight the lost unity of the world." [43] Such a moment is one of higher consciousness, of self-recognition, and its source lies in the feelings; and such numinous moments are in fact one of the most essential preoccupations of Hesse's novels. Such a moment in the *vita* of Peter Camenzind occurs perhaps at his mother's death; the hagiographical associations which the language carries are surely significant: "Also the uncomplaining courage of the dying woman was so sublime that a cooling clear ray of her austere [*herb*] glory also fell upon my soul" (I, 249). It is no accident that his mother's death constitutes one of the pivotal points of the novel; Peter overlooks the life which is behind him and the potential life which lies before him:

At this moment . . . something remarkable happened to me. Suddenly in a single instant everything that I had imagined and wanted and longingly hoped for since I was small seemed compressed together before a suddenly opened inward eye. . . . To learn, to create, to see, to wander—the whole fullness of life shone before my eyes in a fleeting gleam of silver [44] [I, 251].

Naïve and cumbersome though this description may be, it is revelatory both of its author's psychological and of his structural approach—and relevant to an appreciation of all Hesse's novels. Though it lacks the sensuous immediacy which came to be a

[41] He had read the studies of the saints by Sabatier and Bernoulli, for instance; see Ball, *op. cit.*, p. 108.

[42] For instance the "legends" "The Sweet Breads" (1908) and "The Two Sinners" (1911).

[43] *Franz von Assisi*, p. 32.

[44] An old Romantic image (cf. Heine's *Harzreise*), drawn of course from silver smelting, used also in *Hermann Lauscher* and conveying instantaneous transformation or recall.

feature of the typical moment of "awakening" (*Erwachen*), it makes conspicuous use of the relativity of time, by an expansion of *Erzählzeit* (narrating time) and a maximal contraction of *erzählte Zeit* (narrated time). There is a gradation of such moments in Hesse's novels. Though this particular example is rather abstract and unreal, at their most intense and lyrical they have a vital contact with sensuous reality. While by their very nature they are not violent outbursts, they usually exhibit something of the emotional force, and often the poignant strength of memory which characterize the Aglietti passage quoted at the beginning of this chapter. They tend to neutralize reflection. What they express is an instant in which the feelings, instead of raging in blind physical release, meet with the intellectual self, which is no longer disconnected and unreined; there is a blending of mind ("a cooling clear ray") with soul.

If, at the end, Peter Camenzind's self-insight fails, this is paralleled in the style by a thinning out of texture; for the author is now too close to the present moment, is less confident and less secure in his hindsight. In this lyrical *Bildungsroman* (approximately: "novel of education") the development of the *vita* is hesitant and its conclusion unconvincing; nonetheless it establishes the thematic pattern of future books, the depiction of the life of the outsider-artist as secularized hagiography. It prefigures the essential movement of the great novels, the break-out from the closed circle and the return, and it already illuminates the nature of that movement as a psychological *petitio principii*. The actual story itself, for all its autobiographical aspects, is curiously and awkwardly artificial and unreal; Peter's "conversion," his "repentence," and his return home to Nimikon is an evolution which does not grow naturally but is imposed from without, just as Hesse's own life at Gaienhofen was imposed from without (Ruskin, Morris, Tolstoy), the futile labor of a theory and a wrongly formulated longing. In Hesse's maturer works the enlightenment which Peter Camenzind seeks in vain is discovered in a *union* of the mental self with the soul, the "anoetic" self; [45] such moments of union are the nodal points in the

---

[45] For this reason the very interesting comparison made by Max Schmid (*Hermann Hesse: Weg und Wandlung* [Zurich, 1947]) between Hesse and Ludwig Klages is somewhat wide of the mark. Klages' uncompromising disapprobation of the mental, the noetic, function is foreign to Hesse.

structure of the novels as also in the structure of the spiritual Way; they lie like pools of numinous experience in the verbal surfaces of ratiocination and narrative; their occurrence means that the reflective, didactic tract can be the servant of the moment of freedom.

CHAPTER 2

Beneath the Wheel and Gerbersau

ON March 6, 1860, at his boarding school (the famous institution of Schulpforta), that very clever schoolboy Friedrich Nietzsche wrote down the following revealing complaint:

Of course I know full well: school years are hard years,
No burden, effort or labor is ever spared.
Often indeed would the soul tear loose from imprisoning
Fetters, would the sensitive heart take flight into solitude.
But even this weight is relieved by faithful friendship,
Which comes to us, comforts and raises us up.[1]

These words express, with remarkable precision, these sentiments which, decades later, helped to give rise in Germany to a literature of specialized satirical protest, the so-called *Schulliteratur* (school-literature). It consists largely of novels, and it flourished chiefly between 1890 and 1914, though there are some examples later among the Expressionists. These works may be novels about teachers—the outstanding example is Heinrich Mann's *The Blue*

---

[1] Nietzsche; *Werke*, ed. Karl Schlechta (Munich, 1954–1956), III, 77.

Angel (*Professor Unrat,* 1905)—but more typically they deal with the specific problem of the schoolboy in relation to his school, delimiting in this way the sphere of the traditional *Bildungsroman.* Child psychology as a developing science became increasingly significant in literature toward the end of the nineteenth century,[2] and account must also be taken of the general inclination of the Naturalist writers toward the unraveling of organic causes.

The school novel proper deals primarily with the clash between the child and the formal educational system, and in this it was very topical, since the last twenty years of the nineteenth century disclose an ever-increasing agitation in Germany for the reform of the high schools.[3] At the back of a good deal of the controversy lay an unspoken question which Nietzsche's verses clearly pose: did the German school system, with its quasimilitary ethos and discipline, its long school day, and its premium upon intellectual attainment and hard work, not perhaps do irreparable harm to the emotional life of its charges? Or did it not, at the very least, transform them into Nietzsche's execrated "cultural Philistine" (*Bildungsphilister*)? In 1890 Julius Langbehn's *Rembrandt als Erzieher: Von einem Deutschen* (*Rembrandt as Educator: By a German*) created a sensation, being a plea for a conception of education which regards art and the aesthetic experience as central and derogates the importance of intellectual knowledge;[4] too much of the latter, it is maintained, will cripple the harmonious development of the personality. Langbehn lacks the subtlety and scintillation with which Nietzsche had handled this subject in his essays. His book is aggressive, abusive, and also racist; he harps upon the need that the pupil should be guided by "education" to the fullest possible exploitation of his own deepest nature and not pinned down to a Procrustean bed of anti-

[2] Seminal in this connection was W. Preyer's *Die Seele des Kindes* (Leipzig, 1882); we may also note the extreme popularity in Germany as elsewhere in Europe of Ellen Key's *Barnets århundrade* (*The Century of the Child* [Stockholm, 1900]).

[3] The concern was the modernization of the traditional curriculum, still largely based upon the study of the classical languages and mathematics. At a conference held in Berlin in December 1890 the emperor himself delivered an address urging reform, pointing out that the high schools existed to educate Germans, not Romans and Greeks.

[4] Cf. earlier not only Nietzsche in *Thoughts out of Season* (1873–1874), but also the writings of Paul de Lagarde. Langbehn was a disciple of Lagarde.

quated pedagogical theory; he attacks the institutions of public education in bitter terms. The school literature was nourished, furthermore, by the epidemic of suicides among high-school boys which persisted through these years.[5] The best-known German writers of this period are almost at one in their hostility to their own schooldays.[6] The German school system stands condemned by all and sundry as a kind of civilian recruit training which warps the child's soul, nationalizes it, and then loads down the victim with useless knowledge and a false moral outlook. It is the soul as the seat of the feelings ("the sensitive heart") which suffers. At their deeper level, of course, these school novels are a rebellion not merely against the school system, but against the whole ethos of Wilhelminian Germany and against the monolithic intellectualism of the later nineteenth century, the overwhelming preoccupation with fact.

Although the school novel unfortunately sometimes sinks to abysmal depths of Philistinism, crudity, and profanity, *Beneath the Wheel* (1905) must compete for the title of best example of its class with Emil Strauss's *Friend Death* (*Freund Hein*, 1902)—Robert Musil's *Törless* (1906), the real masterpiece of the period, is only tangentially a school novel. In 1904 Hesse and his bride were house hunting, looking for an ideal locality in which to lead the healthy rustic life: "the half-peasant, half-aristocratic country house, with a mossy roof, spacious, beneath age-old trees, if possible with a rushing fountain outside the door." [7] The decision to abandon the search in the Basel district and to look for something near Lake Constance was stimulated by Hesse's first visit to Emil Strauss at Emmishofen, and his wife finally discovered the village of Gaienhofen "while I sat at home in Calw with father and sisters and

---

[5] Frank Wedekind's bitter play *The Awakening of Spring* (*Frühlingserwachen*) (1890) introduces a group of alarmed schoolteachers discussing how they may stem this particular plague, amidst characteristic Wedekindian satirical hyperbole.

[6] Thus Gerhart Hauptmann talks of "permanent tooth-ache," and of the Prussian N.C.O. who, rather than Lessing, Herder, Goethe, or Socrates, was the invisible authority behind the teachers (*Das Abenteuer meiner Jugend* [Berlin, 1937], I, 261). For an extensive collection of such comments see A. Graf, *Schülerjahre: Erlebnisse und Urteile namhafter Zeitgenossen* (Berlin, 1912).

[7] "On Moving into a New House" (IV, 617).

wrote *Beneath the Wheel*." [8] *Friend Death* was a best seller by this time, and its influence upon Hesse's novel is unmistakable. Nonetheless, the earlier "Abderegg" fragment shows that Hesse's wish to deal with this subject matter predates his encounter with Strauss.

Friend Death tells the story of a boy, Heiner, who has exceptional musical gifts, and who as a result of this comes into painful, irresolvable conflict both with his father and with his school, until torments of persecution and repression drive him to suicide. The satire upon school life is savage and wholly uncompromising; the workload, the agony of having to study mathematics—"that evil power" [9]—these things bear Heiner down; when the class reads Homer, Heiner's entranced response is not of the orthodox kind: "He forgot entirely that Homer had written first and foremost in order to demonstrate to the German boy with every word the application of a grammatical rule and the peculiarity of the Ionic dialect." [10] Strauss, evidently, is not a master of the light ironic touch—indeed none of the practitioners of the school novel was. It is Heiner's friend, Karl Notwang—the name speaks dire urgency—who unmasks the teachers, these noncommissioned officers, finally and completely, and denounces them; by their methods they destroy all respect for literature and art and thus for themselves. For Heiner real life, that of the soul, has its roots in the feelings, and his only recourse is to music, or else to "faithful friendship." Karl Notwang contrasts with the nervous, retiring, and melancholic Heiner, he is self-confident and determined and hates schools—from two of which he has been expelled—with a fanatical hatred. He sits next to Heiner in class and by crafty devices helps him to outwit their sworn tormentors: "It seemed to Heiner as if strength itself laughed before him, the teeth between the blood-red, well-formed lips shone with such primal health". [11] Coming fresh from *Peter Camenzind* we might here recall Richard and not be too surprised to find a relative of Richard and Karl in the figure of Hermann Heilner in *Beneath the Wheel*. Karl and Heiner become "blood brothers," but it little avails; the combination of a

[8] *Ibid.* (IV, 618).
[9] *Freund Hein* (9th ed.; Berlin, 1905), p. 123.
[10] *Ibid.*, pp. 150–151.   [11] *Ibid.*, p. 213.

strong father (a successful lawyer) and a tyrannical and mis-
directed school gradually cripples Heiner's soul; we hear of the
"secret of his soul," of the bliss of being able occasionally to forget
"reason, will, and purpose," [12] of recovering the instinctive manner
of existence of plants and animals. We remember Peter Camenzind,
of course; and indeed the extraordinary closeness of Emil Strauss
to the psychological world of the young Hermann Hesse has important implications; for the school novels are not only characterized by their satirical objectives, but also by their cult of "life," of
antireason, of emotion and purposelessness and innocence, above all
of ecstasy and innate biological vitality—in a word, their Nietzsche-
anism; they offer ardent friendship as a compensation for the op-
pressor's wrong, and they offer art, very often, and of course nature,
as ways of escape. Hesse and Strauss write of a wholly similar
psychological situation—the mother's boy, the feminine self, the
soul, throttled and extinguished by an overbearing masculinity, the
father, the *Bildungsphilister*, the school and its noncommissioned
officers, the paramilitary tyranny of the mind. When he resolves on
suicide, Heiner's sole regrets are for the pain it will cause his
mother: "But mother! What could be done? . . . Would it not be
ten times worse for her to have to watch all the wheels gradually
pass over my living body?" [13]

   These last words, one might hazard the guess, first suggested to
Hesse the title of *Beneath the Wheel*. His novel differs from *Friend
Death*, however, in that it is not a *Künstlerroman* (artist novel), at
least not primarily and overtly. This was in itself exceptional, since
most of the school novels deal with frustrated poets or artistic
geniuses of some sort. Hesse uses the motif but, unlike Strauss,
deliberately avoids throwing the central stress upon it, a masking
device which helps him to achieve the detachment he seeks, a detachment which is in fact the key to a deeper understanding of
the novel. On its surface, of course, the book is an unbridled
satirical attack upon the Swabian educational system; the reflective
commentary of *Hermann Lauscher* and *Peter Camenzind* has
hardened into obtrusive polemics, indeed into diatribe. The
novel is written in the third person, providing the narrator with a

---

[12] *Ibid.*, p. 95.   [13] *Ibid.*, pp. 315–316.

firm position of sovereign observation and hindsight, a Kelleresque superiority closer to the situation of the Gaienhofen stories than of *Peter Camenzind*, with scope for direct and denunciatory intrusion on the part of the narrator.

Like many of the school novels, the book evidently rests in very large part upon personal experience; it is based not only upon memory but upon the most traumatic set of memories in Hesse's early life. Hans Giebenrath, the son of a small-town middleman of little education and less sense, is selected by his preparatory-school teachers to be "crammed" unmercifully for the awful provincial examination upon which depends his chance of becoming one of the elect few—on this occasion thirty-six—who were given scholarships at the age of fourteen to the preparatory seminaries of Maulbronn, Blaubeuren, Schönthal, and Urach, and later educated free of charge at the Tübinger Stift for a career in the church, or occasionally in teaching. Hans passes second, and enters the seminary full of a promise which for a time he seems to maintain. But the price is terrible and has already in part been paid; his natural emotional development has been crippled and he is on the verge of a mental illness which will destroy him. Under the effects of this creeping malaise and through the intrusion of a stimulus from without (his friendship with Hermann Heilner), he falls from grace and suffers desperately, while his teachers and his father can think only of applying further violence to his personality. Sick and broken, he returns home from the seminary for a rest, but it is understood that he will never go back. A pathetic coda recounts his first experience of the opposite sex, his three days as an apprentice mechanic, and his death by drowning. At the end of *Friend Death* it was Karl Notwang who, as a kind of *raisonneur*, denounced those responsible for Heiner's ruin to the boy's father; here, at the end of *Beneath the Wheel*, when the teachers attend Hans's obsequies with proper and dignified sympathy, the cobbler Flaig, in conversation with Herr Giebenrath, points an accusing finger at them and their hypocrisy: "There go a few gentlemen . . . they helped to bring him to this" (I, 546).

As a satirical novel, *Beneath the Wheel* lacks subtlety and conviction. Much of the school satire is of the conventional kind—the suspicious aversion to mathematics, the complaint that the seminary aims "to make as far as possible a Roman and Greek dream-world out of the German present" (I, 431), the allusions to suicide as the way which, from time to time, "one desperate boy or another" (I, 457) chooses to go. The allegation that the parents in fact sell their sons to the seminary system for long-term financial advantage is characteristic of the intemperance with which both the teachers and Herr Giebenrath are attacked. The latter is treated less fairly than Strauss treats Heiner's father. The novel begins with a description of him, Kelleresque in method, but banal as satire: he is a typically robust *petit bourgeois,* a tolerable businessman, with an appropriate reverence for money, a front of religious orthodoxy, "appropriate respect for God and the authorities and blind submission to the unbending laws of bourgeois propriety" (I, 375)—the kind of sarcasm of which the minor Naturalist novelists such as Max Kretzer had been very fond.

Herr Giebenrath, almost as much as the teachers, is the civilian N.C.O. He and the preceptors at Maulbronn incarnate that society dissected with such ruthlessness in the works of Heinrich Mann, the militaristic era of economic upsurge, empire, and grandeur whose *Iliad* was the saga of Sedan. In November 1918, a somber enough date, Hesse wrote about these things in the essay "World History," about the legend of the Franco-Prussian War: "As we were credibly and sacredly assured, miracles and heroic deeds had occurred in this war, there had been truly grandiose and world-historical events, it hadn't just been like yesterday or today or any old time." [14] Hesse was fifteen before this fantasy began to fade, strengthened as it was by the annual Sedan festival—"the finest day of the year." In the first flush of his feelings for Emma, Hans suddenly remembers a September day three years before, the eve of the festival, when he and his friend August spent the time adorning flag poles with ivy and the maid Anna baked plumcake—a memory which, the author reflects, is Hans's last sight of his innocent boyhood.

Hesse's own respect for "world history"—that is, the idealization of war and great deeds—declined when he began to see through his teachers: "I knew . . . the world history they taught us was

[14] VII, 121.

probably a kind of swindle of the grown-ups, meant to degrade us and make us feel small." [15] This insight was vouchsafed Hesse at Maulbronn; he noticed the moral masquerade of the teachers, which for him meant the masquerade of that whole society, its façade of culture and heroism disguising a cataclysmic submersion in industrialization, an especial rapacity and devotion to Mammon, aesthetic impoverishment, and general spiritual decay. But still: "The world was round and it turned, and if our grandfathers had written poems and works of philosophy, that was all very fine, but their grandsons wanted to show that in this country there were other capacities too." [16] *Beneath the Wheel*—indeed the entire *Schulliteratur*—is fundamentally concerned to castigate that phenomenon, "the defeat, indeed the extirpation of the German mind in favor of the 'German Empire.' " [17]

There are fringe political implications in the satire of *Beneath the Wheel,* and these are of an anarchistic kind.[18] Those who go to the seminary sell themselves to the state, and the state will ensure that it receives its due. The seminary serves not primarily to educate but to produce good citizens and reliable civil servants. As for the teacher, "His task, given him by the state, is to control the rude energies and natural desires of young boys, to expunge them, and to replace them with quiet, moderate ideals such as the state recognizes" (I, 418). Behind the crude criticism of brutal teachers, dishonest and also arid men of the intellect, lies the idea that no such system, maybe no system of schools at all, could ever provide the education the budding *individual* needs, for he must above all else be free of schools, and his development must not be circumscribed by any set of external conventions. The problems of Hesse's writings from *Demian* to *The Glass Bead Game* are foreshadowed, for the teachers in *Beneath the Wheel* commit the unpardonable sin of planting in the helpless Hans Giebenrath a seed

[15] VII, 122.

[16] "The Empire" (VII, 129).

[17] Nietzsche, *Werke,* I, 137.

[18] Hesse's coeditorship of the periodical *März* (founded 1905) had some political implications. The title of the magazine alluded directly to the March Days. Its polemics were directed "in particular against the personal rule of William II . . . although at bottom I did not take these political goals seriously" (IV, 475).

which is foreign to his nature, that of intellectual ambition. *Gemüt* (the emotional self), it is bitterly observed, is cared for only in the confirmation classes—for the rest we have the materialistic religion of work and success, and it leads to the death of childhood. Hans is devoured by implanted ambitions to surpass his fellows and to penetrate to "true knowledge," but never understands the real nature of these impulses; what the teachers do to his "soul" is expressed in a symbol of unmistakable import: "In the good-looking, delicate boyish face deep-lying restless eyes burned with a dull fire, on the handsome brow fine furrows quivered, betraying intellect, and the arms and hands, thin and lean in any case, hung down with a weary grace which was reminiscent of Botticelli" (I, 380).

The crucifixion, then, of Hans Giebenrath begins with his teachers in his home town, in the Black Forest, where he attends the preparatory school. The rector and the local pastor give him special tuition—they make of him a kind of stalking horse for their own ambitions. In reality Hesse remembered two of his early teachers with respect—Schmid at the school in Calw and Rector Bauer at the school in Göppingen. The latter in particular gave him his first experience of the true pedagogical relationship, "that so infinitely fruitful and at the same time so subtle relationship between a spiritual mentor and a gifted child." [19] Such terms as "veneration" and "spiritual vocation" which Hesse uses in recalling Rector Bauer belong indeed to the world of the later novels in which this particular relationship is constantly sought for and adumbrated. But there is none of this reconciling spirit in *Beneath the Wheel;* Hans's teachers are merely dry civil servants who abuse their power and sometimes even resort to violence.

The cobbler Flaig is their foil. Flaig is portrayed with some irony as a fanatical Pietist of the type Calw and Hesse knew well, a great figure among the absurd—and yet not so absurd—*Stundenbrüder;* [20] the cobbler is a childhood friend of the boy, interprets the Bible to him, and is a shadowy prototype of the genuine "teacher" who

[19] "From My Schooldays" (IV, 604).
[20] Cf. "Walter Kömpff" (1908): "In the people of this district there is a strong tendency toward this sort of thing, and mostly it is the better and more gifted individuals who are drawn to it" (II, 231).

appears in the later novels and teaches only by example and by intuitive contact; but as Hans grows older and comes under the influence of the ambitious professionals, he slips out of the cobbler's sphere. Flaig is largely replaced in Hans's estimation by the pastor, an exponent of the Higher Criticism, the mysteries of which excite the boy's imagination; he begins to aspire after learning and to be proud, to feel contempt for his more stupid schoolfellows, and to become like his mentors.

In one of his intrusive commentaries, the author tells us there are two forms of theology, that which is essentially science and that which is essentially art; whatever the former may achieve, it is always the latter which spreads faith and love. And the satirist sides with art while still respecting science, with life while still respecting the mind; for the Pietism in Hesse's background is paradoxically a principal source of his art. The opposition of discipline and feeling which exists within Pietism itself prefigures the tension of form and freedom in the later novels; but at the time of *Beneath the Wheel* this issue was externalized and only crudely sensed; thus the author would not hesitate in choosing between an extraverted and an introverted theology. Hans Giebenrath chooses the other, or rather it is his tragedy that he has this choice forced upon him, and the guilt is supposed to lie with those who do violence to his personality.

But *Beneath the Wheel* is not a great satirical novel, it is too obvious, too blatant, and has grave formal defects. Like *Peter Camenzind* it was an attempt at escape: "to portray the crisis of those years of development and to liberate myself from the memory of them." [21] Hesse came to perceive that it was a "premature undertaking." [22] The book is not nearly so even as *Peter Camenzind:* the vitriolic tone offends, and the last section of the novel in part degenerates into an irrelevant preoccupation with the minutiae of Swabian small-town life. Critics have not been slow to point out these weaknesses; Ball notes a certain timidity or intentional reserve and complains that the book is ultimately superficial; while the blame for Hans's collapse is laid on the teachers, its real motivation is in fact not at all clear.[23] H. R. Schmid goes

[21] VII, 874.   [22] *Ibid.*
[23] Cf. Ball, *Hermann Hesse*, p. 57.

further: he finds *Beneath the Wheel* to be a typical school novel, yet with the important reservation that Hans's fate is no more than the story of a neurasthenic, a decadent whose vitality is grossly impaired.[24] As Hesse specifically protests, Hans's condition may be ascribed to the influence of the teachers, but a close reading of the novel tends to support Schmid's point: Hans Giebenrath is indeed a neurasthenic, his melancholia related to the disease of Lauscher and Camenzind, he is a stray from the world of the Romantic agony [25]—and the connection is not surprising, for the hostility to the school system in nineteenth-century Germany may be seen as an integral part of the whole Romantic tradition.[26]

On the other hand, it is not right to say that *Beneath the Wheel* shows no advance upon the situation of *Hermann Lauscher* and *Peter Camenzind*; an advance there certainly is, though perhaps into a cul-de-sac. Although Hesse's path, from this point on, has been described as essentially the attempt to lay hold on a sphere in which people like Hans Giebenrath may have the possibility of development and, indeed, survival, [27] this observation misses the most significant point about *Beneath the Wheel*. A closer analysis of the novel's symbolism reveals that this school novel is little better than a façade behind which the story of Hermann Lauscher and Peter Camenzind is continued, but given a very different twist. While *Peter Camenzind* was unmasked as a novel of escape which fails, a physic which temporarily disperses the symptoms but does not touch the disease, *Beneath the Wheel* is almost the opposite, a book which takes up the extreme Romantic position as a base for satirical sorties and yet unconsciously, by its whole tenor, ex-

---

[24] Schmid, *Hermann Hesse*, p. 78.

[25] Cf. K. Weibel, *Hermann Hesse und die deutsche Romantik* (diss., Bern; Winterthur, 1954): "Dieser Romantik aber muss er erliegen, weil er nicht, wie der Dichter Heilner, die Kraft und die Fähigkeit hat, sie zu verwirklichen und zu erfüllen" (He inevitably succumbs to this Romantic strain, because unlike Heilner the poet he does not have the strength and the capacity to bring it to its realization and fulfillment) (p. 34).

[26] Ball notes the difference, in this respect, between the educational traditions of France and Germany: "Gestalten wie Rimbaud sind dort Ausnahmen; bei uns sind sie fast die Regel" (Figures like Rimbaud are exceptions there; with us they are almost the rule) (*op. cit.*, p. 81).

[27] Weibel, *op. cit.*, p. 35.

presses the conviction of successful adaptation to society, of *embourgeoisement* achieved.

Peter Camenzind yearned back to that point in time at which the *patres* had taken him up and sent him to school, for this was the end of his childhood and the beginning of the repression of his soul; this is the moment also, Hesse is later to infer, at which the true teacher should materialize and real education begin. The death of childhood is poignantly portrayed when Hans Giebenrath, in an outburst of violence, chops up his old rabbit hutch. Childhood for Hans means summer and the river, swimming, and above all angling (forbidden him by his father lest it interfere with his work), a world of strong colors and odors, of all the senses wide awake. He steps out of the Rector's house the last night before the examination, and his senses suddenly break out of the cocoon in which he has been living for months:

The big limes on the church hill shone dully in the hot sunlight of the late afternoon; on the market place both large fountains splashed and sparkled; the close blue-black pine hills gazed in over the irregular line of the roofs. The boy felt as though he hadn't seen all this for a long time, and it all seemed unusually lovely and enticing [I, 380].

Hans Giebenrath sits upon the balustrade of the old bridge, stares dreamily and sadly into the water and throws crumbs of bread to the fish. This is a gesture which will be repeated in Hesse's novels, an allegory for the feeding of the famished soul. But it is after he hears of his outstanding success in the examination and is released from his toil for the holidays, that Hans temporarily rediscovers paradise. He is absorbed by this physical world, by its visual and tactile reality and its vitality, and by its nightly blend of quiet and thrill:

The water lay black and still beneath the bridge, in the lower mill there was already a light. Voices and singing ran along the bridges and the streets, the air was a little sultry and in the river every minute a dark fish leaped up with an abrupt jerk. On evenings like this the fish are curiously excited, shoot zigzag hither and thither, spring into the air, crowd around the fisher's line and pounce blindly on the bait [I, 409].

It is no accident that it is the darting fish which subsume the magic of the living moment, or that it is of them and of the dark water that this voice of deep memory is able to speak so lovingly, almost free of the accents of ratiocination. However, even in these passages this last sometimes does intrude and of course it spoils the effect: "Nothing expresses the warmth of a pure day in high summer as well as the few quiet little clouds" (I, 405). For the boy this wonderful summer lasts but a couple of days, for almost straightaway the pedagogues pounce upon him once more with their grammar books, suggesting he prepare himself for Maulbronn; Hans Giebenrath's ephemeral summer is his moment of awakening and enlightenment, when he remembers himself and his soul.

Exactly a year later, when he is sent home sick from the seminary, a reversion occurs, described in a way which is extremely revealing:

The precocious youth, now that he was sick, went through an unreal, second childhood. His feelings, which had been robbed of their childhood, now fled back with a sudden burst of longing into those beautiful, dimming years and wandered bewitched in a forest of memories which had a strength and clarity which was perhaps morbid [I, 495].

The satirical note has now been struck again, and harsh accusations sound. The author is consequently detached once more from his material, suspicious of surrender to dreams and memories, for which the word "forest" becomes a dark symbol; and while Hans Giebenrath that summer evening on the bridge at Calw is no doubt Hermann Hesse, Hans Giebenrath after his rustication from Maulbronn has largely ceased to be.

The author is now preparing the lamb for the sacrifice, for though Hermann Lauscher has often been seen as Hesse's Werther, it is really Hans Giebenrath who plays that role. It is true that the last section of the novel, after the return from Maulbronn, still draws upon the author's own experiences—for instance the cider-pressing, the passionate moments with Emma, the days in the workshop, and the drunken afternoon with the apprentices. But the figure who moves through all these incidents has an invented destiny; for at Maulbronn the author's actual fate is transferred to the shoulders

of Hermann Heilner.[28] The interpretation turns essentially upon
the following passage:

When a tree is cropped it often produces new shoots near the roots, and
in this way too a soul which has sickened in its blossoming and gone bad
often returns to the springlike time of its beginnings and its expectant
childhood, as if it could discover new hope there and join up the broken
thread of life again. The sprigs of root shoot up lasciviously, succulent
and fast, but it is a sham life, and they will never grow again into a
proper tree [I, 495].

The symbol is intensely negative in its implication; the tree of
childhood will inevitably be cropped. The putting out of new
shoots near the original roots is in fact a symptom of doom; for it
is not possible to go back and begin again—the effort to do this is
disease, regression, neurosis. At the end of childhood comes a break
in the thread of life, where no healthy connection can ever again
be made. Thus when Hans Giebenrath, after Maulbronn, goes
back into himself, he finds his way only into a sick forest: "This is
what happened to Hans Giebenrath too, and therefore it is necessary to follow him some way upon his dream paths in the land of
the child" (I, 495).

The sovereign detachment, albeit tinged with pity, could not be
more apparent. And, indeed, *Beneath the Wheel* on its deepest level
is unconsciously the most pessimistic novel Hesse ever wrote, for
it alone denies completely the value of the inward way. It is no
accident that it was written just after Hesse's marriage, as he was in
the act of settling down; it is also no accident that it introduces a
period in his career which shows a steady parochialization, if not
enfeeblement, of his literary talent. Apparently an aggressive,
"Romantic" satire, it is actually a further step outward beyond
Peter Camenzind toward "realism," toward bourgeois compromise.
The book, moreover, has lost the Jean Paulian warmth which many
of Hesse's short stories from this period still possess. Thus the
conventional school novel, the novel which decries that vicious

---

[28] "The Preparatory School Boy" offers further confirmation of the real situation; the maid Babett "had heard about the overworking of young people in
the high schools and had no idea how far her protégé was from overexertion
in his studies" (I, 651). Karl Bauer is not like Hans Giebenrath, but for that
perhaps all the more like his author.

political and social system that attempts to force a "false identity" [29] upon Hans Giebenrath, is a cloak for an act of detachment which sees poor Hans's fate as in the last resort something in himself, his weakness, his decadence. The suggestion that it is all a specific case of heredity, of that psychophysical decay so beloved of *fin de siècle* writers, is in fact made early in the book: "A subtle observer with a modern approach, recalling the frail mother and the family's impressive age, could have spoken of hypertrophy of the intelligence as a symptom of incipient degeneration" (I, 376).

The degree, therefore, to which Hans Giebenrath may be identified with his author, is highly limited, especially in the later chapters of the novel. Even in the earlier chapters he may well be partly a projection of Hesse's younger brother, also called Hans. Hans Hesse differed greatly from Hermann: he was not as clever, much less intellectual, more naïve in his responses to life.[30] Though christened Johannes like his father (whom this lofty name fitted far better), he was "Hans" to everyone, "a near, familiar, dear, and harmless person," [31] though not without his own secrets. Frightened and overawed by the intellectual atmosphere of the house at Calw, little Hans sought his emotional nourishment elsewhere; it was in games, which he invented for himself, that he found his best means of self-expression—he took to them more passionately and certainly more desperately than does the average child. For him school was agony: "The preparatory school, which had also caused me a lot of conflicts, became a tragedy for him as time went on . . . and when later on as a young writer and not without embitterment I had it out with schools of all kinds in the story *Beneath the Wheel*, the painful school career of my brother was almost as much a source of this as was my own." [32] Unlike his brother, Hans Hesse as an adult found no fulfillment at all—"We were both outsiders." [33] He had a meaningless job and no hope for

---

[29] J. C. Middleton, "Hermann Hesse as Humanist" (diss., Oxford, 1954), p. 51.

[30] Cf. "Recollections of Hans" (IV, 690 ff.).   [31] *Ibid.* (IV, 700).

[32] *Ibid.* (IV, 702). Hans had to endure "a beast of a teacher" (VII, 931). Hermann Lauscher, of course, also complains of his treatment at school by obnoxious teachers; school had for him, until his fourteenth year, "the heavy atmosphere of a corrective institution" (I, 112–113).

[33] IV, 714.

the future and his dreams all looked backward, "back to paradise, to childhood." [34] Hans Giebenrath, then, on the novelist's own admission, is almost as much Hans Hesse as he is Hermann; and when Hans Giebenrath listens in worried half-comprehension to Hermann Heilner's Romantic moans, it may well be that we have here the reconstruction of a scene set originally not in Maulbronn at all but at home in Calw.

The symptoms of Hans Giebenrath's nervous decline are gone into in detail. "He had a horror of all external enthusiasm" (I, 439), we are told, and this succinct sentence sums him up well. Naturally introverted, he is driven further in upon himself by circumstance, a fate which befalls many of Hesse's characters. When he goes to Maulbronn, his physical state is already bad, and he suffers perpetually from headaches. As his schizophrenic condition develops, it begins to lead to acute symptoms, loss of memory, loss of attention, and eventually hallucinations. The characters in his history books, his Livy, his Homer, and the New Testament begin to acquire tactile reality for him, in particular their eyes and their hands; thus when reading the sixth chapter of Mark he experiences vividly the welcoming gesture of Jesus' "slim, beautiful, brownish hand" (I, 470); when a professor speaks to him in class he fails to react for he is far away—"He was in the midst of other people, other hands touched him" (I, 475). He begins to have "bright, delicate, unusual dreams" and he feels warm sensations "as if a light hand slipped over his body with a soft contact" (I, 478). His intellectual ability, which seemed indeed like a gift from the gods for it is traceable neither to his stupid father nor to his weakling mother, is now in sharp decline; his childhood has long since expired under a heap of grammars, and he becomes lost in sick memories of what once was real. What is fresh now, and active, is the sexual instinct. The conflicts with school, with the adult environment—"conflicts," Hesse comments, "which no one is spared who is to develop personality" [35]—have their source in part in puberty. A constant motif of the school novel is the awakening of the sexual urge in the hostile environment of the high school. *Friend Death* makes little of this, and in this respect is rather ex-

[34] IV, 715.   [35] IV, 471.

ceptional; other novels work the theme *ad nauseam*, on both the homosexual and the heterosexual side.[36] In *Beneath the Wheel* we hear of "the uncomprehended, dark urging of emergent manhood" (I, 450); in Hans this change is slow, and entirely unconscious. As in so many other things, so also in this, he trails behind his friend, Hermann Heilner; the full outburst comes only toward the end of the novel, after the return from Maulbronn, in the short affair with Emma, Flaig's niece. As they work the cider press together the scent of her hair, the touch of it, the brush of her knee overwhelm him and blur his senses; his heart almost stops, his arms go weak, and he can gaze at her only when she is looking away. Then, conversely, there follows that sudden intensification of sense impressions which is a recurrent motif in Hesse's novels: "The sparrows, grown fat on the husks, hurtled raucously through the sky, which had never been so high and beautiful or so longing a blue. Never had the river had such a pure, greeny-blue, laughing surface, nor a roaring weir of such brilliant white" (I, 512). The water is there, the colors are bright, and there is rapid, animal movement in the picture; the world lights up outside the citadel of the mind and this corresponds to a liberation, however sick and transient, of the soul.

For Hans Giebenrath, at Maulbronn, the erotic is as yet unspoken, unknown. What he does experience is what Nietzsche called "faithful friendship," which begins for him when he and Hermann Heilner kiss. And with this kiss we have the first of a long series of such sacramental acts in this author's work. The motif of friendship, of the pair of high school boys, is all but universal in the school novel; generally the two figures are made to contrast sharply, one of them—as for instance Karl Notwang in *Friend Death*—always being strongminded, usually physically tough, and often even actually successful at school. This, of course, is a device to compensate for the fact that the central character in the school novel frequently makes an impression of abnormality and pathological weakness—and thereby to strengthen the effect of realism, balance, and objectivity. In seven of the eight Hesse novels with which this study is principally concerned the motif of the pair of male friends

[36] For example, Hans Hart, *Was zur Sonne will* (Berlin, 1907); O. Schmitz, *Der Untergang einer Kindheit* (Munich, 1905).

is an integral one and is even present in the apparent exception, *The Steppenwolf*, in a form appropriate to that transvestite work.

Thus this structural feature of the school novel happened to coincide extraordinarily well with Hesse's own creative needs, the impulse to express duality, to make a schizophrenic projection, a device common enough among authors but particularly popular with Hesse.[37] Indeed it is used not once but twice in *Beneath the Wheel*. While in Stuttgart for the examination, Hans meets another candidate at a relative's house, who comes from the Göppingen preparatory school, which has sent up a large contingent for the examination. This slightly cynical "sophisticated Latinist" (I, 391), who apparently fails the examination but is confident he will go on to the high school in any case,[38] is in part a humorous self-portrait—Hesse himself took the examination from Göppingen. We recall of course the doubles who appear in *Hermann Lauscher*. As for Hermann Heilner, there is first of all the play with his name;[39] this name contains several elements—"Hermann Hesse," "Heiner,"[40] and presumably "*heil*" ("whole," "cured") (for Heilner is later "saved" or "cured"; unlike Hans or Heiner, he does not get taken by Freund Hein). At Maulbronn, Hans is slow to make a friend, too easily frightened back into his shell, but like Peter Camenzind always waiting, full of need: "Like a shy girl he stayed in his place and waited to see if someone came for him, a stronger

[37] Hans Mayer observes: "Sie alle, diese Freunde und Gegenspieler, scheinen, wie Leverkühn und Zeitblom in Thomas Manns Roman *Doktor Faustus*, etwas zu verhüllen, 'das Geheimnis ihrer Identität' (um es mit Thomas Manns eigenen Worten zu sagen). . . . Schizophrenie . . . ist ein Ausdruck einer geistigen Erkrankung zugleich aber ein wesentliches Formelement der romantischen Kunst" (All of them, these friends and foils, seem, like Leverkühn and Zeitblom in Thomas Mann's novel *Doctor Faustus*, to conceal something, "the secret of their identity" [to use Thomas Mann's own words]. . . . Schizophrenia . . . is the expression of a mental illness but at the same time it is an essential formal element of Romantic art) ("Hermann Hesse und das 'Feuilletonistische Zeitalter,'" in *Studien zur deutschen Literatur* [Berlin, 1954], p. 230). One might recall Jean Paul's *Flegeljahre*, which meant so much to Hesse.

[38] Hesse, after leaving Maulbronn, attended the high school in Bad Cannstatt for a time.

[39] For something of this favorite occupation of Hesse's, onomastic games, see J. Mileck, "Names and the Creative Process," *Monatshefte für deutschen Unterricht*, LIII (1961), 167–180.

[40] Besides Strauss's hero, Hesse's second son also bore this name.

and bolder person than he, who might carry him along and force him to be happy" (I, 439). The simile of the shy girl is perhaps worth noting. And Heilner has just the required strength, but at first his opinion of Hans is apparently a low one. The initial description is interesting:

A striking, although less complex individual was Hermann Heilner, a Black Forester of good family. On the very first day everyone knew he was a poet and an aesthete, and there was the legend that he had written his essay in the exam in hexameters. He talked a lot and in a lively manner, possessed a beautiful violin and seemed to carry his nature on the surface, and this consisted principally of a youthful and immature mixture of sentimentality and frivolity. But less visibly he also had something deeper in him. He was physically and emotionally precocious and was already experimenting in going his own way [I, 434].

The details of this picture are of course all telltale; the attitude behind it is a mixture of ironic detachment ("less complex," "immature mixture," and so forth) and pride ("something deeper"); from the outset the author is inside as well as outside this character, and from this point on his identification with Hans begins to weaken. Heilner also can find no congenial friend at the seminary, and he needs a listener: Hans fills this role well, as young Hans Hesse may also have done, for *he* was "a pleasant toy, let's say a sort of domestic cat" (I, 449). Heilner is a budding poet in a well-worn tradition, addicted to melancholy wanderings, to autumn and Lenau, and to the violin. The author's increasing detachment from Romantic poetry, or at least from the cult of it, may be noticed here; while *Hermann Lauscher* and *An Hour beyond Midnight* show the influence of Heine, Peter Camenzind uses the poet's "empty verses" (!) (I, 240) as a receptacle for his own feelings, while Heilner's complaints are "after the style of lyrical youths who read Heine" (I, 450). Hans and Hermann talk of clouds, and of wonderful things Heilner has seen such as ships on the Rhine at night. But Heilner is not only a poet, he is also a satirist and critic. Almost exactly duplicating Karl Notwang's views, he complains about the way Homer is studied in school: "There we go reading Homer . . . as if the Odyssey were a cookery book. Two lines an hour, and then every word chewed over and examined till it makes you feel sick" (I, 442). Their dormitory bears the name of "Hellas," a fact which arouses Heilner's ire: "All this classical stuff is a swindle" (I, 442). Another of his remarks—"If one of us should try to live a little in the Greek fashion he'd be thrown out" (I, 442) —is probably to be understood quite naïvely, and without the obvious *sous-entendu*.

Heilner is subject to attacks of melancholia; he has "a sick need to be pitied and petted" (I, 450). Hesse's attitude to melancholia is now much less sympathetic than it was in *Peter Camenzind*. Melancholia is a disease in both novels, but in *Peter Camenzind* it is seen with the eye of the patient, in *Beneath the Wheel* with that of the physician—Heilner suffers from "attacks of a baseless, slightly coquettish melancholia" (I, 449). He, as an artist, has no use for anything abstract and is frightened of mathematics; he responds (as Hans at first does not) to the beauty of the old monastery, he is also (like Hans) "a mother's boy" (I, 450). In fact the identity of Hans Giebenrath and Hermann Heilner is extremely close; as time goes on Hans becomes more like Heilner. An artistic strain in his personality begins to reveal itself as the dominance of the intellect declines. Both come from the mother. Both are really artists, and the junior gradually moves into the room that the senior vacates. The "elder brother" disappears eventually—Hans, the "younger brother," replaces him as the outsider, whom the institution and its officers now regard as beyond the pale. This "principle of succession," of course, is a most significant structural feature in Hesse's later novels.

Heilner is a "genius," which is both less and more than an artist (an issue touched on many years later in the *Steppenwolf* tractate). The teachers are the acolytes of convention, and deviations from the norm, such as are implied by the word "*Genie*," are naturally abhorrent to them. True geniuses, the author tells us, survive whatever treatment may be meted out to them at school, with the ironical result that future generations of schoolmasters are enabled to hold them up as an example: "And so from school to school the spectacle of the struggle between law and spirit is repeated" (I, 466). "Law and spirit" (*Gesetz und Geist*) rings strangely, in view of Hesse's characteristic dialectic; we might have expected "law and soul." In the maturer novels, indeed, "law" and "spirit" often become one, and their rigidity is then contrasted with the fluid soul. But "law," for Hesse, is always an ambiguous term, it may refer to the sublime patterns of the Glass Bead Game, the epitome of "spirit" and of form, but it may also be weighted with the dross of the common world, of society which constantly strives, through the mechanism of convention, to give itelf the appearance of truth and permanence. What rebels against the law, however, "in the dark dormitory" (I, 445) is soul, is "the sensitive heart."

Sometime after Heilner has been lured from his self-assured detachment into a fight with another boy and been seen publicly in tears, he kisses Hans. Hans experiences this as "something strange, new, perhaps dangerous" (I, 445); he knows that its discovery would bring great disgrace. The scene has poetic force, almost entirely dissipated however by the reflective paragraph which is then interpolated: "An adult who saw the little scene would perhaps have taken silent pleasure in it" (I, 446). This insertion reveals the fundamental ambivalence of this novel, the tension between poetic memory and prosaic pose. The relationship between Hans Giebenrath and Hermann Heilner enters a period of crisis when Heilner, in trouble with the authorities, is abandoned in cowardly fashion by his friend. Heilner becomes more and more rebellious, his poems—aptly called "Songs of a Monk"—include bitter satirical verses, while Hans Giebenrath, new and strange forces at work within him, gradually loses not only his ability but also his desire to conform. When one of his roommates, Hindinger, is accidentally drowned (for water, which lies outside the walls of Maulbronn, is the way to both the soul *and* death), the incident acts as a catalyst which makes Hans recognize the inadmirable nature of his conduct toward his friend; this is essentially a moment of self-recognition, for puberty is bringing a new ability to stand outside himself, to view himself objectively, to reflect about himself. This, of course, is the ultimate end of Hans Giebenrath's childhood: "It was as though his soul had been transferred to another country" (I, 462). The homoerotic motif is gentle; the boys experience unconsciously, "with expectant shyness something of the tender secrets of a first love" (I, 465). Hans loses interest in Livy and in Hebrew grammar, despite a warning from the Ephorus that to weaken is to run the risk of coming "beneath the wheel" (I, 468). Heilner's melancholy, like Peter Camenzind's when in his cups, is accompanied by a bitter satirical spirit. Hans's, however, is associated with increasing help-lessness, bewilderment, and meandering in dreams. One of them must die, so that the other may live on.

Therefore Heilner runs away, he breaks out of the prison of Maulbronn by an act of defiant self-will; he is not, as Hans is, eventually relegated because of a nervous breakdown. Before he goes he tells his friend of another kiss, this time with a girl at home. Under this sign his flight takes place, though its ostensible motive is anger that the Ephorus has forbidden him and Hans to associate. It is a short moment of triumphant freedom: "At this same time Heilner lay a few miles away in a wood. He was freezing and could not sleep, but he breathed with deep relief in a profound feeling of freedom and stretched his limbs as though he had escaped from a narrow cage" (I, 482). He takes his solace in the night, the stars, the clouds, the satisfaction that he has asserted his manly will. Captured, after two days of freedom, by a rural gendarme, he re-turns to the seminary defiant; he is without remorse for his escapade and is duly expelled. He departs with a handclasp, and Hans never hears from him again. As time goes on, Heilner's flight from Maulbronn enters the sphere of history and then of legend (*Sage*). Such a deed makes good material for legend; it is the point where the ordinary course of existence is ruptured by the fantastic; and legend becomes, in the context of Hesse's later work, the ultimate refuge of the uncompromising individualist—the legend of the Magister Ludi is just such another case. Of the fate of the hero of the legend, in *Beneath the Wheel*, we do learn a little: "The suffering of life later took the passionate youth . . . under a stern yoke, and if he has not become a hero, at least he has become a man" (I, 484). This destiny, had the boys at Maulbronn known of it, might well have impaired the legend! As for Hans Gieben-rath, he is not so lucky as Heilner; he languishes on in a be-wildered, futile groping after the lost thread of his childhood and eventually finds his way to death. Much as in *Friend Death*, the notion of death begins to enter the failure's dreams. He dreams of Heilner drowned (as Peter Camenzind's comrade *was* drowned), and then in another dream pursues him through a forest, his friend repeating the words of their last recorded conversation: "I have a sweetheart" (I, 490). Hans plans his suicide in detail, but it happens that the time is not yet ripe; a few more experiences—"a few drops of pleasure and vitality each day out of the chalice of death" (I, 492)—are to be his before he himself finally slides into the water and dies. An accident?—or maybe a suicide from exhaustion and fear.

In January 1951, Hermann Hesse, in a reply "to a schoolboy who is reading *Beneath the Wheel* and thinking of suicide," answered the question why he himself, when a seminarian, failed to commit suicide; it was because of instinct, of a will-to-life stronger than the death-wish:

I was, after all, gifted with senses and soul. . . . Moreover, I was not only a man of the senses, I was also an artist; I could reproduce in my memory the images and experiences I got from the world, I could play with them, I could try to turn them into something new and special by means of drawings, hummed melodies, poetic words. And probably it was this artist's joy and artist's curiosity which in spite of everything made me prefer life to death.[41]

Hermann Heilner is the budding artist who survives, Hans Giebenrath the sick prodigy who regresses and dies and thus finds his way back to the long-dead mother whose absence has always haunted him. Art—that is, memory, form, and game—may make life tolerable. But we are not told, in the novel, that Hermann Heilner ever realizes himself as an artist; we hear only, "If not a hero at least a man." In this very terminology we may be surprised to see a laudation of will, albeit only in the service of society. All we learn further about Heilner is that, after bursting out from Maulbronn, he goes on to more turbulent years and eventually to maturity. And if there is still any doubt as to what "maturity" and "manhood" mean in the context of *Beneath the Wheel*, a quotation from the author's portrait of Hans Hesse practically settles the matter:

And at last I had reached the goal, had freed myself first of all from the family, then from my previous profession, had become a writer, could support myself this way, had become reconciled with my family and the bourgeois world and recognized by them. I had married, settled down a

[41] *Letters* (VII, 777).

long way from any towns in a beautiful countryside, lived as I pleased, a friend of nature and a friend of books. . . . For Hans . . . I was a man who had arrived, who was successful.[42]

Compromise with the family and the bourgeois sphere, marriage and material success, a touch of dilettantism—this became the environment in which Hermann Heilner's destiny as an artist was apparently to be fulfilled. Hermann Heilner is the Peter Camenzind who does find a home in the *outside* world, Hans Giebenrath the Peter Camenzind who sinks, hopelessly, into the cold waters of the Nimikon lake; Peter Camenzind himself, perhaps rather shrewdly, did neither of these things.

Hesse's own account of his running away from Maulbronn [43] naturally corresponds closely to the details the novel gives of Heilner's escapade, except for the fact that Hesse was punished *at* the seminary and not immediately expelled. His family treated him with terrifying kindness (and a similar apprehensive consideration on the part of his father unnerves Hans Giebenrath). Especially terrifying was the prospect of an interview with his grandfather, Hermann Gundert, the celebrated indologist. The latter's amiable greeting [44] was an anticlimax which may have reflected that gentleman's own recollection of unhappy days at Maulbronn; [45] and in any case Hermann Gundert was a shrewd old man who knew how to deal with such matters. While the indentification with Hermann Heilner cannot be doubted, its implications were probably never fully clear to the author. Ball's remark—presumably approved by Hesse—that at the time of writing *Beneath the Wheel* Hesse was glad to be Giebenrath, the clever boy, rather than Heilner, the genius,[46] is an extraordinary distortion, though all the same it does reveal an inkling of the fundamental tenor of the work. *Beneath the Wheel* is in fact Hesse's most conformist novel, and its self-insight is very limited. A similar spirit of "reconciliation," but this

---

[42] IV, 714.
[43] Cf. "About Grandfather" (VII, 831), also "Letter to Adele" (VII, 442).
[44] He referred jovially (VII, 831) to his grandson's *Geniereisle;* this almost untranslatable term, which then finds its way into *Beneath the Wheel,* had been current in Tübingen in Hermann Gundert's student days.
[45] Cf. Ball, *op. cit.,* pp. 60–61.
[46] *Ibid.,* p. 58.

time overt and fully conscious, may be discerned in the story "The Engagement" (1908), which certainly contains autobiographical elements and also deals, though without intellectual depth, with the issue of the outsider's cure.

Beneath the Wheel lacks the lyricism of *Peter Camenzind;* the instants of poetry, the characteristic moments of recall, of sensuous and intuitive experience, are scattered rather sparsely in a desert of polemical discourse and almost journalistic banality; the dynamic verbs which are such a feature of the language of *Peter Camenzind* have vanished. Instances of gross Neo-Romantic ornamentalism, such as the description of the Hebrew tongue—"a brittle, dried-up and yet still mysteriously living tree. . . . In its branches, hollows and roots dwell . . . thousand-year-old spirits" (I, 447)—do nothing to rescue the book linguistically. As a work of art the novel might even be adjudged a serious disappointment after *Peter Camenzind*, having all the distinguishing marks of a minor talent.

It is, however, very significant that what is enshrined in the heart of *Beneath the Wheel* is not Hermann Heilner's "cure," only briefly referred to and in any case still in progress when the book was being written, but that traumatic memory of the author's youth, Maulbronn, and the escape from Maulbronn. In the flight from the seminary—irrespective of what may have followed it, either in Hesse's life or in the novel—is symbolized not compromise but the uttermost refusal of compromise, the extreme demand and the extreme situation, the search for that which is called in *The Steppenwolf* "the unconditional," the act of willed self-isolation and of isolated self-will. Coinciding, as it did by chance at this moment of time, with the more general evil at which the school literature pointed its finger, the "neurosis" [47] of the Swabian seminarians had of course an aristocratic lineage. It was a disease widespread among Swabian poets—Friedrich Hölderlin, Wilhelm Waiblinger, and Eduard Mörike all suffered from it. "In Pressel's Summerhouse," one of Hesse's justly famous novellas and a minor masterpiece, was published in 1913. It is a work which sheds light upon the Maulbronn experience and its many reverberations. The novella recounts one afternoon in the life of the demented Hölderlin; Waiblinger

---

[47] *Ibid.,* p. 66.

and Mörike, both students at the Stift, take him for a walk in Tübingen, up on to the Österberg, where they spend some time sitting smoking and conversing in Pressel's Chinese summerhouse. The stormy dispute between Waiblinger and Mörike while the silent Hölderlin looks on with his pipe at the window has touches of poetic grandeur, as has the poignant moment when Lotte Zimmer calls for her charge and leads Hölderlin away down the hill like a child, the tall dignified figure carrying its large black hat. At this point the novella might profitably have ended; aesthetically it is perhaps unsatisfying that it then goes further into the Waib-linger-Mörike relationship.

What it was that attracted Hesse to his three famous predecessors is clear enough—each one of them, in his own way, fought against the apparently irresistible fate which had determined to make a clergyman out of him; two of them came in the end to insanity, and one to a life of uneasy compromise, frustration, and loneliness. The relationship between Waiblinger and Mörike is sketched in against the background of impending catastrophe for the former; Waiblinger is a gross misfit at the Stift and is expecting expulsion; what he says to Mörike, when they argue, is of peculiar interest: "You're also siding with those opposite, and it's wrong for you to do that, Heaven knows you're worth more than that whole gang" (II, 864). Mörike, then, stands accused by the rebel of betraying their friendship and of siding, at the moment of crisis, with the party of orthodoxy and authority, though he heatedly denies it. "You're a low coward, Giebenrath, shame on you!" Hermann Heilner says to Hans Giebenrath, for "he had relied on Hans" (I, 453). And in this case, at least, the charge must be accounted just. It would therefore seem likely that in this aspect of the relationship between Waiblinger and Mörike "In Pressel's Summerhouse" reflects some experience of the author at Maulbronn twenty years before, the same experience of friendship and of betrayal—real or presumed—as is portrayed in *Beneath the Wheel*, an experience, moreover, which Hesse has the artist's ability to understand from both sides, that of the traitor as well as that of the betrayed.

In "Conjurations" (1954) is related a curious story told by Hesse's mother of her schooldays, of her school friend Olga, two years older than herself, whom she venerated. One day Olga is in disgrace, on account of a common enough offense; the pastor forbids anyone in the class to associate with her. Marie Gundert, as she then was, stood by her friend and accepted her share of ostracism. She rebelled against the institution and went through, and later repented of, "a period of worldliness, revolt, and spiritual arrogance"; [48] but her children's sympathies, as they heard the story, did not lie with the school and the pastor, they lay entirely with the youthful rebels. The analogies between this story and *Beneath the Wheel* disclose, at the very least, an odd coincidence. The whole is probably simply a good example of the "overdetermination" of the work of art.[49] It may be, however, that there are further depths in *Beneath the Wheel*, into which we are not equipped to penetrate. We must even hesitate to compare Hermann Heilner with Hesse's Waiblinger and make deductions from the distinction between their fates—such a procedure would be crude or indeed impermissible. But the recurrence of the fundamental situation in the novel and in the novella, not only in outline but even in some detail, is transparent. And "In Pressel's Summerhouse" perhaps reveals the true source of the Maulbronn conflict more honestly than does *Beneath the Wheel:* "Hölderlin had been, just as had Mörike, a pupil of the Theological Institute and was to have become a parson, and he had resisted this, just as Mörike had the idea of resisting it" (II, 869–870).

Old Hermann Gundert had been at Maulbronn when David Friedrich Strauss was a teacher there; he had been unhappy, and his son Paul (Hermann Hesse's uncle) had also rebelled; they had both found painful the clash between the rationalists—Strauss, Vischer, and Hegel—and orthodox Christian doctrine.[50] But for Hermann Hesse the situation seemed worse; he regarded the seminaries as having the function not merely of training the intellects of budding theologians, but also of mastering the rude animal impulses of the student, of bringing the innate wild nature of man to heel, for it was considered "a primeval forest without paths and without order" (I, 418). The novel uses the symbol of the

[48] VII, 885.
[49] Hesse himself speaks of "overdetermination of symbols" as a feature of all poetic works. See "On Reading Books" (VII, 248).
[50] Ball, *op. cit.*, p. 62.

forest for the unpurified nature of man, the archaic self of drives and instincts. The world of erotic longings, too, is called a "thicket" (I, 527); the world of the childish imagination however, being still undiseased, receives the more positive designation "magic forest" (I, 501). These forest images point essentially toward an attitude of hostility to the bodily and instinctive life (which of course is the attitude the teachers also take):

And just as a primeval forest has to be thinned out and purified and forcibly restricted so also school has to break the Natural Man, conquer him and forcibly restrict him; it is its task to turn him into a useful member of society according to the principles approved by authority and to arouse in him those qualities whose full training is then triumphantly concluded by the careful discipline of the barrack room [I, 418].

The allusion to the barrack room is in line with the usual satirical targets of the school novel. Far more interesting, however, is the expression "the Natural Man," which comes straight from the language of the Pietists. The doctrine that the Natural Man must be broken so that the Christian Man, whom he carries within him as within a womb,[51] may emerge, was assuredly the belief of Johannes Hesse, of Herr Claassen,[52] even maybe of the rather more open-minded Gunderts; it was the basic faith of the Basel Mission with which the Hesse family was associated, and it is of course the doctrine of the Swabian mystics, such as Johann Albrecht Bengel and Friedrich Christoph Oetinger. In *Beneath the Wheel* the intention has now been transferred to society, the goal is not the Christian Man but the social conformist, and the satirical effect of this transference is of course considerable. But as generally in this novel, the satirical function of an element by no means exhausts its meaning. When we recall that it is in a "forest" (I, 495) and a "thicket" that the sick Hans Giebenrath gets lost, we may guess with some confidence that the tragedy of Hans springs in part from

[51] Oetinger, with whose work Hesse was familiar, uses this analogy. For Oetinger see, e.g., H. O. Burger, *Die Gedankenwelt der grossen Schwaben* (Tübingen and Stuttgart, 1951), p. 157.
[52] Cf. how Herr Claassen, the "theosophist" friend of the family in Calw, rebuked one of the little Hesses who showed too much eagerness at table: "Das ist die Gier! Das ist das Tier in dir!" (IV, 674) (That's the greed/That's the animal in you).

the author's still unemancipated Pietistic conscience. The regimentation at Maulbronn and the idyll at Gaienhofen are both different but not wholly unrelated variations upon the Pietistic hostility to the Natural Man.

Beneath the Wheel therefore implies a submission to social discipline as well as a rebellion against it. It is the conflict, however, not the compromise, which is the seed of future artistic achievement. The conflict with Maulbronn, divided between the two protagonists, Giebenrath and Heilner, was evidently for the author an extension of the struggle with his family and with his Pietistic heritage. Not for nothing does Hans Giebenrath—"Formerly he had been a mother's boy" (I, 450)—envy those boys, unlike himself, whose *mothers* are able to bring them to school; like his descendant, Goldmund, he has to be content with his father as escort, but Hesse dwells in *Beneath the Wheel* on the motherly affection in the farewells which are lavished on luckier boys. Peter Camenzind's mother was an inconspicuous character; Hans Giebenrath's is dead; of Hermann Heilner's we hear nothing. Hesse seems unwilling, or unable, to portray his own mother even indirectly in his imaginative works, whereas he portrays his father so very often. In all the great novels only Demian's mother has strength and presence, and she is transfigured and mythologized, as Goldmund's dream mother also is. When Hans Giebenrath travels to Stuttgart to take the examination, it is to show "if he be worthy to enter by the narrow monastery gate of the seminary" (I, 380). But this narrow gate does not lead unto life, it leads away from it; it leads into an abstracted sphere where uniformity is demanded both of mind and soul, and where the seminarian acquires "a subtle and sure kind of stigma" and learns to wear "a kind of spiritual uniform or livery" (I, 426). This is the world of the father to which the boys have been delivered up. Ball, commenting on this, stresses the importance of mother-longing as the real source of Hesse's own neurosis [53] and makes a good deal of the allegedly draconian severity of Johannes Hesse.

Hesse has often recalled the attitude of revolt aroused in him by the stringency of his family's Pietism, their acute preoccupation with conscience. Throughout his life his attitude to the Protestant

[53] *Op. cit.,* p. 73.

churches, at least, was affected adversely by the extremism which he had experienced as a child, and that aspect of religion of which he early became most suspicious was precisely "the confessional and in part sectarian forms." [54] But the mystical, feminine streak in the Pietistic tradition functioned for him as a bridge to Roman Catholicism, a religion to which he was inclined to be increasingly sympathetic later in life.[55] His attitude to his parents' religion was "this back and forth between veneration and revolt" [56]—he had an early and permanent respect for people who were prepared to sacrifice their lives in the service of an unworldly ideal. Hesse's childhood in Calw was essentially, as he never ceases to insist, a joyful and lively one; for narrow Pietists though they were, the Gundert-Hesse family was all the same intellectually alive, traveled, and well educated, and their house at Calw received a constant stream of visitors, some of them exotic. But the strait jacket which fitted somewhat loosely at home was tightened suddenly at Maulbronn, and revolt ensued. This intense sphere of discipline, orthodoxy, and intellect excludes the feminine and demands the sacrifice of the feelings, the oblation of the soul.

Above all others the artist must necessarily be destroyed in such a sphere; its brand lies upon those who experience it forever— "with the exception of the wild ones who from time to time break loose" (I, 426). Hermann Heilner is such a "wild one," his act prefiguring a much more extreme, if superficially more considered, act of wildness forty years on—he himself the precursor, indeed, not only of Joseph Knecht but of other intermediaries trapped in the

---

[54] "My Faith" (VII, 371).

[55] H. O. Burger remarks: "Die Eigenart der schwäbischen Geistigkeit vom sechzehnten bis zum neunzehnten Jahrhundert . . . erscheint . . . im Gegensatz zum lutherischen Norden wie zum katholischen Süden als eine innerlutherische oder ausserkatholische Katholizität" (The peculiarity of Swabian spirituality from the sixteenth to the nineteenth century appears in contradistinction to the Lutheran North and the Catholic South as an intra-Lutheran or extra-Catholic Catholicism) (op. cit., p. 23). The observation is relevant to an understanding of Hesse's mind. Cf. also Ball, op. cit., pp. 21, 110. Hesse notes that since he is "Protestant by feeling and nature" he would, given a free choice, select a conservative religion "out of longing for the opposite pole" (IV, 482).

[56] VII, 904.

same charmed circle, Veraguth for instance in *Rosshalde* and then Klein and then Goldmund. It is rather noticeable that, between 1905 and 1914, this rebellious figure does not occur again (if we except Berthold in the fragment of that name), until Veraguth emerges and finally shakes off the chains of Gaienhofen. It has of course often been observed that the pattern of the flight from the seminary repeats itself in Hesse's novels, as if again and again he endeavored to depict "the primary experience." [57] To borrow a term, the escape from Maulbronn might be called an *exemplarische Begebenheit* (exemplary event); [58] the wall which, real or metaphorical, surrounds all of Hesse's major characters is the wall around Kloster Maulbronn. There is a deep-seated paradox in this, for to cross the wall of their neurotic isolation, the wall which surrounds the world of the father and of the mind, is for them to find their way not only to the world of the senses, the soul, and the mother, but also to their true self; to break out, as it was already in the case of Peter Camenzind, is to find the Way Within.

Though *Peter Camenzind* is without doubt the more satisfactory book, no single work of Hesse's before *Demian* is of such crucial significance as is *Beneath the Wheel*. It stands at the beginning (as "In Pressel's Summerhouse" stands near the end) of a decade, spent in Gaienhofen and then in Bern, which is rich in short stories, sketches, and reviews, verse and miscellanea, but which saw the completion of only two full-length novels, *Gertrude* and *Rosshalde*, and of these neither, despite conspicuous technical refinements, fulfilled the promise of the author's earliest writings.

Gottfried Keller's works taught Peter Camenzind how much there was still to learn if he was ever to convert his "immature reveries" into art; and the stories of the Gaienhofen period—especially those

---

[57] Ball, *op. cit.*, p. 59.

[58] Albrecht Schöne uses this term in an ingenious analysis of Lenz's *Der Hofmeister*. See his *Säkularisation als sprachbildende Kraft* (Palaestra no. 226; Göttingen, 1958), p. 88 ff. Schöne's analysis is also concerned with that motif which is of such significance in German literature and especially for Hesse, the Prodigal Son. Hesse's prodigals, being "exemplary" ("*Exempel*"—Schöne, p. 87) disclose something of that didactic streak which is to be found in all his novels.

in the three principal collections, *In This World* (1907), *Neighbors*
(1908), and *By-ways* (1912) [59]—do seem to be written largely under
Keller's sign. Not only the attempt in many of these tales at combining a plastic, a gently poetic and a psychologically penetrating
style reminds us of Keller, but so also do some of the recurrent
themes—such as the disillusionment of the impractical idealist or
the rescue of the incompetent dreamer by a solider creature of the
opposite sex. Hermann Lauscher had been struck by the persistence
of Romantic elements in Keller's technique (cf. I, 200). For the
Hesse of Gaienhofen, however, Keller was clearly a guide who led
away from the quicksands of decadence; both he and Keller
portray, by and large, the *petite bourgeoisie*, both have a predilection for portraits of originals, and both deal lovingly with the things
of the everyday world. In his evocation of the life of children
Keller had been something of an innovator in German literature;
Hesse follows him and goes beyond him, in *In This World*, in developing a deep-sighted, intuitive child psychology. The objective
descriptive writing of "The Homecoming" (1909) and its conclusion—in which two mature people find each other and common
sense triumphs over shyness and obtuseness—also point especially
sharply to the model. Such figures as Agnes in "The World Reformer" (1911), who deplores the enthusiast Berthold's going
astray "in endless deserts of theory and delusion" (II, 441) and who
eventually rescues him, have the same literary ancestry, as well as
ironical connections with the author's own life experience. The
story "Robert Aghion" (1913), which in some ways may be regarded as a serious document of Hesse's attitude to his parents'
sectarianism and missionary zeal, contains farcical elements which
indicate a long-continued groping after the elusive key to Keller's
masterly humor. Sententious observations crowd in in these stories—
for example, "There is a certain sense in the way Nature bestows

[59] All the stories in these volumes had been previously published in a variety
of magazines. Another selection from the works of this period is *Small World*
(1933)—which was included in the *Gesammelte Dichtungen* of 1952, and a
larger one is *Gerbersau* (1949). Gerbersau is Hesse's humorous transfiguration of Calw, his "Seldwyla." Hesse chose to include *Beneath the Wheel* in
the *Gerbersau* selection, as well as a number of sketches and memoirs. The
selection in the *Gesammelte Dichtungen* entitled "Diesseits" ("In This
World") is not identical with that published under this title in 1907.

her gifts" (II, 198)—and generally, though not always,[60] they spring from social and moral attitudes close to Keller's. Such a story as "In the Old Sun" (1905), with its detached, wry and yet slightly censorious portrait of a group of ne'er-do-wells, might almost have come from Keller's pen. Structurally and thematically, however, some of the tales—for instance "Hans Amstein" (1904)—seem to be equally indebted to the Swiss writer's more lyrical North German contemporary, Theodor Storm.

Ultimately, however, Hesse was no mere imitator, if only because to imitate successfully was beyond his capacity. The differences between his work and Keller's are far more striking than the resemblances. Hesse's stories are altogether more lyrical, more often couched in the first person singular, and the music of his language is more important to him than its plasticity. In "The Marble Saw" (1904) occurs the passage: "Sky, ploughed fields, woods and village together with the manifold scents of the meadows and the sound of an isolated cricket still audible here and there all flowed together warmly (*lau*) around me and spoke to me like a melancholy which was beautiful, happy, and sad" (I, 560). The writing is evidently uninspired, but it is its subjectivism, its pursuit of synaesthesia, its oxymoron which are conspicuously unlike Keller. An all-pervasive whimsy in many stories, including exaggerated whimsical personification—the tree in "Harvest Moon" (I, 676–677)—discloses a weakness of which *Peter Camenzind* is not wholly free. It is an all too simple matter to catalogue Hesse's defects as a stylist in these years: his subjectivism is linked very often with a pose of naïveté, with pretentious Eichendorffian metaphors ("as if somewhere afar off the forests and mountains stirred in their sleep and mumbled the heavy, weary words of dreams" (I, 571), and sometimes also with descriptions which lack lyrical effect precisely because they are too carefully constructed—occasionally the "feeling" has had to be added in a separate sentence as a kind of unpersuasive appendage. When Hesse turns to his Italianate manner—for example in "The Dwarf" (1903)—he frequently slips into preciosity, all but recalling Paul Heyse.

[60] The observation which concludes "Walter Kömpff" (1908): "And few people thought how near we all dwell to that darkness in the shadow of which Walter Kömpff had got lost" (II, 259) is a warning unlike anything in Keller.

In general, Hesse's characters are much more passive, more vegetative even, than Keller's, sceptically exposed to fate, lonely and resigned, sharing their author's doubts about the possibility of any kind of community. For all their careful and superficially objective descriptions, the tales of this period disclose a world much less independent of its originator than is Keller's (or even Storm's). Like the perpetual ironizing which goes on in *Peter Camenzind,* so also the characteristic humor of these productions is introverted, lacking for the most part Keller's freshness, his critical impetus, his clear-cut point of view. Instead, yet another influence, as difficult to pinpoint as it is undoubtedly far reaching, must be constated here. Hesse may have ceased to be so preoccupied with Novalis, but he remains under the profound spell of Jean Paul. True, that great writer's fabulous puns, his elaborate, maddeningly elusive jests, his verbal contortions and monstrosities—these things Hesse does not offer, for at this time at least they were beyond his range. But the Sternian vision, the intensely subjective, narcissistic quality of Jean Paul's humor, his loving play with the eccentric, and the occasional grandiose burlesque, interlaced as it all is with such unanticipated poetic beauties, flights of fancy, and cosmic profundities—something of this Hesse has caught, and something of it he retained to the end of his career, for Jean Paul's influence, unlike Keller's, resurged even more strongly at the time of *The Steppenwolf.* Jean Paul Richter's greatness, for Hesse, derived from his constant proximity and openness to the unconscious,[61] to the world of the soul, and it is this very openness which makes some of the Gaienhofen stories (and *Peter Camenzind* also) closer to the heart of the Romantic experience than anything Keller ever wrote.

These stories add little that is new on which to base our insight into the fundamental, organic structures of Hesse's whole work; they do, however, refocus on certain themes and patterns which had previously emerged. Some of them deal with material which is intellectually significant for Hesse, for instance "Walter Kömpff," which displays pathetically and unsympathetically the tragedy of religiomania and the dark side of the Pietistic tradition. "Robert Aghion" satirizes the absurdity involved in trying to impose the

---

[61] "On Jean Paul" (1921; VII, 261). Cf. also "Artists and Psychoanalysis" (1918; VII, 141–142).

austere system of Protestant Christianity upon Hindus. A few of
these tales are biographically enlightening; we may cite in this
respect "Harvest Moon," which illustrates another aspect of the
difficulties of an amatory relationship between a boy and an older
woman, and, more particularly, "The Preparatory School Boy"—
one of the most successful of all—which catches rather well the
experience of calf-love, touches on the school problematics of
Beneath the Wheel, and ends with a sentimental moral not unlike
that of the Boppi episode. Special emphasis may justly be laid
on "The World Reformer," which first appeared in 1911. The date
is certainly significant, since this was the year of Hesse's five-month
journey to India (actually the Malayan archipelago and Ceylon).
This was the most spectacular manifestation of his increasing rest-
lessness; for if, in the years following 1905, Hesse was apparently in
danger of degenerating into a prolific but superficial practitioner of
belles-lettres, he was in fact never wholly immersed in his "idyll"
or at one with his literary success—one of his doubles was usually
uncomfortably at his elbow.[62] The journey to India was confessedly
partly a flight: "I had exhausted Gaienhofen." [63] "The World Reformer," pedestrian in its narrative style and heavy in its irony,
seems to be still imitative of Keller. It satirizes the effort of the
hero, Berthold, to establish himself in an anchoritic existence after
the principles of Tolstoy, it then laughs at the procession of like-
minded fanatics who visit him in his retreat, and it concludes with a
banal moral of marital bliss in the bosom of society. When, however,
we recall Hesse's remark that Tolstoy was one of the inspirers of
his own Gaienhofen way of life, this material appears somewhat
nearer to the bone than at first sight; while the fact that Hesse, unlike
Berthold, was a married hermit only serves to sharpen the concealed point.

It is difficult to read the tales of the Gaienhofen period without hindsight; even such an example as "Ladidel" (1909), in which
the conflict between the stern demands of the world and the playful and inconsequent nature of the artist is parodied in the fate of

[62] Cf. here for example the observations of H. Mauerhofer, *Die Introversion:
Mit spezieller Berücksichtigung des Dichters H. Hesse* (Bern and Leipzig,
1929), p. 35.
[63] "On Moving into a New House" (IV, 626).

a feckless dandy who finds his artist's métier as a hairdresser, seems double-edged. The most characteristic theme of all these volumes is perhaps that of the youth under the necessity of facing the world, its economic, biological, and moral challenge. "The Cyclone" presents the second—and most important—of these challenges with considerable force: its convincing and sensitive portrayal of the half-conscious recognition of departing childhood, of its fading into the light of common day, is an overture to the depiction of a youth's first erotic experience and his disturbed yearning to scale the walls of his suddenly narrow world: "My life was no longer securely and contentedly enclosed within this small area of walls, river, and woods . . . but burst with the waves of longing over these narrow confines into the wide Without" (I, 771). This is not merely a yearning; it is equally an inescapable and agonizing *fate*: "as if I myself had been torn out with all my secret roots and spat forth into the inexorably piercing daylight" (I, 780). This is also the destiny of Heilner; and indeed, after the cyclone the boy leaves town "to become a man and to master life" (I, 780). If there is this going forth, there is equally the return, and several of the Gaienhofen stories deal with it, albeit in sentimental form. This is the case in "An Autumn Hike" (1906), in "The Homecoming," and in "Beautiful Is Youth" (1907); in this last the boy who left home "as a shy problem child" returns years afterward "like a man of position" (*wie ein Herr*) (I, 719), although only to endure a disappointment in love and then to go forth again. Return home from the years of wandering, we are told in "The Homecoming," is the normal course for the citizens of Gerbersau—Hesse's name for Calw, and this story's ideal of a contented settling down betrays once more the bourgeois commitment of this period. What was later to become a mysterious and subtly managed motif, the occult spiral, the spiritual "return" upon a higher level of being, is here still garbed in the mundane clothes of a parochial *Heimatkunst*.

The novel *Gertrude* (1910)[64] is a *Künstlerroman*, a very fashionable genre at the time, though declining; its subject is the suffering of the outsider-musician Kuhn—he bears the outsider's stigma, since an accident in early life has left him lame—who is crossed

---

[64] Waibler's date (and Mileck's). Frau Ninon Hesse, however, states that the book appeared in 1907 (*Prosa aus dem Nachlass*, p. 600).

in love by the singer Muoth. At its center is the white cloud, the familiar goddess-figure—Gertrude, adored and unattainable. An earlier version, a fragment dated to 1905–1906,[65] is evidently the beginnings of a quite different novel; here Muoth is prefigured in the architect Haueisen, but Muoth's suicide (which ends the finished novel) is in the fragment merely the fate of a minor character, Beyer, who kills himself near the beginning of the story. Gertrude, in the fragment, is herself a would-be paintress of intense devotion but uncertain gifts, problematic in a way her later incarnation is not, but still inaccessible, a rather faint *belle dame sans merci*. The novel, though carefully written, is inclined to be insipid and dull, though some of the incidental matter—for instance Kuhn's conversations with the theosophist Lohe—is informative about Hesse's intellectual development. More important is the switch from the plastic arts to music between the fragment and the finished novel; this accentuates a feature already noticeable in the former, namely, a maturing and hardening of Hesse's conception of artistic technique. In the fragment it is insisted that successful composition in architecture demands the association of fancy and inspiration with discipline and mathematical accuracy. In the finished novel we may note the end of the reign of Chopin in Hesse's imagination —perhaps under the influence of his acquaintance with the young Swiss composer Othmar Schoeck—and in general a new understanding of the problem of form. Despite the suicide motif, the novel's moral remains conspicuously that of the era of *embourgeoisement*; there is the notion that "individualism or imagined loneliness" (II, 128) is a fashionable disease of the Central European, related to moral insanity and curable if tackled while the outsider is still young. There is also the very Camenzindian preoccupation with the overcoming of misanthropism, and an almost Schillerian belief in the sublime fortitude of the human soul at the mercy of the powers of chance and violence.

Gertrude points back, *Rosshalde* (1912–1913) distinctly forward. *Rosshalde*, also a *Künstlerroman*, deals with the ultimate self-discovery of a great painter who has been trapped and spiritually all but destroyed by an unhappy marriage; the painter-novel which *Gertrude* was originally intended to be is here realized in a very

[65] In *Prosa aus dem Nachlass*.

different form. Veraguth and his wife live almost entirely separated lives in detached spheres, though both within the walls of their estate, Rosshalde; between them plays the child, Pierre. It is Veraguth's love for his younger son which thus imprisons him within the wall, within the charmed circle of frustration and discord. It is his friend Otto Burckhardt, the strong-minded messenger from without, who first puts it into his head that he must break loose, come what may. In fact it is Pierre's death which finally resolves the issue and leads Veraguth forth into the world, free at last to become a true individual, to live out his own fate. *Rosshalde*, written after the return from India, is a clear-sighted portrayal of an increasingly intolerable situation; Nietzschean ethics evidently play their part in this resolution, but above all the influence of Strindberg is clearly noticeable for the first time.[66] The insights into himself soon to be vouchsafed Hesse by psychoanalysis are to some extent pre-empted in *Rosshalde*: genuine, fresh experiences, we are told, occur only up to the time of puberty and provide a store upon which a man has to live for the rest of his life. The wrench which Veraguth suffers is agonizing, "but with the sacrifice of favorite desires unrest and disunity also died" (II, 569)—a formulation which is distinctly Adlerian. Veraguth, "a man walled-in of

[66] The influence of Strindberg upon Hesse is difficult to document, but it was certainly significant. In 1947 he himself dated his first acquaintance with the Swedish author's work to approximately 1912 (the time of *Rosshalde*), but this date is evidently too late. His remark in 1909 (*Neue Zürcher Zeitung*, no. 22, Jan. 22, 1909) that, despite the efforts of advocates such as Knut Hamsun, Strindberg was still "outlawed here at home by the Philistines," together with his specific praise for the ruthless consistency of this writer's venture in self-analysis, suggest strongly that Strindberg's influence was already helping to undermine the Gaienhofen compromise. For Hesse the Swede was one of those, like Nietzsche and like Dostoevsky, "who did not only perceive critically and experience intellectually the questionable, sick, and imperiled nature of their epoch, that apparently happy era of the long European peace and of progressive liberalism, but who suffered it biologically in their own bodies" (*Neue Zürcher Zeitung*, no. 1289, July 2, 1947). Hesse constantly returned to Strindberg, especially to his so-called "autobiographical" writings, and of these first and foremost to those of the Paris period, i.e., *Inferno*. In these diaries Hesse encountered "not only the lonely, self-adoring suffering of a psychopath, but a representative suffering, one significant for everyone." This last remark is a pointer to *The Steppenwolf*, and indeed the deposits which these grim documents left in Hesse's works of the 1920's, especially *The Steppenwolf* and *Spa Visitor*, are unmistakable.

his own free will" (II, 534), can experience the cool detachment of artistic inspiration even within the stockade; as he sketches his dead son's face we become aware of the supremacy of the demands of art over those of ordinary life; and when he bursts out he leaves behind, later than most, "the sweet twilight of youth" (II, 633) and—now the committed wanderer—turns his back upon the bourgeois world forever.

This last message is also that of *Knulp*, a work which has frequently been highly praised, for instance by André Gide. *Three Tales from the Life of Knulp* appeared in 1915, but were written in the period 1907-1914. The fragmentary *Tales of Quorm*[67]—the first version of *Knulp*—originated even earlier, before *Peter Camenzind*, and the importance of this has already been stressed: it means in fact that the embryonic *Knulp* material provided Hesse's first escape from the exotic musings of decadent fantasy. Poetic identification with the Way of the Vagabond—conditioned by Hesse's temperament, by Romantic prototype, and by the affectionate observation of the dying journeyman life—was the first alternative he found to the exclusive hermeticism and verbalism of the decadent poet, and at heart *Peter Camenzind* had been little more than a socially and intellectually expanded version of this. The doctrine of *Knulp*, however, seems somewhat blunted by the vehicle in which it is conveyed, for this has too many of the features of Romantic pastiche. The vagabond Knulp with his mouth organ and his childlikeness is a very Eichendorffian figure,[68] though precious in a way his prototypes are not; a child and a creature of the soul, his erotic instincts have first set him upon the path of vagabondage, yet, unlike the later Goldmund, Knulp remains a continent gentleman. Though the style of his utterances is rather wearisome, he is psychologically quite an interesting individual; his world is that of the senses and of play, his attitude to logic and learning a mixture of recognition and contempt, his attitude to will one of skepticism. Knulp, in fact, is a fatalist (which is very

[67] In *Prosa aus dem Nachlass*. There are three fragments: "Peter Bastian's Youth" (1902), "Letter to Mr. Kilian Schwenckschedel" (1902-1903), and "Diary of a Journeyman Saddler" (1904).

[68] The Eichendorffian symbols are indeed extremely consciously introduced, e.g., Knulp (following his precursor in *Quorm*) whistles "In einem kühlen Grunde" (III, 21).

significant), although at moments the Gundert-Hesse doctrine of self-abnegation and willed sacrifice still peeps through. He converses with his "double," or rather his complement, Hesse, the intellectual bourgeois. He, Knulp, would wish to regress to his childhood again, but not Hesse, whose aspirations are apparently just the opposite: "No, not I. I once knew an old man, he must have been over seventy, he had such a tranquil, good expression, and it seemed to me as if there could be nothing in him but what was good and wise and tranquil. And since then I sometimes think I should like to be like him" (III, 48).

There is yet more intriguing matter in *Knulp*, besides this early incarnation of Castalia's Old Music Master; Knulp is not only the wanderer, he is the budding saint. Journeymanlike he carries his "legendary guild-book" (III, 16) with him, and the epithet carries its associations too; his life is a "legend" because, like that of St. Francis, it takes place wholly outside the circle of the masculine, bourgeois world of will and purposes, in that vast legendary feminine Without into which Hermann Heilner and his successors break out. But Knulp's exile is not for him a source of agonized tension; it is blissful, gentle, self-absorbed; it is capricious, (*launisch*—no longer such a derogatory word as it was in *Gertrude*, where life is "capricious and cruel" [II, 191]); it is a game: "He knew how to shuffle the cards and sort them like lightning, with playful casualness"; Master Rothfuss "watched with admiration and indulgence, as a workingman and a bourgeois is pleased to watch tricks which earn nothing" (III, 32). Harry Haller, the Steppenwolf, positively refuses to clown for the bourgeoisie in such a fashion; in fact, he bites! [69] But *Knulp* is a work which, for all its cult of aesthetic vagabondage, is still instinct with sentimental compromise; Knulp feels no loathing for the bourgeois who, by and large, treat him so considerately—he is but mildly amused at their stupidities. His conflict with society lacks all surface acerbity, it is a well-mannered hostility to the bourgeoisie.[70] And the language has similar manners, the same kind of precious gentleness or indeed gentility; there is still order, serenity, and meaning in this lamblike wanderer's life, and the work is perhaps best regarded as Hesse's

[69] See especially the humorous story "About the Steppenwolf" (IV, 523 f.).
[70] Ball, *op. cit.,* p. 162.

last attempt to avoid his crisis, by taking the self-searching road of the future in the dress of the minstrel past. *Knulp* is, in the final analysis, a pleasantly written work of self-delusion and of regression into dreams, of romanticizing infantilism; perhaps it is not too unfair to point to the mouth organ as the central symbol of the book.

That segment of Hermann Hesse's career which has been under consideration in these two chapters is peculiarly well defined; it extends from his literary beginnings in the 1890's until 1916. It was a prolific period, one of fairly steady literary success and an increasingly incongruous personal maladjustment. It was a period in which the Romantic heritage which was Hesse's through temperamental affinity and the conventions of *fin de siècle* writing was experienced and transmuted in the last resort superficially, as a cultivated devotion to letters, the commitment of a professional to his traditional art. Many of the fundamental themes of his entire output (the elucidation of which has become the commonplace of Hesse-criticism)—such motifs as the conflict between the bourgeois and the artist, between the mind and the senses, the mythology of childhood, and the cult of the tramp—are introduced in these years and indeed are expansively treated. The essentially Neo-Romantic dilemma of the conflict between feeling and reflection is seen to be intensified in Hesse owing to his didactic impulse; this is the frame upon which Hesse's language is stretched and it explains the pendulation of his style. Less obvious but even more important for an insight into the later, more significant and more lasting novels are certain of the structural patterns which already leave their imprint very early on: first and foremost the interstices of conversion and illumination which mark out the hagiographical *vita*, and second the enclosed circle, the cycle of the breakout and the return. These patterns were to survive the convulsions of the years to come; actually they are still indispensable for the interpretation of Hesse's last novel, published in 1943, *The Glass Bead Game*.

CHAPTER 3

Demian

IN *Demian* there is much that is new, but there is also much that is old, far more that connects, both thematically and stylistically, with the work of the early Hesse than has generally been realized. That the path to *Demian*, and through *Demian*, was arduous and involved a tremendous spiritual upheaval and a far-reaching transformation of long-established attitudes is well known; it was the path of a writer who now found it mandatory to subordinate his art to the uncompromising quest for truth, so that he might become, as the preface to *Demian* declares, one of those "who do not wish to deceive themselves any longer" (III, 102).[1] Externally, what was involved was the total collapse of a way of life, the loss of home and family; internally it was a new stage in self-discovery born from a state very close to mental breakdown.[2] Hesse moved from Gaienhofen to Bern in 1912; his third son, Martin, soon afterward fell seriously ill, with symptoms which are partly reflected in those of Pierre Veraguth in *Rosshalde*; his wife, Mia, now began to show the first signs of mental disease.

---

[1] Hesse was amused by certain objections raised by previous admirers, who disapproved of his new, less harmonious manner: "What do beauty and harmony mean to a man who is condemned to death, who runs for his life with walls falling down about him?" (IV, 481).

[2] Ball regards the Gaienhofen years as an uneasy sham. Hesse has sought to modify this judgment: "There was more warmth in them and more innocence and play than he suggests" (IV, 625).

Then came the war.[3] *Demian* is a war novel, though rather a strange one, the kind which is not *about* the war but *of* the war; and willy-nilly Hesse now became to some extent a political writer. A stream of letters, essays, and pamphlets now commences, and these have a flavor, an urgency, and a message very different from the largely dilettantist literary exercises of the Gaienhofen years. The essay "O Friends, Not These Sounds" (September 1914) voices the complaint that newspapers are actually declining to review books written in enemy languages, and that writers and artists on both sides are deserting the time-honored cause of cosmopolitan humanism in droves. At this time Hesse and Romain Rolland discovered their common sympathies and established their first personal contact; what they had in common was especially their impartiality, their entire rejection of the chauvinistic viewpoint.

Hesse's new political understanding was linked with an "awakening" which was at once more general and more particular: more general in that it was not purely political, more particular in that it directed him to that characteristic view of life for which the temperamental foundations had long been laid—to a conviction of the inevitable irrationality of human conduct, the belief that such political goals as universal peace, like any other meaningful changes in the social or individual condition, could be achieved not "by rational means, through preaching, organization, and propaganda" but only through "insight" (*Erkenntnis* [4]—that is to say, gnosis). Later on Hesse confessed to having frequently felt the urge to active participation in the political fight, remarking that he had been a strong supporter of the 1918 revolution and still had numerous friends on the German Left.[5] But in fact in the essay "World History" (1918) he is skeptical about the validity or the sense of mere external change: "We are blind adherents of a 'transvaluation of all values'—but this transvaluation has to occur nowhere else but in our own hearts" (VII, 125). In the last resort the crises of politics

---

[3] Hesse sums it all up: "the world war . . . the destruction of my freedom and independence . . . the great moral crisis caused by the war, which forced me to find a new foundation for all my thinking and my work . . . the severe illness of our third and youngest son which went on for years . . . the first premonitions of my wife's mental sickness" (IV, 629).

[4] "War and Peace" (1918; VII, 119–120).

[5] *Letters* (VII, 550).

were for Hesse (and always remained) only pointers to the ultimate issues in the inner world of man. He feels that he cannot really be engaged in any political cause, at most in a moral one; poets and artists were always in his view essentially *Aussenweltler* (outsiders). *Littérature engagée* distorts their nature, it is "like using a barometer to knock in nails." [6] His was the revolt of a religious, not a political, conscience; he knew very well that intellectuals and artists could have little hope of influencing men of power.[7]

The extraordinary consistency of his opposition to the political course of his country from 1914 until 1945—in which the *total* attitude is not gradually evolved but stands there clear and whole from the outset—is an impressive (and rare enough) phenomenon in German intellectual life of this period. But always the message is in fact that of *Demian*. The tract *Zarathustra's Return* (1919), for instance, which tries and inevitably fails to recapture the authentic Nietzschean note, preaches the attainment of individuality and freedom through the acceptance of fate, exhorts German youth to eschew self-pity, and requires them to seek their god not in external slogans but in their own hearts.

Within the heart, however, lies chaos—especially the dissolution of every pseudo-objective moral canon; and the acceptance of chaos is combined with the exercise of a most sensitive conscience—this is the antinomy on which thenceforward Hesse's moral outlook is based. The process which he calls "*Erwachen*" (awakening) shatters the shell of convention and opens the Way Within (*Weg nach Innen*); and this Way, ambiguously and profoundly, leads at one and the same time to the stringency of extreme responsibility and to anarchic freedom of the self. The war brought "the second great transformation of my life," [8] the first having been the flight from Maulbronn. The analogy is indeed very close, in that both transformations involved startlingly sudden conflict with the established norms of the outside world: at Maulbronn the "model scholar" changed unexpectedly into a "wild one," a social renegade; in Bern the expatriate became the object of vicious German press attacks during the war.

[6] "Thou Shalt Not Kill" (1919; VII, 237).
[7] "Attempt at a Justification" ('1938; VII, 465).
[8] "A Short Autobiography" (IV, 477).

The war, itself chaos, also emerged from chaos—the "European unconscious." As for the German decision to overthrow the emperor in 1918, this is described as "a deed from the fearful depths of the unconscious, whence all true deeds come." [9] Freud is not mentioned in this context, but some allusion to the Freudian notions of patricide and of the emperor-figure as father-figure seems self-evident. The anarchistic streak traceable in *Beneath the Wheel*—or earlier—is now hardened by the experience of psychoanalysis into an attitude hostile not only to the state and its disciplines but also to those of the conscious, logical mind (and we recall the anathema of mathematics in the school novel).

The world of Keller and his Seldwyla sinks below the horizon,[10] and Dostoevsky suddenly becomes the dominating literary figure in Hesse's imagination. *In Sight of Chaos: Three Essays*, published with a curious irony by the Verlag Seldwyla, Bern, in 1920, contains the vital essay: "The Brothers Karamazov, or The End of Europe: Thoughts on Reading Dostoevsky." This postdates the composition of *Demian* by several years but is intimately connected with the experience which brought forth that novel. In the Karamazovs, Hesse sees how "an age-old, Asiatic and occult ideal begins to become European, begins to devour the European mind. It is this that I call the end of Europe." This means in fact the ideal of moral anarchy, "the turning away from all firm ethical and moral principles in favor of an all-understanding, all-permitting attitude" (VII, 162). This ideal is found to be exemplified in the "Russian Man," "unformed soul material"; [11] the Russian Man (now incarnate, we may presume, as the Bolshevik) rejects the conscious forms of Western culture in favor of an incessant striving to break through the curtain of the world, the *principium individuationis*. Asia is regarded as the sphere of the Mother, and paternally-oriented Europe is now to be swallowed up by her; [12] and Germany is said to stand closer than any other European nation (except

[9] "The Way of Love" (Dec. 1918; VII, 132).

[10] "Seldwyla im Abendrot. Zu Gottfried Kellers 100. Geburtstag," *Vossische Zeitung*, no. 351 (July 13, 1919).

[11] Cf. "unformed infinity of the unconscious" (VII, 142).

[12] The original source of this idea may well have been Bachofen. Analogies with certain passages in Thomas Mann also, of course, suggest themselves.

Austria) to Asia, to Dostoevsky and the Karamazovs. When a culture is in decay, the repression of drives and instincts within it is
weakened, the eventual surfacing of these drives gives birth to
Karamazovs and in so doing sheds a dubious light upon all so-called
objective standards of good and evil. Ivan Karamazov converses with
his Satanic self, his unconscious; from such a conversation alone,
Hesse suggests, might come a new civilization for Europe, maybe
a combination of Ivan and Alyosha. Beyond good and evil new
Tablets of the Law must be laid down by the unconscious, which
is itself the demiurge, both god and devil. For Hesse it did not
seem possible to reconstruct the world which had existed before
1914, on any of its levels, either outside or inside man; the discovery of his own unconscious became for him synonymous with
the end of the old world and the old sham peace, that superficial,
anachronistic delusion of wholeness and coherent entity, of rational,
independent, conscious selfhood.

Hesse's intimate personal acquaintance with psychoanalysis began in the year 1916, when he was treated by Dr. J. B. Lang, a
Jungian analyst, at the Kurhaus Sonnmatt near Lucerne. In May
1916 he had a series of twelve analytical sessions. In June he was
back in Bern, where he was deeply involved in relief work for
German prisoners of war, but during 1916 and 1917 he made some
sixty visits to the sanatorium. The literary fruits of this experience,
Ball suggests, are above all the Märchen and Demian. By 1916,
certainly, and possibly very much earlier, Hesse was well acquainted with the works of Freud, Jung, Bleuler, and Stekel.[13] He
felt that as an artist, particularly, these writers had something to
give him; he found in their writings something new and important,
and "all in all, in their conception of the life of the soul the confirmation of almost all my intuitions gained from literature and my
own observations." [14] Indeed, Hesse's earlier works, with their introspection, their keen interest in dreams,[15] their intuitive symbolism,
were naturally attuned to receive the analytical message.

[13] Ball, Hermann Hesse, p. 161.
[14] "Artists and Psychoanalysis" (1918; VII, 138).
[15] The use of dreams in earlier works, however, is primitive in comparison
with their use in Demian; it is not until Demian that we find dreams consciously constructed according to the tenets of psychoanalytic schools.

Hesse had the greatest respect for Freud, whom he held to be a genius,[16] and also for "Freud's pupil, Jung"; [17] he was acquainted not only with Jung's doctrines about the unconscious as formulated in *Symbols of Transformation* (1912) but also with his theory of types (not yet fully developed in 1918).[18] Hesse's approach to these thinkers was of course not that of the scientist; perhaps he failed fully to understand Freud and saw in him more a kind of clinical referee of Romantic theories of the self than the nineteenth-century empiricist which he fundamentally was; Freud's material-ism, his basic pessimism, not-to-say cynicism, about human nature could scarcely have been fully sympathetic to Hesse; with Jung he had perhaps innately more in common. The essay "Language" (1917), however, clearly shows the influence of Freudian concepts and symbolism. In "On Jean Paul" (1921) we are told that this novelist's greatness derived essentially from his relationship with the unconscious: "Jean Paul had a profound intuition . . . of the harmony of the functions of the mind, a peaceful and fruitful juxtaposition of knowledge and intuition, thinking and feeling" (VII, 262). Jung's theory of the four basic functions—thinking,

[16] Cf. "Notes on the Subject of Poetry and Criticism" (VII, 365).

[17] The date of the remark (1918) suggests that Hesse was not fully aware of the deep-seated split which had already developed in the psychoanalytic movement.

[18] The question of Hesse's primary allegiance to the Freudian or the Jungian school is still in some dispute. The view that *Demian* must be seen chiefly in the light of the ideas of Jung has gained a good deal of currency in recent years; see, e.g., M. Dahrendorff, "Hermann Hesses Demian" (Staatsexamens-arbeit, Hamburg, 1953), and E. Maier, "The Psychology of C. G. Jung in the Works of Hermann Hesse" (diss., New York University, 1956). The issue has, unfortunately, not been greatly illuminated by the publication of the cor-respondence between Dr. Maier, Hesse, and Jung in *The Psychoanalytic Review*, L, no. 3 (1963). In his letter to Maier (March 24, 1950), Jung claimed that his ideas had a direct influence, through J. B. Lang, on the composition of *Demian*. Hesse, in his letter (undated), confesses to a knowledge of Jung's *Symbols of Transformation* and other works, but adds: "I have always re-spected Jung, but his writings have not made the impression on me which Freud's have done" (*loc. cit.*, p. 16). In *The Psychoanalytic Review*, B. Nel-son argues that Hesse's letter—which is undoubtedly cool toward Jung—reflects "his annoyance with Jung, Jung's claims, Jung's style" (*loc. cit.*, p. 12). Nelson also adduces some rather slim evidence in support of the assertion that a little later on, at any rate after 1922, Hesse drew closer again to Freudian circles, Freud being his real love. Through Lang, it is worth noting, Hesse had become personally acquainted with Jung.

feeling, sensation, and intuition [19]—is here reflected or, rather, re-fracted by Hesse's characteristic reduction of them, still just recognizable, to two pairs of almost parallel opposites. The concept of sublimation, Hesse appreciated, came from Freud, though he much later on endorses Jung's criticism of Freud's usage; [20] how-ever, he points out that artists "achieve . . . genuine sublimation, and not from will or ambition, but from grace." [21]

Psychoanalysis can, Hesse came to think, be highly destructive of the artistic personality. At an early stage he became aware that it presented special problems to the creative artist, or indeed to the critic, who might wish to employ either its methods or its supplies of material. In fact, artists and poets had always grasped instinctively what the clinicians now felt they had discovered for the first time; but they had done so not because they were them-selves analysts, but because they were the exact counterpart there-of—namely dreamers, and dreamers they must needs still remain, in spite of the new "science": "The poetic appreciation of the processes of the soul remained as before a matter of the intuitive talent, not the analytical." [22] Hesse's view, in "Artists and Psycho-analysis" (1918), was that psychoanalysis provided the artist with "three confirmations" (VII, 139), establishing for him the objective value of his apparently dubious games and fancies, and—if he were prepared himself to be analyzed—giving him a richer contact with his own unconscious and teaching him how to face his repressed self with honest impartiality. Both Dostoevsky and above all Jean Paul understood intuitively most of what psychoanalysis had to teach; and in citing Otto Rank's reference to an unusually percep-tive passage in one of Schiller's letters, Hesse observes: "Here is a classical expression of the ideal relationship of intellectual criticism to the unconscious . . . loving hearkening to the hidden springs, and only then criticism and selection from the chaos." [23]

Here, in his formulation of what he implies should be the proper

[19] *Psychological Types* (New York, 1933), p. 412 ff.
[20] In a letter to Jung, Sept. 1934, *Letters* (VII, 575 f.).
[21] The term Hesse uses—"*geglückte Verdrängung*"—seems to be near enough the opposite of Freud's "*Missglücken der Unterdrückung.*"
[22] "Artists and Psychoanalysis" (VII, 139).
[23] *Ibid.* (VII, 142–143). Cf. the obvious Freudian influences at work in the essay "Language" (1917).

technique of the artist, Hesse sheds an intense light upon his own relationship to psychoanalysis. The figure of listening to the hidden waters within—one of the most central in Hesse's work— goes back in embryo at least to *Hermann Lauscher*. The analyst and his patient reproduce for Hesse the relationship of ironist and dreamer, the interlocked opposition of reflection and memory. That this structure is itself that of Jung's "introverted type" may add to but certainly does not diminish the significance of the fact that the framework of Hesse's later writings was not given him by psychoanalysis but is largely prefigured in his earliest productions. The impact of psychoanalysis upon him was certainly very real— "an encounter with real powers" [24]—and the transformation of the war years was deep, but of course it was not total. Of the psychological fundamentals, indeed, less was changed than Hesse himself imagined (at least at the time). A more developed self-awareness does, of course, now enter, also a greater determination to avoid evasions and to face the truth. The second "confirmation" is also relevant—memories now become conscious which before operated only in darkness. One of the difficult problems in criticism of *Demian* is the precise delimitation of this ultraconscious use of symbols, especially since analysis and "awakening" did not by any means remove all the veils which screened the artist from the sources and meaning of his own work. But *Demian* is not a psychological tract, though the temptation to treat it as such has always been great; it is, it scarcely needs emphasizing, a work of language, and however consciously the material from analysis is introduced, it must be, and is, modified by the poetic process. Hesse himself bears witness to this elementary truth in his attack upon the exaggerations of the psychoanalytical approach to criticism: he castigates "the misuse of the basic Freudian concepts by witless critics and renegade literary scholars," [25] that illiterate attitude which degrades literature to "symptoms of psychic conditions," an attitude which disregards the whole meaning of the concept of sublimation.

Demian: The Story of a Youth by Emil Sinclair was published pseudonymously in 1919; it created a sensation and won the Fontane prize for first novels. Hesse confessed his authorship [26] only after

---

[24] VII, 802.
[25] "On Good and Bad Critics" (VII, 365).
[26] *Vivos Voco*, I (1919–1920), 658.

Eduard Korrodi had suggested it in the *Neue Zürcher Zeitung* (July 4, 1920), after the prize had been returned. There has been much discussion both of the reason for the pseudonymity and of the choice of pseudonym. Generally the name is thought to have been taken from Isaak von Sinclair, Hölderlin's friend, although at least one other very ingenious suggestion, quite consonant with Hesse's methods, has been made.[27] The answer to the first question is probably very personal; Hesse certainly felt that he had, with *Demian*, become a new writer, that he had sloughed off his former self. Furthermore, he disliked being in the public eye.[28] The name "Emil Sinclair," significantly enough, was appended as a pseudonym to a number of Hesse's essays of these years. The new note so clear in *Demian* was first sounded, Hesse claims, in some of the *Märchen* written just before (this is undoubtedly true of "Iris" and "The Steep Road"); 1915 was a turning point which brought this critic of the war into conflict in unheard of fashion with his country and its government, with public opinion, with conventional intellectual life, and indeed with every form of orthodoxy—both in the world and in himself. He tells us that his attitude to his own earlier works was now at first hostile; [29] only later did he come to recognize in all of them "starting points for later things," which they do in fact disclose. He observes that the figures of Demian and his mother are not fully susceptible of rational explanation, for they are "symbols . . . magical conjurations." [30] A sensitivity to the symbols alone, he suggests, will make possible the critical penetration of this novel. In its interpretation the track of the "psychiatric" symbolism has been all too well trodden, and certainly it is futile to seek in the work of some single thinker or mystagogue (such as Ludwig Klages) a key to its secrets. There are, however, a number of hidden paths which lead to *Demian* from *Peter Camenzind* and *Beneath the Wheel*.

What is left of the Gaienhofen world, or one should say the Gaienhofen vision of the world of Calw, hangs on still in the second

[27] J. C. Middleton, "Hermann Hesse as Humanist," p. 172: an Anglo-French compound, "Sin-clair."

[28] See *The Nuremberg Journey* (1927; IV, 136).

[29] And to some of them it always remained distant; in later life *Peter Camenzind* was to remind Hesse of nothing so much as the famous nineteenth-century verse romance, Joseph Viktor von Scheffel's *Trompeter von Säckingen*.

[30] *Letters* (VII, 515).

paragraph of *Demian*. But this evocation of home and town is already instinct with the mystery and myth of Emil Sinclair's childhood. The two worlds which exist in the child's imagination are
interfused; the one, that of the parents, the light world, and the
other, the dark, fearful, and fantastic world, are inseparably inter-
mingled. The maid Lina, indeed, plays two roles; with her horror
stories, with which she amuses the child, she belongs to the dark
world as well as to the light. The child Emil finds a deep satisfaction
in harmless games with his sisters, in life in the light world, but his
own emotional explosions so often disturb such idylls. The unconscious speaks, and in any case the sights, sounds, and smells of the
dark world are all around him; he slips frequently into it, even likes
to dwell in it, so that return to the light world appears as "return
to the less beautiful, the duller and more arid" (III, 105). Through
Emil Sinclair's life, and through his imagination, there runs a dividing line; it is as though there were two concentric circles; the
circumference of the inner circle is the border between the light
and dark worlds, while the circumference of the outer circle is unknown. It seems always possible, when venturing outside the inner
circle, to take flight back into the security that is within: "It was
wonderful that here at home there was peace, order and tranquillity,
duty and good conscience, forgiveness and love—and also there
was all the other, all those loud and shrill, dark and violent things
from which you could escape with a leap back to mother" (III,
104). The word "*Sprung*" (leap) is to become a key word in
Hesse's symbolic language; while the fundamental pattern of the
two spheres, light and dark, may be traced as far back as "Julius
Abderegg." [31]

The projection of the inner circle along the horizontal line of
time leads to school, where Emil will gradually grow in the image
of his parents and *pass examinations*. This last is an idea the
significance of which was partly concealed in *Beneath the Wheel*—
these tests are essentially validifications of the right to belong to the

[31] Or rather, its inverse. The half-lit dream world which constitutes Julius'
childhood is disrupted by an older boy, "a real street-lad," who tells "a lot
of terrifying stories from the town—about fires, robberies, jails, and that sort
of thing." The episode is summarized thus: "Into this beautiful dawn-light,
rich in imaginings (*ahnungsvoll*), there fell a harsh glare" (*Prosa aus dem
Nachlass*, p. 22).

light world; it is as if Hans Giebenrath, by passing the provincial examination, had given proof of his capacity to repress the dark world within him, the instinctive Natural Man. As might be expected, the school of *Demian* is the bourgeois sphere and a projection of the world of the parents, more specifically that of the father: "The question was still whether with time I would turn into a good son and useful citizen or whether my nature was inclined in other directions" (III, 163). As an older boy Emil is of course a rebel at school; his particular disgrace and dissipation later turns out to be drinking, and like Peter Camenzind—like Harry Haller too—he becomes viciously ironical, indeed masochistic, under the influence of alcohol. It seems then as if he is about to drown in the dark world, as he sometimes used to fear when he was younger, and yet his impulses had always been ambivalent:

There were stories of Prodigal Sons to whom this had happened, I had read them with passionate interest. In them what was always such a release and so magnificent was the return to the father and to the good, I felt absolutely that this alone was what was right, good, and desirable, and yet that part of the story which took place among the wicked and lost was by far the more enticing, and if you could have said this and admitted it, it was in reality sometimes actually a pity that the Prodigal repented and was found again [III, 105].

Such biblical imagery is, not surprisingly, common enough in Hesse, and the Prodigal Son has a most particular niche in his imagination (and in this novel). He functions as a *figura*.[32] On the first page of *Knulp* we find the ditty:

> Es sitzt ein müder Wanderer
> In einer Restauration,
> Das ist gewiss kein anderer
> Als der verlorne Sohn [III, 9].

> (A weary wanderer
> Sits in a café,
> He is undoubtedly none other
> Than the Prodigal Son.)

[32] For a discussion of the concept of the *figura* in this connection see T. J. Ziolkowski: *The Novels of Hermann Hesse* (Princeton, 1965), pp. 118–128.

One might return as a penitent; however, the possibility also existed of returning in triumph, "like a man of position." [33] Emil Sinclair, venturing into the outer circle, encounters water, he is "submerged in foreign waters . . . threatened by the enemy" (III, 113). Escaping eventually from the blackmailer Kromer's terrible persecution, he returns to the bosom of his family: "And now with elevated feelings I celebrated the festival of my reconciliation, the return of the Prodigal Son" (III, 140). He adds: "Everything was marvelous, everything was as it is in the stories." The regular Bible readings at home in Calw are of course the source of all this; it is a scarlet thread in *Demian*, for Pistorius too says of himself: "I am a Prodigal Son" (III, 195). Pistorius is precisely the theologian *manqué*, who rejected the career which his clergyman father had mapped out for him "just before the state examination" (III, 196), just in time; he is the promising boy whom his family now regards as "off the rails and a little crazy" (III, 196). The Prodigal in his many incarnations always appears in Hesse's work as the son who rejects the priestly career, rejects the seminary, and may indeed never return home to repent. In Pistorius's as well as in Emil Sinclair's fate *Demian* touches upon the problematics of "In Pressel's Summerhouse" and also upon those of *Beneath the Wheel*.

In all of this we may draw an analogy with Gide and his *Retour de l'enfant prodigue* (1907). Gide and Hesse, of course, have much in common, both in their lives and in their works. The way of the Prodigal Son is the life pattern of several of Hesse's characters, most obviously perhaps Goldmund. Sometimes they do find their way back home. But home may well be a prison (we have only to recall *Rosshalde*). Flight may proceed in both directions, back to the mother like little Emil or irretrievably into the vast Without. That these two possibilities should contrast is already surprising. In *Demian* in fact a subtle play begins with the two spheres, within and without the wall, though their ambivalent nature was already apparent in *Beneath the Wheel*. The return itself, in fact, may be portrayed as flight. At first Emil flies always back to his cloistered home, with the antique escutcheon of the bird over the doorway: "When we arrived, when I saw our house door, with the thick brass door latch, the sun in the windows and the curtains in my

[33] "Beautiful Is Youth" (I, 719).

mother's room, I took a deep breath of relief. O homecoming! O good, blessed return home, into the light, to peace" (III, 109). H. R. Schmid sees in the house door the threshold of the unconscious mind,[34] but of course a more rigorous Freudian approach would see in such a doorway something else again. At all events it is here, in this entrance, that Emil suffers the first terrible pressures of Kromer; it is here he seeks for refuge with a dirt on his shoes he cannot scrape off. The entrance becomes contaminated, "our hall did not smell of peace and security any more" (III, 110); guilt penetrates the hitherto secure circle. Thus Emil begins to lose his natal home, and becomes a seeker after home.

Near the end of the novel he appears to find what he was looking for: "When I closed the gate behind me, when indeed from some distance away I saw the high trees of the garden appear, I was rich and happy. Outside was "reality," outside there were streets and houses, people and institutions, libraries and lecture rooms—here within, however, there was love and soul, here lived the *Märchen* [35] and the dream" (III, 236). This is the house of Frau Eva, Demian's mother, and she greets Emil "beneath the picture of the bird in the opened door" (III, 232). This parallelism is striking, but the arrangement of the major symbol seems oddly inverted vis-à-vis *Beneath the Wheel*—it is predominantly the world of the mother which is now within the wall, the world of dream and *Märchen*.[36] In entering here Emil shuts out the world outside. The circle is now closed and the paradox is complete. The essay "Refuge" (1917) shows us what view we should take in order to approach the symbol; the true refuge is of course within, in the soul, "a space or point where there is only I, whither the world cannot reach, where I alone am at home. . . . There nothing may penetrate unless it be totally transformed into I. . . . Little chamber within, little coffin, little cradle, thou art my goal" (VII, 68). Hesse knew that, in the deepest sense, he who bursts out from the cloister must always seek to find his way back within, but on a different level of

[34] *Hermann Hesse,* p. 140.

[35] The English term "fairy tale" is frequently a weak translation of the German term "*Märchen*," which is therefore retained.

[36] One might add this one—probably a memory of "Hyazinth und Rosenblütchen"—to the numerous figures from Novalis which have been discovered in Hesse.

being; the true Way is in fact not a circle, it is a spiral; cradle and coffin are one and yet different. As the mystical implications crowd in, however, we have to note that Frau Eva's home is itself not regarded as the ultimate refuge; this it cannot be, for all has not yet become "I," "I" still lies deeper; Emil Sinclair is still to some extent caught in the toils of his own fantasies, in pictures (we may here compare the situation in the *Märchen* "Iris"). Demian and Frau Eva themselves are still present; they have replaced his parents.

It is a possibility that the use of the house symbol in *Demian* was derived from Friedrich Huch's novel *Mao*.[37] It seems at any rate impossible to doubt that the Kromer episode owes a good deal to this book. *Mao* belongs to the genus *Jugendroman* (novel of youth). The little boy, Thomas, has an intense and secretive emotional life, closely identified with the large old house on the marketplace and the long, sheltered garden behind it; his parents (as so often in this type of novel, the father is a successful lawyer) and his extraverted sister fail utterly to understand the nature of the boy's inner life. Then at school Thomas falls into the grip of a blackmailer, who once saw him, in the street, put out his tongue behind a teacher and so threatens to denounce him. He forces Thomas to give him his pen, his pencil, his lunchtime snacks, his castoff clothing (for, as he says, he is poor and Thomas is rich), and finally more valuable items, pressing him to steal his father's stamp collection. The blackmailer summons his victim by whistling outside his house. At the same time Thomas comes to idealize another boy in his class, Alexander, who becomes for him a kind of higher being. In his dreams he sees a face which resembles Alexander's. Over the threshold of the old house there is a worn escutcheon in the shape of the initial of Alexander's name.

In *Demian*, Emil Sinclair is blackmailed by Franz Kromer, his sadistic schoolfellow, to whom he has told—to acquire prestige— an untrue story about stealing apples (the biblical allusion is persuasive). Kromer forces him to rob his own moneybox but finds its contents inadequate; he, also, stresses that he is poor and Emil rich: "You have nice clothes, and you get a better lunch than I do"

---

[37] Berlin, 1907. I am indebted to Dahrendorff's work for first drawing my attention to this novel.

(III, 120). He, also, summons his victim by a whistle, which becomes an obsessive terror for Emil: "Not a single place, no game,
no job, no thought to which this whistle failed to penetrate"
(III, 120). However, while Thomas is rescued by his father's intervention in the affair, after falling ill with fever, Emil is saved by
Demian, who "talks" with Kromer. Emil also, however, is made
physically sick by the tensions of the situation. While the bird
escutcheon over the house door is a major emblem in Demian, the
house itself is not described in detail. In Mao, on the other hand,
the house is the overriding motif—Thomas's dreams circle around
it day and night, and especially around an old picture of a boy
which hangs in his bedroom. Here we may also note that Emil
dreams of the picture he pins up over his bed. For Thomas the boy
in the picture becomes the spirit of the house, an alter ego whom
he eventually deifies in Alexander's stead, and whom, playing with
the three middle letters of his own name, he christens "Mao."

Huch's novel is extraordinarily badly written and its symbolism
crude; evidently, however, it provided Hesse with a good deal of
material, especially the central action of the Kromer episode and the
motif of the escutcheon, but perhaps with more than this. Thomas,
it is worth noting, has the high school boy's contempt for "the comrades who stay behind in elementary school," [38] and the novel deals
to some extent with life in a school, although it is not a school novel
in the proper sense. This connection between Mao and Demian is
yet a further link between the latter novel and the world of Beneath
the Wheel.

There are grounds for the view that the first chapters of Demian,
the evocation of the ambivalent universe of the childish imagination
and its disintegration, are the most satisfying section of the book
and perhaps among the best things that Hesse ever wrote. These
chapters are concerned with the child's growing consciousness of
"sin," of good and evil. The parents represent "goodness and
authority" (III, 106); the child suffers torments from the side of his
superego. The symbol of sin and revolt is theft, first imagined, then
real, and strikingly paralleled in "Child's Soul" (1919). In this
latter story the conflict with the father is gone into in detail: the
boy steals some figs from a box in his father's room—and the

[38] Ibid., p. 155.

significance of the selection of this particular fruit scarcely needs
elucidation.[39] Parental supremacy must indeed be broken, but this
is a painful process accompanied by an obsessive guilt complex.
Emil must learn to accept his guilt; to acknowledge that the dark
world also exists within himself. And curiously his sense of secret
guilt suddenly makes him feel superior to his father, who is ignorant
of this guilt: "This moment was what was important and permanent
in the whole experience, as far as it has been recounted. It was a first
rent in the sanctity of my father, it was a first incision in the pillars
on which my child's life had been founded and which everyone
has to destroy before he can become himself. The inward, essential
line of our destiny consists of these experiences, which nobody
perceives" (III, 115). Emil Sinclair narrates not only with hindsight
and self-knowledge, but with the technical self-knowledge which
comes from analysis. The Kromer episode is by far the most vivid
part of the novel, because, whatever it may owe to *Mao*, it clearly
draws strongly for its atmosphere on Hesse's own childhood memories; and this atmosphere is in some degree one of Pietistic conscience, of struggle with the debilitating notion of sin. In this sense
Kromer is the Devil: "I saw him clearly, one eye was screwed up,
he mouthed a crude laugh, and his evil eye gleamed demoniacally"
(III, 116-117). Emil specifically calls him "Satan," and throughout the episode the author plays upon the double meaning of the
word *"Feind."* Furthermore, Kromer is evidently seen as the
Jungian "shadow" (cf. III, 129)—a motif much used later on which
here makes its first appearance in Hesse's work.

Demian is first and foremost, however, an interpretative novel;
nothing is merely evoked, nothing is presented wholly free of the
author's interpretative hindsight. In this element of ratiocination,
Demian, indeed, goes much further than do any of the earlier
works; this is its most outstanding characteristic. It is noteworthy
that it has an introduction (as *Hermann Lauscher* also has), in
which the narrator states his purpose and his method, and tries to
define his own limitations. He is not God, he says, as writers of

---

[39] It is certainly significant that the boy himself admits he does not know
why he steals the figs. When his penknife breaks off at the hilt and his father
commiserates—"You poor fellow"—the startlingly Freudian nature of the symbolism is again revealed.

novels (and of course he is no novelist) often pretend to be. His insight is not limitless, any more than the novelist's is if the truth were told; but his work is more significant to him than any work of fiction could be to its creator: "For it is my own and it is the story of a person—not an invented, a possible, an ideal or otherwise non-existent person, but of someone real, unique and living" (III, 101). It is very curious how this preface, superficially at least designed to establish the veracity or at any rate the verisimilitude of the story to be recounted, actually exerts its influence in the opposite direction. It distances the reader; it functions as a kind of alienation mechanism, for it makes clear to us that what we are in fact about to read is not a "real life" at all, not genuine memoirs but rather a systematized and formalized biography of the inner man, "the inward, essential line of our destiny," a *vita*. This effect connects *Demian*, for instance, in technique with *The Glass Bead Game*.

And in the form of *Demian* there are also certain elements which may best be defined by the word "tract," not only the introduction but also the conversations between Sinclair and Demian, Frau Eva, and Pistorius. The novel is built up on an interleaving of action and conversation, the action—such as it is—being continually inspired, directed, and finally interpreted by the conversations.[40] Generally, Sinclair's part in these conversations is so small that Demian takes on the appearance of a lecturer delivering himself of his notes— and this despite his expressed aversion from "wiseacring."

It is symptomatic of this structural peculiarity and the approach behind it that Emil Sinclair is able to say of his childhood: "There would be beautiful, tender and worth-while things to tell of my childhood. . . . But I am only interested in the steps which I took in my life to get to myself. All the attractive resting places, islands of bliss, and paradises, whose charm was not strange to me, I leave behind me in the glow of faraway things and have no desire to go there again" (III, 143). Presumably this includes the island of beauty evoked in the first section of *An Hour beyond Midnight* so long before; and dwelling upon childhood for childhood's sake is indeed almost as taboo in *Demian* as it is later in *The Glass Bead*

---

[40] For this point, see what is one of the very best studies of Hesse's work: P. Schiefer, "Grundstrukturen des Erzählens bei Hermann Hesse" (diss., Münster, 1959), p. 86.

Game. It would really seem from Emil's remarks that his analysis has all but cured him; for him paradisiacal states, islands of peace, are now regarded as transitory delusions which must be transcended one after another on the way of self-discovery, while dreams are no longer an escape to hidden memories and longings but the tools of self-development. Emil himself, of course, is not the analyst, though perhaps he would like to be; he is the analyst's counterpart, the dreamer, and his detachment is not absolute. Thus he cannot help speaking with disgust of his boyhood dissipations, of how his childhood finally expired when he became stranded "in puddles of dirt, in back streets full of smells and filth." Between himself and his childhood he himself sets up "a closed gate of Eden with mercilessly radiant guards" (III, 169–171).[41]

Expelled from paradise, Emil Sinclair finds his own angel, the coldly radiant Demian. Sometimes, especially in the conversations, Demian appears to be a pure construct, hypostasized reflection. One might say that at the point at which he intervenes between Emil and Kromer the book turns decisively into a didactic vein. Hans Giebenrath had looked hopelessly for a teacher who would come to him at the end of his childhood; Demian is such a teacher. He is, of course, many incompatible things at once, an imago, a mouthpiece for the reflective, critical mind, and a patchwork of various memories, both literary and personal. Two main strands are joined in him, the one which descends through Kasper Hauri, Richard, Karl Notwang, and, somewhat paradoxically, Hermann Heilner, and the other through the cobbler Flaig, the elderly theosophist Lohe in *Gertrude*, and perhaps Johannes in the novel fragment *Berthold*.

Demian, from the outset, makes an impression of precocious maturity. He is always the master of himself and his environment.[42]

[41] Cf. Genesis 3:24. For the related figure of the tree of life see P. Gontrum, "Oracle and Shrine: Hesse's 'Lebensbaum,'" *Monatshefte für deutschen Unterricht*, LVI (1964), 183–190.

[42] Since, in an analysis by a Jungian analyst, "Jungian" material tends to be produced, and since the association of *Demian* with Hesse's own analytical sessions is clearly very close, the direct use of Jungian parallels for an interpretation of the symbolism of this novel is a more permissible method than it might otherwise be. So it is of interest that Jung, in an analysis of Goethe's *Pandora*, writes: "For Epimetheus . . . Pandora has the significance of a soul-image—she represents his soul; hence her divine power, her unshakable su-

Although like Emil he is merely a schoolboy, he walks about "like a man, or rather like a gentleman" (*wie ein Herr*; III, 122). He is not popular, nor does he deign to take part in games, still less in "brawls," and we recall that Hermann Heilner actually wept when lured into just such a departure from his dignity; but, as is the case with some of his predecessors, Demian's "self-possessed and decisive tone toward the teachers pleased the others" (III, 123). The commentators have generally failed to notice how much of the traditional school novel still survives in this section of the book. Demian seems to be an adult merely pretending to be a child, or else "a prince in disguise" (III, 123). Physically he is powerful, and there are appropriate rumors that he already knows all the secrets of the other sex. Very revealing about the creative process to which this figure owes its "life" is the fact that Emil has to make a special effort of conscious memory to recall much about him, to (re)-construct him: "I am trying to recall what I know of Demian from this period. . . . I am searching my mind for his figure, and now I try to recall him I see that he really was there and that I noticed him. . . . I try to recall, with closed eyes, and I see his image arise" (III, 145).

Clearly, to regard Demian simply as an imago—that is, to apply a purely psychoanalytic method of interpretation—fails to allow properly for compositional features such as this. A page or two later we read the characteristic reflection: "I didn't know that, I didn't feel exactly what I now say about it as an adult, but something of the kind" (III, 147). Emil recalls Demian in various situations, he remembers his face: "the face of a man, a scientist or artist, masterful and full of will, strangely bright and cool, with eyes filled with knowledge" (III, 146). In fact, Demian would have turned out a very one-sided artist, would have been hamstrung by his own brightness and coolness, his *mental* bias. His will, of course, might have been an asset, and will is a subject on which he has revealing views: there is, he maintains, no such thing as free will, and yet if a creature (he draws his example from the Lepidoptera) can will

---

periority. Wherever such attributes are conferred upon certain personalities we may with certainty conclude that such personalities are *symbol-bearers;* in other words *imagines* of projected unconscious contents" (*Psychological Types,* p. 225).

what is in accord with its own nature, it can achieve its goal. Indeed, for Demian, fruitful willing comes only through the discovery of and total identification with one's fate; when a human being is in this condition, his outer and his inner worlds begin to correspond, to revolve at the same rate, to interlock meaningfully, and the element of accident begins to be excluded.[43] As an imago, Demian should be a projection of the soul, but here one senses an artistic deficiency—somehow the novel fails to give him texture, depth, and the necessary femininity, he remains far more a disembodied intellect, a mere voice, than a fully realized imago ought to be. To be sure, when Emil considers Demian's face, this profounder aspect of his nature does begin to be stressed: "It was as if there was also something of a woman's face in it, and for a moment this face seemed to me neither grown up nor childish, neither old nor young, but a sort of thousand-year face, somehow timeless, stamped by eras other than our own. Animals could look like that, or trees, or stars" (III, 146).

It remains true, nonetheless, that the language which describes Demian gives a predominantly masculine, abstract, or even lifeless impression; there are a remarkable number of adjectives—for example, "cool," "masterful" (*überlegen*), "bright," "distant," "lonely," and even "age-old" and "stony"—all of which, in Hesse's work at any rate, invariably point in the direction of intellect, abstraction, and will, and not in that of the "soul." [44] In his trancelike, meditative states it is—unavoidably, since Emil must observe these from without—the same coldness, hardness, and abstractedness which are emphasized; although Emil does indeed remark upon the burning life which there must be beneath this petrified surface. Demian "sat with the stiffness of a picture and, as I could not help thinking, that of an idol" (III, 161)—the allusion to Indian statuary is self-evident. Demian, furthermore, is a magician—"he stood before me like a magician" (III, 134).

Yet that Demian is inadequate as a teacher for Emil is implicitly conceded by the very introduction of Frau Eva, Demian's mother,

---

[43] Such conceptions, of course, are of mystical origin, connected with the Tao and with the *rita* of the *Rig-Veda*.

[44] This language has been adjudged more generally significant as being that of introversion. See H. Mauerhofer, *Die Introversion*, p. 50.

supposedly the epitome of the feminine. On meeting her, Emil is overcome: "Her face—like that of her son—timeless and ageless and full of soulful will, the beautiful, dignified lady smiled at me. Her gaze was fulfillment, her greeting meant homecoming. Silently I held out my hands to her" (III, 232). Her will is "soulful" to be sure, but somehow the scene is far too posed and lifelessly constructed.

Compared with women characters in other works of Hesse's, notably *Narziss and Goldmund* and *The Steppenwolf*, Frau Eva is herself made of stone. She is indeed a goddess on a plinth, a member of that species which is, to use Peter Camenzind's words, "like stars and blue mountain tops far from us . . . and nearer to God," dominant in all the novels up to *Demian*, to be later on supplanted by a quite different creature. Certainly Frau Eva has some touches of the new type of woman to come (Kamala, Hermine, Maria, and Goldmund's connoisseur's collection). Her voice is like sweet wine; the picture of her that Emil carries in his heart becomes "mature and lustful" (III, 233). But this is the secondary, subsidiary impression; primary is her unapproachable transfiguration, and in this ethereal, mythologized quality she is at one with the whole last section of *Demian*, which suffers above all in that the manner of the "interpretative" novel is used to evoke the material of the soul.[45]

The interrelationship between teacher and pupil in Hesse's works requires, in reflection of ancient occult tradition, that the pupil must be raised to the level of the teacher in order that the teacher himself may advance beyond. In a sense *Demian* is hagiographical, and the axis upon which the relationship of Sinclair to Demian turns is that of spiritual emulation (*imitatio*); however, Sinclair's emulation of the *imitabile* (Demian) is not really in the Christian manner, since he has finally to learn not to be another Demian, but to be himself (and we may remember that a grave error of the pupils of Nietzsche's Zarathustra is that they do not grasp this point). The figure of Demian is so rich in implications that it is difficult to exhaust him. He may, for instance, be regarded

---

[45] There is even unintentional bathos: "I turned sharply away from her, walked to the window and stared with blind eyes out over the potted plants" (III, 234–235).

as a Messiah and/or as a symbol of the Middle Way.[46] He may well have connections, in his capacity as an alter ego, with cabbalistic teachings about Habal Garmin, the "spiritual double" (as developed in Gustav Meyrinck's sensational novel *Der Golem* (1915), which may have influenced Hesse). He appears, furthermore, as the synthesis of thesis Sinclair and antithesis Kromer, of good and evil, light and dark, the affirming force and the denying—his exact place in the triad is even marked out for him: "Between me and Kromer there stood something like future, something like hope" (III, 137).

Demian, however, is a work of language, and the figure Demian is a creature of language, a functionary in a fundamental stylistic dualism; but it would be obtuse, in the case of this particular novel, to close one's eyes to the rewards bestowed by the psychoanalytical method of interpretation. The Freudian view of the action of the book requires that we see Demian as the analyst and Sinclair as the patient, the Jungian that we regard Demian as a projection of Sinclair's own unconscious, "a voice which could only come from myself" (III, 135). On this latter view all other major figures in the novel are projections too, with the exception of Pistorius—he being excepted on the assumption that he is the analyst, Dr. Lang.

It must be emphasized, however, that such interpretations fail to make full allowance for what is disclosed through a study of the language and style of the work and fail, above all, to situate the novel properly in series with Hesse's earlier writings. On the contrary they tend to isolate it from the author's literary past. The new power in Hesse's creative art, with *Demian*, was released by traumatic experiences, among these most certainly that of analysis; his art found new goals—spiritual truth at all costs, "magical thinking," and the pursuit of a style in which "magical thinking" might be transmitted. Meanwhile, however, on the way to these

---

[46] Jung writes: "The psychological point of departure for the god-renewal corresponds with an increasing divergence in the manner of application of psychic energy or libido. One half of the libido moves towards a Promethean, while the other towards an Epimethean, manner of application. Such an opposition is, of course, a very great hindrance not only in society but also in the individual. Hence the optimum of life recedes more and more from the opposing extremes and seeks out a middle way. . . . Since the middle position, as a function of mediation between the opposites, possesses an irrational character, it appears projected in the form of a reconciling God, a Messiah or Mediator" (*Psychological Types*, p. 241).

far-off goals, there was temporarily intensified the distancing, critical element which had always been so significant, the capacity for abstraction, for self-analysis, for clear-eyed freedom from the bewitchment of memory and dream. This, in its turn, resulted in the virtual elimination of the conventionally "poetic" element still so strong in *Rosshalde* and in *Knulp*, in favor of a programatic study of the skeletal inner life, a formalized *vita*. The external world has little life in *Demian;* no fish zigzag in the magical twilight, as they do in *Beneath the Wheel*. On the other hand, the hagiographical features of the form connect with numerous references to saints and sainthood in the novel. Demian and Emil sit together in a wine cellar discussing the latter's alcoholic dissipations; Demian remarks that at least this way of life is superior to that of the blameless bourgeois and observes: "And then—I read this once —the life of the profligate is one of the best preparations for the mystic. Indeed there are always people like St. Augustine, who become seers" (III, 180). The remark is crucial for an understanding of Hesse's work, as will emerge. It brings Emil to a vivid moment of truth: "Had I not lived in drunkenness and dirt, in stupor and abandon, until with a new life-impulse exactly the opposite had been born in me, the yearning for purity, the longing for the holy?" (III, 181). He refers to his cult of the girl he calls Beatrice, whom he never approaches; Peter Camenzind undertook the unrewarding "role of the worshiping priest", Emil Sinclair is "a temple servant with the goal of becoming a saint" (III, 175).

In concentrating upon the narrowly psychoanalytic, some critics have been inclined to miss the importance of biblical material in *Demian*. The *figura* of the Prodigal Son is but one example of this. In fact, several of the fundamental steps that Emil takes toward enlightenment, largely under Demian's guidance, involve biblical references or allusions. From the conversation with Demian and others come strange ideas which lead to sudden insights, to dreams, to instants of inner awakening, to moments of inner "death." The first such conversation, about Cain and Abel, has endless reverberations: "A stone had fallen into the well, and the well was my youthful soul" (III, 128). Demian interprets Cain as the strong individual whose "mark"—"something uncanny and scarcely perceptible" (III, 125)—struck fear into society and forced him and his family beyond the social pale, a Nietzschean superman whom the weak banded together to destroy.[47] Pondering the curious implications of this—as he feels—excessively abrupt transvaluation of values, a flash of memory comes to Emil, that moment when his guilt in the Kromer affair had made him feel superior to, indeed contemptuous of, his father and the "light" world. The mark of Cain seemed then momentarily no disgrace, but a high distinction— or so he intellectualizes about his insight later on. Then comes the first significant dream in the novel, in which he dreams he is mishandled, spat and knelt upon by Kromer, given a knife and urged to murder his father; there follows a dream in which it is Demian who kneels upon him, but "everything I had endured from Kromer in agony and revolt I endured from Demian willingly and with a feeling which had in it as much bliss as it had fear" (III, 130). The meaning of such classical dreams is transparent and needs no commentary. From this world of sin, of fear of sin and longing for sin, Emil is brought by Demian to a moment of confession, another instant of light and intense sense of change; he quivers on the brink of confession to Demian—"and a hint of redemption wafted toward me like a strong scent" (III, 137). Yet it is, after all, to his family—above all to his father—that he confesses, and there is duly celebrated the return of the Prodigal Son. Confession is, for all Hesse's major protagonists, an inevitable stage; but to be useful such confession must not be—as Emil's is—"decorative and touching" (III, 141), the self-embroidery of the narcissistic artist-sinner. It is also highly material to whom the confession is made.

The destruction of childhood, that milestone on the Way, is therefore delayed for Emil. Such ideas as Demian's do not eliminate his pupil's respect for religion; as with Hesse, so with Emil it is the

[47] The tone of the argument is distinctly Nietzschean, and there is no doubt that the whole novel follows Nietzsche in its immoralism. However, as Emil's father points out, this view of Cain is ancient enough; he refers to that obscure gnostic sect, the Cainites, who are said to have venerated both Cain and Judas Iscariot. Hesse called Cain (in 1930) "a Prometheus distorted into his opposite" (Letters; VII, 488). His claim, in the same letter, that he did not know any literary sources for his ideas on Cain as expressed in Demian has rightly been called in question by Dahrendorff (op. cit., p. 8); he must at least have known of the Cainites. Jung, in Symbols of Transformation (Collected Works [Bollingen Series XX; New York, 1956], 112), associates the race of Cain with chaotic passion.

model provided by his parents' life which has made the most permanent impression. In the chapter entitled "The Thief," Demian develops the notion that the thief on Christ's left hand is the more worthy of respect of the two—"he's a regular fellow and has some character" (III, 155–156)—this fellow accepts the consequences of his pact with Satan and goes his own way to the very end.[48] Puberty, Emil tells us, is for many people the only moment at which they experience "that dying and being born anew which is our fate"; furthermore, "many always remain suspended from this cliff and adhere painfully life-long to what is irrevocably past, to the dream of the lost paradise, which is the worst and most murderous of all dreams" (III, 144). Here Sinclair-Hesse makes a harsh but scientifically informed judgment about his own life and work.

He has no time, however, to dwell upon the feelings and dreams which attended the end of his childhood, for they are extraneous matter: "Let us get back to the story" (III, 144), that is, to the skeleton, to the stark *vita* itself; and what was significant for this last, at this moment of development, was that the dark world of Franz Kromer had been absorbed into Emil Sinclair. Because it is Within, it attracts its corresponding Without—"and thereby the 'other world' again acquired power over me from outside too" (III, 144). On the Jungian view this change is the first step in the successive assimilation and integration of the projections of the unconscious.[49] The Way, at all events, is a way of moments, of instantaneous inward transformations and shifts, as for instance once in confirmation class when the instructing clergyman comes to speak of Cain and Abel: "With this moment there was a link between me and Demian" (III, 148). After years of separation the adolescent Sinclair finds his guru once more and is introduced more deeply into the magical arts which are at the guru's disposal. The remark about the thief on the Cross makes conscious for him the issue of the God-Satan antithesis, the opposition and perhaps transcendent unity of good and evil, light and darkness, "my own myth, the idea of the two worlds or half-worlds—the light one and the dark" (III, 157).

[48] This ancient idea had interested Dr. Lang. Ball quotes Lang as having written: "I am the justice of the left-hand thief" (*op. cit.*, p. 164).
[49] Cf. E. Maier, *op. cit.* (abridgment of diss., p. 8).

Put like this, strong resonances of Jung but also of Johann Jakob Bachofen are noticeable. The evidence for Bachofen's influence on *Demian* seems to be wholly internal, but it is generally recognized. Hesse certainly knew something of Bachofen's work quite early in life; together with Jakob Burckhardt and Nietzsche, Bachofen was the third intellectual giant whose memory was potent in Basel at the turn of the century.[50] Bachofen's view of myth as the exegesis of symbol is relevant to *Demian*, but it is above all his famous interpretation of the symbolic eggs, half-light half-dark, on the tombs at the Villa Pamfilia, which appears to be reflected in the novel.[51]

But before he can come to an even partial understanding of this duality, which is incarnate in the demiurge Abraxas—"a God who also contains the Devil" (III, 157)—Sinclair has a long way to go: he has to observe, for instance, and to wonder at, Demian's state of self-absorption. This state, of course, is not itself one of "awakening" because it is deliberately turned inward, away from the outside world. It is however, we may say, the precondition of the higher level of consciousness on which Demian moves in active life; it is the contemplative systole which is the foundation of the diastole of an "awakened" *vita activa*. To Emil it appears that Demian is motionless, hard, and immune to external stimuli, a stone god, though full of life deep within; around him there is an aura of "ether and starry space" (III, 161)—here surely a presentiment of Harry Haller's Immortals—and he has, as he himself observes, crept into himself like a tortoise.[52] Emil, who does not know the technique

[50] A definite reference to Hesse's Bachofen studies may be found later in "Aus einem Tagebuch des Jahres 1920," *Corona*, III (1932-1933), 204.

[51] "Der Wechsel der hellen und der dunklen Farbe drückt den steten Übergang von Finsternis zu Licht, von Tod zu Leben aus. . . . In der Religion ist das Ei Symbol des stofflichen Urgrunds der Dinge. . . . Der stoffliche Urgrund der Dinge . . . umschliesst beides, Werden und Vergehen. Er trägt zu gleicher Zeit die Licht- und Schattenseiten der Natur in sich "(The alternation of the light and the dark hues expresses the perpetual transition from darkness to light, from death to life. . . . In religion the egg is the symbol of the material ground of things. . . . The material ground of things . . . comprises both, becoming and passing away. It contains at one and the same time the light and dark sides of nature) (Bachofen, *op. cit.*, pp. 25–26).

[52] "The tortoise can draw in its legs; the seer can draw in his senses" (*Bhagavad-Gita*, tr. by Swami Prabhavananda and Christopher Isherwood [London, 1948], p. 48).

it requires, subsequently exhausts himself trying to reproduce this condition. It is now indeed the end of his childhood, which falls away from him in ruins; the world loses all its charm, the garden its fragrance, the forest its mystery, books and music their value: "So the leaves fall around a tree in autumn, it does not feel it, rain runs down it, or sun, or frost, and in it life slowly recedes into the smallest, innermost place. It does not die. It waits" (III, 162). The tree sheds its greenery, the stark skeletal self is exposed, and yet, like the meditating Demian, it is withdrawn, impervious to external stimuli; it is waiting, to live out in due time the secret of its seed.

This tree finds its way into the novel from the ambiance of *Peter Camenzind* and *Beneath the Wheel*. The Beatrice episode, also, seems to owe as much to the past as it does to the immediate psychological environment of *Demian*. Indulging in what Demian defines later as "flight into community" and soon to become "hero of the wine cellars" (III, 169), Emil is Peter Camenzind down to the very words; people "saw a hypocrite and disagreeable eccentric in me. I liked the role and exaggerated it, and sulked my way into a loneliness which from outside always looked like manly contempt for the world, while secretly I often surrendered to consuming attacks of melancholy and despair" (III, 164). Though he calls himself "a beast," he is in sexual matters more timid than his comrades, and like Peter unable to approach women. Beatrice, the elegant and vaguely hermaphroditic young lady he sees in the park—"a clever boyish face . . . the type . . . I liked" (III, 173)— he christens specifically after a memory of a Pre-Raphaelite portrait (not Dante or Jung);[53] of course, she is yet another white cloud, even more ethereal than Peter's Elisabeth. Her faint masculinity reminds us that in *Peter Camenzind* the hero's affections moved from man (Richard) to woman (Elisabeth) and then back to man again (Boppi), and here also his attachment is first to Demian, then to Beatrice, and then to Demian again. Demian stripped to the waist with a punch ball, moreover, reminds us of Richard playing the piano or cavorting naked as the Lorelei. However, the extent of the

[53] In this figure numerous elements are overlaid; purely literary allusion blends with Jungian analytical doctrine. In *Demian* it is in fact frequently impossible to disentangle such elements. For instance, it has been pointed out that Demian and Frau Eva may well be interpreted in terms of the Jungian theory of the mandala. Cf. E. Rose, *Faith from the Abyss* (New York, 1965), p. 54.

(perhaps temporary) advance from *Peter Camenzind* is measured
by the fact that it is a female figure, Frau Eva, who dominates the
last pages of *Demian*. In Beatrice, Emil does find a Dantesque ideal
once more; he is now able to begin reconstructing the "light world"
by his own efforts, an exercise of worship, self-discipline, and
will; he consciously changes his posture while walking, he goes in
for cold showers at dawn.

Such "spiritual" exercises, however, do not penetrate much below
the surface—something which his painting is still able to do. Painting, of course, is free of will, "this playful activity" (III, 175). As
far as the attempt to paint Beatrice's face is concerned, he can only
do so expressionistically, following inner directives: "It was a dreamt
face which came out of this, and I wasn't at all displeased with it"
(III, 176). Painting directly from the prompting of the unconscious,
he produces a face which is clearly androgynous and which one
morning, awakening from one of his new dreams, he suddenly
recognizes for what it is—"divine image or holy mask" (III, 176)—
Demian's face.[54] When Demian was in his trance state, Emil had
been fascinated by "this pallid, stony mask" (III, 161). This "holy
mask" will indeed not leave us again in Hesse's novels, and is still
there on Tito's face at the very end of *The Glass Bead Game*.
Emil's dreams have in fact returned in strength and with fresh
images, and in them this painting, sometimes beautiful, sometimes
unspeakably distorted, constantly recurs. Looking at this picture
in the setting sun it seems to him to represent neither Beatrice nor
Demian, but himself, "what constituted my life, my destiny or my
demon" (*Dämon*; III, 173); to find one's friend, indeed, is to find
oneself.[55]

To discover and to identify with one's friend, one's "demon",
one's fate, is, as the novel never ceases to insist, to interlock the
world without and the world within in a linked movement and
hence to exclude the element of chance. Emil remarks condescend-
ingly of an early stage in his development: "At that time I still
firmly believed in coincidences" (III, 148); but it is not chance

[54] The Jungian hermaphrodite. In *Mao* a rather similar moment of recognition occurs, when Thomas identifies the face of his dreams, which he has confused with Alexander's, as that of the boy (Mao) in the portrait over his bed
head.

[55] Cf. Hans Mayer (as quoted above, Ch. 2, n. 37): "secret of their identity."

which causes the instructor in Greek to mention Abraxas just when he does. "Destiny and the feeling self (*Gemüt*) are names for one and the same concept"—Emil believes that he grasps the Novalis aphorism. In the text, however, there is really little enough evidence as to precisely what he understands by that difficult word "*Gemüt*"; he speaks of "the music and rhythm of my destiny" (III, 178). Fate must come from inside ("He to whom Fate comes from without is destroyed by it");[56] Fate is carried in the activated symbols within. In true Jungian fashion Emil says of Beatrice: "You are linked with me, but not you, only your image; you are a fragment of my destiny" (III, 178).

Reabsorption of the projected symbols back into the self, which may be regarded as the essential process in Emil's development, is certainly as adequate explanation as any of the central dream of the escutcheon, which is stimulated by the conversation with Demian in the wine cellar. In the dream Demian compels Emil to devour the escutcheon, a bird on a blue ground: "When I had swallowed I felt with tremendous terror that the devoured escutcheon was alive in me, was filling me up and starting to consume me from within" (III, 182). The motif of the escutcheon probably comes from *Mao*, but its use is original. Numerous interpretations have been proposed. The above quoted experience is obviously intensely erotic in quality, and moreover feminine in its essential nature. It has been suggested that the devouring symbolizes an "introversion" of psychic energy to fertilize the psyche and is also, since the sparrow-hawk feeds on animals, a figure for the sublimation of the animal impulses of the soul.[57] It has been proposed that what is symbolized is a process of becoming at one with the god,[58] or that it all goes no further than the sexual desires which Emil is as yet unable to affirm and which thus eat up his inner self.[59] The bird is clearly also to be seen as a traditional symbol for the soul.[60] The figure of the bird bursting out of the egg, which takes shape in Emil Sin-

[56] *Zarathustra's Return* (VII, 206).
[57] J. C. Middleton, *op. cit.*, p. 160.
[58] Cf. Dahrendorff, *op. cit.*, p. 87. The idea is familiar from Freud's *Totem and Taboo*.
[59] R. B. Matzig, *Hermann Hesse in Montagnola* (Basel, 1947), p. 20.
[60] Jung makes frequent allusion to birds in such a connection, as "soul-images." See, e.g., *Symbols of Transformation*, p. 215.

clair's painting: "Now it was a bird of prey, with the sharp, bold head of a sparrowhawk. He half-protruded from a dark globe, from which he was struggling to get out as from a giant egg, on a background of blue sky" (III, 183)—this may well have come from Bachofen.[61] The association of the bird with the soul persists in Hesse's later writings,[62] its association with the libido may be discerned as early as the dreams of Berthold, in the novel fragment of that name (1907–1908). Demian, the interpreter, in a cursory message of somewhat mysterious provenance, has this to say about Sinclair's painting: "The bird struggles out of the egg. The egg is the world.[63] Whoever wishes to be born must destroy a world. The bird flies to God. The god's name is Abraxas" (III, 185). Matzig's view of this, that the libido frees itself by destroying the shell of conventional morality, is a trifle crude;[64] it overlooks the religious, more specifically the gnostic connotations of the image and the general tenor of the novel. It might be more rewarding, and nearer the unattainable truth, to see the egg as the limited world, the closed circle of "light," out of which the soul must escape into that endless outer sphere which is both light and dark.[65] In any case the event represents the breaking through of a wall, the release of the unconscious from its erstwhile bonds [66]—as this had been prefigured in earlier novels.

The god Abraxas is a venerable deity, historically related to

[61] Bachofen writes of the ancient function of the egg in circuses: "Es ist auch in dem Zirkus Darstellung des weiblichen Naturprinzips, und älter als die Vogelgeburt, die aus ihm . . . hervorbricht" (It is also in the circus the representation of the female principle in nature, and older than the birth of the bird, which . . . bursts out of it) (op. cit., p. 33).

[62] Cf. its use in Siddhartha; also the story "Bird" (1932), and the quotation from the Psalms associated with the death of Hesse's father: "Der Strick ist zerrissen, der Vogel ist frei" (Psalms 124:7). In fact the symbol occurs as early as "Julius Abderegg" (Prosa aus dem Nachlass, p. 14).

[63] Hesse may possibly also have had in mind the—admittedly very different—conception of the "world-egg" to be found in the Vedanta, for instance in the Chândogya-Upanishad. Cf. P. Deussen, Sechzig Upanishad's des Veda IV (Darmstadt, 1963), p. 116.

[64] Op. cit., p. 23.

[65] Dahrendorff, who advances this view, points out that it is not wholly compatible with Bachofen, for whom the egg is (as in the Vedanta) the entire primal unity (op. cit., p. 108, n. 187).

[66] Cf. H. R. Schmid, Hermann Hesse, p. 12.

Mithras and having connections with sun myths.[67] Hesse's acquaintance with him may well have been made through J. B. Lang. His
nature is initially explained to the reader in the form of a lucid
lecture delivered by the young schoolmaster who teaches Greek,
which follows directly on the symbolism of Demian's cryptic message, thus partially interpreting it. This god who is also devil, "the
age-old demiurgos," [68] synthesizes all opposites within himself.
Dostoevsky, we are told, was much to the point in portraying Ivan
Karamazov's conversation with his own unconscious as a talk with
the Devil, since the repressed material of the unconscious mind is
precisely "satanic and detested" (here we must needs think of
Franz Kromer); beyond good and evil might lie a new synthesis of
Ivan and Alyosha, since "then the unconscious will not be the
Devil any longer, but the God-Devil." [69] Thus is Abraxas; he may
be seen as the ancient demiurgos who ruled over the world of
anarchy and of gynocratic supremacy, before the severity of the
Roman paternal system and the tyranny of the Jewish-Christian
God overturned his agreeable and harmonious hegemony (certainly
he must be the sworn enemy of that disciplinarian deity who
reigned over the house at Calw). It is Jung who says of libido that
it is God and Devil, and that it manifests "original bisexuality." [70]
Abraxas comes when Emil has need of him, when Beatrice "was
no longer sufficient for my soul" when "the sexual urge . . . demanded new images" (III, 187).

   Emil has a recurrent dream or imagination in which he goes
inward, through the portals of his "paternal home," beneath the
gleaming yellow and blue escutcheon, to meet his mother coming
toward him; but as he is about to embrace her she is transformed
into some tremendous, startlingly new figure which, like Emil's
painting, resembles Demian and yet is wholly feminine. He is
drawn into a deep embrace, an embrace which is both divine
worship and also sin; in this embrace memories of Emil's mother
and of Demian are mingled. Gradually a link is forged between this
recurrent vision and the external notion of the god Abraxas: "And

[67] Cf., e.g., Albrecht Dieterich, *Abraxas* (Leipzig, 1891), a work several times
cited by Jung.
[68] The Karamazov essay also discusses him in these terms (VII, 165).
[69] *Ibid.* (VII, 173).
[70] *Symbols of Transformation*, p. 289.

I began to feel that precisely in this intuitive dream I was invoking Abraxas. Pleasure and horror, man and woman blended, the most holy and most repellent woven together, deep guilt quivering through tender innocence . . . thus was my love-vision, and thus too was Abraxas" (III, 188–189). Love comes to be seen neither as a mere animal instinct nor as austere spiritual veneration but as both and much more, a hermetic union of extremes. Sex is freed from its shackles, the dark world at last faced and absorbed, and the incest theme which had lain deep in the novel rises to the surface.

There can be no doubt that psychoanalysis had made Hesse conscious of the significance for his own development of his attitude to his mother. "Childhood of the Magician" (1937) remarks of father and mother: "At times, full of admiration and eagerness, I strove to be like him, all too eagerly, though I knew that my roots grew more deeply in the soil of my mother, her dark eyes and her mystery" (IV, 456)—an observation which certainly has its relevance for Goldmund, if not for Emil Sinclair. "Dream Traces" (1927) ends with a dream about the "lover" in which the influence of the Jungian doctrine of the anima seems clear. "The Mothers," the sources of all life—"We all come out of the same gorge" (III, 102)—are mentioned in the first paragraph of *Demian*. As the novel moves toward its climax, an old woman shows Emil a photograph of Demian's mother: "That was my dream-picture . . . demon and mother, destiny and lover" (III, 224). The friend, Demian, is the father, fate, the I; the mother is the lover, the soul, and at the same time "vampire and whore" (III, 190). "A Fragment of Diary" (1918) tells of a dream in which the dreamer hears many voices; it is the voice of the mother, however, which speaks the message of *amor fati:* "Take no model. Models are things that do not exist, that you merely invent and impose on yourself" (VII, 147). It had, therefore, been folly to struggle, all too eagerly, to imitate the father, to emulate Demian. Freedom and fate, which are one and the same, come through discovery of and union with the feminine in the self, the anima; thus indeed the relationship of incest becomes a metaphor for the relationship of a man to his soul. The gnostic conceptions of the *Urmutter*, of the phallic god as secondary to her, to "female matter," [71] and of the immortality, through rebirth, which comes from union with her, the act of becoming one's own father, of begetting one's self—all these lie as shadows behind it.

Through all these complexities the novel moves with quite considerable art. The episode with Pistorius [72] adds yet another dimension. Pistorius, the organist, plays a music which is declared to be Classical, but which communicates a Romantic experience to Emil: "Yearning . . . passionate listening to one's own dark soul"—in the characteristic gesture—"ecstasy of surrender and profound curiosity for the marvelous" (III, 192). There can be no chance in the meeting with Pistorius, since it turns out that he already knows of Abraxas. Emil and Pistorius lie upon the floor of the latter's room, peering into the open hearth; the passage descriptive of this contemplation of the fire is intensely reminiscent of Novalis, especially of the opening of *Die Lehrlinge zu Sais.*[73] A mystical experience of immense significance then supervenes:

The contemplation of such shapes, the submission to irrational, intricate (*kraus*), strange natural forms produces in us a sense of the correspondence between our inner self and the will which created the shapes—soon we are tempted to regard them as our own fancies, our own creations. . . . Never so simply and easily as in this exercise do we make the discovery how much we are creators, how great a part our soul always plays in the perpetual creation of the world [III, 198].

The solipsism of the German Romantics joins here with the Jungian doctrine of the projection of the libido, but the imagery strongly suggests the primacy of the former influence. Strindberg, with his obsessional interest in supposed "correspondences," may

[71] Bachofen, *op. cit.,* p. 30.

[72] The origin of the name is obscure, but its oddity suggests that it has some point. It is the Latin adjective from "baker." There was also a sixteenth-century Swabian cleric called Johann Pistorius. Cf. J. Mileck, "Names and the Creative Process," *op. cit.,* p. 172.

[73] "Not observing, but surrendered to their own magic, their intricate (*kraus*), profound language. Long, ossified tree roots, colored veins in stone, patches of oil swimming on water, cracks in glass" (III, 198). (Novalis writes of "strange figures, which seem to belong to that great secret language which can be seen everywhere on wings, eggshells, in clouds, in the snow, in crystals and stone formations.")

also be in the background. As for Pistorius, he is a kind of mid-
wife of the soul; he helps Emil's bird to be born. The character
renders especially doubtful any purely Freudian interpretation of
the novel, since his occupation of the position of "analyst" leaves
no vacancy there for Demian. Theosophical doctrines in various
disguises appear in Pistorius' pronouncements, mixed with Jungian
theories; there may be some reflection of Rudolf Steiner, but the
principal model for Pistorius was no doubt Dr. Lang.[74] Pistorius
develops the doctrine of total amoralism: "Abraxas has no objection
to any of your thoughts, to any of your dreams" (III, 203)—
especially Emil's erotic dreams. This does not however imply a total
permissiveness, no one should *do* everything that comes into his
head, he should, however, accept that it is all in some sense meaningful and should strive neither to repress it nor to moralize about
it. Pistorius gives Emil a great deal; his music alone, for instance a
Passacaglia of Buxtehude—"this strange, fervent music, absorbed in
itself, listening to itself" (III, 203)—teaches him to pay the soul its
due. Emil comes to break with Pistorius because he finds him to be
too much the teacher, the intellectual, above all the antiquarian;
to break with him is (as we would expect, indeed, in view of whom
he represents!) very hard, much harder even than it had been for
Emil to break with his parents; it is an act of Cain. Pistorius is a
Romantic; Emil, however, is on the track of something which goes
beyond the disbursements of the Romantic imagination. Pistorius
has helped to teach Emil something he himself could not learn how
to do—to accept fate. Emil understands the absoluteness of this requirement, there are no new goals to seek and follow, and, indeed,
there is no path except the predestined Way of the awakening self.

The Pistorius chapter is entitled "Jacob's Fight"; at its core we
find Emil's struggle with his most inward vision. Already the
ancient esoteric law of succession is forcing him into a new position,

[74] Matzig also suggests Klages (*op. cit.*, p. 26). Lang, it is worth noting, had
little interest in music (Ball, *op. cit.*, p. 162–164). Hesse remarks in *The Nuremberg Journey* (IV, 143) that on this trip to Baden he has met his old friend,
Pistorius, again. Also relevant is the characteristically Jungian mixture of psychology, biology, and mysticism which we find in the passage about the "air-
bladder" in *Demian* (III, 200–201). Playfulness is consonant with Hesse's
methods, but of course it is not consonant with them to regard *Demian* as
basically a *roman à clef.*

he must himself become a teacher. The youth Knauer approaches him for help, desperate at his failure to achieve self-mastery by white magic, obsessed with the monkish delusion that sexual continence will by itself lead to spiritual progress. He warns Emil not to touch women, tells of his struggle with his own minor perversions. Emil instinctively knows the futility of such techniques as these, which but seek to deprive Abraxas of his rights. Not chance, but a strange inner call leads him one night to a building site where he saves Knauer from suicide, and tells him: "And we aren't pigs, as you think. We are human beings. We create gods and fight with them and they bless us" (III, 214). Knauer becomes his pupil, from whom in turn, as such relationships require, he continually learns. He thinks of Jacob's challenge to the angel as he contemplates his picture of the female figure out of his Oedipus dream. Closing his eyes, he visualizes the picture within; this effort changes the level of consciousness, brings an intense experience of memory to him which penetrates, as memories do in *Demian*, not only "back into the earliest, most forgotten era of childhood" but also "back into forms of pre-existence and early stages of becoming" (III, 212). Later on, Siddhartha and Friedrich Klein are to make visionary contact with pre-existence. No purely psychoanalytic interpretation of the novel can make sense of the mystical experiences which are now more and more introduced and not explained away. When Emil awakes from sleep, however, and cannot find the picture, we are back with a symbol which might seem to come direct from the sphere of the analysts: "Had it been a dream that I had burned it in my hands and had eaten up the ashes?" (III, 212). For the second time in the book devouring is the symbol for absorption.[75]

The outside world, indeed, is gradually absorbed by the inner world of Emil Sinclair; what reality it still possesses in the last chapters of the novel is only as a conventional framework. The Jungian process itself induces this result: "Images, pictures, or desires, arose in me and drew me away from the outside world so that my relationship with these pictures in me, with these dreams and shadows, was more real and more alive than it was with my real

[75] Compare the story "Within and Without" (1920; III, 836 f.). A very recent study of *Demian*, however, has shown persuasively that this symbol too has its Scriptural source; see Ziolkowski, *op. cit.*, p. 130.

environment" (III, 188). It is interesting to see that for Emil, sub-sequently writing his own story, reality has after all remained reality, and dreams have remained dreams; total solipsism has not carried off the victory. But in the novel itself the orientation is now entirely inward; Emil moves from archetype to archetype: "I was only waiting for my destiny to approach me in the form of a new picture" (III, 230).

The ambiguity of external reality has finally struck home, and Emil, staring into the fire with Pistorius, begins to think "magi-cally." In an essay on Dostoevsky's *The Idiot* (dated 1919) Hesse discusses this, for him, central conception. Prince Myshkin in *The Idiot* is a "magical person"; his thinking, owing above all to his close contact with the unconscious, is "magical thinking." "Magic" is the wisdom of the mystic, the experience of the resolution of all antitheses, the perception that all divisions in logic, space, time, and eternity are illusory, that all is One. Civilization depends upon the existence of negation and prohibition as well as of affirmation; but the way of the Idiot is the way to chaos—and there is a resonance of Bachofen: "*The Idiot,* thought through to its end, introduces the matriarchy of the unconscious, dissolves civilization" (VII, 184). Magical thinking is precisely "the acceptance of chaos" (VII, 185), the descent into the unconscious and the unbridling of the instinc-tive life; from this men may proceed (as elucidated in the Karama-zov essay) to a new creative "division of the world." Magical thinking is furthermore "the entire legendary wisdom of child-hood" (IV, 450), and "Childhood of the Magician," from which this last quotation comes, speaks of the child's "dissatisfaction with what was called 'reality' " (IV, 450), which he longed "to bewitch, to transform, to intensify." Magical thinking denies polarity and operates by analogy [76] rather than by syllogism; springing from the ultimate experience of unity—"the moment of experienced paradox, the flash of the instant when separated poles make contact" [77]—it dissolves all barriers, especially the border line between the outside world and that within. "And if the outside world were to dissolve, any one of us would be capable of recreating it" (III, 198)—these

---

[76] Cf. Novalis' phrase in *Die Christenheit oder Europa*: "magic wand of analogy" (*Schriften,* II, 78).

[77] "Exotic Art" (VII, 271).

words of Emil's point not only to Jung but also to that step which
Novalis took beyond Fichte, in making external reality wholly
subject not to the "transcendental imagination" but to the powers
of fancy of the empirical self.

The experience of the process of "magical thinking" is perhaps
the kernel of Emil's awakening. For Hesse the term alone is new;
the crisis of the war years had now brought the experience to
flower, but the seeds had been there lifelong. Peter Camenzind's
inner life had followed a hesitant, awkward path; nonetheless, it
too had its moments of awakening, of conversion, moments when
the "cooling clear ray" of the mind lit up the stuff of the soul; in
Peter's nature mysticism, moreover, the line between the self and
the nonself had been partly smudged away. In the case of Emil
Sinclair the nodal points upon the *vita* are even more obtrusive—
for instance the proud experience of the mark of Cain, described in
language which emphasizes the suddenness, the shock quality of
such moments: "a blazing up of feelings, of strange impulses"
(III, 127–128). And then there is the vivid perception ("suddenly
bright before my mind" [III, 181]) of the connection between
dissipation and sainthood, and then the contemplation of the open
fire, which evokes "an intensification of my sense of self" (III,
198). Such moments of awakening involve, above all else, this
strengthening of the sense of self, and they involve, more often
than not, a reactivation of memories; for memory, as we saw in
Peter Camenzind, is the shaft which penetrates to childhood and the
roots of the soul.

The thought that magical thinking is the key not only to the
basic experience but also to the style and structure of Hesse's later
novels has been formulated by Franz Baumer in the assertion that
the interaction between Hesse's fundamental magical feeling on the
one hand and his rational thinking on the other leads in the end, in
the work of art, to the aesthetic unity of magical thinking.[78] It is
difficult to follow Baumer entirely in this, since the reservation
must be made that the stylistic unity of which he speaks is far more
an aspiration than a reality in Hesse's works. In the last chapters of
Demian, in fact, the artistic achievement certainly diminishes markedly as the language and the experience, instead of coming ever

[78] "Das magische Denken," p. 20.

closer together, move farther apart; numerous critics of the book
have remarked that its conclusion is flawed aesthetically.[79] Emil's
hypermnesia, the memories which flood in when at last he is in
Frau Eva's house, show the author's unifying purpose very clearly,
but this entire episode has about it some quality of artifice; a true
junction of mind and feelings—such a junction as there are several
scattered through *Peter Camenzind*, *Demian* itself, and the later
novels—should light up the language, but in fact here the language
goes dead and loses much of its concreteness. The ratiocinative and
theoretical factors, both in language and narrative composition,
overweigh extremely and perhaps disastrously. The book becomes
sententious, as Demian prophesies about the war: Europe's soul—a
beast that has broken loose—will now conduct itself in violence,
"But the paths and detours are of no importance, as long as the
genuine need of the soul emerges" (III, 238). Demian declares that
he and his circle are the servants of new ideals still to be born,
recalls the task of Cain, "to arouse fear and hatred and to drive contemporary humanity out of a narrow idyll into dangerous open
spaces" (III, 239), a phrase containing an apt analogy with what had
occurred in Hesse's own life. Frau Eva and her son, indeed, vie
with each other in the didactic, exegetical arts; she interprets Emil's
dreams with a recognizable debt to Freud, she tells him an elucida-
tory *Märchen* which communicates the dogma that a man must
have faith in his own desires to make them real. Conversations, in
reality one-sided discourses, sum up the novel's message and make
the thin connection between Emil's self-discovery and 1914.

When Emil first sees his dream figure, Frau Eva, in the flesh, he
recounts as follows: "I had reached a goal, a high point on the way,
from which the rest of the way looked broad and magnificent, striving toward countries and promises, overshadowed by the treetops of
a near happiness, cooled by the near gardens of every desire" (III,
233). These are, it must be said, the images of a desiccated Romanticism, and the language is tired and cumbersomely repetitive. The
whole scene is an artificial construct. On the other hand, when it is
describing a moment of awakening which contains a genuine element of experience, the style still has some strength left: "I felt

[79] Cf., e.g., H. R. Schmid, *op. cit.*, p. 147; Dahrendorff, *op. cit.*, p. 17; and
Middleton, *op. cit.*, p. 168.

that force emanated from me. For a few moments something in me contracted firmly and closely, something bright and cool; for a moment I felt that I was carrying a crystal in my heart, and I knew that this was my I" (III, 250). The crystal in the heart, the cool brightness of mind bonded with feeling—this imagery has the artistic sincerity of which the previous passage is sadly devoid. The description of Emil's love for Frau Eva, however, and of the forms taken by his contact with her, is flat and unconvincing. There are other weaknesses in these last paragraphs of *Demian*—for instance bathos and a certain loss of Hesse's usual discretion and sensitivity. Emil sees in some of the soldiers on the Flanders battlefields "the firm, distant gaze, a little as though possessed, which knows nothing of goals and signifies complete surrender to enormity" (III, 254). *Amor fati*, though no doubt a hard taskmaster, reminds us in this guise of Ernst Jünger rather than Hermann Hesse. "In the depths something was coming into being"—"the will of the future"—"according to the laws of biology and of historical evolution"—yes, the attempt to equate the self-discovery of the individual with the destruction of old Europe undeniably involves Hesse in the jargon of the neo-Nietzschean evolutionists, Ernst Jünger, Moeller van den Bruck and the rest, with whose baneful preoccupations he was in reality so little in sympathy. There is intellectual arrogance, as well as some naïveté, in the application of the symbol of the birth of the bird to the renewal of Western civilization, a kind of arrogance, it should be noted, of which Hesse's psychoanalytic mentors are not entirely free.

For the rest, the novel has the chiliastic vision of the German Expressionists, as it has their mythification techniques. It culminates in the spectacular evocation of the Magna Mater poised over the slaughter on the battlefields (III, 255). On his deathbed,[80] the wounded Demian communicates his last message to Emil, the traditional reassurance of teacher to pupil that he will always be with him, indeed within him. He duly seals this with a kiss passed on from Frau Eva, a hermaphroditic kiss. Demian has been absorbed entirely within, he the friend is now synonymous with Emil's

---

[80] The view (advanced for instance by Matzig) that Emil Sinclair also dies at the end of the book is patently mistaken. Any impartial close reading of the last few paragraphs must surely lead to the rejection of such an idea.

self, his fate. Emil has been admitted to the "Order" of which Frau
Eva is high priestess, the existence of which Demian's original appearance had first disclosed to him—"an Order of the mind and
the personality which must exist somewhere on earth" (III, 159–
160). Indeed, the mark which Demian had recognized on Emil's
brow meant that he had really always belonged to it. The exoteric
fringe of eccentrics he meets at Frau Eva's house is not in itself the
true Order, the inner, the esoteric circle, any more than were the
odd characters who were mocked in "The World Reformer," first [81]
—and ironic—treatment of the idea of the Order in Hesse's works.
Emil, Demian, and Frau Eva, members of the inner circle, adhere
to no external form of confession, but strive only to become themselves. Emil, maybe, remains at the very end still something of a
"virgin gnostic." [82] "But when I sometimes find the key and climb
right down into myself, there where in the dark surface the images
of my destiny slumber, then I need only bend over the black surface and I see my own image, which is now identical with Him, my
friend and guide" (III, 257). This ultimate act of the novel is in a
double sense a gesture of reflection, as the old narcissus metaphor
again recurs; this metaphor is a symbol for the persisting dualism
of the self, an unresolved dichotomy which the language of
Demian inescapably betrays.

[81] Or perhaps we should give pride of place to the "cénacle" which is described whimsically in Hermann Lauscher.
[82] Middleton, op. cit., p. 170.

CHAPTER 4

Siddhartha

HESSE'S journey to the East began in his childhood. His parents' personal experience of Southeast Asia, the indological expertise of grandfather Hermann Gundert with his specimens, books, and mastery of several oriental languages, the Asian visitors who came frequently to the house at Calw—the sources were early and varigated. This was, in any case, the age of the "Oriental Renaissance" in Europe. That movement which began in Germany with the Schlegels and with Schopenhauer had turned into a fashionable cult by the mid-nineteenth century, and in the time of Hesse's own childhood was if anything accelerated and intensified by the reaction against the pseudoscientific banalities of the Naturalist school.

Hesse's conscious, intellectual interest in India came first from a study of theosophical writings, all of which led him back to the same sources, in particular the *Bhagavad-Gita*. He became acquainted with the work of Hermann Oldenberg, Paul Deussen, and Karl Eugen Neumann, as well as with that of Leopold von Schröder.[1] Schopenhauer, whom he began now to prefer to Nietzsche,[2] merely confirmed for him the significance of Indian ideas he

---

[1] The most important translations with which Hesse was acquainted include: P. Deussen, *Vedanta-Sutra* (1887) and *Sechzig Upanishad's des Veda* (1897); H. Oldenberg, *Buddha* (1881; long the standard German work on the subject) and *Die Literatur des alten Indien* (1903); K. E. Neumann, *Die buddhistische Anthologie* (1892) and *Reden Gotamo Buddhas* (1896).

[2] Presumably in the early 1900's. See, e.g., "Kleines Bekenntnis" in H. Kliemann and K. H. Silomon, *Hermann Hesse: Eine bibliographische Studie zum 2. Juli 1947* (Frankfort, 1947), p. 74. Cf. also "Aus einem Tagebuch des Jahres 1920," *Corona*, III (1932–1933), 200.

had already found elsewhere. Translations, however, often seemed to Hesse poor and badly written.[3] Nonetheless, poor or not, those versions of the Sanskrit and Pali scriptures which he read did communicate to him an experience of religion on a par with that which he had received from the faith and practice of his parents: "I experienced religion in two forms, as the child and grandchild of pious upright Protestants and as a reader of Indian revelations in which I give pride of place to the Upanishads, the *Bhagavad-Gita* and the sermons of Buddha. . . . From early childhood I lived just as much in the atmosphere of Indian spirituality as I did in that of Christianity." [4]

In the interpretation of Hesse's works it is inadmissible to suppose these Indian influences largely subordinate to, or simply an intensification of, the stimuli of the German Romantic tradition; [5] India was at least as old as Novalis in Hesse's imagination, each fructifies, at various times, the other. In any case the interaction was not at all a simple one; Hesse remarks that Indian religion offers more food for the imagination than does Protestantism,[6] while Leopold von Schröder noted, not wholly absurdly, that the Indians were in a sense the Romantics of the ancient world.[7]

The journey of 1911, which took in Malaya, Sumatra, and Ceylon, was a severe disappointment to Hesse; it ended summarily that idealization of the East in which the hermit of Gaienhofen was seeking escape.[8] Hesse found the Orient europeanized and having its own momentum of degeneration. Buddhism, with its ludicrous pomp and circumstance, was a decayed religion with which one could not sympathize, although one might feel for the good, gentle, and naïve peoples at whose foolish hands it had been destroyed.[9] Though he was repelled by this, Hesse's attitude remained ambivalent; at least in the East he found a bond of ideal community

---

[3] Cf. "A Library of World Literature" (1929; VII, 338–339).

[4] "My Faith" (1931; VII, 371).

[5] As Baumer, among other authorities, seems rather inclined to do.

[6] "My Faith" (VII, 372).

[7] Leopold v. Schröder, *Indiens Literatur und Kultur in historischer Entwicklung* (Leipzig, 1887), p. 7.

[8] In *Rosshalde*, which in part reflects Hesse's attitude before the journey, Veraguth dreams of the East as offering "a new, still pure, innocent atmosphere free of pain" (II, 504).

[9] Cf. "India" (1911; III, 841).

together with some contact with a magical source, and Demian-like he harps upon the need for the "Northern European" to redis-cover such things in his own culture, "in a higher form." [10] He writes still, to some degree, with the superiority, even the con-ventional smugness of the Western intellectual toward such matters, but as the years passed this shell fell away and a more positive kernel was revealed: "What remains is the experience of a dream-visit to distant ancestors . . . and a deep respect for the spirit of the East." [11]

Retrospect or distance is perhaps the precondition of romantici-zation; whether Hesse subsequently reromanticized the East on the basis of the former, the latter condition having been lost, is a matter of opinion. At all events childhood, fairy tale, and above all home with a nuance of paradise are the imagery with which the Orient remains uncertainly and ironically bound in Hesse's later writings. In 1916 he finds the vital experience of the Indian journey had been that of the oneness of humanity, now thrown so into relief by the war. "Visit from India" (1922) recalls how he still felt in Kandy—just as he had felt in Europe before setting out—that identical homesickness for a contact with the true spirit of India, and how at length the realization came that physical contact was unnecessary, that a teacher was unnecessary, the fundamental insight into the universality and ubiquity of the magical sphere. "Here my education in magic began"; "Buddha and the Dhammapaddam and the Tao Te Ching [sounded] pure and familiar to me and had no riddles any more." [12] India, he eventually found, was all around him everywhere: the same magical thinking as in the Upanishads might be discovered in the novels of Dostoevsky; yoga belonged not only to those Indian practitioners he had personally known but was also, for example, the key to the personality of that curious Pietist who used to visit the Hesses in Calw, Herr Claassen. The magical bridges to the East were really built, however, in the time of Dr. Lang and *Demian*. And then the year 1920 apparently sees Hesse moving back from the Vedanta

[10] III, 850. Cf. Hesse's review of the new, cheap edition of Neumann's *Die Reden Buddhas aus der mittleren Sammlung:* "When we Westerners have finally learned how to meditate we shall get quite different results out of it than do the Indians. For us it will not become an opiate, but will lead to a deepened self-knowledge" (*Neue Rundschau*, XXXII, i [1921], 118).
[11] "Recollections of India" (1916; III, 852).
[12] "Visit from India" (1922; III, 858).

and the Buddhist scriptures toward "the true religious India of the gods, of Vishnu and Indra, Brahma and Krishna." [13]

Siddhartha is the pinnacle of Hesse's orientalism; perhaps it is the high point of his art in the novel as well. It is the culmination, all but successful, of that struggle for a new style which characterizes this author's most productive, most impressive period, the years 1916–1925. Of Hesse's earlier and later novels probably only *The Steppenwolf* stands comparison with it as a formal achievement, and then for other reasons. It shares its high position in his life's work, however, with productions which are themselves not novels, with "Iris," with *Pictor's Transformations,* with "Klingsor's Last Summer" and "Klein and Wagner," and perhaps with the "autobiographies" of *The Glass Bead Game.* "Iris" and *Pictor's Transformations* are both *Märchen;* it is indeed practically only in the *Märchen* form that Hesse seems able to approach what in *Demian* recedes the farther the more it is pursued, namely, some resolution of the fundamental stylistic dualism, a language fit to render directly the constatations of magical thinking, the numinous experience of the soul. The approximation—which is all it can be—is principally achieved by surrendering mind to the hegemony of *Märchen,* by making of reflection the servant, and no longer the discursive critic, of dreams.

"Iris" (1918) is a story in which the reflective commentary is present only in a subtly muted form. When Anselm gazes into the calyx of the iris, "then his soul looked through the gate where things become mysteries and seeing becomes intuition" (III, 367). Only the sudden present tense lifts this sentence gently onto the plane of the reflective. The next paragraph—"Every earthly object is an image"—and that which shortly follows—"All children feel this way"—are generalizing language, but this is little more than the age-old moralizing of the *Märchen,* the distilling of wisdom. There is no tension between the narrating and the interpreting mind; the dualism, though not extinguished, is softened to the point of incipient harmony. Indeed, "Iris" is impressive just because of its harmony, its oneness, its being cast in a single mold. The debt to Novalis is

[13] "Aus einem Tagebuch des Jahres 1920," *op. cit.,* p. 201. In his review entitled "Hinduism," Hesse writes of the new Western interest in the many-armed gods now penetrating "by many routes, by the routes of occultism . . . of collectors . . . of scholarship" (review of H. v. Glasenapp's *Der Hinduismus, Neue Rundschau,* XXXIV, ii [1923], 669).

decisive, but yet the story is no mere pastiche. Few works of its author, in fact, are so strikingly, so intimately his own work, the deepest expression of himself.

Hesse's central, poignant theme of childhood is here wholly translated into the fragile tissue of *Märchen*. Anselm (the name recalls E. T. A. Hoffmann) has one or two points of contact, in his childhood, with Hans Giebenrath; Iris, the bride "older than he would have wanted for a wife" (III, 371), has no doubt some qualities of Maria Bernoulli; but the autobiographical approach would be a total desecration of such a work as this. In the magic world of Anselm's childhood, in the entrancement of the garden, it is the iris which casts the deepest spell, arouses the deepest dream. He gazes into the calyx of the blue flower:

Long rows of yellow fingers grew out of the pale-blue flowery ground, between them a light path ran away and down into the calyx and the distant blue mystery of the flower . . . [He] saw the yellow delicate members sometimes as a golden hedge by the park, sometimes as a double line of beautiful dream trees which no wind stirred, and between them bright and interlaced with glassy delicate, living veins ran the mysterious way down into the interior [III, 364].

In his dreams Anselm goes into this fairy palace and the whole world with him, "drawn by magic, down into the lovely gorge where every anticipation must be realized and every presentiment become truth" (III, 367).

It is of this dream of childhood, long lost, that the girl Iris, difficult, withdrawn, musical, and flower-loving, unconsciously reminds him when the subsequent professor and man of the world seeks a wife. But she hesitates, for she perceives that this young intellectual—successful, worldly, ambitious, furrows already upon his brow—is far from being at peace with himself and cannot harmonize with her soulful inner world. We have heard before, in *Demian*, of the music of fate—"the music and rhythm of my fate" [14] (III, 178)—Iris speaks of "the music in my heart" (III, 373), and she will only marry a man whose "inner music" harmonizes with her own. She sets Anselm the task of searching in his memory to discover what it is of which her name always reminds him, and in this task he now

[14] *Demian* actually postdates "Iris."

sacrifices his entire empirical existence; in the pursuit of lost memories he forfeits forever his worldly posture, his material aims, his acquisitive will. He becomes a vagabond, but immersed in memory and thus close to wisdom, to nature and to truth. Finally, as an old man, he comes across an iris growing miraculously in the snow and, gazing into the calyx of the flower, he at last remembers his childhood dream. Iris herself is now long dead, but soon Anselm comes upon the spectral gate opened by the spirits only once in a thousand years. He goes within and down into the earth: "Anselm walked past the sentinel into the crevice and through the golden pillars down into the blue mystery of the interior. It was Iris into whose heart he made his way, and it was the iris in his mother's garden into whose blue calyx he stepped" (III, 382). The world within is that sphere in which there are no symbols, no images, no archetypes any more, but only reality, the I, the self.

This story, dominated by blue, is altogether rich in colors, as fairy tales often are, as Hesse's anoetic style invariably is. Yet it has the insubstantiality of a dream. The subjective mystery of the childish self, and its synesthetic mode of experiencing, are effectively evoked. This is the inward home, and its loss sets the human being off on that spiral journey—"the long, hard detour" [15] (III, 369)— which is the course of the soul. For Anselm a modification of his childhood relationship with his mother was the first sign of the great sea-change. Adulthood also brought the impoverishment of memory. When Anselm eventually begins to re-enter his memory world, it is like uncovering a series of concealed frescoes; experiences rise from the past, sensations of spring and winter days, nameless and dateless, moments of childhood which were awakened moments and therefore stored up: "the gorges of memory" (III, 378)—we think not only of the "lovely gorge" of the iris itself but of the preface to *Demian* ("We all come out of the same gorge"). There are also here, as in *Demian*, allusions to the possibility and the nature of pre-existence. The path which Anselm treads is that which goes inward into the womb; and as Iris tells him upon her deathbed, he takes this path not for her, but for himself. Within him he becomes aware of a pres-

---

[15] "The winding path (*Umweg*) of the libido seems to be a *via dolorosa*" (Jung, *Symbols of Transformation*, p. 54). Hesse is very fond of the word "*Umweg*" at this period, and it may well be a Jungian resonance.

ence, a voice which directs him. A vagabond in search of his soul, he discovers anew how to converse with the things of nature, with trees and stones, as he could as a child (and as his Romantic forbears were able to do). If this verges on pastiche, the bird which sings to him and leads him to his final goal belongs intimately to Hesse's own symbolic vision. The bird finds its way inside him, its song comes from within his breast. It directs him to the spectral gate, the cleft in the rock, the way into the heart of the iris, and away from that sphere of mere phenomena in which men live.

The psychoanalytic approach to this work would constate the significance of the cleft which leads into the earth; but then, even more so than the biographical, it would destroy "Iris," without understanding it. Novalis—above all "Hyazinth und Rosenblütchen" —might help us more discreetly. But "Iris," in the last resort, lives in its own symbols, Hesse's symbols, the blue orifice and golden stigma of the flower, the mystery of memory, the song of the bird in the seeker's breast.

Pictor's Transformations (written 1922; first published 1925) is an equally intimate work; it was originally published in a limited edition of 650 copies, and is now available as a facsimile complete with Hesse's curious illustrations.[16] The story of Pictor unfolds entirely in paradise, "in the home and source of life," in the garden where grows the tree of life [17]—"it was both man and woman." Here Pictor enters full of longing, and here metamorphosis is the controlling law. The bird of paradise is transformed into a "bird-flower"; the "bird-flower" turns into a butterfly; the "bird-flower-butterfly" into a ruby crystal, a magic carbuncle which threatens to sink away into the earth until Pictor hurriedly makes use of it, at the serpent's bidding, to transform himself into a tree. Years pass, and as a tree he is happy, until he finds that he is somehow excluded from the flow of the river of metamorphosis, he cannot transform himself any more. He has been trapped by the serpent's advice into assuming an immutable and therefore an agonizing form, since it is subject all the same to time, to sadness and decay. The fatal difference lies in the fact that the tree of life is androgynous, whereas Pictor is not.

[16] Frankfort, 1954.
[17] Cf.: "I told him I was on my way to Asia to see the holy tree and the serpent" ("India"; III, 806).

Then a girl enters paradise and sits beneath Pictor's tree, drawn to Pictor, in whom now new dreams are stirring. When the bird brings the carbuncle, her longings too are realized and she is united with the tree—"sprouted from his trunk as a strong, young bough." For Pictor this monoecious state is "eternal transformation"—"He became a deer, he became a fish, he became a man and a serpent, a child and a bird. But in all his forms he was entire, he was a pair, he had moon and sun, man and woman in him, flowed as a twin river through the lands, hung in the sky as a double star."

Pictor's Transformations is no doubt among other things a prose-poem on loneliness, and the hope of surmounting it (and we may think of Hesse's eventual—unsuccessful—marriage to Ruth Wenger in 1924), but biography helps no further than this. At the heart of *Pictor* stands Peter Camenzind's tree, its mythical identity at last fully revealed; the bird of the soul flies through the air of paradise, while the twin river of metamorphosis is Siddhartha's stream. All Hesse's works from this period, from "Iris" through *Demian* to *Siddhartha* and ultimately *Pictor* are intimately interwoven, linked by "symbols of transformation." In *Pictor* at times the rhythmical prose of the tale slips over, with its meter and internal rhymes, into undisguised verse. *Pictor's Transformations* is indeed a highly sophisticated *Kunstmärchen*, designed to convey "magical" insights; in a sense it is more hermetic still than "Iris," in a sense also less overtly personal, for the fragile connection in the former with the world of common experience has in *Pictor* finally been abandoned. The story seeks to portray objective reality, that is, eternal change and flow.

Ensconced between these two *Märchen* lies *Siddhartha*, but not alone; apart from *Demian* itself, "Klingsor's Last Summer" and "Klein and Wagner" are the other principal works of Hesse's middle period, and in comparison with the *Märchen* both move on an external plane. Into both of these, the reflective, critical mind—which in the verbal context (at least) of *Pictor* finds no place—obtrudes.

"Klingsor" is a unique and outstanding work; its weakness is a certain imaginative overstrain, its harlequinade of self-dissipation is perhaps in some degree a theoretical speculation and its language a concession to Expressionist fashions.[18] But the splendor of the language of "Klingsor" is, after all, unparalleled elsewhere in Hesse;

[18] Ball, who argues in this way, is perhaps a trifle severe.

the intoxicated, burning summer of 1919 in Tessin lives vividly and poignantly in such sketches as the walk to Kareno (Carona), while the scene in the grotto achieves a force rare in this often passive, slowly contemplative writer:

Klingsor, king of the night, lofty crown in his hair, leaning back in his stone seat, conducted the dance of the world, gave the beat, summoned forth the moon, vanished the railroad. . . . Painting was fine, painting was a fine, sweet game for good children. A different thing—grander and more massive—to conduct the stars, to project the beat of your own blood, the colored rings of your own retina out into the world, to let surges of your own soul rove forth in the wind of the night [III, 583].

This drunken solipsist is wholly enmeshed and entranced by his own monologue; though famous, he is in reality the artist whose public has disappeared. This was Hesse's condition of mind in 1919, doubt in his public, desperate doubt in the sense and purpose of his own "profession." [19] Klingsor is moreover an artist in physical decline, an artist already ultimately engaged with death, for whom this is now his greatest source of inspiration; with the missiles from his palette Klingsor takes aim at death, with empty wine bottles for cannon he tries to shoot down time, death, and suffering. Around him as he moves through the sultry, virulent months of summer there is only "music of doom" (III, 588). "I believe in one thing alone: in doom. . . . All over it is the same: the great war, the great revolution in art, the great disintegration of the states of the west. . . . We are perishing, friends, this is our destiny, the key of Tsing Tse has sounded" (III, 591–592).

The gaunt figure of Klingsor, caught wandering ecstatic and lonely through these fabulous days, is already self-portrait enough; so also, however, in a sense is Li Tai Pe, is the Armenian astrologer, are the poets Hermann and Thu Fu, even Louis the Cruel (though the model was Hesse's friend Louis Moilliet). There is fragmentation of the ego. The powerful dialogue between the astrologer and Klingsor–Li Tai Pe is that between magical insight and death-wish, acceptance and frenzy, the seer and the artist. Klingsor's last picture of himself has many faces, even "prehuman, animal, vegetable, stony"

---

[19] Hesse later points out (IV, 867–868) that previous generations of writers still had some sense of community with their audience; Keller had it, and Hesse himself had still felt it in his earlier works.

ones (III, 611). Once again the metamorphosis motif is introduced and combined with allusions to prehuman forms of existence—both motifs from *Demian*, both occurring later in *Siddhartha* and *Pictor*; indeed, one of Klingsor's faces resembles Demian's—it is "like an idol's" (III, 609). Throughout the whole sounds the drunken music of fate, in which the Armenian magician's words ring out: "There *is* freedom of the will. It is called magic" (III, 595).

Hesse writes of that vital year, 1919: "Three circumstances combined to heighten this summer into an extraordinary and unique experience: the date of 1919, the return from the war to life, from the yoke to freedom, was the most significant, but to this was added the atmosphere, climate, and language of the South, and as a blessing from heaven there came in addition a summer like very few I have experienced." [20] In May 1919 he had taken up residence in the Casa Camuzzi in Montagnola, entirely alone and impoverished, convinced that the only possibility of further existence which remained to him was to live in and for his literary work.

"Klein and Wagner," also, was composed in those days (it was the first work written in Montagnola); it is a novella of escape, of wrenching loose, escape over the wall of the Alps to the south, the feminine Without, yet another repetition of the "exemplary event" in which the innate death-wish apparently at last fulfills itself in Klein's suicide by water. "Klein and Wagner" is probably one of the most ruthlessly direct and merciless pieces of self-exposure in the whole range of modern German literature, of the same stuff as the later *Crisis* poems and *The Steppenwolf*. Friedrich Klein sees in flight from his marriage and flight to the south "the two most burning desires of his life" (III, 472); he has become a criminal, a refugee from justice, and the whole act seems to him "crime and revolt, abandonment of sacred duties, leap (*Sprung*) into cosmic space" (III, 477). While the word "*Sprung*" indicates the unconditional nature of this act, the adjective "sacred" is also telltale, pointing to its deepest sources, resonant of the past. Klein's theft and subsequent flight were in fact a milder substitute for a fearful blood bath modeled on that of the South German schoolmaster Wagner who murdered his entire family, and whose specter haunts Klein. But Wagner is also the name of that composer whom Klein

[20] "Recollection of Klingsor's Summer" (1938; VII, 412).

now hates so intensely,[21] thereby hating his own lost youth.[22] For Klein has struggled all his life to repress his drives, to be a good husband and citizen; it is this moralizing Klein, whom painted women and sensuality still revolt, who now has to die, for he has been throttling his own soul.

Here lies the essential theme of the story, which follows Klein—through his casual affair with the elegant Teresina—on his concentrated course in ultimate self-insight. Klein's face is a mask, like Demian's and like Siddhartha's. When he gazes into a mirror, it is the face of Wagner he sees there. The narcissus figure with which *Demian* ends repeats and repeats in the works of these years; but in "Klein and Wagner" a new element is added, for this experience belongs to the "Wagner theater," "the theater with the sign 'Wagner'" (III, 529). Klein's dream of *Lohengrin* is the descent into the unconscious mind, the world of instincts unmasked and unbridled, in fact the "Magic Theater" of *The Steppenwolf*. In the long account of Klein's suicide the *Erzählzeit* expands to contain the expansion of Klein's consciousness, at the moment of bursting through the *principium individuationis*, of entering the magical sphere, the sphere of endless flow, of union with Brahman. For this is "the world-stream of forms" (III, 553)—many creatures and faces swim by. Moreover, it is also "a transparent sphere or dome of notes, a vault of music, in the middle of which sat God" (III, 554), not the throttling divinity of Calw but rather the Krishna of the *Gita*, beyond good and evil.

"Klein and Wagner" has something of the verbal pyrotechnics of "Klingsor," the same dire mood of transience, combined with the claustrophobia and cacophonies of *The Steppenwolf*; it is of course not really a Schopenhauerian relapse vis-à-vis *Demian*, but just the other side of the very same coin, its doctrine the living out of fate. The neurotic criminal Klein, the thief who would steal freedom, has something in him of the saint; in this his Way is like that of the rake and the drunkard. In the figures of both Klein and Klingsor, moreover, other specific prototypes shine through, distant and distin-

---

[21] Hesse is several times critical of Wagner; cf., e.g., *Zarathustra's Return* (VII, 225) and *Letters* (VII, 571).

[22] In *Rosshalde*, Wagner is referred to as the great musical love of Veraguth's youth (II, 538).

guished luminaries remodeled at several Romantic hands, Don Juan
and Faust. Klingsor at the end, as he paints his self-portrait, has been
shrewdly diagnosed as a Faust with traits of a Buddha, as "already
Siddhartha." [23]

The first half of *Siddhartha* (up to the point at which Siddhartha
leaves Buddha and Govinda behind) was written during 1919 and
appeared as a fragment in the *Neue Rundschau*,[24] with a dedication
to Romain Rolland. The second section, up to the point at which
Siddhartha is saved from suicide, was composed in the winter of
1919–1920 and the rest of the book not until a year or eighteen
months later. The author could go no further for a time, he had
exhausted his own experience: "When I was finished with Siddhartha
the endurer and ascetic, the struggling and suffering Siddhartha, and
wanted to portray Siddhartha the victor, the affirmer, the conqueror,
I could not go on." [25] In the intervening months, in which he almost
despaired of finishing the novel, Hesse occupied himself with painting, with the study of Bachofen, and with his reawakened interest in
the Indian pantheon.[26]

The complete work is written in a strongly rhythmical, sensuous
prose with ritual features. The use of leitmotifs, parallelism, and the
repetition of phrases and of single words (especially threefold repetitions) in the liturgical manner is constantly reminiscent of the
Bible, the Psalms, or—perhaps more directly—the Pali Canon. In
none of Hesse's novels is the style more material to the nature of the
act of communication sought after in the work; referring to the
extreme parataxis and the apparently endless repetitions of Buddha's
canonical preachings, like prayer mills, which had led to some
ridiculing of Neumann's translations, Hesse explains: "Buddha's sermons are in fact not compendiums of doctrine, on the contrary they
are examples of meditations." In this special sense the language of
Siddhartha may be characterized as *meditative;* the purpose of meditation is defined as "a shifting of the state of consciousness, a
technique the highest goal of which is a pure harmony, a simultane-

[23] K. Weibel, *Hermann Hesse und die deutsche Romantik*, p. 60.
[24] *Neue Rundschau*, XXXII, ii (1921), 701–724.
[25] "Aus einem Tagebuch des Jahres 1920," *op. cit.*, p. 193.
[26] Cf. *ibid.*, p. 204.

ous and uniform functioning together of logical and intuitive thinking." [27] The function of the language of *Siddhartha* is to correspond
to this purpose; each phrase (as, later on, each ideogram in the Glass
Bead Game) is a possible threshold of meditation. Rhythm is the
essential feature of this language, an undertone of chant; there is a
predilection for adverbial openings to sentences because of their
rhythmic effect: "Wonderfully did he feel the joy surge in his
breast" (III, 690), and also for resonant inversion combined with
repetition, alliteration, and assonance: "Dead was the singing bird of
which he had dreamed. Dead was the bird in his heart. Deep was he
snared in Sansara, disgust and death he'd sucked up from all sides,
as a sponge sucks water till full. Full was he of ennui, full of misery,
full of death" (III, 681). In that it is appositional, the style also
betrays its sources: "Know ye, in Jetavana, in the garden of Anathap-
indika, tarries the exalted one" (III, 636); poetic meter, in fact,
constantly recurs, while there are many stock epithets.

The language of *Siddhartha*, however, is unmistakably Hesse's
own; "your wondrous doctrine" (III, 641), for instance, has an
affective quality the ancestry of which is evidently German Romantic rather than Pali, and such touches are common both in the
vocabulary and the cadences of the prose: "Sweetly sounded the
legend of Buddha, magic wafted fragrantly from these tales" (III,
632). The unresolved stresses and disharmonies of *Demian* are
replaced by a style much closer to "Iris" and *Pictor*. Its concreteness
has frequently been remarked upon;[28] it is indeed a curious inter-
fusion of the tactile and the intuitive-visionary, a product of the
esemplastic imagination. It might be possible to characterize it by
that rather dubious term "magic realism," since it does indeed seem
to express magical insights, to circumscribe the "inner" world, in a
language owing a debt both to this world and to "external reality,"
having points of reference in both, but closer to the latter perhaps
than would be appropriate in the *Märchen*.

And indeed *Siddhartha* is precisely not a *Märchen;* it is a species
of legend, and as such it has marked hagiographical features. As

[27] *Neue Rundschau*, XXXII, ii (1921), 1118.

[28] Ball notes an attempt to integrate the religious devotion wholly in the objective world of symbols and points back to the technique of *Peter Camenzind*
(*Hermann Hesse*, p. 32). Weibel argues that the love of things in *Siddhartha* is
an anti-Romantic characteristic of the novel (*op. cit.*, pp. 66–67).

Hesse remarked while in the course of composing this novel, "Now the fact is that the saint is the strongest and most attractive of models for me." [29] Almost timeless and unhistorical, *Siddhartha* is the presentation of an exemplary *vita*, and in this alone no *Märchen*. Like *Demian* it is constructed upon the basis of interleaving conversations and moments of enlightenment and insight. The apparent realism of *Siddhartha* is in the last resort a superficial thing; both characters and background are to a high degree stylized. What Hesse is concerned with above all else in the work is the depiction of a series of moments of awakening, in which the *vita* is borne forward. Sometimes the description is cursory; sometimes, however, the *Erzählzeit* lengthens extraordinarily—these are the moments of freedom when the curtains draw back from the magical reality which it is the true purpose of this partially didactic novel to disclose.

The Sanskrit word "*siddhartha*" was the personal name of the most recent of the Buddhas, Gotama, bestowed on him by his father King Suddhodana, and means approximately "he who has achieved his aim." Siddhartha is indeed the first of Hesse's heroes of which such a great claim might be made and almost the only one. The hesitant, scarcely discernible *vita* of Peter Camenzind took this form partly because he did not know his aim; in *Demian*, where the aim is much more conscious, the lines of the *vita* are starker. Siddhartha knows his own aim from the outset, and there is in the novel no element which does not directly subserve the tracing out of his Way. Siddhartha grows up on the riverbank, "in the shade of the Sal forest, in the shade of the fig tree" (III, 615)—sacred trees (the Sal Grove in Buddhist scripture) and also another tree which suggests, in Hesse's emblematics, the sensual and the profane. At the very beginning his achievements are not inconsiderable; he understands the use of breathing exercises, knows how to say "*Om*," [30] and knows that within him is the indestructible Atman, at one with Brahman,

[29] "Aus einem Tagebuch des Jahres 1920," *op. cit.*, p. 200.
[30] Siddhartha (III, 621) recites (with a minor variation) three lines from the Deussen translation of the *Dhyânabindu-Upanishad:*
"Om ist Bogen, der Pfeil Seele,
Das Brahman ist des Pfeiles Ziel,
Das soll man unentwegt treffen . . ."
(P. Deussen, *Sechzig Upanishad's des Veda,* p. 661).

the universe. He has been impressed with the deep wisdom of the Samaveda Upanishads.[31] He burns with a longing for knowledge, and his father hopes of him that he will become a prince among Brahmans; his mother, on the other hand, sees in him above all "the strong one, the beauteous one, he who walked on slim legs, he who greeted her with perfect seemliness" (III, 617–618). Demian too was physically impressive; and like him Siddhartha finds an admirer of his own sex, Govinda, "his shadow" (III, 618)[32]—whose life is consumed in emulation, *imitatio.*

Siddhartha is dissatisfied, the waters of the river send him dreams and restless thoughts; he is dissatisfied with ritual and the worship of the gods. He wishes to find his way to *experience* the Atman, but to this no one can help him—the Upanishads merely bestow abstract knowledge. Like Faust, it is his revolt against the frustrations of the intellect which sets him on his path. Deciding to cast his lot with the Samanas, itinerant ascetics, he is involved in a conflict of will with his father, "the pure one, the learned one" (III, 620), and in this he conquers. The Way of the Samanas is, however, ironically enough, really only an intensification of the father principle in Siddhartha's heart. In search of the spring of the self, the *"Urquell,"* Siddhartha joins these ascetics; their method involves a total rejection of sense experience, its suppression, the achievement of a condition of apparent emptiness. While killing the senses, the novice must learn to project himself, by meditative techniques, into the selves of other things; he must use multiple "ways away from the ego" (III, 627). But for Siddhartha these are all a disappointment; he shocks Govinda by the remark that such escape from the self may be obtained "in every tavern" (III, 628). The Faustian "Auerbach's Cellar," as Hesse's protagonists mostly well know, is a kind of premature surrogate for the spiritual Way.

"Much time have I needed to learn and am still not at an end of

---

[31] Many of the references in the first chapter of *Siddhartha* seem to be traceable to the *Chândogya,* the principal Upanishad of the Samaveda.

[32] Here we must again take note of Jung's doctrine of the "shadow." The "shadow," the suppressed alter ego, "can manifest itself . . . in the guise of a figure from our field of consciousness, e.g., our elder brother (or sister), our best friend, when this person represents our opposite, as for instance Faust's famulus Wagner does" (Jolande Jacobi, *The Psychology of C. G. Jung* [New Haven, 1951], pp. 145–146).

learning, O Govinda, that nothing can be learned" (III, 630). Like Faust, Siddhartha expresses his disillusionment. But Govinda is more patient than he; Govinda already knows a good deal: "We do not go in a circle, we go upward, the circle is a spiral, already we have climbed many a step" (III, 629). It is of course not such a crass self-confidence, but there seems to be a resonance of Faust's famulus Wagner here; the irony is in the parallel implicitly drawn, that the rationalist Wagner is reincarnate as Govinda, apostle of gradualism upon the *mystical* Way. Siddhartha is his Faust, impatient and absolutist, demanding all at once, contemptuous of the method of knowledge, inevitably seeking nothing less than "the Way of Ways" (III, 630). Knowledge may indeed exist, but learning is impossible—this paradox demolishes, in Siddhartha's eyes, the whole philosophical structure of the Wagner-Govindas. In the eyes of Govinda, however, such iconoclasm also destroys the very dignity of the hierarchical system and thus of all pedagogy—"What . . . then," he protests, "would become of everything . . . which is venerable?!" (III, 631) —and a thought of the preceptors at Maulbronn is not too far removed.

Siddhartha, like his author, has discovered that comforting secret that a teacher is unnecessary. Hence he is prepared to refuse to accept even Gotama Buddha. What the Samanas hear of Buddha is first of all "legend," and "*Märchen*"—the two spheres of the consummate saint. Here is one who is enlightened, who has reached Nirvana and need never descend again into "the turbid stream of forms" (III, 632)—apart from the significant adjective, these are the very words of "Klein and Wagner." To refuse Gotama is tantamount to refusing all teachers, a decision already discernible in *Beneath the Wheel*. The conversation Siddhartha has with Gotama centers on the Buddhist doctrine of the unbroken chain of cause and effect; Buddha's teaching makes immensely clear the unity of the world, as Friedrich Klein had experienced it at the moment of death. But Siddhartha finds a logical flaw in this closed, apparently coherent system, the crack through which slips the doctrine of redemption, of the possibility of Nirvana. Gotama praises his perspicacity, but does not resolve the ambiguity; he merely emphasizes the pragmatic nature of the system, warning Siddhartha against "the thickets of the intellect" (III, 642).

Buddhism makes a moral judgment upon existence, a negative judgment which Siddhartha proves unable to accept. That Hesse could only laugh (in 1925) at being so often called a Buddhist is not surprising; overt world-denial is indeed nowhere to be found in his work: "At bottom I knew I was further from this confession than from any other. And yet there was something that was right, a particle of truth hidden in this that I only recognized somewhat later." [33] The reservation is intriguing; perhaps it refers to this renegade Protestant's insight that Buddhism itself was a reform religion, the Protestantism of ancient India.[34] Hesse had believed in Buddha "for a while in my youth very faithfully," had been interested in the Sankhya, and had understood Nirvana to be "the redeeming step back behind the *principium individuationis,* that is, expressing it in religious terms, the return of the individual soul to the universal soul." [35] But the notion that it was the individual's primary task to find his way back to this condition was counterbalanced in Hesse's mind by the doctrine of "letting-oneself-fall," the true meaning of which is thus expressed: "Or should I not rather fulfill God's will precisely by letting myself drift (in a story I called it 'letting-oneself-fall'), by doing penance with Him for His love of breaking Himself up and living Himself out in individual beings?" [36] Now "letting-oneself-fall" was the ultimate doctrine of "Klein and Wagner," and it is therefore implied that this was really the expression of an incipient "heresy against Buddha," whose extreme rationalism and godlessness was perhaps revelatory of a certain unwillingness to submit fully to the fate of living and thus to the fatherhood of God.

Siddhartha as a whole must therefore be seen in the context of Hesse's movement away from Buddhism, not toward it, characterized also by the reference to his increased interest in the multiple Indian gods. Hesse was throughout his life probably more influenced by Hinduism than by Buddhism; he apparently found that yoga answered better the needs and yearnings of himself and his contemporaries than did the Eightfold Path.[37] Yet *Siddhartha* differs in the

[33] "A Short Autobiography" (IV, 482).

[34] "Aus einem Tagebuch des Jahres 1920," *op. cit.,* p. 201.

[35] *Ibid.* p. 206.

[36] *Ibid.*

[37] "The general longing is not so much for Buddha or Lao-tzŭ as for yoga" (*Neue Rundschau,* XXXII, ii [1921], 1117).

end from all such faiths and systems by the extremism of its derogation of the intellect. Certainly, Siddhartha's experience leads him
away from Buddhistic "pessimism"; it leads him away from ethical
judgments to the total amoralism of chaos; while the doctrine of
universal love points away from Indian teachings altogether toward
that of St. Francis. We may note that Hesse remarks at this time that
Jesus, with his doctrine of the childhood of men before God, was
perhaps further advanced than the Buddha.[38] The actual description
given in *Siddhartha* of Gotama Buddha is not without its interest:
"With a hidden smile, still, peaceful, not unlike a healthy child, the
Buddha walked by" (III, 637). The harshness, the stoniness of
Demian's trance face has been softened; the hermaphroditic smile of
the Buddha speaks a serenity which in a later novel is to be transformed into laughter.

To leave Gotama and to leave Govinda, now Buddha's "shadow,"
is a turning point in Siddhartha's life, a moment like a snake's
shedding of its skin (a symbol beloved of the Upanishads). Now he
seeks neither teachers nor a teaching, but only self-knowledge. This
had been his error: in the pursuit of the Atman he had striven to
escape from the self, but it is precisely the self which he must come
to know, what the Vedas cannot teach, what no teacher can teach,
"the secret called Siddhartha" (III, 646). At this point something
happens:

He looked around him as if he were seeing the world for the first time.
Beautiful was the world, colorful the world, strange and baffling the
world! Here was blue, here was yellow, here was green, sky and river
ran, forest stared and mountain, everything beautiful, everything
bewildering and magical, and in the midst of it he, Siddhartha, the
awakening one, on the way to himself. All this, all this yellow and blue,
river and forest, entered Siddhartha's eyes for the first time, was no
longer the spell of Mara, was no longer the veil of Maya, was no longer
the meaningless and accidental multiplicity of the world of phenomena,
despised by the deep-thinking Brahmans, who scorn multiplicity, who
seek unity. Blue was blue, river was river, and even if in the blue and the
river in Siddhartha the One and the Divine lived concealed it was
precisely the nature and sense of the Divine to be here yellow, here blue,
there sky, there forest and here Siddhartha. Meaning and being were not
somewhere behind things, they were in them, in everything [III, 647].

[38] "Aus einem Tagebuch des Jahres 1920," *op. cit.*, p. 207.

This must be placed side by side with a passage from "Klein and Wagner":

The wave went through him like pain and a thrill of pleasure, he shuddered with feeling, life resounded in him like surf, everything was incomprehensible. He tore open his eyes and saw: trees on a road, silver flakes in the lake, a running dog, cyclists—and everything was strange, a fairy tale and almost too beautiful, everything as though brand-new out of God's toy box, everything solely for him, for Friedrich Klein, and he himself only there to feel this stream of marvels and pain and joy shudder through him. Everywhere there was beauty, in every pile of dirt by the wayside, everywhere there was deep suffering, everywhere there was God. Yes, this was God, and unimaginable ages ago as a boy he had experienced Him this way and sought Him through his heart whenever he thought the thoughts "God" and "omnipresence." Heart, burst not of your fullness! [III, 515].

The moment of inward enlightenment involves, indeed often begins with, an awakening of sense impressions; remembering themselves, Siddhartha and Klein remember the world, and vice versa; the colors of the world light up, movement ("a running dog") leaps to the eye, it is suddenly a world of concrete particulars, not just the hypothetical veil of Maya. It may certainly be regarded as an epiphany, but it is more important still to note that it involves a total change in the mode of consciousness; in Klein's case (and this reminds us of experiences of Emil Sinclair's) it results in a state of hypermnesia: "Once more there poured up from all the forgotten shafts of his life liberated memories, countless ones" (III, 515). A passage from "Dream Traces" adds rewardingly to our general insight:

He blinked out of a narrow crack between his closed eyelids and perceived, not merely with his vision, a light wafting and gleaming . . . somehow valuable and unique, transformed by some secret content from mere perception into experience. What flashed multi-rayed, drifted, blurred, surged, and beat its wings was not just a storm of light from without, and its theater was not just the eye, it was also life, a rising urge from within, and its theater was the soul and his own fate. This is the way in which the poets, the "seers" see, this is the delicious and devastating manner in which people see who have been touched by Eros. . . . Everything was eternal moment, experience, innermost reality [IV, 424–425].

"Life resounded in him like surf"; "it was also life, a rising urge from within"—the connection between the world within and the world without, that of the affects and that of the senses, which connection Emil Sinclair experienced first and foremost as a linked movement of fate, can also be a bond of consciousness. The process may indeed begin in the senses or in the soul, but it eventually embraces both of these. It involves the feelings, but equally it involves the memory and the insight.

Above all, it is a state of awakened presence, magical thinking, the experience ascribed to Dostoevsky's Prince Myshkin: "The highest experience for him is that half-second of highest sensitivity and insight which he has known several times, that magic ability to be for a moment everything, to feel everything, to suffer everything, to understand and affirm everything that is in the world." [39] This is a condition in which perceptions are transformed into experience. The passage from "Dream Traces," it is worth noticing, is anything but naïve experience; in fact, the account which precedes it of the author enjoying the spring as he sits in a park is markedly intellectualized. A certain formal stylization in the *Siddhartha* passage is also undeniable—the colors are not from Klingsor's rich palette, they are representative only; in neither Siddhartha's case nor in Klein's is the outside world experienced wholly with naïve sensuality, but still with a certain detachment, and *sub specie aeternitatis*; Siddhartha's objects are no longer merely the veil of Maya but yet they are not just objects, like Klein's they have a soul, they have God within them as Siddhartha has; in this the things are replicas of the man, Siddhartha. For the magical realists, precisely, "objective reality" can never be simply "a storm of light from without" but must also be subjectively conditioned, by an awakening within the self; the *locus in quo* is essentially within, "its theater was the soul and his own fate." This is, as we are told, the vision of poets, a form of mystical vision; it is intimately bound up with contact with Eros, and of course Siddhartha stands, at this moment, on the brink of his plunge into the erotic world. Thus each nodal point upon the *vita* may be regarded *inter alia* as a moment of poetic inspiration.

Siddhartha walks out of the grove of Jetavana, the grove of the Buddha, with the intention of returning home, to his father. But the

[39] VII, 182.

ambiguous feast of the Prodigal Son is not for him. He stops short, "as if a snake lay before him on the path" (III, 647). Between him and home there lies a barrier of a spiritual, but evidently also of a specifically sexual kind (the snake symbol recurs again at a much later point in the novel). For the first time Siddhartha really feels his solitude, his homelessness; he belongs to no community, has no place even among Samanas, hermits, or monks. Out of the coldness of this experience "Siddhartha came to the surface, more I than before, more tightly coiled," resolved to go on, "not home any more, not to his father any more, not to go back" (III, 649). The world of the senses is now evoked—"for the world was transformed" (III, 650)— the description, though vivid and colorful, is perhaps more like the *Märchen* than like "Klingsor"; all is subordinate to the laws of metamorphosis, that is, to Siddhartha's changing consciousness, to his "liberated vision." Flickerings of archaic memories rise from the depths of the author's work; there is the characteristic animal movement as the pike hunts; the orgiastic force of "Klingsor" and "Klein and Wagner," Eros, and even Dionysos is not far away: "Siddhartha saw a ram pursue a sheep and cover it" (III, 651). The world is beautiful when it is experienced thus, "without searching, so simply, in so childlike a way" (III, 650).

In fact, the second part of *Siddhartha* turns upon the paradox of enlightenment and childlikeness; in a sense these are one and the same, in a sense infinitely different: the Way is a spiral indeed, not a circle; and the world of the magician (cf. "Childhood of the Magician") has deep analogies, but no identity, with that of the child.[40] Siddhartha now goes to dwell among the "child-people," an ambiguous term. Their childlikeness both is and is not that spoken of in the New Testament; theirs is the sphere of reality, with which the magical reality of Siddhartha can never coincide. As the magical realism of the novel differs from realism, in some such way does Siddhartha differ from the "child-people" among whom he now lives. This first night of freedom he dreams of Govinda, who in embracing him is transformed into a woman, from whose breast Siddhartha drinks the intoxicating milk; the characteristic transition from male to female, that fundamental structural element in Hesse's

[40] "We do not want to go back to the child, the primitive, but onward, forward, to personality, responsibility, freedom" ("On the Soul"; VII, 72).

novels, may now be noticed again. The erotic motif now becomes dominant, but not before the ferryman Vasudeva (one of the many names of Krishna) has borne Siddhartha over the barrier of the river into the wide world. Vasudeva speaks briefly of the teaching which it is the river's to bestow, predicts Siddhartha's return, and makes a childlike impression upon the wanderer: he reminds Siddhartha of Govinda, but Siddhartha is to learn painfully of the ambivalence of childlikeness, and is with time to come to see the gulf which separates Govinda from Vasudeva, the perfected one.

Klingsor, on the road to Kareno, had had an encounter unlike any which had occurred in Hesse's work before: "Out of a dark stone room as though out of a primeval cave a woman appeared. . . . From her dirty clothes her brown neck emerged, a firm broad face, sunburned and handsome, a full broad mouth, large eyes, a rough sweet charm, her large Asiatic features spoke expansively and silently of sex and motherhood. . . . She was everything, mother, child, lover, beast, Madonna" (III, 575). Such words as these had, it is true, been used of Emil Sinclair's dream lover, but the physical reality had turned out somewhat contrived. This woman, however, is *seen;* and now a figure takes shape—in this book of Klingsor, Hesse's first Don Juan—fit at last to wrest to herself the hegemony which Peter Camenzind's statuesque Elisabeth had so long held. She is born at the same time as Klein's Teresina, is in fact her dissimilar twin; we may note that the peasant woman who comes to Klein when he stays the night in her hovel does so when he has just been dreaming about the elegant Teresina. It is a gypsy girl who later introduces Goldmund to the experience of love; and Siddhartha, once across the river, has a similar encounter, feels for the first time stirring "the spring of sex" (III, 654), but the call of some inner voice disperses his entrancement, he recognizes the animal in the woman, and his virginity is spared for Kamala.

Kamala herself,[41] the courtesan, belongs to the school of Teresina and of Harry Haller's Hermine. There is more naïveté, more of the animal, in Teresina than in Kamala, whose oriental sophistication is of subtler kind; it is hard to imagine Teresina being converted, as

---

[41] Kama is the Hindu god of love and of sensual experience; the peasant girl's attempt to entice Siddhartha with "the tree climb" is, of course, a reference to the *Kama Sutra* of Vatsyanyana.

Kamala eventually is, to Buddhism. Nevertheless, both are the type
who always used to make that conscience-shackled bourgeois, Friedrich Klein, both disgusted and afraid. When Teresina first appears,
Klein sees "a girl, strong and rhythmic, very upright and challenging, elegant, haughty, a cool face with painted red lips and dense
high hair which was a bright, metallic yellow," and then again "a
calm and clever face, firm and pale, a little blasé, the painted
mouth bloodred, gray eyes fully alert, a handsome, richly formed ear
on which an oblong green stone shone. She was dressed in white silk,
the slim neck sank away in opal shadows, encircled by a thin necklace
with green stones" (III, 499). Kamala is unquestionably the same
figure; the hair style, the eyes, the vocabulary, and the structure of
the portraits are astonishingly similar; only race, and therefore some
of the coloring, is different: "Beneath black upswept hair . . . a
very bright, very delicate, very clever face, a bright red mouth like
a freshly opened fig, eyebrows trained and painted in high arches,
dark eyes clever and alert, light high neck emerging from a green
and golden tunic, still bright hands long and narrow with broad
gold bangles on the wrists" (III, 655). Kamala assures Siddhartha
that she can dispense love at her will alone, as the Samana and
Brahman can dispense spiritual truth. She can teach love, the gradu-
ated wisdom of kissing; on this Way too there are many stages, it
is a hermetic mystery.

To be initiated, Siddhartha, who has just left one grove, must now
enter another, Kamala's pleasure grove—"to go into the grove" is
the emblematic phrase. Siddhartha now plunges into the world of
sex, of the "child-people," into the game. Friedrich Klein had let
himself fall into the waters of the lake, but the truth was he could
just as well have let himself fall into life—"letting-oneself-fall" *in
life*, the doctrine of *Demian*, and of the Tao. Siddhartha now lets
himself fall into life. He has understood the paradox of determinism,
the nature of action. Real doing is the same as suffering; both are the
execution of fate;[42] to wait, to submit—this is the teaching of the
Vedanta and of Lao-tzŭ. On those who have understood this most
elusive truth and converted it into a way of life, as Siddhartha has,
fortune smiles: "Siddhartha does nothing, he waits, he thinks, he

---

[42] "Doing and suffering, which together make up our existence, are one whole,
one and the same" (*Zarathustra's Return;* VII, 212).

fasts, but he goes through the things of the world like a stone through water" (III, 663).

This is magic, and through it Siddhartha succeeds in the commercial world of the "child-people," where it astonishes his mentor, Kamaswami.[43] He becomes rich, learns the life of the merchant detachedly, "like a game" (III, 666). Unlike Kamaswami, neither time nor money cause him the least concern. He is participant and spectator at one and the same time—the positive aspect of Klein's decadent schizophrenia. The life of ordinary people, child-people, seems to Siddhartha only a passionate game, with which, however, they are wholly identified. Kamala, for whom love is a game, is more like Siddhartha himself; like him she is inwardly detached, she has "a quiet place and refuge" (III, 671) within her. However much she teaches him, he does not really love her; as he says: "I am like you. You do not love either—or else how could you treat love as an art? People of our sort perhaps cannot love. The child-people can, that is their secret" (III, 672). Sexual love is an art, and art is a game; every game is dangerous, for the player may sooner or later forget it is a game.[44]

To let oneself fall, to submit, to play—like all great spiritual secrets this one too has its hellish converse. That which can liberate can also bind all the faster. Thus Siddhartha begins to forget, to lose the all-important power of discrimination, to lose awareness of the distinction between the game which he practices and the source, the stream, "the spring of his nature" (III, 670), which flows, or used to flow, within him. What he experienced at the peak of his youth—"that lofty, bright wakefulness" (III, 673)—this is no more; his soul, filled with world and sloth, falls asleep. His decline, like Hans Giebenrath's, is compared to that of a tree: "as dampness penetrates the dying tree trunk" (III, 673). Like Faust, whom he so often resembles, he all but succumbs to *"flache Unbedeutenheit"* (triviality). For the first time, pointing backward to *Hermann Lauscher* and forward to *The Glass Bead Game*, Hesse openly develops

---

[43] Again a name with a meaning, presumably "master" (*swami*) of the "material world" (*kama*).

[44] H. Mauerhofer points out the tendency of the extreme introvert to seek refuge in "game" and then: "Es ist eine geschaffene Welt, in der nun der Introvertierte lebt" (It is an *invented* world in which the introvert now lives) (*Die Introversion*, pp. 20–21).

the symbol of the game as a figure for the aesthetic existence. Those who but play the game, be it in art or be it in life, in the end are lost in the game. However unsatisfactory the asceticism of the Samanas was, it remains a fact that without some degree of self-discipline, of self-recall, the spiritual life is impossible.

Siddhartha, becoming like the "child-people," acquires only their painful, negative side, "the soul-sickness of the rich" (III, 675), their animal emotional life. He remains intolerably without their comfortable blindness, their anaesthetic self-confidence, the "tranquillity" of perpetual identification with purposes. He ends by being possessed by greed and by taking to dicing (apparently to demonstrate his contempt for money!), to wild gambling—most degraded of all forms of game. So he comes to feel—though at first in a superficially pleasurable form—that emotion which is characteristic of the "child-people" and which reduced Klein's life to hell, anxiety. Like Klein, haunted by Wagner, and like Klingsor, Siddhartha stares at his own face "in the mirror" (III, 676), stands outside himself and watches his decline, his "*Wagnerization*." It is in this form, the mirrored or painted face, that the motif of the double, introduced into *Hermann Lauscher*, recurs most often in Hesse's later works.

A dream warns Siddhartha, the aging Kamala's wish to be told more about the Buddha strikes home with him; one day, she thinks, she will hand over her pleasure grove to the monks of Gotama. Into their lovemaking there comes a new element, fear of old age, of autumn, of death. In his disgust with himself Siddhartha sleeps and dreams of a bird, Kamala's singing bird, which he finds dead in its cage, extracts and throws into the gutter; then suddenly it seems as if he has thrown away everything that has value in existence. He surveys his life, he discovers the terrible truth that for the partially enlightened one to seek to be again like ordinary men makes him in fact far worse off than they; in truth, there is no reversal possible, no way back at all. Not even the game which Kamala plays can be endured any longer; and his mango tree, his pleasure garden, his riches—all is but a stupid game which he leaves there and then, without more ado, in the very same hour of the night. When Kamala hears of Siddhartha's disappearance she opens the golden cage, takes out her bird and lets it fly away. When Hermann Heilner fled from Kloster Maulbronn he breathed deeply and stretched his limbs, "as if he had escaped from a narrow cage" (I, 482). There are many varieties of cage; but Hermann Heilner and Siddhartha have at least this much in common, they both go on and not, like poor Hans Giebenrath, back.

On the bank of the river, beneath a huge cocos tree, Siddhartha contemplates suicide, death by water. He thinks of it in terms such as those which ran through the mind of Klein, "to smash to pieces the unsuccessful form of his life, to throw it away" (III, 682). Klein was pursued by the detailed vision of his body pulverized beneath the wheels of a train.[45] His eventual suicide seemed to him "a child's trick, something no doubt not evil, but comic and pretty foolish" (III, 548); as for Siddhartha, his mind awakes in time and he perceives the absurdity of seeking peace through the destruction of the body. Looking into the mirror of the water, he perceives his own emptiness and spits at his own face. At this moment the word "Om," rising from the depths of the self, stays his hand, as Faust's hand is stayed by the Easter chorus. The dreamless sleep (Tiefschlaf [III, 620]) [46] which now overcomes him and which, as the Upanishads teach, takes him temporarily to Atman, separates him utterly from his previous life, just as Faust is separated in the scene "Anmutige Gegend." The moment of enlightenment which precedes the sleep, described at some length, is, however, summarized as "just a moment, a flash" (III, 683).

Immensely refreshed, joyful, awakened, and inquisitive again he is now confronted by a man in a yellow robe, Govinda, who has been watching over his sleep. For a short moment his friend, his former "shadow," has reversed his role, has been his guardian and protector. To Govinda he relates about his rich and worldly life, now gone, for the Wheel turns. Govinda, full of doubt, goes on his way, watched by Siddhartha with love; the woman, Kamala, has duly given place to the man, Govinda, but Govinda is now a symbol for humanity, the object of a new kind of love. Now at last Siddhartha can really love; that is, he is free of the game, for those who

---

[45] Wilhelm Stekel (Die Sprache des Traumes [Wiesbaden, 1911], p. 536) observes: "Unter die Lokomotive wirft sich nur der Neurotiker, der einen andern auf diese Weise zermalmt sehen wollte" (The only neurotic to throw himself under a locomotive is the one who would like to see someone else crushed like this).

[46] The term is evidently taken from Deussen, op. cit., p. 470 and passim.

only play cannot love. Siddhartha has lost his ascetic self, he has lost his worldly self, he must begin again as a child, a situation which brings him to laughter, "to laughter about himself, to laughter about this strange, foolish world" (III, 689).

At this moment of utter destitution, which is the beginning of freedom, Siddhartha's *vita* brushes against the author's life as it was in these lonely years, and indeed a note of Klingsor's "music of doom" sounds: "He was going downhill" (III, 689). In a passage extraordinarily close to the language and mood of "Iris" (III, 689) Siddhartha's life seems to him to have been a long and strange detour (*wunderliche Umwege*); these circuitous paths have brought him to be a "child-person"—the word is full of *double-entendre*—and the bird in his breast is not dead after all. It is an errant, maybe a foolish Way (*närrisch;* III, 690), perhaps even a circle, but he will continue to follow it. Recognition of this brings joy, as does something else, his escape like a bird from the cage, the charmed circle of Kamala's pleasure-grove: "that I have escaped, that my flight is a fact, that at last I am free again and stand here like a child beneath the sky. Oh, how good it is to have fled, to have become free!" (III, 690). Heilner's flight from the teachers, Klein's flight from marriage, Siddhartha's flight from Eros—all three coalesce; but it is above all the figures from "Iris" which are dominant here: "you have done something, you have heard the bird sing in your breast and you have followed it" (III, 691).

The dark night of the soul is past; Siddhartha now feels only joy that the bird is still alive, the bird whose voice is now identified with the source itself—"the bird, the merry spring and voice" (III, 691). Siddhartha no longer merely *knows about*, he *understands* the evils of the worldly life, that is, they are a part of his experience; he listens to the song of the bird in his breast and realizes that what has really died is his egoistic pride, his small willful self, that unconquerable enemy with which his haughty intelligence, his priestly knowledge, his self-mortification, and spiritual insight so long contended in vain. The reason for his erstwhile failure is really not far to seek, though inobvious: "Into this priesthood, into this arrogance, into this spirituality his ego had crept and had hidden itself there" (III, 692). Siddhartha told Gotama of his perceptive fear that his ego, instead of finding dissolution in Nirvana, might batten on to

Buddha's teaching, or on to the pupil's veneration for Buddha, and thus grow fat. Now he has discovered, and thereby escaped from a similar, profounder, snare upon the Way—that the mainspring of spiritual development, the will-to-change itself, should become the ultimate hiding-place of that which is resolved to remain the same.

Siddhartha the Brahman and the Samana are long dead. Siddhartha the slave of the senses has now followed them. The first of these deaths is that we find prefigured in "Klein and Wagner," in the liberation of the inhibited conscience-ridden Klein; the second is the final exorcism of Wagner, achieved by Klein only through suicide, by Siddhartha through satiation and enlightenment. Vasudeva the ferryman, with whom Siddhartha now comes to live and work, is already fully enlightened. He has understood the fundamental secret of listening: "I know only how to listen and to be devout, I've learned nothing else" (III, 697); this is "hearkening with a quiet heart, with waiting, open soul" (III, 698). Hermann Lauscher had in a sense been right after all; in a sense also the passivity of the Neo-Romantic impressionists was right; one must listen, it is, however, very material *how* one listens. Listening may appear to be purely a passive function; performed correctly, however, it is an active function of the rare genuine kind (here we may compare Josephus Famulus in *The Glass Bead Game*), for what men call active is really passive, while acceptance is true activity. *Amor fati* is active, submission is active; Vasudeva has learned through serenity what Klein discovered only in tumult: "that it is good . . . to sink, to seek the depths" (III, 697). Through the river, moreover, the river of life, this paradox of endless change and changeless presence, Siddhartha comes to penetrate the illusion of time: time, Klingsor's demon, does not really exist. The river, the flow, is indeed all things; in its sound may be heard all existing sounds, blended into the holy syllable "*Om.*" Siddhartha's illumination now commences, he becomes like Vasudeva, "childlike and aged" (III, 699), as the years pass. Then monks go by, on their way to the dying Buddha, from whom Siddhartha himself no longer feels in any way separated; once more the thought is formulated that teachers and teachings can only lead astray: "No, a true seeker could not accept any doctrine. . . . But he who had found could approve every doctrine" (III, 701).

Kamala, pilgrimaging with Siddhartha's son to the scene of the dying Gotama, expires in her former lover's arms of snake bite;[47] she recognizes him and reads in his eyes that he is now at peace. The boy whom she leaves behind is to be Siddhartha's final trial; as he once struggled with the will of his father, so his own son now revolts against him. Siddhartha resists Vasudeva's recommendation that the boy be released to go out into the world, since this would mean committing him to Sansara—at which objection the river laughs, for Sansara is indeed the lot of all and cannot be avoided. Thus the issue of the Prodigal Son is apparently resolved—the father perceives the inevitability of the son's departure, of his son's corruption by the world. The lesson is harsh, for Siddhartha for the first time feels truly possessive love, strongest of all the passions, characteristic emotion of the "child-people," belonging truly to "the turbid stream of forms," for it is "a turbid spring, a dark water" (III, 710), a necessary folly, however, upon the Way. Saintliness does not captivate the boy; he runs away, resolved rather to be a robber and a murderer than a saint like his father. Siddhartha goes after him, as far as Kamala's pleasure grove in which the yellow-robed monks now walk, and then returns, empty and wounded, to the place of his meditation; his son has not to become like his father, any more than Emil Sinclair had to become like Demian; he has to become himself.

The paradoxical term "child-person" at last discloses its full significance: "Although he was nearing his perfection . . . it still seemed to him that the child-people were his brothers" (III, 715). Their passionate, darkened lives are also Brahman. A necessary and lofty stage upon the Way is the pilgrim's realization that he is after all no different from other men.[48] Perhaps even the great secret itself, knowledge of the One, is nothing but "a childishness of the think-people, of the think-child-people" (III, 716). Staring into the water at his own reflection, Siddhartha this time sees in it his father's face. Wisdom is indeed knowledge of the One, of endless repetition too, "this running in a fateful circle" (III, 717), again and again the same conflict of father and son, the same suffering. Siddhartha's pursuit

[47] Once more the snake. The psychoanalytic interpretation seems cogent—she pays the penalty in the end for her way of life, dies from the poison of that for which she has lived. Hesse thus, unconsciously, judges Kamala.

[48] This, of course, is also a paradox, true and not true. In *The Glass Bead Game*, Dion Pugil makes a sharp distinction between child-people and partially enlightened ones. Cf. VI, 636.

of his son toward the city had itself been a kind of flight, he himself a "childish refugee" (III, 718), for what repeats, repeats on many levels. Thus he confesses to Vasudeva, that "confession to the father" to which Hesse's protagonists so often come, Vasudeva listening silently like the later Josephus Famulus, sucking in his confessions "as a tree does rain" (III, 718). This seems like, and is, a confession to the eternal, to God.

Vasudeva, in love and serenity (*Heiterkeit*), takes Siddhartha to the river, bids him watch and listen again: "And the river's voice sounded full of longing, full of burning pain, full of invisible yearning. . . . All things together made up the river of events, the music of life" (III, 719–720). These are the many voices of Klein's universal stream, over which rises God's temple of music; more, it is suddenly the language of the German Romantics again, a language which describes no music better than it does that of Richard Wagner. Siddhartha, now "seeing," and thus united with the One, bids farewell to the departing Vasudeva, now Sri Krishna leaving this incarnation: "Radiant he departed" (III, 721).

Siddhartha remains for his ultimate task, the meeting with Govinda, with the "friend" who has not yet found salvation, which we may understand as the final confrontation with his own intellect, his questioning, reflective self. Govinda has made the mistake of too much searching, while to find is precisely "to be free, to be open, to have no goal" (III, 723). Siddhartha cannot teach Govinda anything, for truth cannot be taught; his highest secret, with which he permanently confounds the logical faculty, is the paradox of paradoxes, that of each truth the opposite is equally true. The apparent flaw in Buddha's coherent system, the unfounded division of the world into Sansara and Nirvana, was merely a teaching device. It is taught that the sinner at this moment of time will one day, in some later incarnation, evolve into a Buddha, but since time itself is an illusion this can only mean that the world is already complete in every moment of its existence, all is Brahman. While Siddhartha might previously have venerated a stone because of its divine potential, he reveres it now because all levels of existence, including the divine, are already contained within it. At the same time, he loves the stone because it is a stone, he loves things, and not doctrines, ideas, or words. Govinda intellectualizes; he protests that this "loving the world" is the very opposite of the Buddha's teaching: "He commands benevolence, consideration, pity, tolerance, but not love" (III, 729), but Siddhartha dismisses the objection as a theoretical confusion. Govinda, though impressed by his friend's saintly appearance, finds his doctrine foolish (*närrisch*), which for such as him is a serious matter. Kissing Siddhartha's brow, with that symbolic kiss which links the two "friends" in novel after novel, he looks into his face: there he sees many faces, first of all fish—Hesse's favorite figure for the prehuman stage—then, Wagner-like, the face of a murderer as he drives his knife into his victim's body (his execution follows), then men and women in acts of sensual frenzy, animal faces of all kinds, gods—Krishna and Agni —a stream of faces in constant metamorphosis behind a mask, a smiling mask of water, Siddhartha's face smiling the masked smile of Gotama.

So *Siddhartha* concludes with the confrontation of the two "friends," two students of the eternal, the one who, by turning his back not only upon family but also upon teacher and tradition, by bursting into the vast Without alone, has found serenity and wisdom, the other who has failed because he remained with the other monks within the grove of Jetavana, celibate within the walls of the Spiritual Academy.[49] It is not in fact an idle allusion to compare Govinda with Faust's famulus, Wagner, for at the very least the comparison illuminates Hesse's fundamental, ironical analogy between the ladder of the traditional pedagogical hierarchy and the ladder of the "conventional" spiritual Way—that is, the Way which depends upon the relationship of pupil and guru. On the basis of this analogy, throughout this author's works, that monastic tradition which has always yoked divine and secular knowledge is constantly alluded to; but over and above all this a third kind of "knowledge" is proposed, which cannot be learned in the Christian monastery or in its Indian equivalent.

In 1931, in the essay "My Faith," Hesse delivered himself of a categorical assertion: "I once attempted, a little more than ten years ago, to express my beliefs in a book. The book is called *Siddhartha*, and its convictions have often been examined and discussed by

[49] "Platonic academies" are mentioned in the same breath as yogic schools. See *Letters* (VII, 640).

Indian students and Japanese priests, but not by their Christian colleagues" (VII, 370). It is a fact that no other novel of Hesse's (with
the possible exception of *The Journey to the East*) gives such expression to his deepest insights, for in none is the form, that of
legend,[50] so perfectly adapted to the experience conveyed. Other
effects, perhaps equally admirable, are achieved in *The Steppenwolf*
in quite a different manner, by a new tension between matter and
form. *Siddhartha* discloses finally and unmistakably the significance
of hagiography, of the saintly *vita*, as a formal conditioning factor
in Hesse's work; the book's doctrine of love is not Indian at all,
but Franciscan, or at the very least Christian.[51] The conception of
spiritual development which the *vita* form implies and involves,
having its roots in Calw, is linked with the trans-Darwinist dogma
of "psychic evolution" so popular in Hesse's youth,[52] and promi-
nently reflected in the Karamazov essay, which itself suffers from
the inextricable ambiguities of these doctrines, their inability to
distinguish clearly between the evolution of the individual and that
of the race. "On the Soul" informs us that man is to be seen as "the
special order of beings whose present task it is to develop soul"
(VII, 69). This very ambivalence lends a certain arrogance and
artificiality to the last pages of *Demian*; but *Siddhartha* is free of
such things, and its individualism is the more intense for this, its
self-revelation the more genuine.

Hesse's theoretical framework for the spiritual evolution of man
is laid down in "A Bit of Theology" (1932): the first stage is a state
of no responsibility, called paradise or childhood, succeeded by the
demands of culture and ideals, religion and morality with the cor-
relate experience of sin and guilt; if this second stage is fully experienced, it leads inevitably to the realization of the inadequacy of

---

[50] For an attempted definition of "legend" as a specific literary form see
André Jolles, *Einfache Formen* (Halle, 1930).

[51] Hesse notes this Christian element, even calling it "a truly Protestant trait"
("My Faith"; VII, 372).

[52] Given a great impetus by Nietzsche, who transmutes Darwinist conceptions
much in this way. The idea, of course, is found widely in the *fin de siècle*, frequently linked with traditional occult and gnostic notions (for instance, in
Germany, in the works of Johannes Schlaf). Nietzsche had pointed out the
ambiguity of the idea of health, and we may compare Hesse's remark "that the
diseases of today may be the healths of tomorrow" ("On Good and Bad
Critics"; VII, 369).

the will, hence to despair—a condition which may mean destruction. "This despair leads either to destruction or to a Third Kingdom of the Spirit, the experience of a condition beyond morality and law, an advance to grace and redemption, to a new, loftier kind of irresponsibility, or in short: to faith" (VII, 389). This is not unlike the conventional, triadic structure of most mystical systems. Hesse finds that faith, irrespective of the particular religious garb it wears, is essentially a realization of the need for submission to the forces which rule man, a state of confident acceptance. He finds his formulation "European and almost Christian" (VII, 389); Brahmanism, together with Buddhism, constitutes the loftiest achievement of Theological Man, but has different categories from the Christian—first, the condition of childish or naïve man, then the stage of yoga which corresponds to that of "works," and finally enlightenment, in Christian terms "grace." In such analogies between systems Hesse finds "my suspicion of a central problem confirmed" (VII, 390). The second stage, that of the end of innocence, of the beginning of polarity, of the struggle of the will—that stage, indeed, with which *Demian* begins—terminates always in despair; it may lead "to destruction or redemption: that is to say, not backward beyond morality and culture to the paradise of the child, but forward beyond them to the capacity to live in faith" (VII, 391). This is the vital transition, the point of hazard between self-realization and infantile regression. *Beneath the Wheel* was also in this respect the early psychological paradigm of the later conceptualized spiritual Way; for Hans Giebenrath, after the desperate struggle of his will, regresses. The breakout (which *he* did not make), the "exemplary event," therefore, may be seen as the qualitative leap from the second to the third stage. This issue is also cardinal at the end of *The Glass Bead Game*, where the transition is seen to be full of ambiguities.

For the understanding of *Siddhartha* it is, however, of importance to notice that the theoretical pattern, as adumbrated in "A Bit of Theology," does not fit very well; the episode with Kamala, the approach to the life of the "child-people," falls out of the pattern, and it is much too negative to regard this episode as being simply a regression to paradise. Perhaps Siddhartha's experience with the Samanas, with Buddha, and with Kamala and the "child-people" should all be regarded as part of the meandering *via purgativa;* the syllable *"Om,"* then, is the overture to the *via illuminativa* which follows. The important distinction between *via illuminativa* and *via unitiva* is blurred in Hesse's writings; but *Siddhartha* scarcely corresponds even to his own system, since illumination eventually comes to the hero through a despair which springs, not from the breaking of the will, but from satiety and disgust with the world.

"The Third Kingdom of the Spirit"—Christian dogma, Novalis and *Heinrich von Ofterdingen,* the old dream of the Third Kingdom, the chiliastic visions of the turn of the nineteenth century and of the Expressionists here combine in a term which has interesting applications in all Hesse's later novels. It refers to the condition of faith, of chaos, of magical thinking, of perception of the One. Fundamental to its attainment is submission to an inner autocrat, the law of the self wheresoever it may lead, just as the tragic hero, with his "self will" (*Eigensinn*), follows his star.[53] Willfulness[54] is one thing, it leads away from fate; true will, however, is identical with fate. The most successful exposition in allegorical *minuscule* of these basic ideas is the little-known *Märchen* "The Steep Road" (1917). This story has some stylistic and thematic affinities with Franz Kafka; it tells of a man who is led by a guide to climb an insurmountable mountain. They are teacher and pupil setting out together upon the Way, and the pupil painfully follows his teacher out of the pleasant valley of flowers and sunshine, picks up his chant: "I will, I will, I will" and significantly changes it to "I must, I must, I must" (III, 325). There is, once started on the Way, no turning back; there is no choice but to go on. Sometimes through effort, if it is strong enough, a change of state is produced and real will is born: "Now the climbing became easier, I did not have to any more, but really wanted to. . . . Within me it became bright" (III, 325). In this transformation is symbolized the rewards which may be bestowed from time to time on those who follow the Way of works, of yogic schools, or of extreme asceticism (fakirdom), which are, on their deepest level, all one and the same; but therefore

[53] VII, 196.
[54] "Unclean and distorting is the gaze of the will." "On the Soul" (VII, 68). Hesse, in the same essay, speaks of a "net, woven of mere distractions from the soulful" (VII, 71).

all lead to the same end, which is an intolerable end, the summit of the mountain:

That was a strange mountain and a strange peak! On this peak . . . a tree grew out of the stone, a small, thick-set tree with a few short, tough boughs. There it stood, unimaginably lonely and strange, hard and rigid in the rock, the cool blue of the sky between its boughs. And at the top of the tree sat a black bird and sang a hoarse song.
    Still dream of a moment's rest, high above the world: sun blazed, rock burned, tree sternly stared, bird sang hoarsely. His hoarse song was: Eternity, Eternity! The black bird sang, and his hard shiny eye gazed at us like a black crystal [III, 326].

In this fascinating passage, likely enough reflecting memories of Nietzsche's *Zarathustra*, the figures for the soul and the self, bird and tree, appear terrifyingly petrified; they are "in a stringent, ludicrously thin air," in the mocking ether, indeed, of Harry Haller's Immortals,[55] and the sky is a cool blue. For this summit is not the true goal—a moment of awakening, certainly, immense and lucid (the dropping of the article—"Tree sternly stared," and so on—is often a feature of such passages; compare the *Siddhartha* excerpt quoted on page 138. This moment as the high point of willed effort is the ultimate incarnation of the father, the mind, a mere half or, worse, a dream surrogate ("still dream") for the full self; it is that state of tension before the hermetic union has taken place which is the sense of *Pictor's Transformations*, in effect, before grace. To bring about this ultimate union, first the guide and then the pupil, following the bird, hurls himself into endless space: "And already I fell, I hurtled, leaped, I flew: I shot . . . downward through infinity to the breast of the mother" (III, 327). Only through the unbearable intensification of the father principle can the breasts of the mother be found; it was only Demian who could lead Emil to Frau Eva.

    Thus it is that Siddhartha went first to the Samanas before he found himself and so found Kamala; this detour was indispensable. Later still he discovered how to unite the two in one, like Pictor's tree. Hesse is, despite certain ambiguities of statement, evidently

[55] We may compare also "The Rainmaker" in *The Glass Bead Game*, where the stars are "so ludicrously superior to him with their grand cold majesty and eternity" (VI, 590).

traditional in his mystical formulations; there is nothing new in these conceptions, a fact which implies nothing at all as to either their depth or their fatuity. The act of submission, "letting-oneself-fall," this is also, "as the German mystics called it, 'de-becoming' (*Entwerden*)," [56] diastole. It is all the "perennial philosophy," and it may be interpreted without difficulty in psychological terms, without the aid of metaphysical postulates. The parallelism of religious ideas and Jungian doctrines is a conditioning factor in Hesse's art at this period, of which he was well aware: "There be-
√ gan in me what the Christian calls 'contemplation,' the psycho-analyst 'introversion.' " [57] It is not at all surprising to find the mother-figure of his analyzed dreams in conscious association with the Madonna, when he confesses wryly to his own form of mari-olatry and, *à la* Jung, to "my own cult and my own mythology." [58] There is much justification, however, for the view, to which he him-self held,[59] that the mainspring of his work was the religious impulse, an impulse corresponding, moreover, to an objective metaphysical correlative (though he may use the word "God" but rarely).

Out of all this, for Hesse's art as a writer it is the momentary experience of awakening which is of primary significance. Sidd-hartha's awakening on leaving the grove of Jetavana is the culmina-tion of the first section of the novel and sets the lines for all that follows. The experience is one to which Govinda comes only at the very end, in contemplation of his friend's face. "No longer sure whether time existed, whether this vision had lasted a second or a century" (III, 732)—the destruction of the time sense, reflected in the style in the sudden expansion of *Erzählzeit*, is the telltale feature. This is that state which is localized both without and with-in—"as though wounded in his innermost self by a divine arrow, a sweet-tasting wound, bewitched in his innermost self and dis-solved, Govinda stood for a little while longer bent over Sidd-hartha's face which he had just kissed, which had just been the theater for all the forms, for all existence" (III, 732). The analogies

---

[56] *Letters* (VII, 545).
[57] "World History" (VII, 122).
[58] "Madonna Festival in Tessin" (1924; III, 896).
[59] "We poets and other outsiders . . . we religious people" (VII, 123); also: "I myself consider the religious impulse to be the decisive characteristic of my life and works" (*Letters;* VII, 497).

between this passage and that which describes Siddhartha's first moment of awakening are close, and with that which describes Klein's perhaps closer still. Not the surface of objects only but their spiritual texture, their inner divinity is opened to insight. In Govinda's experience the sensual has succumbed to the visionary, to the "magical," not, however, to the reflective. This numinous translucency of the material world is more than the intrusion of reflection.

It is also very interesting that the last chapter of *Siddhartha* shows a change of standpoint: suddenly the author has moved out of Siddhartha and stands behind Govinda's eyes. "Deeply Govinda bowed down" (III, 733), for Siddhartha is now the image of the divinity, that archetype in Govinda's own soul before whom Govinda must bow. In "A Bit of Theology" Hesse had set up an elementary theory of types, dividing men into two classes, "the devout" and "the rational." Govinda, to some extent still "rational," has to learn like Siddhartha to be wholly "devout." Veneration is said to be the chief characteristic of the devout,[60] and in Govinda's heart there is now "the feeling of warmest love, of most humble veneration" (III, 733). At the end of *Demian*, Emil Sinclair climbed down inside himself, bent and regarded his own reflection in the dark mirror of the water within, and saw in fact the face of his friend. This was an act of narcissism, of reflection indeed. But now when Govinda bows down before *his* friend there is change and maybe progress: for one who has always been cursed with reflection this offers a possibility of escape, that the act of reflection become the act of worship.

[60] VII, 397.

CHAPTER 5

The Steppenwolf

ONE of the doors of the Magic Theater, one which Harry does not choose to enter, carries the inscription: "The essence of art. The transformation of time into space through music" (IV, 386). For the solution of this particular enigma one might well turn first to "Old Music" (1913):

There, a high strong note from the organ. Growing, it fills the immense space, it itself becomes space, envelops us totally. It grows and lingers, and other notes accompany it, and suddenly they all rush in hasty flight down into the depths, bow down, worship, also defy and tarry subdued in the harmonic bass. And now they are silent, a pause like the breath before a storm moves through the halls. And now once more: powerful notes arise in deep, magnificent passion, swell tempestuously on, cry out in lofty devotion their lament to God, cry again and more urgently, more loudly and fall still. And once again they go forth, once again this daring and self-absorbed master sends forth his powerful voice to God, laments and invokes, weeps out his song mightily in charging files of notes, and rests, spun in his mesh, and praises God in a chorale of reverence and majesty, spans golden arches through the high twilight, raises pillars up and ringing groups of columns and builds the vault of his adoration until standing it rests in itself, and it still stands and rests and encloses all of us after the notes have died [VII, 41–42].

This was an evening in the cathedral at Basel, quite possibly the very place where later Harry Haller (IV, 325) was to hear a similar music. The imagery prefigures the vision of the drowning

Friedrich Klein—"a transparent sphere or dome of notes, a vault of music, in the middle of which sat God." Music—that is, time—is transformed into architecture, into space—"it itself becomes space." A dome of worship is built, and golden arches are raised in the high twilight. Then follows a melody rich in arabesques, which seeks only to express the harmony of this earthly world, and "the beauty of a contented, happy soul." Finally Bach transcends all these limits, builds at a much higher dome, "lifts up and rounds out his edifice of notes far above the church into a starry space full of noble, perfect systems, as though God had gone to rest and had handed over his staff and his cloak" (VII, 43). The vision opens out onto the starry vault of the universe, perhaps the most persistent and potent figure in the whole complexity of *The Steppenwolf* (1927). Time and space as alternative manifestations of music, the moment of transcendent freedom which music may bestow and which is colored gold, music as form for the passionate impulse of worship—in this short passage from "Old Music," indeed, much of the essence of the later novel is already incapsulated in a quite extraordinary way. And there are yet other associations: what the drunken Klingsor, in the grotto, had achieved in the imagination only, the domination of the heavens, this composer has actually attained in the work: "He thunders in massed clouds and then opens up free and clear spaces of light, triumphantly he brings forth planets and suns. . . . And he ends splendidly and mightily like the setting sun and subsiding leaves the world behind him full of brightness and soul" (VII, 43).

Upon the dualism of "brightness and soul" (*Glanz und Seele*), surface brilliance of form and fathomless depths of being, turns Hesse's view of music. "I was in music," he tells us, "inclined to be conservative, like most writers," [1] with a long-lasting attachment to the great Romantic composers. Never an *avant-gardiste*, the course of his relationship with musical tradition was sharply different from that of Thomas Mann, had indeed a different starting point, Chopin rather than Wagner. In *Peter Camenzind*, Wagner's *Meistersinger* is a symbol of health, but tensions did later arise not unlike those in Mann, as the dubious light in which the composer appears in "Klein and Wagner" shows. Already in *Rosshalde*, in the argument between Albert Veraguth and Otto Burckhardt, we may note the

[1] "Recollections of Othmar Schoeck" (IV, 652).

beginning abandonment of the Romantic position, although there was never a clean break. The significance of music as a vehicle of austere religious experience is already pre-eminent in the virtuoso performances of Pistorius, and yet Emil Sinclair's reaction to these pre-Classical offerings has much about it that is both Romantic and sensual, as the language at this point betrays.

One suspects that it may well have been the religious feeling of the Bach chorales which first drew Hesse toward the music of the eighteenth century, to the music, it is worth recalling, of the great age of Protestant Pietism. And as his interests move in this direction, music becomes for him less a prop of poetry and the poetic temperament, and more an objective entity, a paradigm of transcendent harmony. The contemplation of such paradigms sometimes seemed to Hesse the true object of the aesthetic impulse; they might be discovered in a statue by Michelangelo, a Tuscan cathedral, or a Greek temple, or else a composition by Mozart. Moreover, the "Northern European" could experience, for instance in the music of Bach, something of what the Moslem and the Buddhist, secure in their religious traditions, were vouchsafed every day: the feeling "of belonging to a transcendental community and of drawing strength from an inexhaustible magical source." [2] Music became for Hesse a symbol of spiritual community as well as a source of magical insight; its paradigmatic aspect turned it into a sort of hieroglyphic of the soul, a hieroglyphic giving only "the approximation of what we have heard," as Hoffmann had said,[3] its highest content an austere fervor, "the genuine serenity (*Heiterkeit*) of the soul." [4] For the Schlegels, architecture had been conceived of as frozen music, in Hesse's later work the characteristic design of music in space is the gothic arch, but it also may be said to form patterns in ice, diagrams of feeling coolly drawn by mind, or as *The Steppenwolf* has it, it becomes "time frozen into space" (IV, 347).

Spa Visitor (1924), a work originally more informatively entitled

[2] "India" (IV, 850).

[3] "Johannes Kreislers Lehrbrief," in E. T. A. Hoffman, *Das Kreislerbuch* (Leipzig, 1903), p. 365.

[4] To quote from one of the prime sources of this view of music, Wilhelm Heinrich Wackenroder. See Wackenroder and Tieck, *Herzensergiessungen*, ed. A. Gillies (Oxford, 1948), p. 134. Music, for Wackenroder, is "the land of Faith" (p. 131).

Psychologia Balnearia and which is close to *The Steppenwolf* in both date and mood, tells of the author's exacting struggle to achieve a musical form in his writing, an invertible counterpoint, "this two-voicedness and eternally progressive antithesis," a form "where constantly melody and counter-melody should be simultaneously visible," a form which would give expression to his own experience of duality: "For life consists for me exclusively in the fluctuation between two poles, the back and forth between the two fundamental pillars of the world" (IV, 114), the duality, moreover, of phenomena and noumenon, multiplicity and the One.

Hesse several times compared the structure of *The Steppenwolf* to a musical prototype; he said that the novel was constructed around the "Tractate of the Steppenwolf," the intermezzo, "as strictly and tautly . . . as a sonata," [5] and also that "the *Steppenwolf* is as strictly constructed as a canon or a fugue and has been given form to the utter extent of my capacity. It even plays and dances." [6] Sonata form, indeed, would appear well adapted to display the fundamental dualism on which the novel is founded, as to a lesser extent might the canon and the fugue or double fugue with its contrapuntal structure. The introduction, the first section of Harry's journal and the tractate may be regarded as the first movement, having a tonic and a dominant, a development and a recapitulation; [7] perhaps the "wolf" is the tonic, the "bourgeois" the dominant. Certainly in his musical analogies the author seeks to stress that the texture of the novel must be regarded as woven of two principal subjects set forth, restated, developed, and contrasted, and eventually resolved.

A curious remark of Hesse's, however, leads to a deeper level of interpretation than this; the novel dances: "But the serenity out of which it does this has its energy sources in a degree of coldness and despair of which you know nothing.[8] There is no form without faith, and there is no faith without previous despair, without

[5] *Letters* (VII, 495). The "musical" form of *The Steppenwolf* has been analyzed in detail by T. J. Ziolkowski, "Hermann Hesse's *Steppenwolf:* A Sonata in Prose," *Modern Language Quarterly,* XIX (1958), 115–133.

[6] *Letters* (VII, 525).

[7] Ziolkowski, *op. cit.,* p. 120.

[8] I quote from a somewhat ironical letter in reply to a lady inquirer (Oct., 1932) (*Letters;* VII, 525).

previous (and also subsequent) acquaintance with chaos." Faith, earlier novels teach, is the acceptance of fate, the sometimes side-long recognition of a secret order in chaos; this order, when imposed upon the material of the imagination, is the form of the work of art (itself therefore an act of faith). The form of *The Steppenwolf*, then, is in some way intimately related to the spiritual agony from which the novel springs. Certainly it discloses the genetic pattern discernible in all the author's works, to which he inevitably submits despite the yearning to resolve this dualism in a new stylistic synthesis. The strictly devised, musically conditioned form of the novel itself introduces an austere, an ascetic element which leads away from *Märchen* and legend, away from synthesis and magic realism as attained in *Siddhartha*, toward the intensest possible expression in novel form of the irresolvable counterpoint of the self. (The resolution we are offered is, not to put too fine a point on it, spurious.)

The difference from *Siddhartha* is apparent from the very outset, for *The Steppenwolf* has a preface or introduction. It is a revealing fact that those three novels of Hesse's in which the reflective aspect predominates, namely, *Demian*, *The Steppenwolf*, and *The Glass Bead Game*, are all framework novels and all have such a preface; there is a note in the introduction to *The Steppenwolf* which reminds us at once of the preface to *Demian:* "I do not want to recount my confessions or *to tell stories*" (IV, 192; my italics); within a framework of common sense we have a set of memoirs which may or may not be "fiction" (IV, 203), may or may not be "pathological fantasies" (IV, 205). Both *Demian* and *The Steppenwolf* are, within the framework, first-person narratives; *The Glass Bead Game* is not, but here the renewed importance of the element of legend makes a great difference. Whether the existence of the introduction in *The Steppenwolf* actually results in an intensification of the novel's realism is open to doubt, as it is in the case of *Demian;* the introduction equally (or correspondingly) has a distancing, depersonalizing effect. The tractate, the novel's most curious formal feature, goes much further than the introduction in objectifying and universalizing the problems of Harry Haller; like the introduction it is remarkable for the sobriety and matter-of-factness (which to Harry merely seems crudity) of its presentation. Except here and there, where for instance the bourgeois narrator talks in the introduction about a "sickness of the age," the portentous note of the preface of *Demian* is missing; the use of imagery is restrained in both introduction and tractate. The bourgeois narrator, an elder cousin of Mann's Serenus Zeitblom, is duly reticent about himself; the author of the tractate is both reticent and mysterious, although a little familiarity with Hesse's earlier novels serves quickly to identify him. The problem of the novel's form, and hence the understanding of the work as a whole, turns really upon the nature and function of the tractate.[9]

What has happened here is that the element of tract discernible in the style of earlier novels has been hypostasized as a specific entity; Schiefer points out acutely the analogy between the tractate and the Christian tracts of the Protestant missionary societies.[10] The Calw printing house where Hesse's father worked published such things; their style was a matter of poignant familiarity to the novelist, as was their purpose—to preach the truth and the gospel, to awaken and convert. Thus we have the valuable insight that the tractate derives from the Pietistic tradition; we may even note in Harry's own journal reminiscences of the Pietistic tradition of the examination of conscience; the dissociation of the personality which occurs in Hesse's works has its roots here too. None of Hesse's novels is so clearly indebted to his Pietistic heritage [11] as is *The Steppenwolf;* the form is the imposition by faith of order upon chaos, the theme is the reflections of a Pietist upon the way of life of a profligate with aspirations to sainthood. The saint, in any case, Hesse defines as one "in whose soul-state the chaos of the world is turned into meaning and music." [12] The choice of music

---

[9] In all editions of the novel the tractate is printed differently from the remainder of the book, and in some early ones had its own colored binding.

[10] P. Schiefer, "Grundstrukturen des Erzählens bei Hermann Hesse," p. 73 a. There are other significant features; for instance, the opening of the tractate is a parody of *Märchen* style: "Once upon a time there was a man called Harry . . ."; and the ironic question is posed whether Harry was "sometime, maybe before his birth, changed by magic from a man into a wolf" (IV, 225).

[11] Which he had earlier contrasted negatively with the "healthy" Roman Catholic religion. "Aus einem Tagebuch des Jahres 1920," *Corona*, III (1932–1933), 200.

[12] *Ibid.*, p. 197.

as the paradigm could be, but of course is not, wholly adventitious, for such music not only offers discipline, austerity, ascetic control, but is also itself connected with the appropriate religious sources [13] (the question of jazz, naturally, is a somewhat separate one). The book is saturated with allusions and symbols drawn from the Pietistic sphere, the tractate itself makes use of significant parallels —for example, "as no rule is without its exception and as a single sinner may be dearer to God than ninety-nine of the just" (IV, 227)—and reveals from time to time a faint but detectable puritanism. Not only the tractate but also the novel which contains it preaches a gospel, teaches a lesson; interpretative and reflective like *Demian*, and equally aspiring to normative definitions, the formally more consummate *Steppenwolf* is at heart a didactic novel.

The roots of its form, therefore, lie in the Pietistic view of the world, so it is not surprising that its theme should be that of the outsider. The English term first occurs in *Spa Visitor*, [14] then again in *The Nuremberg Journey* (1927)—and here a second time in the outlandish compound *"Outsiderwurstigkeit"* [15]—twice in *The Steppenwolf* and later on also in *The Glass Bead Game*.[16] *Spa Visitor* and *The Nuremberg Journey* may both be regarded as prolegomena to the major novel. The former deals with Hesse's first stay as a sciatica patient, taking the waters, at the Swiss spa of Baden, the second with a reading tour he undertook in Bavaria.

Spa Visitor is a work of some importance; Hesse later characterized it as "a mood of contemplation and self-examination, halfway from *Siddhartha* to *The Steppenwolf*." [17] An ironic stocktaking and mannered self-persiflage, *Spa Visitor* owes something to Jean Paul, to whose humorous vision—as well as to his eccentric narrative techniques—Hesse turned for inspiration in these years. It states and restates theoretically a number of propositions central to

[13] Music, however, is the direct analogue of the *moral* condition—and therefore the developing destiny—of a civilization, a point Hesse makes strongly by allusion to the appropriate Chinese sources (*Letters* VII, 571). Both Novalis and Fichte had identified the supremacy of the inner over the outer with the triumph of the *moral* principle.

[14] IV, 58.

[15] IV, 161 (for both instances).

[16] Cf. also "poor outsiders and steppenwolfs," in *Letters* (VII, 730). How this word found its way initially into Hesse's vocabulary has not been cleared up.

[17] "Notes While on a Cure in Baden" (1949–1950; IV, 914).

the author's outlook, for instance the notion of fate—cited in those very words of Novalis already once used in *Demian* [18]—and the concept of unity. The gambling motif (gambling may be spiritually reinvigorating, it may restore the lost delight of childhood) links with *Siddhartha*, more specifically with "Klein and Wagner," where the description of high life has a similar luster; one passage at least points directly forward: "And now at isolated moments my soul trembles alarmed and recalcitrant, like an animal of the steppes which suddenly awakens prisoner in a stall" (IV, 79). Return home to Montagnola from Baden is "return to my steppe" (IV, 79). In its depersonalization and its hostility to the self, *Spa Visitor* is positively Strindbergian. There are, indeed, direct analogies to be made with *Inferno* (which certainly influenced Hesse), for instance the neurosis of hotel living, but of course the persecution mania is less frenzied in Hesse than in Strindberg and the scatological obsessions are absent; *Spa Visitor*, though it is by no means gentle, lacks the matchless misanthropy of *Inferno*.[19] Humor is the solvent for the agony of outsiderdom here, as it is in the major novel, and the rituals of spa life are viewed comically as a banalization of religious exercises: "I had wanted to achieve by the way of penance, punishment, and good works, bathing and washing, doctors and Brahman magic, what can only be achieved by the way of grace" (IV, 103–104). Burlesqued though it is in this case, the association of bathing and washing with spiritual exercises points to a significant symbolic motif in Hesse's later novels. *Spa Visitor*, to sum up, may be regarded as a rather wry discourse upon the futility of good works as well as an aggressive attack, in the footsteps, though scarcely the mood, of *Siddhartha*, upon the curse of the intellect.

The rather slighter *Nuremberg Journey* takes up once more the question of the nature of humor, debates the justification of literature in this modern age, expresses horror of technology, and may be summed up as a commentary, both overt and oblique, upon the

[18] "Yes, just as fate and the feeling self were names for one and the same concept" (IV, 17). Recent major studies of Hesse (Ziolkowski and Rose) have indicated the important debt to Romantic writers—Novalis, Jean Paul, and also Hoffmann—discernible in both themes and forms of *The Steppenwolf*.

[19] Hesse reviewed the German translation of *Inferno* (Berlin, 1919) in *Vivos Voco*, I (1919–1920), 270.

incapacity for naïve experience, the chronic condition of self-observation which the author constates in himself, whether this be
incipient "contemplation," the *sine quâ non* of self-development, or
merely sickness, schizophrenia. Of the *Nuremberg Journey*, Hesse
wrote later that it had been composed "in a critical and often
virulent period of my life, when catharsis by means of *The Steppenwolf* had not yet been achieved." [20]

The pessimism, aggression, and self-denigration of this period are
most acutely caught in the remarkable collection of poems entitled *Crisis*, original confessional literature which, though crude at
times, is astonishingly strong.[21] The *Crisis* poems certainly provide
a rich fund of material for the psychoanalyst's casebook; when the
work appeared, as Hesse wrote to his future wife, the despair
which had given rise to it was already past [22]—*The Steppenwolf* was
already finished. The link between the poems and the novel is
extremely intimate.[23] The poems, Hesse said, dealt with "the misery
and despair of physical life" [24]—itself a very Halleresque theme.
Crisis reflects a desperate and vain effort to drown the corrosive,
cauterizing intellect in sensual experience, the blur of wine and
dancing, perhaps above all the former; Harry Haller stands "in the
sign of Aquarius, a dark and damp sign" (IV, 202), and *Crisis* adds:

> Ich will zum Wassermann und zu den Fischen
> Und heim in das gewohnte Elend gehen.[25]

[20] *Letters* (VII, 932).
[21] *Krisis: Ein Stück Tagebuch* (Berlin, 1928). There were 1,150 copies, of
which 1,000 were put on the market. Hesse's uneasiness about the degree of self-
exposure in these quite untypical poems is evident in that the majority (and
many of the best) were not reprinted. A number appeared in the *Neue
Rundschau*, XXXVII (1926), 509–521, under the title "Der Steppenwolf: Ein
Stück Tagebuch in Versen," and also as "Aus einem lyrischen Tagebuch" in
the *Neue Schweizer Rundschau*, XX (1927), 625–627. Some were even thought
harmless enough to find their way into *Trost der Nacht* (Berlin, 1929) and the
later *Gesammelte Gedichte*. See also *Gesammelte Schriften*, V, 688–702. The
original volume is now rare.
[22] Cf. *Letters* (VII, 478).
[23] "A new dance, a foxtrot," writes Harry Haller, "called 'Yearning' con-
quered the world that winter" (IV, 363). The use of the word "that" (*jenem*)
inadvertently destroys the immediacy of Harry's journal and reaches the true
standpoint of retrospect and hindsight occupied by the author.
[24] *Letters* (VII, 572).
[25] "Nach dem Abend im Hirschen," *Krisis*, p. 18 (also V, 689).

(I go to Aquarius and to the fish
And home as always to my misery.)

The poem "Missglückter Abend" [26] recounts almost exactly that
same incident which is made a pivotal point of *The Steppenwolf*—
the visit to the professor's house. Harry Haller's maddened hatred
of the bourgeoisie and of their sham religiosity is reflected in the
story of the master baker who runs the poet down in his car and is
himself killed but of course goes to Heaven (as the poet does not),
for he is a Catholic.[27] There is a sarcastic detachment from the new
self-knowledge and the poet's erstwhile guru, Dr. Lang,[28] while the
theme of the profligate sounds strongly:

> Rot blüht die Blume der Lust,
> Rosig lächelt die Knospe auf deiner Brust,
> Schaudert bebend unter meiner Zunge.
> Einst war ich ein kleiner Junge,
> Lernte Griechisch und ging zur Konfirmation,
> Eines frommen Vaters vielversprechender Sohn.[29]

> (Red blooms the flower of desire,
> Rosy is the smiling bud upon your breast,
> It shudders trembling beneath my tongue.
> Once I was a little boy,
> Learned Greek and went to confirmation,
> A devout father's promising son.)

But the Promising Son became the Prodigal Son, the criminal, the
masochist, the potential sex-murderer:

> Ich bin heraus aus eurem Garten gebrochen,[30]
> Schweife flackernd umher in der Wildnis,
> Noch verfolgt und gequält von jenem Jugendbildnis,
> Das ich mich mühe zu tilgen und langsam zu morden.
> Vielleicht morde ich's, Mädchen, in deiner Seele.
> Vielleicht, noch eh' diese Stunde der Lust verglüht,
> Drück' ich die Hände um deine zuckende Kehle.

[26] *Krisis*, p. 15.
[27] "Besoffener Dichter," *ibid.*, p. 73.
[28] "Abend mit Dr. Ling," *ibid.*, p. 51.
[29] "Der Wüstling," *ibid.*, p. 62 (also V, 695).
[30] Cf. Gide in *Le Retour de l'enfant prodigue;* there is here a similar contrast
between garden within and desert without.

(I have broken out of your garden,
Errant I roam in the wilderness,
Still pursued and tormented by that picture of youth
Which I struggle to erase and slowly to murder.
Perhaps, my sweet, I will murder it in your soul,
Perhaps, before this hour of pleasure fades
My hands will press around your quivering throat.)

The Prodigal is constantly referred to in these poems:

> Nun ziehe ich vor, gleich dem verlorenen Sohn
> Brüderlich zwischen den Schweinen zu sitzen [31]

> (Now I prefer, like the Prodigal Son,
> To sit in brotherhood with the swine.)

He even appears in conspicuous association with another notable figure:

> Legen Sie ab Ihre werte Persönlichkeit
> Und wählen Sie sich als Abendkleid
> Eine beliebige Inkarnation,
> Den Don Juan oder den verlorenen Sohn [32]

> (Discard your worthy personality
> And for your evening suit select
> Any old incarnation,
> Don Juan perhaps or the Prodigal Son.)

The wall which separates the poet from the universe must be pierced, the open cosmos is the world of the Immortals, the great sinners:

> Und hinübertreten zu den grossen
> Sündern . . .[33]

> (And to cross over to the great sinners . . .)

The way into "starry space" may be through crucifixion, but then the note of scepticism typical of *Crisis* intrudes:

[31] *Krisis*, p. 61.
[32] *Ibid.*, p. 49.
[33] "Ahnungen," *ibid*, p. 67 (also "Gewissen" [V, 694]).

Aber diese kühlen Sternenräume,
Diese Schauer der Unendlichkeit
Sind ja leider nur geliebte Träume.

(But these cool starry spaces,
These shivers of eternity,
I'm afraid they're just beloved dreams.)

"Am Ende" repeats the words of *Spa Visitor*, the sounding of the retreat:

Packe meinen Koffer, fahr' zurück
In die Steppe, denn es gilt zu sterben.[34]

(Pack my case and travel back
To the steppe, for there's dying to be done.)

For *Crisis* has none of the optimism of the novel itself; it mixes pessimistic longing for extinction with masochistic contempt, and all under the supreme sign of blasphemy. It reflects:

Wer des Lebens Wonnen kennt
Mag das Maul sich lecken.
Ausserdem ist uns vergönnt
Morgen zu verrecken.[35]

(He who knows life's pleasure
Can slobber at his leisure.
We've another grace as well:
Tomorrow we can go to hell.)

This sums up the mood. The depression is in truth partly anchored in physical despair, in the pains and frustrations of middle age.[36]

Harry Haller is Hermann Hesse's "fifty-year-old man"; Hesse made the association with Goethe's novella of that name quite consciously: "The 'fifty-year-old man' has little reason to collect congratulations."[37] Harry harps upon his age, his physical decline;

---

[34] *Krisis*, p. 79.

[35] "Zu Johannes dem Täufer/Sprach Hermann der Säufer," *ibid.*, p. 25.

[36] Hesse suggests that this is a reason for the constant misinterpretation of *The Steppenwolf*, especially by young people. Cf. VII, 413.

[37] "Nachwort an meine Freunde," in *Krisis*, p. 81.

his proposal to cut his throat is compared with Adalbert Stifter's act. This note is by no means new; in "Aus dem Tagebuch eines Wüstlings" (1922–1923) it is sounded strongly: "Aging as I am," groans the diarist, "I dissipate my days like a student." [38] Perhaps the most intensely personal of all Hesse's imaginative creations, there is in Harry something of almost all this author's previous protagonists, Peter Camenzind's Rousseauism, Hans Giebenrath's morbid regression, Knulp's introverted vagabondage, Klingsor's frenzy, and Klein's decadent self-crucifixion on the cross of introspection.

The Neo-Romantic issue of the justification of the artist has evolved into the question of the justification of the psychopath: "whether in certain historical and cultural circumstances it is not more important, nobler and more right to become a psychopath than to accommodate oneself to these circumstances by sacrificing all one's ideals." [39] As the tractate points out, those who begin to perceive the true nature of their own ego are frequently locked up by the majority as schizophrenics. The characteristics of the outsider may often seem identical with those of the psychopath, or those of the artist, or those of the genius *per se*. The lone wolf artist is a well-known type with particular advantages over those of his colleagues who are *engagés*, but many lone wolves lack special artistic gifts, they have only "a plus in mind and imagination, a capacity for experience, for empathy, for resonance." Such individuals are those in whom the highest possibilities of humanity are periodically realized, they justify the vanity and the waywardness of genius. One day, confronted by a call which they cannot respond to in any other manner, they immolate themselves and thus become saints: "These are they who truly love, the saints." [40] The outsider is therefore justified in the last resort because he is a potential saint, and we see that his goal is decreed by his origins, is perhaps innate in the Pietism of Calw.

Hesse's fifty-year-old man bemoans the loss of his youth, his poetry, his ideals; now he is bitterly involved in "the crisis in a man's life around his fiftieth year." [41] He has gout in his fingers,

[38] *Simplicissimus*, XXVII (1922–1923), 19.
[39] *Spa Visitor* (IV, 58).
[40] *Letters* (VII, 719).
[41] *Letters* (VII, 545).

his walk is that of a sick man. The bourgeois narrator, proud of his own healthy instincts, is inclined at first to dislike Harry, suspicious of his manner, his style of life, his fear of the police; he concludes from the mobility and sensitivity of his features that he is "a genius of suffering" (IV, 193), as Nietzsche was. A gifted intellectual, disillusioned with men, sad at their insincerity, their pretention, and their histrionics, Harry has habits which are very much those of his type: he has no regular work, sleeps late, lives in a room stamped with eclecticism and chock full of symbolic miscellanea—photographs of home, a Siamese Buddha, a reproduction of Michelangelo's "La Notte," a picture of Mahatma Gandhi, a whole library of eighteenth-century literature including the memorable *Sophiens Reise von Memel nach Sachsen*, a well-thumbed Goethe, Novalis [42] and Jean Paul, volumes of Dostoevsky, of Baudelaire, the odor of cigars, empty Chianti bottles.

Not only are his eating habits irregular and his digestion bad— he is "an evening man" (*Abendmensch*, punning the prefix "Abend—" in its sense of "Western")—but the drinking is evidently central, as one might expect of a budding saint, especially in the era of the author of *Crisis*, "Hermann the Tippler." The "old-style tavern" (IV, 216) which he frequents is a hideaway for crusty, nostalgic, and would-be bachelors, "lonely lads like me who'd gone off the rails" (IV, 217). The word "lad" is quite enough here to summon up Peter Camenzind, and it is no surprise to find that Harry's taste is for "light, modest local wines without particular names" (IV, 217). Later on in the book we have it again: "Dear to me was my hard seat, my peasant glass" (IV, 353); there is a romantic atmosphere reminiscent of Harry's boyhood where inn, wine, and cigar were still forbidden delights. Those youths Peter and Emil, as may have been suspected, were bourgeois after all! They too suffered, it is true, from melancholia, and between their headaches and hangovers had but a few tolerable days; they

---

[42] In 1925 there appeared *Novalis: Dokumente seines Lebens und Sterbens*, eds. Hermann Hesse and Karl Isenberg. In his postscript to the edition Hesse describes the work of this poet as "the strangest and most mysterious . . . in the history of the German mind" (VII, 282). *Spa Visitor* also discloses the revival of interest in Novalis at this period in Hesse's career—as also Jean Paul, to whose writings *The Steppenwolf* makes direct allusion (IV, 218). Cf. T. J. Ziolkowski, "Hermann Hesse and Novalis" (diss. Yale University, 1957).

too had talked themselves into their loneliness, as Harry into his; but still they were both *young* tipplers, both had their teachers and helpers, some sort of providential guidance or at any rate the remains of a poetic youthful faith in themselves. But this fifty-year-old man has used up all his placebos; demanding absolute freedom, he has all but obtained it. The iron justice of the *Märchen*, of which genre Harry's life is in some sense a parody, has him in its vice— what he longs for he gets, but "more than is good for human beings" (IV, 230); the "magic wish" (IV, 231), once wished, cannot be taken back; as Hesse's protagonists all learn: "There is no way back at all" (IV, 249). In the inn, under the wine, the rich memories flood in; memory alone—the aesthetic experience and its recall— seems to make the Steppenwolf's existence valid: "Who still thought"—in this treeless novel, at any rate— "of that tough little cypress high on the hill above Gubbio? . . . The Steppenwolf did" (IV, 219).

The Steppenwolf is a novel of the city (either Zurich or Basel)— although Harry does live in a garden suburb, this is scarcely evoked at all. His is the sharp and intolerable loneliness of the city streets; he has found that he cannot have community, not any more, however much he may desire it. People may not dislike him actively— indeed, he casts a certain spell to which the aunt and later her nephew, the bourgeois narrator succumb—but they all avoid him. He knows full well, as a partly awakened man, that it is hopeless for one like him ever to try to fulfill the demands and obey the commands of society.[43] For him there is only the coldness—and the wondrous silence—of absolute loneliness, "wonderfully still and great like the cold, still space in which the stars revolve" (IV, 220).

With this there sets in the imagery of the cosmos, later to be developed so richly in what can be called the main section of the novel, that is, that part of "Harry Haller's Notes" which follows the tractate. These memoirs are "only for madmen"; nothing in them is quite on the level of reality of the prosaic introduction. But there are several levels of reality in *The Steppenwolf*. The tractate also, and the Magic Theater, are "only for madmen"—the latter, in the reflection of the illuminated sign on the asphalt, being "only—for—mad—men!" (IV, 215). *Ver-rückung* ("de-range-

[43] Cf. "In Memoriam Christoph Schrempf" (IV, 773).

ment")—this is the process by which the novel proceeds from the
real to the superreal: to receive the message of the Magic Theater
one must be "crazy . . . and far removed from 'everyman' " (IV,
258).

At the end of the first movement, if we follow the musical analogy, comes the tractate, a summing up constituting the chief attempt in Hesse's entire work at a theoretical statement of the nature
of his protagonists' conflict with society and its conventions, with
the bourgeois outlook. The bourgeois narrator, in the introduction,
shows us Harry from the outside, recalls his ambivalent first impression of the Steppenwolf, the latter's tristful features at the
celebrity lecture at the Aula, their encounter on the stairs where
Harry sits entranced before the potted araucaria, the symphony
concert at which the Steppenwolf seems transported by a work of
Friedemann Bach. The bourgeois narrator is himself a type, portrayed with a certain dry objectivity, his satirical potential scarcely
explored; in comparison with him, the author of the tractate is
clearly of a totally different origin. Harry compares his own
poem

"I, the Steppenwolf, trot and trot . . ." [44]

with its significant mixture of aging weariness and blood lust, with
the tractate, and finds the former a sad, subjective picture, whereas the latter is a cool analysis, "seen from without and above," composed by "one who stands outside" (IV, 253), outside the charmed
circle of introversion, an Immortal, as one presumes. Thus it
seems to him, but in fact, of course, the author of the tractate sees
Harry not from without but from within, the voice is the voice
of his "friend," the higher reflective self, the "invisible magician"
(IV, 258). He speaks to Harry rather as the Armenian astrologer
speaks to Klingsor, though more sharply; what he relates is not the
socially conditioned observation of the bourgeois but the truth of
an esoteric gospel. Thus the tractate is on a different level from
the introduction, and is written in a different style, self-assured in
its diagnosis and coolly ironical.

The world of the bourgeoisie is etched in in its contrasts with

[44] Cf. also the same poem, entitled "Steppenwolf," in *Krisis*, p. 34 (also V,
692–693).

Harry's world by the employment of symbols of cleanliness and order; when Harry first enters the aunt's house he sniffs appreciatively—"Oh, here it smells nice" (IV, 186). This nasal reference, like others—"I stood for a minute sniffing" (IV, 221),—points to that ubiquitous specter, the wolf; the various allusions to teeth throughout the novel are also signs of the omnipresence of the beast. The two cleaned and dusted plant pots on the landing which contain the araucaria (or *"Kinderbaum"!*) and the azalea are pillars of a bourgeois temple; in this house Harry finds "a superlative of bourgeois cleanliness, care, and precision, dutifulness and fidelity in small things" (IV, 197), all that he could possibly want, things he both loves and needs, for his mother was a bourgeoise. It seems that the Steppenwolf loves the bourgeois world as he says he does, without any irony; however, Harry, having neither family life nor social ambition, also regards this bourgeois sphere with a good deal of contempt, although he cannot do without it, has money in the bank and supports his relatives, dresses discreetly and respectably, tries to live at peace with the tax office. He is willy-nilly drawn by a "strong, secret longing for the small world of the bourgeoisie" (IV, 235), he lives in the province of the burghers, and all that he does stands in some relationship to them, be it only one of revolt. Dwelling in such clean middle class homes is, he thinks, simply "an old sentimentality of mine" (IV, 210).

The tractate censures him for this cowardice; for those with some understanding of the teaching of Gotama Buddha it is absurd and unforgivable to live in a world "in which common sense [Hesse uses the English expression], democracy, and bourgeois culture rule" (IV, 251). This is to serve false gods—an idea expressed vividly years before *The Steppenwolf* in "The Hiking Trip" (1920): "You cannot be a vagabond and an artist and at the same time a bourgeois and a respectable, healthy person. You want the ecstasy, so you have to take the hangover" (III, 409). The tractate points out, and the Steppenwolf later comes to understand, the concealed and shabby compromises and philosophical inanities on which the life of Harry Haller has so far been founded; educated in a *petit bourgeois* milieu, he has prejudices against prostitutes, thieves, and revolutionaries, as Friedrich Klein had.

The tractate proceeds to a normative definition of the term

"bourgeois": "The 'bourgeois,' as a permanently existing condition
of man, is nothing else but the attempt at an equilibrium, the
striving for a balanced middle position between the countless extremes and antithetical poles of human conduct" (IV, 236). Characteristically, the author of the tractate selects saint and profligate as
his exemplary pair, and sets up a typological model. A man can
choose between devotion (*Hingabe*) to the aspirations of the saint
or else to the drives of the senses, he may elect to martyr his instincts or his spirit; between both poles stands the bourgeois, characterized above all by the wish not to surrender his own ego to
anything at all but to contain it, appalled by the postulates of any
kind of ethical absolutism. Intense experience is only possible at
some cost to his ego, rudimentary though this ego may be. Here
and there the Nietzschean tone is unmistakable; Harry has to learn
"that 'man' is not something already completed, but a challenge of
the spirit" (IV, 247): bourgeois are all weak and fearful creatures,
a herd of lambs who survive solely because of the vitality of the
Steppenwolfs amongst them.

These "wild ones" are the prisoners of the bourgeoisie, held to
it by "infantile feelings" (IV, 238); the reverse of the act of
transcendence is, as we have seen before, infantile regression. The
dominant cosmic imagery leads to an analogy between the bourgeoisie and Mother Earth, for the tractate speaks of "the heavy maternal planet of the bourgeoisie" (IV, 239), which is then contrasted
with "soaring into free, wild cosmic space" (IV, 239). The author
of "The Hiking Trip" remarks that he is partial to neurotic extremes and dislikes the golden mean, what Harry calls contemptuously "comfortable room temperature" (IV, 209). Unable quite to
achieve sainthood, despite breathing exercises and the rest, Harry's
ascetic impulse shows its fundamental masochism, turns him into a
potential suicide, an assassin of his own ego. His aggression upon
the outside world is in reality only self-destruction, encompassed
by symbols of lupine savagery, blood, and murder. Even the act
of eating has the bestial nuance (cf. IV, 217). Or of another act,
as we have it in *Crisis:* "Blood blooms in bed." [45] In fact, it is not to
be denied that murder lies in the pun which stands at the very
opening of Harry's journal (*herumgebracht/umgebracht*). In

[45] "Der Wüstling."

Harry's polemics against the bourgeois world, the language is always harsh, ugly and shrill, full of ill-contained violence: "Those bad days of inner emptiness and despair, in which, in the middle of an earth destroyed and sucked dry by joint-stock companies, the world of men and so-called civilization grins at us at every step in its concealed and debased rubbishy fair-ground luster like an emetic, concentrated and intensified to the peak of intolerableness in our own sick ego" (IV, 208).

By and large Hesse attributes to two megalomanias, that of technological progress and that of nationalism, the present condition of man.[46] He regarded it as his life's work to help defend the individual existence against the threat of mechanization. That new invention, the radio, of which the technologists are so proud, merely causes Harry to think of the ancient Indians, who knew all about ubiquity and uchronicity; the relativity of space and time is no new discovery. In any case, Hesse's community of Romantic castaways, infantilists all, are not really hostile to the railway and the automobile so much as to "the forgetting of God and the trivialization of the soul." In that they have faith in something real, they have perhaps more genuine hope and longing for the future than do the "devout apostles of progress"[47]—and he thinks amicably of Knut Hamsun (though perhaps he should have thought rather of Naphta in *The Magic Mountain*). In *The Steppenwolf*, Romantic aggression is turned particularly against the automobile, a neurosis which was prefigured in *The Nuremberg Journey* (IV, 175).

Cars and the death-wish are closely associated. The Catholic master-baker in *Crisis*, transcendental in his smugness, reappears in just this context in "Dream Traces"[48] in the same year as *The Steppenwolf*: "It could happen that the automobile of one of the lords of this world, a newspaper publisher or a rich master baker, might run over him at a street corner" (IV, 423). In the novel itself we hear of these pseudo-Christians, "the taciturn business-faces of these merchants and master bakers" (IV, 260)—the subject was clearly much on Hesse's mind. Eventually, in the Magic Theater,

[46] Cf. "Expression of Thanks and Moralizing Reflections" (1946; VII, 457).
[47] "Madonna d'Ongero" (III, 891).
[48] "Dream Traces" itself appeared under the title of "Inner Experience" ("Inneres Erlebnis") in *Die Horen*, III (1927), 11–20.

Harry Haller dreams his automobile hunt, a war to the death between man and machine. In the company of his boyhood friend
Gustav, who has subsequently become a professor of theology but
is now glad to exchange this role for one of actual violence, the
pacifist Steppenwolf commits mayhem among carowners. Harry's
meditation that such insane actions as theirs may help to re-ennoble
a life reduced to cliché by the American and Bolshevik rationali-
zations is disposed of by the pragmatic Gustav as "a bit too dreamy"
(IV, 383). The pretty prisoner, Dora the secretary, gets kissed on
the knee, and this gesture leads on to a Freudian fall in which the
dream concludes.

Satire of the bourgeoisie, of its twentieth-century hypostasis in
technology, and of the outside world in general is but an inverted
form of attack upon the self. All comes back to the critical contemplation of the ego, the tormenting of the libidinous will. Even
the bourgeois narrator is under no illusions as to the origins of it
all in Harry: "[he] was brought up by strict and very devout parents and teachers according to that approach which makes the
'breaking of the will' the basis of education. . . . Instead of erasing
his personality this had merely succeeded in teaching him to hate
himself" (IV, 193); self-hatred, indeed is the Steppenwolf's form
of piety, his Christianity. Harry's disgust when he witnesses the
sanctimonious sham of a funeral ceremony sends him on one of his
meaningless peregrinations through the gray streets of the city.
Meeting a youngish professor of his acquaintance, an orientalist,
Harry accepts an invitation for that evening, a folly which, as he
shaves himself morosely, leads him to meditate upon all the
mechanical functions of life which protect men from self-insight
and upon the social activities which cannot mean anything to him,
"as if I still belonged to that delightful childlike world of eternal
play" (IV, 265). The social life, the elegant life, the life of the
theaters, bars, and cafés is a frivolous, childish game from which
wolves are by definition excluded. As for the professor, he is
satirized as an example of the devoted scholar half buried from
reality, understanding nothing of the great changes, such as the war
and the theory of relativity, which have recently overturned the
whole world. Worse, he is a chauvinist. He abuses a publicist name-
sake (as he thinks) of Harry's, "that traitor Haller" (IV, 267), who

had ridiculed Kaiser Wilhelm and blamed Germany for the war. His wife possesses an appalling portrait of the older Goethe, thoroughly *embourgeoisé.* All this arouses in Harry the "Steppenwolf with grinning fangs" (IV, 268); sick and feeling his age, Harry hits out, predicts with bitter anguish the approach of another war brought on by the chauvinists, and confesses that he himself is the aforesaid treacherous publicist—having first of all angrily deplored the disgraceful treatment that Goethe has received at the hands of the portraitist. It is of special note that he declares his interest in things oriental, in Krishna and such antiquarian rubbish, long since at an end.

His precipitate departure from his host's house is no triumph, however, but rather a retreat and a flight. The imagery now becomes characteristically physiological and violent: "I had taken my leave of my former world and home, of middle-class life, propriety and learning, just as a man with a stomach ulcer takes his leave of roast pork" (IV, 271). He apologizes for his behavior—after all, he is a schizophrenic.

The poem "Missglückter Abend" tells us of this dismal withdrawal:

> Traurig bin ich davongezogen,
> Um irgendwo ein kleines Mädchen zu kaufen,
> Das nicht Klavier spielt und sich nicht für Kunst interessiert.

> (Sadly did I take my leave,
> To go and buy a little girl somewhere,
> One who doesn't play the piano and has no interest in art.)

Harry's escape from the professor's house onto the dark streets of the city is a total victory for the wolf in him. The typical act of flight, the rush to suicide, which, however, ends in the beginnings of enlightenment, the encounter with Hermine—these features may even recall Siddhartha's flight from Kamala. But in this case the flight is *to* woman. Encounter with the "shadow" (that is, the wolf) is but the first stage in a Jungian analysis, is the approach to something deeper, the anima. There is thus a sense in which the escape may be compared more closely with Siddhartha's flight from the Samanas and from his "shadow" Govinda. Harry finds his way to a dive, The Black Eagle, and there he discovers his *dame aux camélias;* she does indeed wear the appropriate flower and she has moreover certain appropriate additional qualities—"She was indeed like a mama with me" (IV, 279). The bourgeois Harry, the compromising Harry, appears finally to have been torn to pieces by the wolf; what Hermine, "the wonderful friend" (IV, 290), has to offer is of course neither the Way of the bourgeois nor the Way of the wolf, but some third Way, that which leads to the Third Kingdom of the Spirit. Of Hermine, Harry says: "She was the little window, the tiny light aperture in my dark cave of fear. She was redemption, the way outside" (IV, 294). The imagery is familiar; Harry the outsider is outside all walls except that which he has built around himself.

A situation of considerable complexity obtains here. The "wolf" is defined in the tractate as "a dark world of instincts, of savagery, cruelty, unsublimated, raw nature" (IV, 242). The tractate chides Harry for the crude mythology in which he divides himself into "man" and "wolf," points out that the wolf, though healthy, is also no ideal savage, but has his longings and his sufferings just as the child has his: "There is no way back at all, neither to the wolf nor to the child" (IV, 249).[49] Clearly the "wolf," in one of his aspects, is the Jungian "shadow," the "inferior self," which "stands, so to speak, on the threshold of the way to the "Mothers," to the collective unconscious."[50] Harry makes the mistake of idealizing those impulses he also consciously represses, this is the source of much of his sickness. But the meaning of the wolf is scarcely exhausted by these explanations; Harry Haller's is an inverted world, and the fearsome wolf with his teeth and his blood lust is not only Wagner, but in a sense is also his opposite, Klein. For the wolf is the instrument of masochism (it is the wolf who tears to pieces the "bourgeois man" in Harry); and the masochist is the frustrated saint. Thus the wolf may be seen in his inverted aspect as a terrible perversion of the Pietist's will-to-God, his rending of Harry Haller as a satanic variant of the struggle to destroy the Natural Man;

---

[49] Cf. again in "On the Soul": "Not back to the child, the primitive . . ." (VII, 72).

[50] J. Jacobi, *The Psychology of C. G. Jung*, p. 146. Jacobi notes specifically (p. 144) that Hesse's *Steppenwolf* is an example of the artistic use of the shadow motif.

he is, maybe, the repressed world of the mother, but he is also a bestialization of the demands of the father in Harry's heart. In his savaging of Harry, the bourgeois, he tends to represent not one extreme, but *the* extreme.

Harry's error in dividing himself, in his own imagination, into only two is of course a baneful crudification of the richness and subtlety of human nature. It has been remarked before that this reveals a Lutheran heritage in the novel;[51] the tractate points emphatically to original sin—"all created things, even the apparently most simple, are already guilty" (IV, 249). Harry's meeting with Hermine might therefore for this reason also be called his escape from the Samanas, from the clutches of asceticism. Hesse's writings are full of commentaries upon that condition of consciousness in which there are two I's, an observing and an observed: "In each one of us there are two I's, and whoever could know where the one begins and the other ends would be infinitely wise." First of all there is "our subjective, empirical, individual I," and then a second I not fully separated from the first: "This second, lofty, sacred I . . . is not personal, but is our part in God, in life, in the whole, in the unpersonal and the superpersonal."[52] In practice a distinction must be made, and indeed emerges quite clearly from Hesse's writings, between the genuine moment of enlightenment, self-centered detachment, and the obsessive self-observation of the decadent for whom naïve experience is but a dream. In the former case everything falls into place, for there are differences of level; in the latter everything jars, for all is on the same level. Harry's stupid error of dividing himself into ego and id—"the fairy tale of the wolf" (IV, 251)—the secondary delusion that the personality is dualistic whereas it is manifold, this derives from the primary delusion that the personality is a unity. All make this mistake, which is caused largely by the apparent oneness and permanence of the body; here the classical drama with its unity of character contrasts with the ancient Indian epic, the heroes of which are "not characters but groups of characters, successive incarnations" (IV, 245). Modern authors frequently portray uncon-

[51] Anni Carlsson, "Vom Steppenwolf zur Morgenlandfahrt," in Hugo Ball, *Hermann Hesse*, p. 252.
[52] *Letters* (VII, 635–636).

sciously the same disunity of the personality, their characters being fragments of a higher unity—"if you like, the writer's own
soul" (IV, 245). Here the author of the tractate mentions *Faust* and
may also have had *Peer Gynt* in mind, for he compares the personality to an onion. I's succeed each other in time, moments of
transformation occur in which whole selves are sloughed off, each
change triggered by a moment of self-confrontation. The Steppenwolf knows this as Siddhartha did, but he finds it an agonizing process from which he would fain escape forever; he is afraid to look
in a mirror, he maneuvres to avoid this very self-confrontation.[53]
Only suicide offers him the hope of achieving his aim permanently.

Immortality, says the tractate, can be hoped for only through
nonattachment and through "eternal surrender of the ego
to metamorphosis" (IV, 248). It is just this sacrifice of the will of
which the Steppenwolf is incapable. To go on living seems to him
quixotic; suicide constantly hovers therefore before him, now
nearer now farther, as the only way out. The bourgeois narrator,
observing Harry's habits, remarks with unconscious irony that he
is leading "the life of a suicide" (IV, 203). In fact for one of his
type suicide is quite clearly the ultimate form of inverted aggression,
and a total surrender to the delusions of Maya besides. Like Siddhartha and like Klein, Harry must know that suicide "is after all
only a rather shabby and illegitimate emergency exit" (IV, 233),
but nevertheless he sets his fiftieth birthday as the day on which to
decide whether to kill himself, and when he meets Hermine he had

[53] The highly important mirror motif (and the related motif of reflection in
water) occurs—as has been shown—in almost all Hesse's major works. It happens that it is also inseparable from the problematics of Goethe's novella *Der
Mann von fünfzig Jahren*. Goethe's Major imagines he is experiencing "the
return of spring," and yet, when he stands before a mirror, he is most dissatisfied with his appearance and is persuaded to undertake a course of facial
and general physical rejuvenation. Cf. here "Bei der Toilette":

> "Einst war das Auge klar, die Stirne licht,
> Wange und Lippe lachender und weicher,
> Da braucht ich Puder und Pomade nicht"
> (*Krisis*, p. 40; also V, 700).

> (Once my eye was clear, my brow was light,
> Cheeks and lips more laughing and more soft,
> Then I needed neither powder nor pomade.)

in mind to hasten the deed that selfsame night. Psychologically all this is acutely enough observed.[54]

The treatment of suicide throughout Hesse's work offers an intriguing pattern; a clue to it all may be found where it occurs in "Child's Soul." In his bitter desperation the little fig thief wishes he were dead: "One ought to take poison, that would be best, or hang oneself" (III, 442); then this is transformed into the kindred impulse toward an act of externally orientated violence, "something horrible but liberating" (III, 443), revenge on the world, to set fire to the house, or—to kill his father. Suddenly Franz Kromer is conjured up before us, offering the knife to Emil Sinclair; worse the awful specter of schoolmaster Wagner butchering his whole family, and his pupil Klein about to stab the sleeping Teresina ("Child's Soul" was written in January 1919, in Basel; "Klein and Wagner" in May-June of the same year, in Tessin; the two works certainly have much in common, especially the main theme—theft— and the bloodthirsty undertones). Govinda's vision included a murder and the execution of the criminal, and so also the boy in "Child's Soul" visualizes his own execution and his Cain-like glorying in his crime. "Der Wüstling," in *Crisis*, takes up the theme again, as does "Sterbelied des Dichters": [55]

> Liege bei den jungen Weibern,
> Reibe meinen Leib an ihren Leibern,
> Kriege sie satt und drücke ihnen die Gurgel zu,
> Dann kommt der Henker und bringt auch mich zur Ruh.

> (I lie with the young women,
> Rub my body on theirs,
> Tire of them and throttle them,
> Then the hangman comes and quiets me too.)

Thematically, these aggressive dreams are manifestly linked with childhood experience, and that such notions play so significant a part in Harry's imaginative life is striking confirmation of the

---

[54] "But anyone who refuses to experience life must stifle his desire to live—in other words he must commit partial suicide. This explains the death-fantasies that usually accompany the renunciation of desire" (Jung, *Symbols of Transformation*, p. 110).

[55] *Krisis*, p. 10.

sources of his neurosis. As late as the second "autobiography" in
The Glass Bead Game, "The Father Confessor," we find a condemnation of the idea of suicide as the work of the Devil (VI, 615).

In *The Steppenwolf* the firm resolution to cease being "the noble
Don Quixote" (IV, 256) and to kill himself, sends the hero to bed
in a calmed state of mind:

> At the ultimate instant, however, at the final limit of consciousness, in the
> moment of going to sleep, that curious section of the Steppenwolf
> pamphlet flashed before me, where it speaks of the "Immortals," and with
> this was linked with a sudden start the memory that I had often and
> indeed quite recently felt myself near enough to the Immortals to
> experience with them in a bar of old music the entire, cool, bright, hard
> smile of the Immortals' wisdom. This rose up, gleamed, died away, and
> sleep laid itself as heavy as a mountain on my brow [IV, 256].

The second-long lightning flash of memory, of recalled aesthetic
experience, is a moment of awakening alongside the intention of
suicide; it is a close parallel to Siddhartha's recollection of *"Om,"*
as he bends suicidally over the water, and like that it is at once
followed by sleep "heavy as a mountain"—*Tiefschlaf*. In Harry's
case this does not rescue him at once from the threat of self-murder,
but it points to the source from which salvation is to come. In the
tractate there is a discourse on that whole class of people [56] who
are designated "suicides," whether or not they ever lay hands upon
themselves; they are those who live constantly exposed at the edge
of existence in a sense of imminent danger, "on the narrowest of
rock pinnacles" (IV, 232), Romantic at root, "inflicted with the
guilt feelings of individuation" (IV, 232), longing for the mother,
yearning to be reabsorbed into the universal flow. When Pablo
enjoins Harry to commit "a little sham suicide" (IV, 371) as a
necessary preface to entering the Magic Theater, suicide has become a figure for the sacrifice of self-delusion prior to descent into
the soul. The death-wish, indeed, is intimately connected with
something else, with *"Om,"* with enlightenment.

Such moments are defined by the author of the tractate, in a
central passage, as containing the real meaning of the Steppenwolf's

---

[56] In "Aus einem Tagebuch des Jahres 1920," Hesse talks of the various
journals he is writing or should write. One should be "a suicide's journal" (*op.
cit.*, p. 195).

life: "Even in this man's life it seemed at times as if all the ordinary, everyday, well-known, and regular things merely had the function of undergoing a second-long pause, of being interrupted and giving way to the extraordinary, to miracles, to grace" (IV, 228). This is "the froth of the happiness of the moment," "precious fleeting froth of happiness," it elevates a man for an instant so high above his fate "that his happiness shines like a star" (IV, 228). Harry Haller remembers that moment of bliss which the bourgeois narrator, at the concert, had observed from without:

> I had flown through Heaven and seen God at his work, had suffered blissful agonies and no longer struggled against anything in the world, no longer feared anything in the world, had affirmed all things, surrendered my heart to all things. It hadn't lasted long, perhaps a quarter of an hour, but that night it had returned in my dreams and since then, through all the barren days, it had occasionally secretly flashed out again, sometimes I saw it clearly for minutes pass like a golden, divine trace through my life [IV, 212].

There are the expected figures here from religious poetry—flying through the heavens, for instance. The color gold, in association here—as in 1913—with music, is evidently an epithet for the experience of the awakened soul. For the religious source of the epithet we must turn to the scene in which Harry takes Hermine's head in his hands and kisses her on the brow; as he does this the sunlight plays on the golden inscriptions on the spines of his books [57] and recalls what she has just said about the communion of saints: "this was formerly portrayed by the painters in a golden sky" (IV, 346). And we may note yet another account: "By happiness I understand something quite objective, that is: the totality itself, timeless being, the eternal music of the world, what others have called the harmony of the spheres or the smile of God. This essence, this endless music, this full-ringing and gold-gleaming eternity is pure and perfect presence." [58] From the delighted moment of 1913,

---

[57] Cf. in "Old Music" (VII, 39) "the golden letters." The adjective is, of course, extremely common as a cliché of Romantic language and occurs frequently in *An Hour beyond Midnight* and in *Hermann Lauscher*. It is, in general, a secularized religious epithet, but the point is that in Hesse the religious nuance is still quite detectable: Hermann Lauscher's mother used to tell "stories of Jesus with a golden background" (I, 101).

[58] "Happiness" (1949–1950) (IV, 891).

through the dry prose of the tractate and the passionate memory of Harry Haller, to one of Hesse's last essays, the pattern is the same, the object of description the same, an experience of totality both aesthetic and religious, a condition of pure and perfect presence. From one such experience to another, by way of Maya and Sansara, stumbles the *vita* of the profligate-saint.

The motif of the "golden trace" occurs several times in the first section of Harry's memoirs; aggressive hatred of society gives way over wine to a moment of glorious memory: "The golden trace had flashed, I was reminded of the eternal, of Mozart, of the stars" (IV, 219).[59] Equally significant is the longing which possesses Harry for a friend, in some attic somewhere, complete with violin, with whom he might while away the nighttime hours; but Pistorius was rejected in an earlier novel, and *Crisis* is very skeptical about "Dr. Ling." [60] To see through his "crude simplification" of himself, to penetrate the nature of his own ego, it is necessary for Harry to observe himself from another level, to break the vicious circle of one-level thinking in which it is so easy to drown.[61]

The tractate points out the possibility of self-knowledge for the Steppenwolf, "be it, that he lays hands on one of our little mirrors, or be it that he encounters the Immortals or perhaps discovers in one of our magic theaters what he needs for the liberation of his derelict soul" (IV, 241). *The Steppenwolf* is a novel full of mirrors, from the wet asphalt, when Harry first paces the streets, onward. The whole world in which Harry Haller moves may be interpreted as merely the reflection of his own mind. It is no surprise that Harry's friend, when he finds one, is really but a piece of himself, though it is new that this "friend" turns out to be a woman.

Hermine's first words to him, it has been well observed, are no more than "precisely what one would expect from a prostitute with

[59] Mozart's name is associated with such an experience at least as early as 1920; cf. "Aus einem Tagebuch des Jahres 1920," *op. cit.*, p. 192.

[60] Cf. "Abend mit Dr. Ling" (*op. cit.*).

[61] Cf. Novalis, "Die meisten Menschen wollen nicht eher schwimmen, (als) bis sie es können" (Most people aren't willing to swim until they can swim) (*Schriften*, III, 217). Harry quotes this aphorism to the bourgeois narrator with approval. The idea actually comes from Fichte, whose Idealism was indirectly a significant source of Hesse's thought. Harry compares learning to swim to learning to think: to think means to leave solid ground behind for the water, and eventually to drown (IV, 199).

long experience in handling drunks and mothering would-be suicides." [62] It is perhaps worth adding that Harry talks to her with some touches of condescension, which she resents. In the episodes with Hermine and Pablo the novel is indeed moving on two, if not more, levels of reality and gives in some degree "the effect of a sustained pun." [63] Just how far one should go, however, in assigning the prostitute Hermine to the "real" world and the ideal Hermine (and all her mantic utterances) to Harry's projective imagination is an uncertain matter. She has, of course, her unmistakable forbears: "I saw her clearly, the pale, firm face with the blood-red painted mouth, the bright gray eyes, the smooth cool brow, the short stiff lock of hair before the ear" (IV, 274). The identity of this description with that of Klein's Teresina is extraordinary: the pale face, the blazing lips, the gray eyes, the allusion to the ear. The fascinating, complex conversation between them when Harry takes her out to dinner slips from one level to another, at first almost imperceptibly but then with a quite conspicuous change of style: "Slowly, as though producing each word unwillingly, she said . . ." (IV, 298). Hermine herself is described as extremely changeable and "always only moment" (IV, 302); even when she is but her frivolous self she can be extraordinarily perceptive, as for instance when she designates Harry "you Prodigal Son" (IV, 301). We may recall that Kamala turned into a Buddhist, that the religious vein in the life of the prostitute is a cliché since Dostoevsky, and we may therefore find Hermine's confession about her former piety and her enduring preoccupation with the saints entirely in character: "The saints, they are the genuine human beings, the younger brethren of the Saviour" (IV, 345). Nonetheless, there is without doubt a great deal in the view, which Harry himself asserts, that many of the utterances of Hermine and Pablo are but projections of his own higher self; the constant emphasis upon the change of level—"All the same I could not leap back into the probable and the real with the same tightrope walker's facility as Hermine could" (IV, 301)—must charitably be interpreted as a deliberate pointer to the "double perception" [64] on which the novel is based

---

[62] Ziolkowski, "Hermann Hesse's *Steppenwolf*," *op. cit.*, p. 125.
[63] *Ibid.*, p. 124.
[64] *Ibid.*, p, 123.

and not as the uneasy effort to remedy a sensed weakness of composition.

Hermine puts out a hand and rescues Harry; Hermine is the first human being "who shattered the opaque glass globe [65] of my deadness and stretched in her hand, a kind, beautiful, warm hand" (IV, 290). She is a "child," she understands how to play the moment. She introduces the Steppenwolf to jazz, which used to appear to his raw lupine imagination "like the steam from raw meat" (IV, 220), as "American" (symbol for Harry of all that is streamlined and intolerable), and as a music of doom. She introduces him to dancing, with a strong emphasis upon the sexual pleasure thereof, the world of *boîtes* and cafés, night life in the superlative; one of the *Crisis* poems remarks that this is no place for one who used to be "brother of the trees, friend of the lakes and the rivers":

> Nun, altes Männlein, kämme hübsch den Scheitel,
> Rasier dich gut und schlüpf' ins Abendhemd!
> All dein Bemühn ist doch vermutlich eitel,
> Du bleibst in dieser Welt doch immer fremd.[66]

> (Now, old fellow, comb a nice parting,
> Have a good shave and slip into your dress shirt!
> But all your efforts are doubtless useless,
> In this world you'll always be strange.)

He is too old:

> Traurig seh' ich ein, ich alter Knabe:
> Dieses Tun ist lächerlich und nichtig,
> Das ich viel zu spät begonnen habe,
> Nicht einmal den Onestep kann ich richtig! [67]

---

[65] Mauerhofer points out the frequent occurrence of glass imagery in the thoughts of introverted and schizoid personalities (*op. cit.*, p. 29).

[66] "Bei der Toilette," *Krisis*, p. 40.

[67] "Kopfschütteln," *Krisis*, p. 13. Hermine's horror at his ignorance: "Not even the one-step?" (IV, 275) may be compared. The dance is, as it was for Nietzsche's Zarathustra, the supremely unreflective form of self-expression. In "Nachwort an meine Freunde," Hesse asserted that *Crisis* was to be understood as a reassertion of the sensual element in his nature, "this half of me up till now repressed" (p. 82). He then adds, recalling for us the confessional doctrine of *Demian:* "One cannot have the ideal of honesty and always display only the attractive and significant side of one's nature" (p. 82).

(Sadly I perceive, boy that I am grown old,
These doings are absurd and vain,
Which I've started much too late,
I can't even do the one-step properly.)

Hermine tells him that he has always occupied himself with the most complex and difficult matters, and hence cannot cope with the simple ones such as dancing—and unless he has first tried these simple things he has no right to say he has found nothing worth having in life. Harry the "hermit" (IV, 320) puts up some resistance to the suggestion of importing a gramophone into his "cell," but eventually gives way. Then on a night after he has been listening to music in the cathedral his initiation is continued by an emissary from Hermine, Maria, a sensuous little creature whom he finds in bed in his lodgings, and gradually, instead of the church music "which once had been my home" (IV, 326), he becomes at home in "the world of dance and entertainment halls, cinemas, bars, and hotel lounges" (IV, 330). Maria's naïve enthusiasm for an American hit song tears great holes in Harry's aesthetics; from all sides fresh and jolting experience forces its way in—"New things, feared things, solvents into my life which up till now had been so sharply circumscribed and so strictly shut off" (IV, 319). He feels, indeed, that what he needs is "experience, decision, a push and a leap (*Sprung*)" (IV, 294); his escape over the wall of his enclosed self is facilitated in that the Without comes a great way to meet him, forces its way into his hermitage and begins to dissolve it from within. Like Siddhartha, he has to learn to play; this Hermine can teach him; he has to learn how much of him is still bourgeois, for instance his fear of death; once again he must needs slough off a skin. He has to rediscover the delights of concrete things, of luxury articles and toiletries, all of which help one to live in the present. In Maria's arms, "out of the well of this night of love" (IV, 333), rises a whole host of memories of things past, mother and childhood, "stars and constellations," "experiences turned into stars" (IV, 332), all the women he has ever loved, and his own wife who fell victim to mental illness. Above all he recalls a legendary figure, the "legendary Hermann" (IV, 332), the friend of his youth with whom he committed his first "spiritual excesses and dissipations" (IV, 315) and of whom Hermine at once reminded him. In rousing

these memories, Maria also shows that she is able to give him naïve
experience, it is the lesson "to entrust myself like a child to the
game of the surface, to seek the most fleeting pleasures. To be child
and beast in the innocence of sex" (IV, 350), "playful sensuality"
(IV, 299)—for the first time in his life Haller-Klein has sexual
experience which is free of a feeling of guilt; with Maria he finds
himself in a warm garden, a pleasure garden like that of his Indian
precursors, a state of bliss which he realizes, however, is but a
transitory stage: "Once more I ran flickering and full of desire
through all the paths and thickets of her garden, sank my teeth
once more into the sweet fruit of the tree of paradise" (IV, 351).

As for the saxophonist Pablo, [68] "this handsome *caballero*" (IV,
314) for whom music is not to be talked about but only to be
played, he is the representative, in a curious sense, of the outlook of
l'art pour l'art, an expert in the most licentious refinements of the
"game." It appears to Harry that Pablo's creole eyes hide "no
romanticism, no problems, no thoughts" (IV, 314); he is surprised to learn that Pablo has remarked of him: "Poor, poor fellow.
Look at his eyes! Can't laugh" (IV, 315). Pablo is a "metaphysician
of the body"; he uses narcotics (as indeed Harry himself is not
averse to doing), he plays with the senses, he offers homosexual
as well as heterosexual delights; he organizes orgies—for example,
"a love orgy for three" (IV, 336)—and Harry peremptorily
declines participation, as he also affrontedly refuses the offer to sell
one night's rights to the circulating Maria in return for twenty
francs. Hermine asks if Maria has as yet shown the Steppenwolf "a
particular game of the tongue while kissing" (IV, 338), and admits
to a Lesbian connection with the other girl.

These manifold new relationships and possibilities recall to
Harry the thousand I's of which the tractate spoke. Hermine's
"boy-face" (IV, 296), her boyish lock of hair, remind him constantly of Hermann, of which name, of course, hers is the feminine
form. It is indeed a hermaphroditic spell which she casts, she is

[68] He appears in the poem "Neid" as an ideal:
 "Wenn ich doch Banjo könnte spielen
 Und Saxophon in einer Jazzband blasen"
 (*Krisis*, p. 28).

 (If only I could play the banjo
 And blow the saxophone in a jazz band.)

Harry's anima—hence the authority which she can exercise over him—"all too near to me . . . my comrade, my sister" (IV, 315). The legendary Hermann takes physical shape at the masked ball, when Hermine is dressed as a youth. What they all of them, Hermine, Maria, and Pablo, teach Harry might be regarded as merely what the young Siddhartha contemptuously dismissed as "ways away from the ego," obtainable in every tavern and brothel; they introduce him to the experience of orgiasm, "the ecstasy of festival, the secret of the submersion of the individual in the crowd, of the *unio mystica* of joy" (IV, 362). Pablo—his teacher—duly kisses him; and Harry also impresses a sacramental kiss on Hermine's brow. The deep anoetic state which Harry reaches—"in this deep, childlike, fairy-tale happiness" (IV, 362)—has evidently connections with the world of the child and the *Märchen*, both of which are the sphere of the hermaphrodite: "For she often talked to me about Hermann and about childhood, mine and hers, about those years of puberty in which the youthful erotic capacity embraces not only both sexes, but everything, the sensual and the spiritual, and endows everything with the love-spell and the fairy-tale power of metamorphosis which returns occasionally in later times of life solely to the elect and to poets" (IV, 360). Transvestism is the Steppenwolfian form of metamorphosis; Pictor's paradise reappears in this novel in the guise of orgy; and all is under the sign of increasing age and of—to use Goethe's phrase—"recurrent puberty."

No wonder, therefore, that Goethe has his part to play in all this. If *The Glass Bead Game* is Hesse's *Wilhelm Meister*, *The Steppenwolf* is perhaps his *West-östlicher Divan*.[69] Both Hesse's novel and

---

[69] A comparison with *Faust* has also been made by E. Schwarz: "Zur Erklärung von Hesses Steppenwolf," in *Monatshefte für deutschen Unterricht*, LIII (1961), 191–198: Harry and Faust are both "elderly" men rejuvenated by magic and led into the world of sense experience; Harry and Maria is a relationship reminiscent of Faust and Gretchen (?), and the artists' ball is seen as a kind of Walpurgisnacht. This scholar also notes analogies with *Wilhelm Meister*: Hermine resembles Mignon, while the Magic Theater has something in common with the Society of the Tower in Goethe's novel. However, the much more striking relevance of "Der Mann von fünfzig Jahren" has been overlooked. What is really of dominant interest throughout these analogies—and what might make further comparison with the *Divan* particularly apt—is the emphasis on the recovery of potency in the fifty-year-old man and the problems raised by this event.

Goethe's book of poems parody another style (in Hesse's case a musical form), both glorify the temporary resurgence of potency, both unite the mystical and the sensual in a peculiar blend and above all both are hermaphroditic in their innermost sense and structure. The history of Hesse's changing attitude to Goethe is interesting. "Gratitude to Goethe" (1932) tells us that Goethe, though not his favorite author, was the one who—with the possible exception of Nietzsche—had stimulated and provoked him most. As a youth in Tübingen, Hesse had been much preoccupied with that poet he later called "the star of my youth," [70] and there are important references in *Hermann Lauscher* and *Peter Camenzind*. A recurrent discrepancy between Goethe the poet on the one hand and Goethe the humanist, teacher, and man of letters on the other plagued Hesse's judgment until the First World War; Goethe, it seemed, had never quite succeeded in blending Tasso with Antonio, "and at times this made him really disagreeable and embarrassing for me".[71] Then during the war Goethe became a symbol for international truth, for the European spirit above all partisanship and contemptuous of all chauvinisms—Hesse's position and that of Romain Rolland.[72]

But the real secret of Goethe revealed itself only later, as an esoteric mystery, disclosed to the perceiving eye here and there in the works of the older Goethe, in his letters, in sections of *Faust* Part Two, above all, and the *Novelle:* this is that wisdom of Goethe's which is impersonal or superpersonal: "no longer will and no longer intellect, but piety, reverence, readiness to serve, Tao." [73] The analogy between Goethe's wisdom and Chinese thought was drawn already in "Goethe and Bettina" (1924): the older Goethe "produces all around him like a Chinese magician that double atmosphere, that air of Lao-tzŭ, in which doing and non-doing, creating and enduring are no longer separable." [74] Geniuses of the Goethe type are precisely those who do not burn up young, they are positive and affirmative; but at the same time Goethe, Leonardo, Rembrandt, Frederick the Great, they all in old age

[70] "Gratitude to Goethe" (VII, 380).
[71] VII, 377.   [72] Cf. "O Friends, Not These Sounds!" (VII, 44 f.).
[73] VII, 382.   [74] VII, 289.

become "depersonalized": "Affirmers of life, affirmers of nature, they are however all of them deniers of themselves, of man. The more they 'perfect' themselves, the more their life and work takes on the tendency to dissolve in the direction of an apprehended distant possibility which is not called man anymore, at the most superman." [75]

Depersonalization in this sense of the word becomes an essential element in the solution which is eventually proposed for Harry Haller. At the professor's house the Steppenwolf reacts antagonistically to the bourgeois characterization of Goethe—there was enough of the bourgeois in Goethe, as there is enough of the bourgeois in Harry, to bring about this painful crisis of conscience. Humored by Hermine into a drunken sleep, he comes to dream of Goethe: received by the Olympian, Harry—embarrassed by the attempts of a dream scorpion to run up his leg—speaks to this stiff little man with the *star* on his "classic's breast" (IV, 283), rebukes him for his dishonesty, for his sins of suppression and aversion: "You have rejected and suppressed the voices of the depths . . . in yourself just as in Kleist and Beethoven" (IV, 284). Goethe defends himself; the discussion begins to turn upon time and death, Goethe's fear of death, the Faustian issue of transience—a theme Hermine then goes on with when Harry wakes up. Goethe talks of his own innate childlikeness, his "play impulse," says slyly that such games are now at an end, then, however, warns Harry not to take the pompous older Goethe too seriously, for the Immortals like fun above everything: "Seriousness, my boy, is an affair of time; it arises . . . from an overvaluation of time" (IV, 286). To show what he means he discloses a lady's leg of diminutive proportions contained in a leather and velvet case, which then transforms itself into the somewhat too symbolic scorpion.

On the way to the masked ball, the local annual artists' jamboree, Harry calls in at a cinema and watches an Old Testament epic. His contained outrage at this degradation of the holy tales of his

[75] VII, 290. Cf. "Aus einem Tagebuch des Jahres 1920": "Then what is higher could also follow, what is superpersonal and supertemporal, art would be transcended, the artist would be ripe to become a saint, or at any rate a priest" (*op. cit.*, p. 197).

childhood puts in a nutshell the essence of his outsiderdom. We now enter the concluding movement of the novel, the "theme with variations," [76] as the Magic Theater has been called. Don Juan now descends into hell. The Strindbergian motif of hell, essential to the novel, is first concretized by the bourgeois narrator, who defines the Steppenwolf's memoirs as "quite literally a passage through hell, a sometimes nervous sometimes bold passage through the chaos of a darkened soul-world, undertaken with the will to traverse hell, to face up to chaos, to endure the evil to its end" (IV, 205). This attitude of truculent, persecuted resolve is exactly that of the author of *Inferno.* Hermine tells Harry that she has snatched him up and saved him even before the very gate of hell. After an exhausting and fruitless evening at the ball, Harry—the observing "I" who sees behind "falsifying masks of feeling" (IV, 241) as the tractate calls them, and who therefore alone is both unmasked and uncostumed—receives a message: "Hermine is in hell" (IV, 357). Waylaid for a time by a Spanish dancing girl (Maria), Don Juan presses on as fast as he can toward his goal: "Never has a sinner been in such a haste to get to hell" (IV, 358). "Hell" is in fact a basement room of the hotel, appropriately decorated: "on pitch-black walls sinister glaring lamps, and the devils' band playing feverishly" (IV, 359). Here Harry meets the transvestite Hermann, recognizes and for the first time definitely falls in love with Hermine. "Masque . . . *Märchen* . . . game and symbol . . . dream paradise . . . ecstasy . . . *unio mystica* of joy"—in such terms as these Harry now describes the experience of the ball.

Meanwhile the prospect of the Magic Theater looms—"Entrance costs your sanity" (IV, 357). On the first night of his narrative Harry recounted how, tramping along the rainy streets, he had noticed the gothic portal for the first time, cut unexpectedly in the familiar old monastery wall (certainly not an accidental association), contrasting so sharply with the doors leading down into the ubiquitous *boîtes de nuit,* and then the flickering lettering like an illuminated advertisement: "Magic Theater: Entrance not for everybody" and "only for madmen" (IV, 215). The light on the glistening black asphalt had momentarily brought the "golden

[76] Ziolkowski, "Hermann Hesse's *Steppenwolf*," *op. cit.,* p. 132.

trace" to mind and filled the Steppenwolf with a longing, "for the door to a magic theater, only for madmen" (IV, 216).

Now as the ball shrinks to its conclusion, as room after room empties, Hermine reappears disguised as a pierrette; with her as she is now dressed, that is, with his feminine self, Harry can dance a wedding dance, the preamble to the preordained hermetic union. At the end of this: "Entranced we gazed at one another, my poor little soul gazed at me" (IV, 366), the personification of the self in Hermine has now become transparent; even Pablo's eyes are those of Harry's soul, now characterized by that old epithet "the lost frightened bird" (IV, 367). Pablo takes them both into a strange circular room, where they sit "in a layer of very thinned-out reality" (IV, 368); the opium cigarettes, now handed round, have—we are hardly surprised to learn—a smoke which is "thick as incense" (IV, 368)—even in these circumstances, or perhaps especi-ally now, the dominant orientation of the novel is retained in this simile. Drugs will take Harry into the world of his own soul; reality is within. Pablo says: "I can give you nothing which does not al-ready exist within you. I can open for you no other hall of pictures but that of your soul" (IV, 368–369). Mirrors—Pablo's "tiny mir-ror in the hand" (IV, 371) (for *The Steppenwolf* constantly parodies the *Märchen*)—and then an enormous mirror in the Theater itself, now dominate the action; in them Harry sees the reflection of the shy wolf within him. Pablo laughs; the purpose of the whole performance is said to be to teach Harry to laugh, to mock his own self-delusion, to destroy it, to commit in fact a "sham suicide" (IV, 371)—much more sensible, and so much more efficacious, than the real thing.

Looking into the mirror, at his laughing face, Harry sees it dis-solve into many faces, innumerable fragments and separate egos, a heterosexual and a homosexual self. Harry's visits to the penny sideshows of the Theater now begin with the "Automobile Hunt"; passing over various suggestively inviting prospects, he then selects "Introduction to the construction of the personality. Success guaranteed" (IV, 386). Here sits a man cross-legged, with a kind of chessboard before him; by the use of another mirror this man again breaks Harry's personality into pieces, assembles the pieces, and demonstrates the great error conventional psychology has made in assuming that these can be combined only in one valid order. It is the old error of the teachers, and there is a touch of the sarcasm of more than twenty years back in the remark: "its value lies solely in the fact that the officially appointed teachers and educators find themselves spared their labor" (IV, 387). That this is an error means of course that "insane" and "normal" [77] are highly unreliable terms; it also means that anyone who has once experienced the dissociation of his personality can reconstruct it as he likes, "and that thereby he can achieve an infinite variety in the game of life" (IV, 387–388). Life is a game, and as the chess player plays it, it reveals itself, through the analogies employed, as a musical game. As insanity (in the loftiest sense) is the beginning of wisdom, so schizophrenia is the root of art; and the handling of the personality, precisely, is "the art of living."

In contradistinction to this learned and incisive exposition, the next booth in the Theater offers something much more Grand Guignol: "Miracle of Steppenwolf training" (IV, 389) is an ironic horror peep show in which the animal trainer, resembling Harry, trains the wolf and then gives the animal the whip hand, falls to the floor, and himself *acts* the wolf, tears the clothes off his own back with his stopped teeth, bloodily rends a rabbit and a lamb. This is the bestiality of hell, and Harry flees in terror, with a mingled taste of chocolate and blood in his mouth; 1914's "O Friends, Not These Sounds" echoes in his memory, and he has a vision of piles of mangled corpses in gasmasks. The world of the unconscious is evidently hardly paradise unalloyed, though being the home of the memory it can also offer the fragrant atmosphere of youth, longingly evoked in "All the girls are yours" (IV, 392). In this particular dream there is the boy of fifteen again, looking down from the hill upon Calw; all is alive with sense-experience as he recalls his first love for Rosa Kreisler and his mistake in failing to tell her of it, an error he puts right in the dream. In this dream the Steppenwolf lives out to the full a frustrated side of his personality, the lover within him. Hesse's work and especially *The Steppenwolf* is constantly concerned with just this rediscovery

[77] "Normal," Hesse says in effect, is merely a term for the conservative function: cf. "Fantasies" (1918; VII, 153).

of the "shadow," that part of the self which has been denied its rights. It is life in a magic garden, a river, "a playful, childlike swimming in the stream of sex" (IV, 398), and in this richness of self-discovery Harry even develops a belated taste for Pablo's orgies. He emerges from this immersion transformed, and the language is much like that of *Siddhartha:* "Out of the infinite stream of enticements, of vices, of ensnarements I came to the surface again, quiet, silent, prepared, sated with knowledge, wise, deeply experienced, ripe for Hermine" (IV, 399).[78] What we have here is adult baptism, by total immersion.

"How to kill by love" (IV, 399)—the title of this booth brings to Harry's mind Hermine's dark words about the last command she will give him, the command one day to kill her. In his pockets he rummages for fragments of his personality but finds only a knife. In the giant mirror he sees a wolf, then himself, with whom he converses. At this moment the music from the last act of *Don Giovanni*, which heralds the approach of the Commendatore, begins to be heard. Don Juan is to be called to repentance; the music of the Immortals is icy. The poem "Die Unsterblichen," which Harry once wrote on the back of a wine card, sums up this motif:

> We however have found ourselves
> In the ice of the ether bright with stars [IV, 348].

Mozart, now materializing, points out the laughter which is in such music. A conversation about Brahms and Wagner, once held to be so different but now both of them souls in purgatory, convicted of that foul sin of the late Romantics, "thick instrumentation" (IV, 402), leads Mozart to talk of original sin, and of salvation as being attainable only in the eventual achievement of the superpersonal state. Salvation is synonymous with depersonalization—and think-

---

[78] Hesse's use of the word *"tauchen"* is interesting. We may compare, e.g., "aus diesem Augenblick einer Kälte und Verzagtheit tauchte Siddhartha empor . . ." (III, 649). The etymological relationship between *"tauchen"* and *"taufen"* seems to have been everpresent in Hesse's mind as an assonance. Figures of baptism constantly recur. So later, Goldmund "tauchte . . . in den frommen Übungen wie in einem tiefen, kühlen Wasser unter" (V, 295). Cf. also Wackenroder: "oh, so tauch' ich mein Haupt in dem heiligen, kühlenden Quell der Töne unter" (*op. cit.*, p. 131).

ing of the *personal* nature of his own literary endeavors, of his endless articles and reviews, the Neo-Romantic Steppenwolf has to shudder with guilty apprehension. Depersonalization is a state of total detachment from existence, which is a symptom, of course, of acute introversion but which, in its positive connotation in Hesse's novels, is the distinguishing characteristic of successful players of the game, from the cool manipulations of the gambling Teresina to the austere and sovereign meditations of the best exponents of the Glass Bead Game. For his sins Harry Haller must go to hell—and the pointed suggestion (IV, 404) that he is not merely an epigone but a plagiarist to boot is too much for the Steppenwolf; he seizes Mozart by his pigtail, and is duly transported on this "comet's tail" just where he has always been so eager to go, outer space, the freezing vacuum in which the Immortals live. Before losing consciousness, he experiences "a bitter-sharp, steely-bright, icy serenity, a desire to laugh just such a ringing, wild and unearthly laugh as had Mozart" (IV, 404).

But he reawakes in his old miserable Steppenwolfian world, looks once more in a mirror at the dilapidated features of this fifty-year-old man, and is filled with his old self-contempt again and an upsurge of aggression. Armed with his knife he sets off in search of Hermine, finds her and Pablo together, naked and asleep, and stabs her beneath the breast. Pablo wakes up, half covers the body with a carpet, and makes a cool exit; Harry remains with the debris of what is left of all his love and happiness, of his entire life: "a little red, painted on a dead face" (IV, 407).[70] The body radiates a

[70] Cf. the poem "Mit diesen Händen":

> "Alles lässt mich im Stich,
> Jetzt ist auch meine Geliebte kaputt,
> Es war so schauerlich,
> Sie hiess Erika Maria Ruth.
>
> . . .
>
> Ich wollt, ich wär tot, ich wollt, ich wär
> Das Messer, mit dem ich sie totgestochen.
>
> . . .
>
> Doch von all den erloschenen Sonnen
> War kein Abendrot mehr . . ."
>   (*Krisis*, p. 78).
>
> (Everything leaves me in the lurch,
> Now my lover is done for.

terrible, musical frigidity—"The cold . . . was deathly and yet beautiful: it resounded, it vibrated wonderfully, it was music!" (IV, 407).
Mozart (really of course Pablo—both address Harry as "Monsieur")
has still to teach the Steppenwolf a lesson, and he does this by re-
appearing with a radio; in this instrument Handel's Concerto
Grosso in F Major, broadcast from Munich, sounds like a mixture
of "bronchial phlegm and chewed rubber" (IV, 408). This technical monstrosity represents the ultimate bourgeois corruption of art,
"the triumph of our era, its last victorious weapon in the war of
annihilation against art" (IV, 408). But Mozart points out that
through all the distortion and interference the "original spirit" of
this music can still be heard, and thus the radio is symbolic of the
whole structure of existence, of the perpetual tension and conflict
between ideas and phenomena, eternity and time, the divine and
the human. That Platonic note characteristic of the finale of *The
Steppenwolf* sounds here. Mozart's own detachment is dubious,
his dislike of modern civilization is as intense as Harry's, but he does
deliver a timely admonition: "People of your sort have no right to
criticize the radio or life. First of all learn to listen!" (IV, 410).
To learn to listen, like Siddhartha, is the foundation for an understanding of action. To act—especially if it means to knife a pretty
girl—is pointless and absurd. Harry's defense—that it was Hermine's
wish that he should kill her—is a weak one, for, as he well realizes,
he is unable to distinguish at all clearly between Hermine's wishes
and his own. The murder from which Friedrich Klein shrank back
at the last moment is in *The Steppenwolf* committed in a dream.
Mozart derides what inevitably follows—Harry's offer of himself
for retribution, for the guillotine, but lets him go through with this
in the hope that it may end by instilling in him a sense of humor,
"gallows humor" (IV, 411). At Harry's "execution" judgment is

---

It was so horrible.
She was called Erika Maria Ruth. . . .
I wish I were dead, I wish I were
The knife I used to kill her. . . .
But from all the dead suns
There was no sunset any more. . . .)
Erika is the name of Harry's girl (IV, 259). Maria and Ruth may recall Maria
Bernoulli and Ruth Wenger. *The Steppenwolf* also uses the sun image in this
way: "Had I extinguished the sun?" (IV, 407).

first read out: he is convicted by the Immortals of mischievous and humorless misuse of the Magic Theater. Harry's murder of Hermine is evidence that he has failed; he succumbs to the illusion of Maya (that is, magic), an illusion within an illusion, since the Theater itself is an opium dream. Although, as the tractate says, he had no theoretical objections to prostitution, he was unable "to take a tart seriously and really look upon her as someone like himself" (IV, 236). He discovers in Maria the type of women, naïve sensual creatures, who fulfill him in a way their intellectual predecessors in his life had never been able to do. But all the same he remains unfree, throttled by his bourgeois conscience. His murder of Hermine is not simply motivated by common jealousy (as Pablo, taking the long view, vainly hopes) but is rather a disastrous reversion to his bourgeois self, an upsurge of disgust with the sensual.

He still divides the world into irreconcilable halves. In that the Immortals ridicule this attitude they reveal themselves as of the same stuff as Demian,[80] acolytes of Abraxas; and yet we are forced to take account of the fact that the world these Immortals inhabit is totally beyond the sensual, is that icy cosmic vastness which belongs so obviously to the emerging scientific mythology of the age, a Third Kingdom much less linked than Siddhartha's was to experience through the senses. The suspicion arises that—in spite of Goethe's toy leg—their fulfillment is somehow but a surrogate for the real thing. Here lies the root point, the problem of interpretation which the conclusion of *The Steppenwolf* presents. Harry is condemned by the court of the Immortals "to the penalty of eternal life and a twelve-hour withdrawal of entrance permission for our theater. Also the accused cannot be excused the penalty of being laughed at once" (IV, 412). He must learn to overcome his masochistic impulse to self-analysis, the descent into himself is duly forbidden him for a time, and he is introduced to the weapon of humor, the awful "laughter of the Beyond" (IV, 412). Since he was ready only for punishment full of pathos and devoid of wit, he is condemned to go on living forever and listening to the radio-

---

[80] *Demian* also uses the image: "the loneliness and deathly cold of cosmic space" (III, 144); in this case it describes the condition at the time of puberty, of the death of childhood.

music of life. Mozart now turns into Pablo, who looks so much like the chess player. Pablo scolds Harry for his indecorous violence; he has not yet learned what he must learn, "to play the figures game better" (IV, 415), the technique of the "game."

The Steppenwolf, then, differs radically from *Siddhartha* in that it affirms the ultimate value and psychological necessity of the game, *in nuce* the aesthetic existence, on the spiritual level implying a condition of life in which the controlling will is all-dominant—in Hesse's terminology, therefore, a masculine bias rather than the true androgynous union. The "humor" of *The Steppenwolf* (it is after all a remarkably unfunny novel) has been variously interpreted; central must be the statement of the tractate: "Humor is always in some respect bourgeois, though the genuine bourgeois is incapable of understanding it" (IV, 239). Humor is conceived of as a state of sovereign superiority above the polar tensions of life, tending toward resolution, harmony and balance, its elevation above the melee making it all but synonymous with Romantic irony—which vertical polarity in turn implies an unresolved duality. The aim of outsiders is "to burst out into starry space" (IV, 239); a few indeed do find their way through "to the unconditional" (IV, 239) [81] and are destroyed; "for the others however, those who remain bound . . . for them a third kingdom is open, an imaginary but sovereign world: humor" (IV, 239), a sphere which embraces saint, profligate, and bourgeois in an imaginary reconciliation. Yet—somewhat inconsistently perhaps—humor is also declared to be the key to the Tao: "To live in the world as were it not the world, to respect the law and yet to stand above it, to possess 'as though not possessing,' to renounce as though it were no renunciation" (IV, 240)—the Steppenwolf's only hope is to distill this fairy-tale "magic potion" (IV, 240) in the hell of his night-mind. Thus the meaning of Goethe's sly humor, thus Jean Paul; thus also Hesse is able to speak of "the divine humor of Asiatic yogis" [82] and in *The Nuremberg Journey* to describe humor

[81] Cf. Ziolkowski, "Hermann Hesse and Novalis" (pp. 133–134). Novalis uses this term in *Blütenstaub* (*Schriften*, II, 15). We may compare Hesse's comments on the nature of heroism in "On Hölderlin" (1924; VII, 279). At the end of *The Glass Bead Game*, Joseph Knecht tells Master Alexander that what he yearns for is "the unconditional" (VI, 503).

[82] "Herr Claassen" (IV, 686).

as "a crystal which grows only in deep and lasting pain" (IV, 128).

The image of the crystal fits well into the patterns of *The Step-penwolf*, the symbolism of coldness, clarity, translucent hardness, the brightness of the musical dome of the cosmos, the luminosity of dark streets and of stars:

The Immortals, as they live in timeless space, removed, turned into images and crystal eternity poured over them like ether, and the cool, starlike radiant serenity of this extraterrestrial world—what made all this so familiar to me?" He reflects, and he remembers the music of Bach and Mozart: "and everywhere in this music, this cool, starry brightness seemed to shine, this ethereal clarity to vibrate. Yes, this was it, this music was a sort of time frozen into space, and above it vibrated endlessly a superhuman serenity, an eternal divine laughter [IV, 347–348].

So persistent is the imagery of the cosmic dome, of eternity, time, and space in *The Steppenwolf*, that it is probably no accident that the novel actually refers to the theory of relativity and to Einstein by name; the poet's imagination has been caught and held by the scientific imagery of his own day. Depersonalization, as in Goethe's case, is achieved when the individual has passed through all the vicissitudes of common life and has burst "into the Eternal, into cosmic space" (IV, 347), where time has been redeemed, has undergone that metamorphosis of which "Old Music" had spoken in 1913, "its transformation back into space."

The Steppenwolf is an optimistic work [83] and a Strindbergian catharsis of crisis years. Like his predecessor in *Inferno*, Hesse is experimenting with faith. Hermine's own philosophy is a curious mixture of transcendental optimism and death-wish, highly remi-niscent of Novalis, to whom it no doubt owes a good deal. She draws parallels between her own unsought fate as a courtesan and Harry's; they both have "a dimension too many" (IV, 343); maybe

[83] As Hesse must have grown weary of protesting. Many readers failed to see "that over and above the Steppenwolf and his problematical life there rises a second, higher, immortal world." "Postscript to *The Steppenwolf*" (VII, 413). While the novel certainly aimed to reveal the desperate problem of existence, it also sought "to give some sense nonetheless to this apparently sense-less, cruel life" (*Letters;* VII, 490). It is Mozart and the Immortals "who are the real content of the book" (*Letters;* VII, 493). The message of the book is how to endure life and overcome time (*Letters;* VII, 501–502).

outsiders—"people with a dimension too many" (IV, 344)—are themselves only epiphenomenal and will eventually vanish from the face of the earth. Meanwhile all they can call their own is death and eternity—by eternity, she says, she means what the pious call the Kingdom of God. This is defined as the world of the real and the true, of music, poetry, miracles, genuine feelings and actions, beyond time, of the communion of saints. The essential Platonism [84] of this outlook is manifest; the suggestion made in *Siddhartha* that knowledge of the One might itself be merely "a childishness of the think-people, of the think-child-people" shows that Hesse was fully aware not only of the ambiguities inherent in the term "child-person" but also of the epistemological difficulties in his concept of "magical thinking." Whereas *Siddhartha*, in effectively moving away from the abstractions of Buddhism and of the Vedanta [85] toward the Hindu pantheon—its intellectual chaos and the earthiness of graven images [86]—partially bypassed these difficulties, *The Steppenwolf* remains seized with them, as in the last resort the thought of Novalis, with its critical heritage, also is. Hermine echoes the latter yet again: "Oh, Harry, we have to grope through so much dirt and senselessness, to reach home. And we have no one to lead us, our only guide is our home-sickness!" (IV, 346).

Thomas Mann remarked of *The Steppenwolf* that it was a book not inferior in its experimental boldness to *Ulysses* or *Les Faux-monnayeurs*.[87] Certainly it depends for its effect upon an artistic principle very different from that which informs *Siddhartha*. The extremely conscious structure, the massive intrusions of reflective commentary through the bourgeois narrator, through the tractate,

[84] Plato is ranked with Jesus, Buddha, and Lao-tzŭ. See "War and Peace" (1918; VII, 120).

[85] Cf. Max Schmid, *Hermann Hesse: Weg und Wandlung*, p. 61: "Die Upanishad-Philosophen suchen die Einheit von Mensch und Natur. Dass sie diese Einheit wieder herstellen müssen durch das Wissen um sie, zeigt, dass sie bereits von ihr gespalten sind" (The Upanishad-philosophers seek the unity of man and nature. That they have to reconstruct this unity by knowledge of it shows that they are already cut off from it).

[86] Gods and magic, we are told, may be just as necessary as "pure" teaching: Shiva and Vishnu are a requisite counterweight to Buddhism. Cf. *Letters* (VII, 616).

[87] "Hermann Hesse: Einleitung zu einer amerikanischen Demian-Ausgabe," *Neue Rundschau*, LVIII (1947), 248.

through Harry's obsessional process of self-diagnosis, the discourses of Hermine, Pablo, and the chess player, and a speculation about music as a German heritage in which Harry's reflection all but cracks the taut framework of the novel [88]—all this shows the bent of the book. Furthermore, we have to note a good deal of political matter, an only partly integrated left-wing polemicism, predictions of war, an attack on that old *bête noire*, "world history," and finally some pontifications *à la Demian:* Harry's memoirs, says the bourgeois narrator, are not just the fantasies of a paranoid but "a document of the age, for Haller's sickness is . . . the sickness of the age itself, the neurosis of that generation to which Haller belongs" (IV, 205). The widespread use of rhetorical questions is a feature of a style which has in general a marked rhetorical nuance. The existence of at least four narrators—the young bourgeois, the author of the tractate, Harry Haller, and then by prominent implication Hesse himself—all this is ostentatious artifact. Hesse experiments in the novel in a greater degree than heretofore with montage techniques, but it is no doubt important to remember in this connection the debt *The Steppenwolf* owes to Romantic narrative art, especially the writings of Hoffmann and Jean Paul. In its very structure the book is Platonic, representing the nexus between matter and idea, life and faith, the radio and the music beyond (the analogy is apt because it requires that we should see the radio as the matter of the narrative and the original music as its form). The Platonic way of thinking is not, ultimately, "magical thinking," for the latter is a genuine monism best found in the *Märchen* and *Siddhartha,* Hesse's least Platonic works. *The Steppenwolf,* one must sum up, is an act of faith imposing form on chaos, time on space, and music on life, by the sovereign *acceptance* of the old Calw dualism, by the apotheosis of irony ("laughter of the Beyond"). It is indeed the eternity of the father which here finds its form; the senses are denied by the very language in which the acceptance of sensual experience is enjoined. The "depersonalized," though they may treasure ladies' legs in caskets, must find sense experience rather difficult of access, or at

---

[88] "In the German spirit matriarchy reigns" (IV, 326 ff.)—a passage reading a good deal more like Mann than Hesse and fitting none too well into the general conspectus of Harry's views on music.

any rate subordinate to that superior form of game which Siddhartha *finally* abandoned only on leaving Kamala, finding eventually that the warm, naïve experience of the "child-people" (of
which, despite flickerings of it in Maria and elsewhere, there is not
a word at the end of the novel) was essential to samadhi. "Eternity,
eternity! The black bird sang, and his hard shiny eye gazed at us
like a black crystal"—these words from an earlier story are worth
quoting here once again, for the tractate ends: "We take our
leave of Harry, we let him go his way alone. If he were already
with the Immortals, if he were already at that place to which his
steep road seems to lead, with what astonishment would he look
upon this wild, indecisive zigzagging path" (IV, 251–252; my italics). The world of the Immortals, therefore, lies at the very end
of the Way, of "The Steep Road," where there is not merely the
bird song of eternity but also cold laughter. Yet even the tractate
had its reservations—perhaps after all the only Way *is* that of
martyrdom, leading "to still greater sufferings, to proscription, to
the last renunciation, perhaps to the scaffold" (IV, 248). Indeed,
one may well feel that the vision of the scaffold is not effectively
exorcised by the mockery of the Immortals. Harry knows, at all
events, that he is still far from being at one with them; another
saison en enfer still awaits him, perhaps over and over again; *unio
mystica* he may have briefly experienced, but *unio mystica sub-
stantialis* is reserved for the saint. There remains the suspicion that
the point Harry Haller has now reached is not the well of space
but rather only a certain mountain peak; humor, confessedly the
key to an *imaginary* reconciliation, will prove an inadequate
panacea. The ultimate "leap (*Sprung*) into the universe" (IV, 240),
will be still to come, as inevitable as Klein's "leap into cosmic
space"; and to follow the analogy a trifle further still, Harry may
yet discover that it is not Mozart and Pablo but rather his own
mother who awaits his eventual fall.

CHAPTER 6

Narziss and Goldmund

IN the "Preface of a Writer to His Selected Works" (1921) Hesse compares the great novelists and narrative artists of the nineteenth century, such as Dickens, Turgeniev, and Keller, with himself, concluding that he is not really a novelist at all. In this situation he finds that he is not alone: "Modern German literature, for the last hundred years, has been full of novels which are not novels, and of writers who behave as though they were storytellers but are not" (VII, 251). He cites Josef von Eichendorff, who wrote "ostensible novellas"; he feels at one with writers such as this, in their sins of commission: "The story as disguised lyric poetry, the novel as a borrowed label for the attempts of poetic personalities to express their experience of themselves and the world, this was a specifically German and Romantic matter, in this I at once realized myself to be involved and to share responsibility" (VII, 252). Poets such as Eichendorff, Hölderlin, and Nietzsche wrote prose because German prose can indeed provide a superb outlet for that musical impulse which is the true source of the lyrical. "But few, extremely few were strong or sensitive enough to deprive themselves of the advantages which derived from using the story form on loan (and one of these advantages was that of a larger public). . . . And so I also, without being fully aware of it, had played the role of the storyteller as a deceiver who was himself deceived. . . . Of my tales—there was no longer any doubt about this—not a single one was pure enough as a work of art still to deserve mention" (VII, 252).

Such self-doubt, first coming to the surface in "Klingsor," becomes a recurrent theme of Hesse's writings in the twenties. To obtain a public by stealth, by disguising lyric poetry in the form of novels, is seen as an impermissible procedure which revenges itself by the impure sediment which it deposits in the works themselves. Hesse perceived that his monologues were not novels at all, any more than the prose productions of Hölderlin and Novalis had been, but he found that the company he kept was still no excuse. In *The Nuremberg Journey* a related issue is aired: "I do not believe in the value of the literature of our age. . . . Invariably I can only feel that the attempts of contemporary German writers (naturally including my own) at real creation, at genuine works, are somehow the inadequate efforts of epigones, everywhere I imagine I can see a glimmer of routine, of models which have lost their living qualities" (IV, 156).[1] Feeling the dead hand of tradition upon him, he thoroughly approved of much of the extremism and the conscious and crude iconoclasm of the younger generation who desperately strove to escape the clammy hold. He himself was caught in a conflict which had first become manifest at the time of *Demian*, the conflict between uninhibited confession and fine writing: "Between the demand for honesty, for confession, for the ultimate in self-revelation, and that other requirement—with us since our youth—for beautiful expression . . . the entire literature of my generation oscillates desperately back and forth" (IV, 157).

The conventional Neo-Romantic style cannot, by definition, cope with the demands of the *Expressionist* will, for Expressionism is the laying bare of the archetypal. The style that can do this has not yet been found and perhaps will never be; psychoanalysis, on which great hopes were set, has proved too academic a tool to liberate the poets. Side by side with thoughts and implications such as these, it is characteristic that we should find in Hesse a certain readiness to approve and applaud his own Neo-Romantic heritage: "I have, I think, always been a traditionalist as a writer, with few exceptions I was content to use a conventional form, a current

---

[1] Cf. a similar comment in "The Beggar" (IV, 844); "The Beggar" first appeared in 1948.

routine style, a schema, I never cared about producing anything that was formally new, about being in the avant-garde and an originator. That harmed quite a number of my works, and it was equally beneficial to others, and I am happy to admit to it." [2] He knew very well what the psychological basis of the epigone in fact was, and also that many of those who threw stones at such targets themselves dwelt unwittingly in glass houses. A lyricist disguised as a novelist, Hesse might be defined as a self-confessed Romantic epigone who yearns for raw truth, for the purity of absolute self-disclosure, but who knows that artistic advantage may sometimes lie in the very failure to attain this end; for the struggle for confession at all costs leads even further "out and beyond the good and fine tradition of storytelling" [3] and eventually into a formless world.

Highly relevant is the contrast which Hesse has drawn between the *Confessions* of Rousseau and those of Augustine: Augustine surrenders himself openly and completely and becomes a saint; Rousseau succumbs to some degree of self-justification and becomes a poet. The confession of the artist is never an unsullied one, for he always values it in the wrong way: "Confession is overrated by the artist, he devotes to it more love and care than to anything else in the world, and the more honest, the more careful and complete, the more ruthless his confession is the more is it in danger of once more becoming wholly art, wholly work, wholly an end it itself." [4] One may guess that Hesse had in mind not only Rousseau but also Strindberg when he wrote these words. The artist remains trapped in the magic circle of the self, inevitably exaggerating the importance of his work, since in this alone does he find the justification of his life, entranced—as for instance was Marcel Proust—by the beauty of his own confession.

Hesse called both *Peter Camenzind* and *Beneath the Wheel* a "novel"; *Demian* was subtitled "The Story of a Youth" and *Siddhartha* "An Indian Poetic Fiction" (*Dichtung*); while *The Steppenwolf*, that most unconventional of Hesse's works, had no subdesignation at all. *Narziss and Goldmund*, however, is called a "tale" (*Erzählung*). This might suggest a conscious attempt to find a

[2] *Letters* (VII, 683).
[3] "Interrupted School Lesson" (IV, 868).
[4] "Aus einem Tagebuch des Jahres 1920," *op. cit.*, 198-199.

home within a tradition, to turn away from whatever experimentation there may have been in *The Steppenwolf*, and furthermore an effort to overcome the supremacy of the lyrical impulse. Indeed, certain features of the novel, its narrative breadth and the technique of the good raconteur which distinguishes it, support such a view, and there are good reasons why it has become perhaps the most permanently popular work of Hesse's later period; the public which had recoiled in aversion from *The Steppenwolf* showed itself receptive, once more, to *Narziss and Goldmund*. But this may not have been altogether a good sign, and Hesse himself seems to have preferred the earlier work, perceiving that it probably represents a much higher level of artistic achievement, although its content is evidently too disturbing for the average reader. Even in the case of *Narziss and Goldmund* there was no lack of those who found it "unheroic . . . soft . . . erotic and shameless." [5]

On rereading the novel after twenty-five years, the author discerned a number of faults in it; in particular he found it long-winded. His limitations as a formal artist seemed linked with what was perceived to be a repetitiousness of motifs and characters— "Thus my Goldmund was prefigured not only in Klingsor, but already even in Knulp, as were Castalia and Joseph Knecht in Mariabronn and Narziss." [6] (These are only a few, of course, of the comparisons that might be drawn.) After twenty-five years what Hesse felt closest to in *Narziss and Goldmund* was, most significantly, "the cadences of this writing, its melody." [7] All these ponderings over the limitations of his art are surely rather more than merely that pathetic honesty of self-depreciation which a hostile critic of Hesse, K. H. Deschner, would see and applaud in them; [8] they pose the whole issue of tradition in literature, of the modern gulf between language and experience, the Nietzschean antinomies of truth and art, and in a narrower sphere, in the history of styles, the problems involved in the transition from the new Romanticism to Expressionism and beyond, as they may be seen reflected in the work of so many writers, for instance Hofmannsthal.

No appreciation of *Narziss and Goldmund*—indeed no study of

---

[5] "Engadine Experiences" (VII, 864).   [6] *Ibid.*, 866.   [7] *Ibid.*

[8] Karlheinz Deschner, *Kitsch, Konvention und Kunst: Eine literarische Streitschrift* (Munich, 1958).

Hermann Hesse—can really avoid this issue. Deschner seeks to compare this author (unfavorably) with Hermann Broch and Hans Henny Jahnn, a critical procedure which might be questioned; he picks Hesse out, in fact, as perhaps his most eminent example of an inflated reputation, finding in him little but the meretricious, the imitativeness of the epigone. The obvious weaknesses in Deschner's logical arguments do not, however, dispose entirely of this polemicist's strictures. One might feel inclined to deny outright that the novel in question is merely *Goldschnittsirup;*[9] however, *Narziss and Goldmund* is by no means free of sentimentality—for instance the unfortunate episode of Marie, the lame girl who vainly adores Goldmund, which is, frankly, reminiscent of Paul Heyse. In point of composition, the novel is inferior to *The Steppenwolf*, while its language, which resembles that of *Siddhartha*, fails to achieve the same smooth, ritualistic perfection. The repetitiousness of theme and imagery, which the author himself regarded as a flaw, goes so far that it suggests a certain weariness of the artistic imagination, a degree of carelessness, which last criticism is further attested by an actual narrative error.[10] The objection that the book lacks depth, however, derives from a misunderstanding of the function in it of the reflective element and poses a fundamental issue, relevant to Hesse's work as a whole, to which we shall return. Suffice it to note at the outset that *Narziss and Goldmund* is a "tale" by a writer who has denied that he is a storyteller in the true sense—a "tale" by a lyricist in whom the religious yearning for truth at all costs has for more than a decade been in bitter and ambiguous contest with the will to form, and in whom the drive to uncover the fundamental and the new conflicts with a passionate sense of tradition and of historical affinity. It is a work composed by an artist who is devoted to play, but whose deepest necessity was not to play but to confess.

It is a *Künstlerroman* with religious sources; its forming energy derives from the friction between the religious and the aesthetic impulses. When Goldmund, after his life of dissipation, returns to

[9] *Ibid.*, p. 127. The term "Goldschnitt" alludes to the epigonal poetry of the middle and later nineteenth century; it is totally misapplied as a stricture upon *Narziss and Goldmund*.

[10] "Konrad" should surely read "Adolf" (V, 87).

the monastery, the abbot, Narziss, hears his confession and awards him a penance, which is a conscious and meticulous repetition of prayers and hymns. Narziss adds the admonition that he must not speculate about these exercises: they are to be performed "in the same way as for instance when you are singing and playing the lute you do not pursue any clever ideas or speculations but try to produce each note and pressure of the fingers one after another as purely and perfectly as possible" (V, 296). Music is—as Pablo made clear to Harry Haller—not synonymous with musicology nor with passive appreciation; it belongs neither to the feelings nor to the intellect, but to the will; it is really valid only as active performance, "*Handwerk*"; and so it is with the exercises of the Spirit.

The *tertium comparationis* is, of course, artistic technique in general, or rather form, that in which inspiration is sublimated, as Goldmund's is in the exercises of penance. It is good, says Narziss, that Goldmund went out into the world, that he did not remain within the monastery walls and try to become a thinker; for had he done this, he would inevitably have turned into a mystic; and mystics are, one and all, "secret artists . . . all without exception unhappy people" (V, 287). Unacceptable, no doubt, as a diagnosis of the mystic, the remark yet sheds great light upon the sources of *Narziss and Goldmund;* if the mystic is secretly an unhappy artist so is the artist secretly an unhappy mystic—though false in logic, this was psychologically true for Hesse, at least. "Artists," says a priest to Goldmund, "are not in the habit of being saints" (V, 154), and Hesse had certainly found that the Way of the artist and the Way of the saint were very different in practice, although the former ought ideally to lead into the latter through depersonalization, through "de-becoming" (*Entwerden*), the surrender of the tormented ego. And yet Hesse finds this Way of depersonalization, which Augustine followed but which eluded Rousseau, impossible for him too, even though he declares "the saint" to be his chosen model. He attributes his incapacity to the debilitating consequences of his Pietistic upbringing, to the fact that he has never belonged to a "genuine" religious tradition (such as the Roman). The tradition to which he did belong was essentially an aesthetic one. Thus *Narziss and Goldmund* should primarily be understood as the conversion of confession into music, into cadences, and as the refuge-seeking of the disappointed mystic in art.

In its ritual repetitions, its "triple impulses," [11] the prose of *Narziss and Goldmund* harks back to that of *Siddhartha*. In structure the novel is of course "contrapuntal" (always bearing in mind that musical terminology as such adds little to the understanding of literary forms); it is the most obvious example in Hesse's work of "the two-voicedness of the melody of life," [12] a study of the life of the artist in its mobile relationship with the hieratic life. In *Siddhartha* already, as perhaps even in *Demian*, there was the counterpoint between the wanderer, the "world-traveler," the Faustian figure, and the rationalist (Gide's "*frère aîné*") who remained within the grove, practicing his methods, his rational mysticism. In *Narziss and Goldmund*, Govinda has become dignified as Narziss and is even given a temporary primacy of place—Goldmund begins by being (and in a sense always remains) *his* "shadow." In Harry Haller both extremes, Wagner the famulus and Faust himself, were blended in uncomfortable company; thus Anni Carlsson's observation that Goldmund, had Narziss not liberated him by analysis, was set fair to turn into a Steppenwolf [13] is capped by Max Schmid's perception that it is in fact in combination that the twain would form (or *do* form) a Haller [14] (and since this is clearly right, any interpretation of the novel based upon the view that some sort of "harmony" of Narziss and Goldmund is ultimately achieved is transparently absurd).

Contrapuntal though it is, *Narziss and Goldmund* lacks the relatively strict conditioning by musical prototype which has been noticed in the case of *The Steppenwolf*. On the other hand, it has just that interleaving of nodal incident and interpretative conversation which is to be found in all the major novels, especially *Demian*; it resembles *Demian* also in the pattern of its action—a pupil, in whose early life a spiritual teacher makes a radical intervention,

[11] Max Schmid, *Hermann Hesse: Weg und Wandlung*, p. 112.
[12] *Spa Visitor* (IV, 115).
[13] In Ball, *Hermann Hesse*, p. 260.
[14] *Op. cit.*, p. 100. He adds (and this one doubts, since it appears to contradict the premise) that between them they can be expected to support successfully the existence of a Steppenwolf.

who then goes out into the world, and returns in the end to a tryst with his teacher and friend. In its external realism (which has been compared with Stifter's),[15] its panoramic breadth so unusual in Hesse, the novel is apparently more extraverted than either *Demian* or *Siddhartha;* but in no sense could it be deemed a realistic novel in the classical nineteenth-century sense. It remains a lyrical "tale," a species of *Bildungsroman*, in which the external world stays distinctly subordinate to the exposition of the pivotal moments of the *vita*. Like Eichendorff's *Taugenichts*, with which it has a good deal in common, it makes great use of the technique of summary to bridge gaps and form links in what is essentially a lyrical fantasy; it too—were it not so long—might well be designated an "ostensible novella."

Very material to any discussion of *Narziss and Goldmund* is the fragment *Berthold*,[16] the beginnings of a historical novel set in the period of the Thirty Years' War. The hero, Berthold, is educated in a monastery for the priesthood; his powerful instincts, however, conflict with his vocation, lead him to dissipations and eventually, in an act of wild jealousy, to the murder of his friend, the sceptical intellectual Johannes, his "teacher." The fragment then breaks off with Berthold's flight to the wars.

The analogies between his case and that of Goldmund force themselves upon us. Like Goldmund, Berthold cannot remember his childhood. His erotic awakening contests, as was conventional in the school novel, with the embattled academic self, as it does with all the external criteria of social success and worldly acceptance. But of course this is an awakening not only of the sexual instincts, but also of the whole soul, and characteristic figures are employed: "In blissfully drifting dreams his depression was transformed into the smiling release of winged happiness, which took away all the hardness and dissatisfaction of his haughty soul and turned it into a child playing in the grass and a little bird rejoicing in the air" (I, 858). The haughty soul of the would-be priest becomes that of a child again, and the bird is born. Love is a "garden

[15] By Weibel, but surely unjustifiably. There is in *Narziss and Goldmund* nothing like the objective sweep of *Witiko*.

[16] 1907–1908; first edition, however, Zurich, 1945.

of Venus" (I, 858), a closed garden,[17] the opulent warmth of
which contrasts sharply with the cold of early Mass in the dark
church. On the amused advice of Johannes, Berthold addresses himself to a servant girl, Barbara, unaware in his innocence of the
freedom with which she casts her favors,[18] shows some enterprise,
then discovers the truth, and eventually becomes disgusted at his
own degradation. A period of abstinence parallels the onset of
academic decline (in this resembling several school novels). Finally
Berthold falls in love with Agnes, a blond merchant's daughter,
several times observed in Cologne cathedral; and when Johannes,
half selfishly, intervenes with her, Berthold kills him.

It is a small matter that Goldmund's last lover is also Agnes, "the
blond lioness" (V, 245). More interesting is the murder itself. For
Johannes, though in his worldliness and his taste for lubricious
anecdotes very unlike Narziss, is still the teacher and awakener,
the father-figure whom Berthold slays—entirely appropriately—out
of sexual jealousy; what is more, "Johannes" is Narziss' name in
religion. Goldmund himself commits a couple of murders (and in
error almost kills Narziss!). Various other murderers or would-be
murderers populate Hesse's tales, such as schoolmaster Wagner,
Friedrich Klein, and Harry Haller; there is also a rumor of this
kind about Quorm. Thus it has been observed that, in the figure of
Berthold, Harry and Goldmund are both contained, both living together tolerably until the moment when homicide splits them apart.[19]

One may even suspect that the novel remained a fragment partly
because, for the Hesse of Gaienhofen, Berthold's behavior has already gone a shade too far; he has committed that crime from
which much later characters shrink back, of which they only
dream. *Berthold* has several features which betray the style of the
Gaienhofen years, especially the gnomic reflections; a certain tendency to conscious breadth of portrayal, to the accumulation of
thematically irrelevant material, points to the intention to write a
wholly naturalistic, historical novel. Such a style was not really

[17] Cf. also "The Cyclone": love is "a closed garden" (I, 768).
[18] "Good old Barbie! . . . Now she'll have to ordain this clod too" (I, 861).
The popular profanity displays the characteristic Hesse nexus.
[19] Otto Basler, writing in Ball, *op. cit.*, p. 296.

natural to Hesse; it is questionable whether it was ever in his capacity to create a broad canvas in this mode, and for this reason also the novel remained unfinished.

Berthold bursts forth into the wide world, the world of the Thirty Years' War; a fugitive, he has murder on his hands. Goldmund's flight takes place in somewhat less dramatic circumstances. He is brought by his father, a stern, unsympathetic official, to the monastery of Mariabronn to be educated for the priesthood; his life, as it turns out, is conceived of by his father as a penance for the sins of his mother. He is named after St. John Chrysostomos, the most eloquent preacher of the Greek church.[20] "He had a golden mouth and with his golden mouth he spoke words, and the words were little swarming birds, they flew away in fluttering crowds" (V, 66). The color gold is again primarily that of iconography, and the birds are the eloquence of the soul. Here, at Mariabronn, Goldmund comes under the influence of the brilliant novice Narziss, so exceptional a Greek scholar that he is allowed to teach during his novitiate.

Narziss is intended as far more than a mere foil to Goldmund, though Hesse's assertion that they are equally significant[21] is not quite true in terms of the novel; and it is to some extent counterbalanced by the impression given in "An Evening of Work" where Goldmund is arrayed after Camenzind, Knulp, Veraguth, Klingsor, and Haller as "a new incarnation, a somewhat differently blended incorporation of my own nature in words."[22] If it be allowed that Goldmund is the central personage of the action, that whole action yet remains meaningless and indeed inconceivable without its starting and finishing point, Narziss. Goldmund's *vita* begins with the artist's aspiration after sainthood, the striving to emulate Narziss, the exercise of the will. As for Narziss, the very name of

[20] Perhaps meant in part as a symbol of extraversion. Cf. Max Schmid, *op. cit.*, p. 107.

[21] "Narziss is to be taken just as seriously as Goldmund" (*Letters*, VII, 584). The formulation is rather curious.

[22] VII, 305. An important passage in *Spa Visitor*, in its implications, supports Goldmund's priority of place: "There are two ways of redemption: the way of righteousness, for the righteous, and the way of grace, for the sinners. I, who am a sinner, have once again made the mistake of trying the way of righteousness. I shall never succeed in this" (IV, 104).

course suggests introversion; his poise, his remarkable self-containment, his deliberate stunting of his own self-expression, his search for realization within, all these are classical features of the type as described by Jung. He is "awake" (V, 50); a scintillating teacher of Greek, he is contrasted with the simple, pious, humble abbot Daniel as well as with Goldmund, who vainly attempts to combine as the goal of his existence these two irreconcilable ideals. Narziss has one destiny, Goldmund another; if the former is St. John, then the latter is Judas [23]—and the implication of this analogy shows that Narziss is indeed "awakened" in his understanding of the Christian drama, to have been able to make it! In Narziss we have the "handsome youth with the elegant Greek, with the chivalrously immaculate bearing" (V, 11), a nobility of appearance reminiscent of Siddhartha's. He incarnates both intellect and will. This is Mariabronn, not Maulbronn, and thus Narziss is no mere stuffy academic. In that he is not a committed pedagogue, Narziss has the chance (and the ambition) to become a teacher in the deeper sense; he is aware of the similarity between himself and Goldmund, and also of their extreme polarity. Between them arise magical connections, "a language of the soul and of signs," and Narziss would have liked to "lead him . . . to help him bloom" (V, 46). Narziss has the gift of insight into others; he perceives that Goldmund was never intended by fate for the tonsure, and that a false personality is being forced upon the boy. The analogy with Hans Giebenrath is rather close: "He saw this boy's nature as encased in a hard shell, consisting of false fancies, pedagogical errors, paternal decrees. . . . His task was clear . . . to liberate him from the shell" (V, 36). The image of the kernel which must be extracted from the shell recurs in this novel; Narziss finds in service of the Spirit the "kernel and sense of life" (V, 25), and then, in conversation, Narziss and Goldmund approach the "kernel and sense of their friendship" (V, 47).

Goldmund, the antithesis of Narziss in everything, suffers from his inability to make himself the same. On his first visit to the Greek class he falls asleep, and is deeply disturbed by his failure to concentrate for long. He even has emotions of revolt "against the Latin teacher" (V, 24). In this world of paternal discipline, guilt feelings

[23] Cf. V, 48.

are unavoidable. And yet Mariabronn is by no means paternity unalloyed. The very name suggests all that is feminine in the Christian
system, and the water of the soul. Abbot Daniel—and later Goldmund himself—is particularly devoted to Mary.

At the gate of the monastery, at the very opening of the book,
stands the chestnut tree: "In front of the archway of the entrance
to the monastery of Mariabronn with its twin pillars, close by the
wayside there stood a chestnut tree, an isolated son of the South,
brought back many years ago by a pilgrim to Rome, a noble chestnut with a strong trunk; tenderly its rounded treetop hung over
the path" (V, 9). This stranger from the South is the maternal
sign over the entrance to Mariabronn,[24] which Goldmund notices at
once; moreover, with the old Romantic parallelism, the tree is "related in concealed affinity with the slender sandstone twin pillars of
the portal and the stone carving of the window arches" (V, 9), for
what is the sculpture of men but a reflection of the patterns of
nature? The full significance of the art of the monastery is revealed
to Goldmund only many years later after his return from his
wanderings, when he finds that all of it—and all Mariabronn's
thinking and teaching besides—"was of one stem, one spirit, and
fitted together the way the branches of a tree do" (V, 285).

Many generations of seminarians had studied at Mariabronn before Goldmund came, and were divided into those who remained
to become monks and those who returned in due course to the world.
Goldmund is to fall into neither category, for he breaks out. The
"exemplary event," the flight over the wall, is approached gradually
and carefully motivated. Goldmund has aspirations to be a "model
pupil" (V, 22), but after a year at the monastery, like his prototypes in the school novels, he suffers from headaches and feels
constantly sick. His comrade Adolf, with whom he had fought an
affaire d'honneur on his first day at the school, now suggests that he
join in the traditional sportive defiance of monastery rules, described as "going into the village" (V, 27); they slip through a
window in the wall, then over a stream, Siddhartha's Rubicon; they
are in search of adventure, "something in which you could forget
headaches and apathy and every kind of misery" (V, 27).

---

[24] We recall the maternal farewells, at the opening of the Maulbronn term, in
Beneath the Wheel.

For Goldmund this is to be the first overt contact with sensual passion, which for him will be the characteristic form of love. But love has many forms and levels; love of God is perhaps rather close to love of the body, an issue adumbrated in *Demian*, and the line between *caritas* and *concupiscentia* is thinner than may be thought.[25] Narziss, basing his life on the former, is not wholly free of the latter, whereas Goldmund later discovers the transfiguration of the latter in his feelings for Lydia, his Donna Anna. When he goes "into the village," however, he experiences simply, and traumatically, the magical effect of woman upon him and of him upon woman. The kiss he receives, reluctantly, from the village girl arouses a desperate conflict within him, and in struggling to forget and to repress he becomes really ill.

Narziss takes personal care of him, and their friendship flowers; learning of the escapade, he discusses it with Goldmund, points out to him that he is no monk, and endeavors to exorcise the other's crippling sense of failure and guilt. In their relationship Narziss is the leader, the clear-sighted analyst, and upon him Goldmund duly transfers his repressed urges. Carried away, in one of their conversations, by his own enthusiasm, Narziss touches the secret spring of Goldmund's being: "You have forgotten your childhood, it woos you from the depths of your soul" (V, 50); he himself is a thinker, Goldmund an artist: "Your peril is drowning in the world of the senses, ours is suffocation in airless space" (V, 51). Drowning is of course the lurking threat outside the wall, as we know from *Peter Camenzind* and above all from *Beneath the Wheel;* airless space, on the other hand, points to *The Steppenwolf*, to the principal disadvantage of the sphere of Harry Haller's Immortals—the fact that one cannot breathe there. Goldmund is shocked, he staggers into the cloisters, and in this novel in which all things are explained an analysis of the situation is duly offered: Narziss "had called the name of the demon which possessed his friend, he had confronted him" (V, 52–53). In the cloisters, stone faces of dogs or wolves seem to swoop down into Goldmund and tear at his bowels. Narziss has already suspected the boy's secret; his obsessive devotion to the path of asceticism, his inability—despite his powerful plastic imagination—to evoke for Narziss his father, this "empty idol"

---

[25] Cf. here also Jung, *Symbols of Transformation*, pp. 63–64.

(V, 43): these facts point to the total repression of the world of the mother in him. His love of church music, of Marian hymns, of his horse Bless, and of all the things of nature are symptoms which seep through the shell; but his father had conscientiously filled the boy's soul with dreams "which were so foreign to the kernel of this soul" (V, 43).

Fainting in the cloisters, Goldmund remains a long time unconscious. This, once more, unlikely though the occasion may appear, is the *Tiefschlaf* of the Vedanta, slept before by Siddhartha and by the Steppenwolf. Returning to himself, he captures again a little of the ebbing dream world, what he has now at last *seen:* "He saw Her. He saw the Great One, the Radiant One, with the full flowering mouth, with the gleaming hair. He saw his mother . . . unspeakably beloved" (V, 59–60). The face of his mother, the wild dancer of heathen origins who had brought shame into his father's life by her desertion, is later to modify gradually in Goldmund's imagination, to take on the quality of archetype, to become "Eva, the primal mother" (V, 40). To him so far his mother has been only a legend, a "terrible legend" (V, 63)—the legendary is again the sphere of the free, the "feminine" and the soul. By the resurgence of this memory Goldmund is liberated from the clutches of the father-world, so foreign to his real nature: it seemed as if "that touch of playfulness, of premature wisdom, of falseness in Goldmund's nature had melted away, that somewhat precocious monkishness" (V, 63). The Way of the monk, as Hesse conceives of it, must always remain in some sense a game, for it depends on will. Goldmund will escape the fate of the priesthood, for him a misshapen destiny in any case (and we recall "In Pressel's Summerhouse"). The kernel stands revealed, and Narziss now feels himself "like a discarded shell" (V, 64); his superiority is gone; he and Goldmund are now full equals. For Goldmund the path is clear; the mother leads him in one direction only: "Into the uncertain, into involvement, need, perhaps death. She did not lead to tranquillity, softness, security, the monk's cell and the lifelong community of the monastery" (V, 64–65).

As suddenly as did Siddhartha, Goldmund realizes that on leaving the monks behind he will not return to his father. The way over the wall leads into the vast feminine Without, and a whole array of symbols now comes to life: there is Goldmund's singing tone of voice, bewitching like that of Chrysostomos. There are Goldmund's dreams—"these many-threaded webs of senses suffused with soul" (V, 65)—he dreams of a paradise like Pictor's. There are the flowers, birds, and above all the fish which people his imagination; then there is the tree with the hair beneath the branch as in the depths of an armpit—hair is, throughout *Narziss and Goldmund*, the supreme figure for the sensual. And there is still ambiguity, hermaphroditism; "tranquillity, softness, security" —these scarcely seem very masculine characteristics. The great Without is also Janus-faced: it contains "childhood and maternal love, the radiantly golden morning of life" but also "everything that was terrifying and dark" (V, 65). The escape over the wall is a flight into purposelessness, into sin. Goldmund encounters the gypsy girl, Lise, when he is sent by Pater Anselm to look for herbs in the woods; this encounter teaches him that in sex experience, and perhaps in that alone, there lies for him "the path to life and the path to the meaning of life" (V, 85)—it is, however, perhaps worth noticing that this is still explicitly only the way and not the goal. He goes out again to spend the night with Lise in a haystack, after apologizing to Narziss for the shame of his act. Goldmund's escape, unlike the first trip "into the village," is this time effected without any fear; he walks naked through the deep, tugging waters of the stream. On the bank behind him he leaves his "false home" (V, 87), Mariabronn.

Lise had first come upon Goldmund asleep and had approached him "with a little burning-red wood-pink in her mouth" (V, 79). The image is evocative. And yet the language which describes their first lovemaking does not have this vivid sensuality at all: "The lovely, short bliss of love arched above him, flared up golden and burning, subsided and died away" (V, 80). In characteristic rhythm and delicately toned, this sentence still has a curious emptiness; there is a *vault* above them, the red flower has given place to the color gold; the "lovely short bliss" and the sacramental fire which burns here in fact suggest religious ecstasy. In particular the word *"glühen"* has this *double-entendre* in Hesse, and we may recall the euphemism "to ordain" (*die Weihen geben*) as used in *Berthold;* the sensual is subsumed in the religious; erotic and divine love are indeed close in Hesse; and very frequently the language which tells of Goldmund's seductions disguises the spiritual passion of the mystic. The night with Lise passes almost wordlessly, and when they awake it is to sadness; for she must return to her husband.

Goldmund is left alone in the great wide world, in the forest. His senses always were alive to the fascinating beauty of natural things, the art of God; he had peered amazed at the "minute, starry heaven" (V, 77) embroidered in the leaves of the St. John's wort, at the miraculously formed spiral in the empty snail's shell. Like Siddhartha after his first moment of illumination, Goldmund *sees;* all around him is color and rapid animal movement: "He met many a hare, they shot suddenly out of the undergrowth when he approached, stared at him, turned and fled, their ears flattened, bright hued beneath their tails" (V, 95). Then the forest is transformed in Goldmund's fancy, and he wishes himself metamorphosed into a woodpecker. He recalls how at school he had often drawn flowers, leaves, trees, animals and human heads upon his slate, blending the forms of the species indiscriminately. These illustrations to *Pictor's Transformations* (V, 94–95) evoke paradise and confirm that the Pictor *Märchen* is, on one of its levels at least, an allegory for the processes of art, of play.[26] Nature responds to Goldmund's urge for life, and the imagery of "Iris" reappears gently sensualized: "He picked a little violet flower in the grass, held it close to his eye, peered into the narrow little calices, there were veins there and tiny organs as thin as hairs" (V, 103). Goldmund spends in the forest (exactly as Hermann Heilner did) two nights and two days; then he arrives at a village, where he addresses himself to a farmer's wife—he as wordlessly as before, though she makes feline noises in her throat.

Goldmund's wanderings commence, and the central narrative of the novel opens out. His adventures are arranged in five main sections, of which the first (Lydia and Julie), the third (Meister Niklaus and Lisbeth), and the fifth (Agnes and Narziss) take place within the walls of a castle or a city and are moments of pause (or in the last case the culmination and conclusion) in the years of vagrancy which are evoked in the second (Viktor) and the fourth

[26] In the actual illustrations to *Pictor's Transformations* we have a flower with eyes and mouth, and a tree with human head and shoulders.

(Robert, Lene, and the plague). Goldmund is Don Juan, all things to all women, although they almost all hasten back to their security after a night or two spent with him; and true to type he prefers his freedom. In the calyx of the violet flower Goldmund had seen "how in the bosom of a woman or the brain of a thinker life moved, pleasure trembled" (V, 103); equally revelatory of the parallelism upon which this novel is constructed is the analogy between the development of Goldmund's powers of sensual discrimination— between various kinds of skin and hair, "this capacity for recognition and discrimination" (V, 107), and Narziss' definition of the work of the intellect, of scholarship as "the obsession with the discovery of differences" (V, 47).

Tramping through his medieval world, Goldmund first comes to rest at the castle of a knight for whom he works for some months as a secretary. With the elder daughter, Lydia, he has a melancholic and all but chaste affair and learns that desire is not the whole of love. Then he is put to the test in extraordinary fashion by the younger sister, Julie, who threatens to wake her father unless he admits her to the bed he is sharing with Lydia. Goldmund of course yields, and caresses them both with either hand; he has a gay abandon no other lover in Hesse's novels ever remotely approaches, and there is piquancy and comedy in many of his exploits.

Expelled by the indignant knight, he sets off again through "strange parts" (V, 132), "distant and arid places" (V, 224), and, as he comes to learn, the kingdom of "the great fear" (V, 141). He has much in him of the eternal vagrant. Lying in the wood beside the sleeping vagabond Viktor, Goldmund feels "more strongly than ever before the feelings of the homeless one who has built no house or castle or monastery walls between himself and the great fear" (V, 141). It takes him only a short time to discover what really lies in wait outside the wall, a secret which, though some may have suspected its nature, none of Hesse's previous protagonists ever clearly formulated for himself. What is beyond the wall is simply death: " 'Are you afraid, Narziss,' he talked to him, 'do you shudder, have you noticed something? Yes, honored friend, the world is full of death, full of death, he sits in every hedge, he stands behind every tree, and it is useless to build walls and dormitories and

chapels and churches, he peeps through the window!' " (V, 145).
The sexual act and death, intimately linked, dominate Goldmund's
world. Perhaps the central section of *Narziss and Goldmund* may
be seen in some degree as a parody of the *Abenteurerroman,* the
picaresque novel. Goldmund is the vagabond, the wandering
scholar, and also the *picaro;* certain of his adventures have something of the picaresque outtrumping of the secure and the great.
Hesse several times noted the possible relationship between vagabondage, or indeed the pursuit of travel experiences nowadays
called tourism, and the erotic impulse.[27] *Narziss and Goldmund*
contains a reflective discourse on the life of the vagabond and
perpetual wayfarer: these are the sons of Adam, "who was expelled
from Paradise" (V, 199), loathed by the possessing classes because
they remind them of transience and death, of "the ice of space,"
"the remorseless icy death which fills the universe all around us"
(V, 200). How different, how much more negative is the use of
this frigid imagery here from that in *The Steppenwolf!*

At heart the vagabond is a child (as Knulp was), "his maternal
origins, his deviation from law and the mind, his exposure and
secret perpetual proximity to death had long ago taken deep possession of Goldmund's soul and had shaped it" (V, 200). Eichendorff's Taugenichts was also only a child, and Goldmund, like
Taugenichts, remains perpetually attached to his starting point
as it were by the tails of his coat. But proximity to the Eichendorffian model is refuted by the overt eroticism and above all the
violence of life as portrayed in this novel. Tough-minded beggars
are not uncommon in Hesse's works, and for their rascality and
rapacity the author betrays a certain sympathy.[28] The thieving Viktor, with whom Goldmund journeys for a while and whom he has
to kill in self-defense, is a more genuine vagabond type than Goldmund is himself; Viktor predicts that one day Goldmund will creep
back "in some walls or other" (V, 141), and the latter knows that
this is probably true, though it does not imply that he will ever
feel secure and at rest.

[27] See especially "The Hiking Trip" (III, 394). Cf. also "Engadine Experiences" (VII, 852) and its reference to travel, in a passage which mentions
Goldmund's "privileged moment."

[28] Cf. the figure of Alois Beckeler in "Walter Kömpff."

Goldmund's slaying of Viktor teaches him the need to fight tooth and nail for survival, a thing he is physically well equipped to do. Alone in the savage winter, he defends himself against death "with lust" (V, 147), and all but succumbs. True sympathy with death he aquires only when he comes upon the first signs of the plague. The expansive account of the ravages of the Black Death is in the best Romantic tradition, and one might well think of the wanderings of Renzo and presume the influence of *I Promessi Sposi*. In the peasants' hut, where Goldmund finds five corpses, is an appalling stench of death; his eager eyes are caught by curious details, for instance the dead wife's hair, which seems to refuse to submit to its demise—a far cry, perhaps, from the hair in Julie's armpits. Goldmund is relentlessly attracted by these new sights; understanding the inevitability of death and corruption, he remains gripped but unafraid. Filled with a bitter *amor fati*, Goldmund has come to understand the intimate connection of pleasure and pain, while looking at the expression on the face of a woman in labor; now he grasps the link between the life-urge and the death-wish. The pilgrim Robert—exiled to the highways and byways because his family failed to welcome him back from his Rome pilgrimage "like the Prodigal Son" (V, 202)—teams up with Goldmund, is terrified, however, by the risks he takes and by his monstrous curiosity. There is a short idyll in a hut in the forest with a new paramour, Lene, until she dies of the plague, having been bitten in the breast by a rapist whom Goldmund slays. Life with Lene desperately affirms the generative against a back cloth of decay, though Goldmund is inclined to dismiss the whole episode, with sad irony, as "playing at homes" (V, 221).

The wayfarer continues his dreadful peregrination through the land of death, the land of the mother; he studies a fresco of the dance of death, which captures the ruthlessness and the harshness of it, but Goldmund "would have wished for another picture of it, the wild song of death had a quite different music for him, not bony and severe, but rather sweet and seductive, enticing homeward, maternal" (V, 228). For him death is no stern masculine judge, no executioner, but a motherly embrace, an invitation to incest. Goldmund's journey through the countryside of the plague is his "passage through hell" (V, 227), but his is not the hell of

Harry Haller, it is the hell of Klingsor, the *homme sensuel*, the artist.

The Way of the body, of "wide open senses" (V, 228), teaches first and foremost the lesson of transience. Lydia sees in the depths of Goldmund's eyes "nothing but mourning; as if your eyes knew that there is no happiness and that all beautiful and beloved things do not stay with us long" (V, 120). Goldmund's eyes linger constantly upon the signs of transience: in the fish market there are the gaping, expiring fish, while the fishmongers all-oblivious loudly call their wares; there is the question of Viktor's hair—does any still remain upon his buried skull? And above all there is Goldmund's particular pastime, gazing at a certain moment into his lover's eyes, Lise's eyes (V, 104) and Agnes' eyes (V, 250). The flicker of the woman's eyes at the moment of orgasm is like the shudder of the dying fish and reminds Goldmund also of one of his deepest moments of insight into the soul. Lovemaking has its paradigm in music, Goldmund being the minstrel, the player: "I am a minstrel, if you like and you are my sweet lute" (V, 250). In him culminates the Don Juan motif which first appeared in Hesse's work in "Klingsor's Last Summer" and "Klein and Wagner," as Goldmund moves from lover to lover in search of that permanence which is never to be found.[29] That he can—or must—stand back from his entrancement and make his observations points to the artist in him.

The episode with the Jewess Rebecca, whose family have just lost their lives in a pogrom and who rejects his advances with scorn, stresses the need for a man to see and accept his fate, especially when that be imminent death. It stresses also the invincibility of evil, the inevitable working out of original sin.[30] Goldmund's "Hail

[29] Cf. Jung, *Symbols of Transformation*, p. 205: "The heroes are usually wanderers, and wandering is a symbol of longing, of the restless urge which never finds its object, of nostalgia for the lost mother." Cf. also Stekel's observation that Don Juan is perpetually unfaithful precisely because of his unchanging mother-fixation. However, Goldmund is not normally disappointed by his women; and his metaphysical attitude is not the cosmic hostility which, for instance, Hoffmann notes in his "Don Juan." And yet the revolt and the metaphysical despair are undeniably there.

[30] This section caused Hesse some trouble. He rejected Nazi suggestions that he cut the passage out, and the novel thereupon vanished from the German book market.

Marys," his veneration of the Immaculate Conception, speak of his sense of sin; but step by step his faith declines and is lost in the very excess of evil.

Before the onset of the plague year, he had already found his vocation. The thought that Goldmund may be a born artist first comes to Narziss and is expressed with the undisguised directness typical of this novel. Some years after the flight from Mariabronn, the wanderer first suspects his goal. The motivation of this development is interesting—it begins with a Mass he attends in a monastery which stirs his memories, and he feels a vague impulse to be rid of his past, to change his life, to confess. He goes to confession, and receives gentle treatment from the priest. Just then, in his absolved state, he finds his destiny: his gaze lights upon "a Virgin carved in wood . . . more living, more beautiful and intense and soulful than he thought he had ever seen before" (V, 153). The priest, observing his wonder, refers him to Meister Niklaus in the city, the sculptor of the Madonna. Goldmund is "transformed" (V, 154), in his purposeless life he now has an aim. To Niklaus he relates how the face of the sculptured Virgin held the same secret he had himself once found, the identity, the simultaneity of suffering and serenity in a single smile. Rather unwillingly the master, having tested his skill as a draughtsman, agrees to accept him as a pupil, though not as an official apprentice, for he is too old.

As he begins to learn, Goldmund also observes Meister Niklaus and perceives his inner contradictions. Niklaus is not as Goldmund had imagined the author of that statue must be; he is "older, more modest, more sober, much less radiant and attractive and not at all happy" (V, 159); his face contrasts with his hands, which have a life of their own. The hands indeed are the hands of the artist, the face is the face of the bourgeois. Goldmund's years in the city, rich as they are in learning, in experience of art and sex and fighting (he acquires the reputation of a dangerous customer on the streets), are rewarding and yet frustrating, for he cannot acclimatize himself to his master's outlook or way of life. He is not an industrious pupil, wastes time, plays truant and sleeps; for which waywardness, however, in Niklaus' eyes, his extraordinary natural talent compensates. The born outsider, Goldmund cannot admire the great sculptor's "tranquil, moderate, extremely orderly and respectable life" (V, 168). Niklaus lives a solitary existence, keeping a jealous eye upon his daughter, Lisbeth, the challenging innocence of whose chaste beauty makes Goldmund long to see her face distorted in ecstasy or in pain. Niklaus, his pupil notes, represses drives which are still powerful, and occasionally on a journey can be temporarily rejuvenated and transformed. He accepts commissions for reasons which Goldmund regards as shabby—money and fame. *Gelegenheitskunst* means nothing to Goldmund, it is a "trivial game" (V, 172); he has no use for "the fat bourgeois" (V, 194), nor for compromise of any kind in the sphere of art. While he waits, on the first day, for the master's decision in his case, Goldmund has a moment of self-contemplation, gazing into the well in the yard: "In the dark surface of the well he saw his own reflection and thought . . . that he and every human being flowed away and constantly changed and ultimately dissolved, while his image, created by the artist, always remained unchangeably the same. Perhaps, he thought, the root of all art and perhaps of all the things of the spirit is the fear of death" (V, 162).

Again and again the novel returns to the motif of the inner image, the vision in the soul which is the root of the work of art. In his subsequent wanderings Goldmund stores up a hoard of such images, to pour them out later in his drawing and his wood carving. Memory—"this entire picture book" (V, 254)—is to be rescued from death. These "genuine images of the soul" (V, 172) are free of will, of purpose, and of function; the "original image of a good work of art," as Goldmund later tells Narziss, "is not flesh and blood, it is mental" (V, 278–279), which the latter finds to be "exactly what the old philosophers call an 'idea.'" In practice, Goldmund's theory of art is Schopenhauerian rather than Platonic, just as Goldmund's world is characteristically Schopenhauer's "world as will," his Sansara.

As he advances in art, so Goldmund surrenders more and more completely to the hegemony of the senses. We recall one of his earlier dreams: "Once he dreamed: he was big and grown, but sat like a child on the floor, had clay before him and like a child was kneading figures out of the clay. The kneading amused him, and he gave the animals and men absurdly large sexual organs, in his dream this appeared very witty to him" (V, 67). He becomes totally at the mercy of women, even those who are no longer young and beautiful; they are all that gives warmth to life, and the transience of their love is the source of his hidden but changeless melancholia. Pleasure gives place to melancholy, which in its turn gives way to desire. Life is seen as a function of tumescence and detumescence, death and delight are one, the mother of life is love and lust, or else corruption and the grave. The eternal Eva perpetually gives birth and destroys. With the wisdom of his blood Goldmund knows that he belongs to her and not to the father.

Yet he defines art as the unity of father and mother, spirit and flesh: "it could begin in the sensual and lead to the most abstract, or it could originate in a pure world of ideas and end in the bloodiest flesh" (V, 176–177). At this point there is a curious, and highly significant, equivocation: art may offer Goldmund the possibility of the reconciliation of his deepest conflicts, or failing this only the possibility "of a magnificent, perpetually fresh analogy for the schism of his nature" (V, 177). Art is hermaphroditic; this does not mean, however, that it is necessarily a true *coincidentia oppositorum;* it may be, it is here admitted, but the simulacrum of the perpetually unresolved polarity of the self. Here lies the reservation of a writer who knew a great deal about sham harmonies; the whole of *The Steppenwolf*, indeed, is just such a simulacrum. Inspiration is one thing, essentially erotic in its origins, as is the sense of transience, as is despair; form is quite another thing and it belongs, as *The Steppenwolf* showed, not merely to the father, but to faith, the divine, to God. Thus we hear of Goldmund's spiritual exercises, which, properly performed, have the austerity of musical technique: "Often during his work smoking with anger and impatience or else in a trance of lustful bliss he ducked down in the pious exercises as in a deep, cool pool of water, which washed from him the arrogance of inspiration just as it did the arrogance of despair" (V, 295). These are cleansing moments, recurrent baptism; at the same time they provide the form which, apparently and always temporarily, resolves the chaos of the soul. Temporarily, for form, like faith, may decay. Art is, as Narziss ponders, surveying Goldmund's work, "perhaps a game, but certainly no inferior game to that with logic, grammar, and theology"

(V, 299). For *Narziss and Goldmund* is by no means, as has occasionally been thought, merely a paean to the mother; it is an affirmation also of the formal, the aesthetic will, both in Narziss' life and in Goldmund's art. Both in himself and in Goldmund, Narziss finds the working of the same "spirit"—"it is this that will show you the way out of the gloomy confusion of the sensual world" (V, 279). And at the same time the inadequacy, the temporariness of the achievements of "spirit" *in life* are deeply felt. Goldmund's art is an act of faith *par excellence*—"Credo, quia absurdum est." In this lies the tragic undertone of the novel.

The Way of the artist, then, has much in common with the Way of the monk; both depend on will and also on unsevered contact with the spring of the soul; the work of art itself is a simulacrum of the perfected life, and it alone does not decay. The practice of art, as we learn, is connected with a state which is almost a kind of nonattachment. Goldmund experiences this as he works upon his figure of St. John the Evangelist, whose features are those of Narziss.[31]

Art is also similar to the religious path in that in the end it requires great sacrifice, the sacrifice of life; Goldmund yearns to avoid the price which Meister Niklaus has had to pay: "To create without having to pay the price of life for this! To live without having to renounce the nobility of being creative! Was that impossible?" (V, 255). Goldmund now finds that art is a harder taskmaster than Niklaus: "To it he had sacrificed the wild freedom of the forests, the ecstasy of the wide world, the bitter lustful pleasure of danger, the pride of misery" (V, 177)—once again there is a wall around him, the intolerable wall of the artist's ivory tower, to be bolstered—as Niklaus hopes—by the wall of marriage. For art, too, is will. But the harsh ecstasy outside the wall, an orgasm which has the savor of death, is Goldmund's indispensable nourishment, without which, for him at least, there would also be no art. At death's door he talks once more to Narziss about what he thinks are the origins of art: "And I have also had the good fortune to experience the fact that sensuality can be suffused with soul. Out of that arises art" (V, 317–318). However, the artist—unfortu-

---

[31] Again we note the significance of the name "Johannes"—Narziss' name in religion and also that of Hesse's father.

nately—rarely finds peace and harmony in his art (Goldmund venerates and envies the peace of Narziss, without realizing that this too is in reality a condition of perpetual tension). The artist relapses constantly into a sensuality which is not "suffused with soul" (*beseelt*), he finds himself again and again returning to a situation which is an agony of transience, and of hypnotization by the specter of death, upon the very floor of his being. The transience of orgasm is the "kernel of all experience" (V, 175), and it is the germ also of the "kernel of his frequent tendency to sadness and disgust" (V, 175); for the difficulty of the Way of the artist is that the completed work of art fails to resolve the polarity in the artist's soul: "Nowhere was there inhaling and exhaling, being male and female at once" (V, 255).

This distinction between the nature of art and the nature of the artist is central to a deeper understanding of *Narziss and Goldmund*. In the insight it has into the fate of the artist lies the real theme of this essentially tragic novel. Of course all his art fails to save Goldmund from choking fear as eventually, caught red-handed in his escapade with Agnes, the governor's mistress, he sits in his dungeon, awaiting dawn and the coming of the hangman. He is confronted by the end of the Romantic pursuit of experience, just as the cosmic pessimists of the Romantic era had envisioned it, "the abyss, the end, death" (V, 261), the horror of the corruption of the body: "Tomorrow he will no longer be alive. He will hang, he will be a thing that birds sit on and at which they peck" (V, 261). What Goldmund cannot endure, besides, is the thought of the loss of sense experience *per se;* and in a torment of nostalgic grief he surrenders his life "into the maternal hands" (V, 263). Long before this he had come to understand that for him art was *not* the end and purpose of existence (an understanding which also came to his closest relative, Klingsor): "Art was a fine thing, but it was no goddess and no end and purpose, not for him; he did not have to follow art, but only the call of the mother" (V, 192).

Narziss and Goldmund is, then, a *Künstlerroman* in which dark doubts shadow the redemptive validity of art. Goldmund broods over the relationship between the sphere of art and that of the soul. He sits gazing into the river, deeply attracted, of course, by water: he gazes "at the dark, vague bottom," at the unrecognizable, gold-glinting things below, refuse or fish, "this cursory subdued flicker of sunken golden treasure in the wet black ground. It seemed to him that all genuine mysteries were just like this little mystery of the water, all real, genuine images of the soul: they had no outline, they had no form, they merely suggested it as a distant, lovely possibility, they were veiled and ambiguous" (V, 188–189). The color gold alerts us—it is a numinous experience which is being described. Goldmund stares down into the deep of the soul, where the fish swim, borrows come crumbs of bread from a passing youth and, like little Hans Giebenrath, throws them food. What Goldmund sees is mystery, the sparkling of the formless ultimate ground. It is not the god of Narziss that Goldmund perceives here, the god of Calw, of form, to whom music and exercises may appear to lead. This trembling, fertile mystery, "inexpressibly golden and silvery," this may be caught also in the magic stuff of which dreams are woven, Jungian dreams, "a pool in whose crystal the forms of all human beings, animals, angels, and demons lived as perpetually wakeful possibilities" (V, 189). Goldmund recalls how once at Mariabronn he had seen the letters of the Latin and Greek alphabets undergo "similar dreams of form and magical transformations" (V, 189). He is puzzled that the formless beauty of the river of the soul conveys an experience like that obtained from the perfectly formed work of art. He concludes that in both cases the essential is mystery; art at its highest can express the mystery of the soul. But form is, therefore, not primary; both art and spiritual work are secondary to the mystery of the mother. This vision of the Great Mother, in which his memory of his own mother is enclosed "like the kernel in a cherry" (V, 191), remains inexpressible; and the ultimate destiny of the would-be artist-saint is evidently not form, not self-realization, but its opposite, the embrace of Nothingness, of the dissolute, random world. Thus an issue which was already essentially posed in the antithesis of Demian and Frau Eva becomes perhaps the central problem of Hesse's later novels, both of their message and of their form.

Narziss and Goldmund, it has been noted, has its analogies with the *Abenteurerroman* of the seventeenth century (*Berthold* is set in that period), a type of novel in which the Way of the profligate hangs suspended, as that of Grimmelshausen's Simplicissimus does, between hermitage and hermitage, the innocence of the child and the illumination of the saint. In Grimmelshausen's novel every worldly event is seen *sub specie aeternitatis*, and stands therefore under judgment. So it is with Harry Haller, whose judges—except perhaps for the bourgeois narrator—are all projections of that fiercely cruel judge he carries within himself. Goldmund's way—between the flight over the wall and the return to Mariabronn—is never long free of the thought of home and the memory of Narziss. In this he is not unlike Eichendorff's Taugenichts, whom he resembles also in that extreme oscillation of feeling, between exultancy and melancholic depression, upon which Narziss is drawn to comment.

The motif of male friendship, in this novel, discloses its undeniable erotic quality; Hesse commented: "First of all, as far as the friendships Goldmund-Narziss, Veraguth-Burckhardt, Hesse-Knulp, etc., are concerned. That these friendships . . . are totally free of eroticism seems an erroneous view. . . . In the case of Narziss it is especially clear. Goldmund means for Narziss not only the friend and not only art, he also means love, the warmth of the senses, what is desired and forbidden." [32] As much as this, in fact, Narziss actually says himself; he is in any case a monk for whom love in the sense of *caritas*, the ideal of service, is the principal goal; in his rejection of purely intellectual, scholarly purposes he differs from many of his brethren (as does Joseph Knecht in *The Glass Bead Game*). That Goldmund represents a certain peril for him, this Narziss well knows; he is, as he says, merely repelled by those not-infrequent cases of monks and teachers who fall in love with novices and students. Goldmund transfers his repressed physical longings to Narziss; he even goes so far as to stroke his friend's hair. Narziss is fully awake and aware: "You are an artist, I am a thinker. You sleep at the mother's breast, I watch in the desert. The sun shines on me, moon and stars on you, your dreams are of girls, mine of boys" (V, 51). The course of Goldmund's love-life, as is the case with earlier heroes, goes from man through woman and back again to man. Agnes, the last stage before the return, has evidently in her something of Hermine, the sister, the *anima*: "At the basin of a well he paused and looked for his reflection. The picture bore a brotherly resemblance to that of the blond woman" (V, 246). In the figures of Narziss and Goldmund are caught many contrasts, that between the priest and thinker, and the artist and Don Juan; that between the homosexual and the heterosexual; the hermetic opposition between *animus* and *anima*, and, further, two contrasting attitudes toward the "exemplary event." In his carving of St. John Goldmund portrays his friend, a figure in whose hands is expressed total serenity, free of all "despair, disorder, and revolt" (V, 179); Narziss lives wholly within the Order: "He had committed himself" (*sich verschrieben*) (V, 74). The phrase "*er hatte sich verschrieben*" has, however, curious overtones, even sinister ones; to commit oneself, this may be of God, but it may also be of the Devil—and one thinks here of Hesse's ambivalent attitude to the Roman Catholic church. Unlike Narziss, Goldmund must leave behind him, just as his mother did, "house and home, husband and child, community and order" (V, 74), following his inner drives alone. He quits "la Maison," [33] he leaves the "father" behind. When these two meet again, many years have passed; [34] as though by chance the new abbot's opportunity to intervene with the outraged governor then saves the seducer's life. Here Narziss appears as the polished diplomat, finely combining his spiritual empathy with the exercise of political influence, as Joseph Knecht is also called upon to do. The scene of reunion and recognition is a strange one: ostensibly it is to be a moment of confession. Confession is the river bed of the entire novel; moments of confession form turning points (*Wendepunkte*) in the story. Goldmund goes to confession before he first notices Niklaus' Madonna in the side chapel; then on his exhausted return to his master's city years later, through the plague-ridden countryside, he also seeks to confess. This time, however, he finds only empty confessionals, for all the priests have died or fled, and he confesses in the end in

[33] Cf. Gide, *Romans, Récits et Soties* (Paris, 1958), p. 478.
[34] It is unclear just how many; no satisfying chronology of Goldmund's career can be established. There are contradictions: it is "a good ten years" (V, 219) since Goldmund last saw Narziss; yet soon thereafter he returns to the city which he first visited "so many years ago" (V, 235); though Julie, when he sees her again, has not yet lost her beauty, his first visit to her château now belongs to his "legendary youth" (V, 282). Chapter 13, in particular, involves much compression of time.

one of these, confesses his total loss of faith: "I have lost my confidence in you, Almighty Father, you have made the world badly, you keep it in order ill" (V, 234). Cast into the dungeon, Goldmund awaits the dawn and the priest who will come with it, formulating a desperate plan of escape: to kill the monk and flee in his robes. Thus he plans, albeit unwittingly, the murder of his "father," Johannes, Narziss.

This dreadful, perhaps ultimate, crime is not perpetrated. Pardoned by the governor, Goldmund returns with his friend to Mariabronn, for the last years, for the elucidations of the final conversations, which have a tractlike function.[35] The Prodigal Son, as Viktor predicted he would, crawls back between the walls and confesses to his "father," who is now both priest and abbott. (Of significance here is Goldmund's expressed desire at the beginning of the novel to confess only to Narziss and not to his official confessor.) As Narziss remarks: "You have led the usual worldly life, like the Prodigal Son you have kept the swine, no longer do you know what law and order mean" (V, 280). But as Hesse observed of the act of return: "He who returns home is not the same as he who has never left it."[36] Goldmund, indeed, comes back in triumph, and not as the abject capitulant. Thus the "exemplary event" is transformed; there is a total reversal of the fundamental movement of the old novel of redemption (such as *Simplicissimus*). "Do you not know," Narziss had once asked Goldmund in the words of Demian, "that one of the shortest ways to the life of a saint can be the life of a profligate?" (V, 38). This Siddhartha also comes to understand and to live out. But not Goldmund. The vagrant peregrinates in sin, but he does not find the error of his ways.

The novel is not cyclic, it is not the occult spiral; it is by no means the case that Goldmund returns at the end to the state in which he began though on a higher level of insight; he does not progress from *tumb* to *wîs* in the traditional manner. Goldmund does not even, in returning to the world of the father, contrive to blend this with the world of the mother in a lofty synthesis; for what synthesis there is for him really lies only in the achievements

[35] Cf. P. Schiefer, "Grundstrukturen des Erzählens bei Hermann Hesse," p. 89.
[36] "The Hiking Trip" (III, 412).

of his crayon and his chisel, and not in his life. Though his Way hangs suspended between the Alpha and the Omega of Mariabronn, yet he is not judged against, and forced to submit to, some supreme standard outside himself; on the contrary, his several confessions point in quite a different direction. In the first of these, to the priest in the church where he finds the Madonna, he is astonished by the mildness of his reception: "But the confessor seemed to know the life of the vagrants, he was not horror-struck, he listened calmly, he censured and admonished in a grave and friendly manner without a thought of condemnation" (V, 153). In the second, to the empty confessional, what should be confession turns into a grumbling remonstration with God. In the third, to Narziss, Goldmund is definitely disappointed: "To Goldmund's amazement, indeed disappointment, the confessor did not take his real sins too seriously, but admonished and chastised him unsparingly for his neglect of prayer, confession, and Communion" (V, 294). Here the penance awarded is a set of exercises which will draw off some of the dross from Goldmund's soul and give a little form to his spiritual life. Worldly sin, however, as Dion Pugil in *The Glass Bead Game* later pronounces, is *childish;* it is not real sin, which is reserved for those with insight. The actual course of Goldmund's worldly life, therefore, all that he felt obliged to confess, is simply not judged against the standard of Mariabronn and Narziss. In fact the opposite is the case; in a very real sense it is Goldmund who is the presiding judge at the end of the novel, sitting in judgment over Narziss. As instinctive man, and as the artist, he carries the justification of his way of life into the very citadel of the will.

In one of their last conversations, Narziss and Goldmund discuss the idea of self-realization (*sich verwirklichen*), which is the approach, step by step, to the unattainable condition of perfect being that is God. The analogy, fundamental to this novel, between the creation of the work of art and spiritual work upon the self is specifically drawn: "If you have freed the image of a person from accidental elements and converted it to pure form—then, as an artist, you have realized this image" (V, 288). Narziss remarks that Goldmund's way of self-realization has been much harder than his, but that he has found it, all the same—the Way of the artist. The conversation is then sidetracked into an argument about the possibility of thinking without images, in which Narziss undertakes a rather naïve defense of pure mathematics, and old resonances of the school novel sound again.

A superficial reading of the book's conclusion might indeed give the impression that Goldmund has realized himself, whereas Narziss has not. But such a view overlooks the deeper tide of the novel. It may well be that the key to an understanding of the place of *Narziss and Goldmund* in its author's development is to be found in a letter dated August 9, 1929, that is, in the period when Hesse was composing the novel:

In my case it has always been, as you know, a matter of longing for life, for a real, personal, intensive life which has not been mechanized and reduced to norms. Like everyone else I had to pay for the plus in personal freedom which I took for myself partly by renunciations and privations, partly, however, by increased achievement. So with time my profession as a writer became not merely an aid in approaching my ideal of life more closely, but almost an end in itself. I have become a writer, but I have not become a human being. I have reached a partial goal, but not the main one. I have failed. With respectable remnants and smaller concessions, maybe, than other idealists, but I have failed. My writing is personal, intensive, for myself often a source of joy, but my life is not, my life is nothing else but readiness to work; and the sacrifices which I bring by living in extreme loneliness, etc., I have been bringing in fact for a long time no longer for life, but only for writing. The value and the intensity of my life lies in the times when I am poetically productive, therefore precisely those times when I am giving expression to the inadequacy and despair of my life.[37]

The artist who "realizes himself" as an artist often does so with a bad conscience. To the question: where is Goldmund's bad conscience? the answer must be: it is in the whole novel. *Narziss and Goldmund* with its burning anguish over transience and its apprehensive wooing of death, its seesawing moods—"this oscillation between lust for life and sense of death" (V, 277)—is closer in feeling to "Klingsor's Last Summer" than to any other of Hesse's works; and "Klingsor" was written in Montagnola a few months after the total collapse of the author's family life. Despite contra-

[37] *Letters* (VII, 487).

dictory evidence,[38] it appears that in the late twenties, before his third marriage, Hesse experienced another attack of disillusionment and loss of faith (later reflected in part in *The Journey to the East*); he ceased to believe in self-development. Just as, when he fled from Bern to Tessin, he felt that devotion to his literary work alone could give his life meaning, so also now in 1929 he holds to the same idea; except that this is no longer a notion but a *fait accompli*. Hesse says that it is no longer possible to reach his ideal aims in life—he means, of course, the goal of spiritual self-perfection; the conclusion of *Siddhartha* has revealed itself, with time, to be an utterly unattainable wish-dream. Even *The Steppenwolf*, that optimistic catharsis, ended with a touch of resignation; for Harry perceived that progress along the Way would be very gradual and would involve, maybe, many seasons spent in hell. Now we find Hesse confessing that his spiritual aspirations have been broken upon the wheel of reality: he has reached only a partial goal; only in his writing has he really achieved something; only in his art, now an end in itself, is there meaning; and in his art, therefore, even by the fact that he still creates it, he gives expression to the inadequacy and despair of his life.

Narziss and Goldmund is, then, superficially, a novel of self-re-

---

[38] The assertion in the important letter to Rudolf Pannwitz (January 1955) that this period was one of "tolerable comfort after a serious crisis" is an example (*Briefe: Erweiterte Ausgabe* [Frankfort, 1964], p. 437). However, it is vital to see on what the relative tranquillity of Hesse's intellectual and emotional life during these years was apparently based: it was founded on humor, that is to say, essentially on resignation and compromise, on the abandonment of lofty spiritual aspirations without denying the existence of a higher world. A poem written in 1929 may be adduced in further support of this argument: "Gedenken an den Sommer Klingsors" declares: "no longer to wish for the unthinkable/Is now my wisdom . . ." and affirms as present desire and purpose a purely artistic function:

> "nichts als Spiegel sein,
> Darin für Stunden, so wie Mond im Rhein,
> Der Sterne, Götter, Engel Bilder rasten" (V, 716).

> (to be nought but mirror
> In which for hours, like moonlight in the Rhine
> Rest images of stars, gods, angels.)

In a recovery of personal spiritual hope *The Journey to the East*, which stands at the end of this period, tries to show that this very resignation itself is a stage upon the Way.

alization, but in its essential tenor much more one of tragic resignation, its conclusion is still instinct with aggression against the world-view of the "idealists," of Plato and the theologians. It is all very well for Narziss to pour the balm of "thinking" upon Goldmund's accumulated "spite against us theologians" (V, 276); it remains true that Goldmund dies declaring he has and wants no peace with God: "Do you mean peace with God? No, that I have not found. I do not want peace with Him. He has made the world badly, we don't need to praise it, and it will not be of much concern to Him whether I extol Him or not" (V, 318-319). The conclusion of the novel, properly understood, presents precisely the attainment of that "partial goal" of which Hesse speaks in his letter. The two friends are of course not united in any harmonious entity, but remain utterly separate and different to the very end. Goldmund may have blended mind and matter in his art, but he has scarcely done so in his life. And as for Narziss, the message which his counterpart brings back from the world may incite his wonder but cannot help him to be saved.

On his return to Mariabronn, Goldmund sees his *vita* spread out before him in three great divisions: "the dependence upon Narziss and its resolution—the period of freedom and wandering—and the return, the homecoming, the beginning of maturity and the harvest" (V, 280). We recall "A Bit of Theology" and certain discrepancies between its rigid triadic structure and the actual course of Siddhartha's life. In Siddhartha's case the *via purgativa* was not taken to the point of the breaking of the will and the coming of grace; illumination came to Siddhartha only by way of total submersal in the life of the senses. For Goldmund the *via illuminativa* is replaced by art, which also comes to him through the senses; Narziss remains upon the *via purgativa*, upon which Goldmund had so erroneously set out, and follows it to its highly uncertain end. Thus it is evident that in this novel, as in *Siddhartha*, Hesse distorts the traditional mystical framework to accord with his own permanent dualistic dilemma. The aspiring saint is divided into two halves, which proceed in parallel upon what should be successive stages of the Way. The third step of Goldmund's life, described here as "the return, the homecoming, the beginning of maturity and the harvest," is full of ambiguities. It appears that

Goldmund becomes, to use the *Siddhartha* term, "perfected." Working at his sculptures in the monastery, he even acquires a pupil—a sure sign of advancement on the Way—Erich, the smith's son. His retirement, in order to create, parallels exactly Narziss' retirement to commence the spiritual exercises which precede ordination: "For the monastery it was as though he had vanished" (V, 292) may be compared with the previous: "A few days later, already, it was as though Narziss had vanished" (V, 74). Goldmund's smile belongs only to those figures in Hesse's novels who are perfected; it is a smile "which looked so old and fragile and which seemed sometimes a little half-witted, sometimes had the appearance of pure kindness and wisdom" (V, 321). He is illuminated; he accepts that his dream one day of portraying Mother Eve will never be realized; she does not wish her mystery to be revealed; instead of him giving form to her, her fingers now mold him.

Some play is now made with Goldmund's aging. He is alarmed to be repulsed by a girl he approaches who finds him old; restless, after two years in the monastery, he sets off on his travels again, secretly in search of Agnes, who then in her turn rejects him. He comes back sick and exhausted, aged by many years; true to his pattern, this suddenly old middle-aged man studies his face in a mirror, finds therein, for the first time, a touch of equanimity. He is perhaps "no longer quite present" (V, 314)—beginning to be depersonalized. His depersonalization, however, is unlike that of Harry Haller's Immortals; for it is a sinking back—for this sensualist who believes in no afterlife—into a formless void. There was ambiguity, in *Demian*, between the will-to-be and the desire to dissolve into nonbeing (the ultimate sense of Frau Eva); in *Narziss and Goldmund* the will-to-be has been sublimated in works of art, while the life succumbs.

Goldmund's last journey is not recounted as his previous journeys are; this last breakout has about it the quality of legend: "A few fragments from Goldmund's accounts and confessions were transmitted by Narziss, others by the assistant" (V, 315). A switch of point of view occurs, such as was noted in the middle of *Beneath the Wheel* and at the end of *Siddhartha;* when Goldmund leaves the monastery this time, Narziss with his thoughts remains behind, pondering whether Goldmund's Way is not after all a better one than his own. The author has ceased to write from within Goldmund's mind; we read not "he was weary" but "he seemed to be terribly weary" (V, 311). For indeed Goldmund now takes on some of the qualities of the saint and his life those of legend; for a short moment before his hagiographical death he becomes the *imitabile* whom Narziss would fain be like; he is Siddhartha, Narziss Govinda; Narziss kisses Goldmund on hair and brow. The canonization of Goldmund to some extent disguises the truth, that this novel uses the Way of the artist as a despairing *pis-aller* for the Religious Way, that its glorification of art and form is but the surrogate of the disappointed mystic, while the sinking into the arms of the mother, into the formless ground, is the love-death of the Romantic pessimists relived.[39] As art is supposed to substitute for life, so the polished, melodious language exorcises the burning and and all-too-poignant confession and transforms it largely into music. This sublimative process throws a good deal of light on the novel's style; it is the style of an author who always believed that content by itself was of no significance.[40]

Though the book lacks the stridency of *The Steppenwolf*, it is at bottom an equally painful and indeed a more pessimistic work. It is a veiled, elusive novel; false comparisons in regard to it may lead to gross misinterpretations. The conversations between Narziss and Goldmund should not be compared, for instance, with those between Naphta and Settembrini in *The Magic Mountain*; such ana-

---

[39] Cf. Gerhard Mayer, "Hermann Hesse: Mystische Religiosität und dichterische Form," *Jahrbuch der deutschen Schillergesellschaft*, IV (1960), 545: Klingsor and Goldmund are seen both to be seduced, by their veneration of Mother Eva, to a point at which they abandon their efforts after spiritual "perfecting" and seek "unconscious extinction in the arms of Mother Nature." However, the phrase "to the heart of the mother" (*Spa Visitor*, IV, 105) is confessedly a figure for the state of grace. "The Steep Road" has "breast of the mother" (III, 327). This ambiguous identity of rebirth and oblivion is characteristic of all Hesse's work.

[40] "And I thought . . . that my book, like every poetic work, does not just consist of content, that rather the content is relatively unimportant, just as unimportant as whatever the author's intentions may be, but that for us artists it is a question of whether, à propos of the intentions, views, and ideas of the author, a work has been formed, woven of the material, the yarn of language, whose immeasurable value is high above the measurable value of the content" "Notes While on a Cure in Baden"; IV, 925–926).

logies (which are inclined to be tendentious anyway) lead to the
certainly unjustifiable derogation of Hesse as a thinker and moreover to a total misunderstanding of the book. In the formal world
of this novel the conversations are not primarily profound philosophical analyses of specific and—as is often the case in Mann's
novels—sometimes slightly extraneous issues; they should rather be
seen as restatement in reflective form of the two life patterns, the
twin themes, now wooing, now marrying, now divorcing. Both the
reflective and the symbolic modes are equally important, both
variations on the same motifs. While the book's so-called realism [41]—
the description of the plague, Goldmund's killing of the rapist,—is
constantly muted by the lyricism of words and structure, the most
striking feature of the style is the predilection for direct or—as it
may often appear—overdirect statement. There are the beginnings
of *Altersstil* (style of old age) here. Time and again the symbol is
not allowed to speak for itself, but is interpreted by commentary;
but this technique, as has been shown, was always an integral
feature of Hesse's work, for these lyrical novels are also all didactic
novels, poem and tract are combined in them. Schiefer has observed
(in connection with *The Glass Bead Game*) that it is unreasonable
to reproach this particular writer for the fact that he constantly
resolves the poetic image by interpretation and reflection; for in
Hesse's mature work no figure, no image, no action is portrayed for
its own sake, but everything subserves the exemplification of a convinced and uncompromising view of the world.[42] That is to say—
Hesse can only be properly evaluated as a didactic writer. No
doubt, this overstates the case. It is, however, true that works which
spring simultaneously from the lyrical and the didactic impulses
court certain risks, both subjective hazards of composition and objective hazards of critical judgment. Goldmund's terrible, dying
question to Narziss: "But how will you die one day, Narziss, if
you have no mother?" (V, 322) may be construed as a warning to
the mind. As the reflective mind and the didactic will may damage
the lyrical work of art, so the tyranny of the father threatens Narziss. A synthesis is needed, and it cannot be found, neither in the

[41] The evocation of the Middle Ages is tentative and poetic, and in no sense
does it have the texture of the historical novel proper.
[42] *Op. cit.,* p. 96.

work nor in the life. Perhaps the real "sense" of *Narziss and Goldmund* lies in its confession: "I have become a writer, but I have not become a human being. I have reached a partial goal, but not the main one. I have failed."

CHAPTER 7

The Journey to the East
and
The Glass Bead Game

MOST critics are agreed as to the considerable importance of *The Journey to the East* (1932) in the totality of Hesse's work.[1] A little masterpiece of allegory and irony, it both summarizes all that has gone before and stands as a kind of preamble to what is to follow, namely *The Glass Bead Game*. The emphasis shifts from the preoccupation with the nature of the ego (*The Steppenwolf*) and the metaphysical justification of the artist's life (*Narziss and Goldmund*) toward the issue of the relationship of the individual with the ideal community, the "Order."

Already in "The World Reformer" (1911) the notion of the community of idealists—as represented by vegetarians, primitive Christians, Tolstoyists, and the rest—had been eyed ironically from the standpoint of common sense. Such enthusiasts, it had been noted in *Demian*, formed only the exoteric circle at the house of Frau Eva. A much later letter points out to a young seeker after truth the

---

[1] Hesse himself once asserted that *The Journey to the East* was the work in which he first attempted to formulate his faith "in poetic fashion" (*Letters;* VII, 595).

danger inherent in such groups: "Even these smaller and more ideal associations want to form you, stamp you, educate and integrate you prematurely," [2] the comparison here being with larger political organizations which aim at a similar but even more nefarious standardization. In fact, personal development is of supreme importance. And beyond such communities as these there is indeed another sort, esoteric and elusive, in which are permanently joined together all those whose ultimate devotion is only to the evolution of the self: "Therefore it is good for those who bear the mark to know that they have comrades and to feel themselves a part of the procession of the creative and the suffering which passes through history. This is our communion of the saints, poor Villon belongs to it and poor Verlaine as does Mozart, Pascal as much as does Nietzsche." [3] Already on the Indian journey a metaphor for this thought had been found: "Asia was not a continent, but a quite definite though mysterious place somewhere between India and China. Thence the peoples had come and their doctrines and religions, there lay the roots of all humanity and the dark spring of all life, there stood the images of the gods and the tablets of the law. Oh how could I have forgotten this even for a moment! After all I had been on my way to that Asia for so long, I and many men and women, friends and strangers." [4]

The Order of the Travelers to the East is, then, a "communion of saints," of unfathomable antiquity, a scarlet thread through history, in whose latest materialization and manifestation of activity—the mysterious "Journey to the East" of the previous decade—the author, H. H., himself took part. The historical moment of the Journey is therefore fixed, it is in the years after the First World War, years of the cult of Indian religions and of Taoism in Europe, of the influx of exotic art,[5] of desperate escapist yearning. Many writers, we are told, have by their publications given the impression that they took part in this fabulous undertaking—for instance Count Hermann Keyserling and Ferdinand Ossendowski; but this

---

[2] *Letters* (VII, 563).   [3] *Letters* (VII, 565).
[4] "India" (III, 805). Cf. Novalis, "Religion is the great orient in us" (*Schriften*, IV, 592).
[5] Cf. the essay "Exotic Art" (VII, 270 ff.), also in *Neue Rundschau*, XXXIII (1922), 385 ff.

is often untrue. The extraordinary event of the Journey to the East is integrated into this strange postwar era when, especially in the case of the defeated nations, there was in people's thinking "an extraordinary state of unreality, of readiness for the unreal, even if only at very few points were frontiers actually crossed and advances made into the kingdom of a coming psychocracy" (VI, 10). As for the actual participants in the Journey and members of the Order, they are bound by an oath of secrecy; they may disclose nothing about the true purpose, function, and structure of the Order itself; they may merely relate their own personal experiences insofar as these do not impinge upon the "League mystery." Under these severe limitations, then, H. H. begins to write.

He observes that the Journey to the East is a voyage through time as well, a road to Xanadu which leads back into the land of childhood. Each participant is admitted only if he has his own aim, distinct from that of the Order; he must have his "childish dream," his "secret game in the heart" (VI, 21). In the case of H. H., this is the youthful aspiration "to see the beautiful princess Fatme and if possible to win her love" (VI, 13). This lady is eventually turned up as a reference in the archives of the Order: "princ. orient. 2/ noct. mill. 983/ hort. delic. 07"; [6] and under her number the archives contain a beautiful medallion evocative of all the delight and fantasy of the long-dead imagination of youth. The scent of the delicate violet cloth in which the medallion is ensconced magically arouses memories of the very beginning of H. H.'s Romantic pilgrimage, of the shipwreck of dreams and the descent into despair.

[6] Cf. in "Klingsor": "Where dwells Fatme, the pearl among women?" (III, 577). The reference "noct. mill. 983" apparently alludes to *The Thousand and One Nights*. There is, however, no Fatme in no. 983—hence perhaps stress should be laid on her new incarnation ("princ. orient. 2"). "Hort. delic." may refer to the *Hortus Deliciarum* of the twelfth-century abbess Herrad von Landsberg (an illustrated compendium of religious and secular knowledge), as is suggested by the principal commentator of *The Journey to the East*, Siegfried Wrase ("Erläuterungen zu Hermann Hesses *Morgenlandfahrt*" [diss., Tübingen, 1959], p. 18), but a much more probable source is surely the Hieronymus Bosch triptych "The Millennium" with its central vision of an innocent harmony of spirit and senses in a prolonged Eden. The view that much of this is largely whimsical mystification on Hesse's part is strengthened, however, if we note that a later reference—"Chrysostomos, Cycle V, verse 39, 8"—blithely uses a different arrangement of the same numerals.

Out of the sphere of despair of the Steppenwolf this journey leads
"back home," into "the home and the youth of the soul" (VI, 24)
and even to the collapse of time, "the unification of all eras" (VI,
24); the bliss which the Journey to the East bestowed and which
H. H. has now lost "consisted in the freedom of experiencing
everything imaginable all at once" (VI, 24). Thus *The Journey to
the East* itself confounds and disintegrates time, in speaking of
these dreams of long-lost childhood as if they had been something
new. In fact they were first dreamed much earlier than the period
of the journey; the eastern yearnings of the *Siddhartha* years
had themselves been a resurrection of the poetry of adolescence, of
Hermann Lauscher and *An Hour beyond Midnight* and the
capacity for uchronic experience, we may recall, lay at the heart
of Siddhartha's own awakening. By the outside world, inevitably,
the Journey is regarded skeptically as a "children's crusade"; over
it all stands the sign of Novalis, in the ascendancy once more since
1924—"Indeed our whole host and its great march was only one
wave in the eternal stream of the souls, the eternal homeward
striving of the spirits towards the East, to their home" (VI, 23).

   The Journey to the East, then, might be regarded as the inward
voyage of the practitioner of the Tao. It is also the voyage into
tomorrow (*morgen*), for Hesse is punning again. In the purpose
of the enigmatic servant Leo, "according to the key of Solomon to
be able to understand the language of the birds" (like St. Francis)
(VI, 22–23), there occurs once more the metaphor of the bird, and
at the end of the Eichendorffian evocation of the splendrous and
fantastic feast at Bremgarten (in real life Schloss Bremgarten near
Bern) there appears again the metaphor of the fish, now fed with a
more festive food and drink than Goldmund had to offer, with
pastries and wine. Like Heinrich von Ofterdingen, H. H. has an
underwater dream; as Goldmund ducked down into his spiritual
exercises so the protagonist of *The Journey to the East* goes down,
borne by mermaids, and returns "deeply cooled" (VI, 26) from
that crystal sphere where they, dreamy and unredeemed, toy
with their treasures, play their golden games.

   The narrative is evidently instinct with symbols of the sacramental and the numinous. In contrast with the anathema of "the
preachers of little Pietistic sects" (VI, 10), the Journey moves on

the level of Saviour, Apostles, and Holy Ghost; leader of the expedition is Albertus Magnus, patriarch of the Swabian mystics. H. H. speaks of his own novitiate and of the ring which each member of the Order must wear; the Superior of the Order has his "high chair" (VI, 14). The analogy with the Roman church is in fact elaborately drawn, and eventually Leo, bearing his impressive regalia, appears "like a devout pope" (VI, 64). The theme of *The Journey to the East,* an aspect of the problem of faith and grace, is of course partially formed in a secular mold; the Journey is a descent both into the soul and also into the imagination and memory of the Romantic epigone; in that it conveys the religious essence by the secularization of religious forms, the book has just the irony of *The Glass Bead Game.*

Literary allusions are legion: Heinrich von Ofterdingen, Don Quixote and Sancho, Witiko, and also Parsifal ride together in the party, as well as figures of Hesse's own creation, Hermann Lauscher, Goldmund, Pablo and Anselm; Arnim's *Kronenwächter* obstruct their progress. There are sardonic political allusions (for example, to monarchism in the Weimar Republic) and playful references to living people, some very close to Hesse. One participant, influenced, oddly enough, by an encounter with one of his old Swabian schoolmasters, deserts the party, abominating many of its ways and practices, especially "the confounding of life with poetry" (VI, 18); thereby he is cut off from salvation, perhaps forever. It is indeed a perilous thing, since Hoffmann's *Goldener Topf,* to be deficient in poetic imagination; for Archivarius Lindhorst is also loose in this story, making a more substantial impression than does his neurotic-looking creator, who is present too. Then there is the astrologer Longus sitting in the wood, with a book of magically mutating letters—but this is not Hoffmann's student Anselmus, it is Dr. Lang.[7] These magic letters, inspired by that old memory—Goldmund's memory—of schooldays, come later to be transformed into "senseless ornamentation" (VI, 59), in fact the pointless fantasy of H. H.'s poetic diction, his "fine style," in which

[7] Dr. Lang spent a great deal of his later life in the study of the Semitic languages and of theology. He produced a work entitled *Hat Gott die Welt erschaffen? Zur Theologie und Anthropologie von Genesis 1 bis 11, 4a. Ein exegetischer Versuch* (Bern, 1942).

the truth of things is embellished rather than revealed. For the author of *The Journey to the East* still stands where the author of *Narziss and Goldmund* stood, upon the shifting sands of the artist's self-doubt. He knows, also, "that the characters in literature have the habit of being more living and more real than their authors appear to be" (VI, 76)—as evidenced by the contrast between Hoffmann and his Archivarius. And yet there is change here, and a vital change; a new ideal is in the process of being born; and the gross agony of *Narziss and Goldmund* is apparently forgotten, for all is now suffused with sovereign irony.

The main action of *The Journey to the East*, such as it is, principally concerns the "servant" Leo.[8] The obscure account of the Journey itself ends with the disaster of Leo's disappearance in the pass of Morbio Inferiore and the dissolution, in dissension and uncertainty, of that particular party of travelers to which H. H. belonged. After years of despair, the disappointed pilgrim again makes contact with Leo, in the big city, discovers to his astonishment that the Order still survives (and, still later, that Leo is its Superior); he is examined, tried for desertion, reprimanded, and finally enlightened by the Supreme Ones (*die Oberen*), and is thereby restored to revivifying contact with the Great Spiritual Source and lifted up to be one of Them. Hesse's letters of this period (1932)[9] constantly reiterate to those who are in search of a "leader" that leadership is not what is required, but service: "We think little of leadership, everything of service. Above all virtues we cultivate veneration, but we do not offer this veneration to individuals" (VII, 518). Thus Leo, "this unpretentious man" (VI, 22), is an ideal servant; much later, when he conducts H. H. through the city streets he is, in significant synthesis, "wholly

---

[8] Various interpretations have been offered of the figure of Leo, one of the most recent—and original—being that he was inspired by Hesse's pet cat (see R. H. Farquharson, "The Identity and Significance of Leo in Hesse's *Morgenlandfahrt*," *Monatshefte für deutschen Unterricht*, LV [1963], 122 f.). More important, perhaps, is the consideration that Leo is a common name of popes, and there may indeed be an allusion to Leo XIII (1878–1903), a great figure of Hesse's youth. In Rosicrucian symbolism, Christ is "the Lion." In the general context of Hesse's works we can have no difficulty in identifying Leo as the "friend," the hierophant, the higher self.

[9] A note of Hesse's about *The Journey to the East* tells us "Begun summer 1930, finished April 1931." Quoted by Wrase, *op. cit.*, p. 167.

leader, wholly servant of his task, wholly function" (VI, 55). While they are still on the Journey, Leo imparts to H. H. "the law of service. Whatever will live long must serve. Whatever will rule, however, does not live long" (VI, 28). There are, of course, occasionally natural rulers, but those who achieve power through *effort* end always in nothingness, in the sanatorium.[10]

Leo's disappearance in Morbio Inferiore, which the narrator now (that is, from the standpoint Chapter 2) imagines to have been a link in the chain of devilish interventions to the detriment of the Journey, later reveals itself in fact to have been a test. The Travelers fail the test; with Leo, somehow the symbol of their hopes, having disappeared, controversy breaks out among them. H. H. experiences a sudden loss of faith, deepened by the curious discovery about Leo's baggage: in his small rucksack he appears to have carried off some indispensable valuable from every member of the group. No matter that this alarm turns out to have been false, the symptom of panic itself is grave enough; these objects do gradually reappear again, and in any case it is soon apparent that they are none of them indispensable; the Travelers have deceived themselves. What is finally lost, however, is the most precious article of all, the "league charter," about which there is dispute whether the original was not burned with the body of the "master" long ago, and perhaps Leo has merely made off with one of the various copies and translations. H. H., however, always the realist, concludes with grim resignation (though, as it transpires, wholly absurdly) that it is indeed the original which has just been lost forever.

H. H. returns from the frustrated Journey with nostalgia but without faith. His despondency is more than mere mood; it is symptomatic of a metaphysically based despair, the Dark Night of *Crisis*, the resigned skepticism of the late nineteen twenties too. Leo was a blooming, red-cheeked young man; but the healthy Hesse, it appears, has now finally vanished from his author's life and his pages, leaving the aging, sickly Harry behind. This contrast recurs vividly when H. H. comes across Leo again; the two figures walk through the evening light in the rain, H. H. haggard and ex-

[10] "The way of the millionaires is a different one, and it ends in the sanatorium" ("On the Soul"; VII, 77). Leo says: "They all end in nothing. . . . For example in the sanatorium" (VI, 28).

hausted, desperately wooing his serene "friend," who has such an elastic step (like the later Joseph Knecht!—cf. VI, 520). It is through the assistance of an acquaintance, Lukas,[11] that he finds Leo. Lukas, of course, like other external observers, is skeptical of the whole matter of the Journey; but the two have a point of contact with one another: H. H.'s difficulties in writing about the Journey are paralleled by those of Lukas in writing about his experience of the war—something he had to do, however it should turn out, for it was a psychological necessity. So H. H. also resolves "to force my will through. Even if I have to start my untellable story ten times or a hundred times from the beginning and always reach the same abyss, I *will* start again a hundred times" (VI, 36–37). The folly of this undertaking, of the Way of the will, is something which, in Chapter 3, H. H. has not yet realized. Lukas is a practical man; he looks up Leo (a surname) in the telephone directory, and discovers an address, "Leo, Andreas, Seilergraben 69a" (VI, 41). Here the allegory becomes not only intricate but very likely impenetrable; to begin with, the choice of the number is very probably not adventitious;[12] Leo, moreover, not only lives in the Seilergraben (in Zurich?), but also wears rope-soled shoes, wherein several allusions, some very abstruse indeed, may possibly lie enshrined.[13]

H. H. paces the Seilergraben for days on end, until one evening he is rewarded by hearing Leo's well-known birdlike whistling

---

[11] "Lukas" is a pseudonym for Martin Lang, the Swabian poet and editor. It was derived from the name of the author of a book on gardening which Lang consulted when he used to look after Hesse's garden at Gaienhofen (as Ludwig Finckh disclosed). Cf. for this Wrase, *op. cit.*, p. 77. Such impenetrable and apparently pointless play with pseudonyms, etc., as characterizes this work may seem exaggerated, but it remains only a superficial element in a poetic and profound tale.

[12] There have been many suggestions, e.g.: "The number 69 also remains 69 when stood on its head; and it is thus a symbolic number for the Heraclitean conception of the voyage" (J. C. Middleton, "Hermann Hesse's *Morgenlandfahrt*," *Germanic Review*, XXXII [1957], 303).

[13] E.g., Nietzsche's "rope across an abyss," in *Also sprach Zarathustra;* perhaps the *Brhadaranyaka-Upanishad* (Middleton, *op. cit.*, p. 305) or, more likely, Oknos the Ropemaker as elucidated by Bachofen (Ziolkowski, *The Novels of Hermann Hesse*, p. 279). The shoes are so stressed that the detail is clearly intended to hide some meaning. We may recall also the mountain guide in "The Steep Road."

coming from the building. Leo emerges into the twilight, out of the dark house, lithe and boyish as ever, and the sight cramps H. H.'s heart with nostalgia for youth: "O how everything has changed since those days, the air, the seasons, dreams, sleep, day and night!" (VI, 45). And nonetheless, the youthfulness is "of evening" (*abendlich;* VI, 45)—like Harry Haller, Leo is an *Abendmensch;* he sits down in a park near St. Pauls Tor, and here, in the shadow of a pun, H. H. commits his "folly," he approaches Leo and accosts him, still unaware of his holiness; for the moment on the road to Damascus still lies ahead. They talk about music; H. H. has sold his violin, and Leo censures him for this action, which is construed as a function of his despair. H. H. has made the mistake of the Steppenwolf; he is altogether too inclined toward the pathetic, he does not grasp that life is a game: "That is exactly what life is if it is beautiful and happy: a game!" (VI, 49). Leo refers to the story of David and Saul; David the bard charming Saul with his music is a more attractive figure than David the king. It is in vain that H. H. accompanies Leo through the wet evening; he is handled with cool irony, all his direct questions are evaded; he (a Steppenwolf?) is even growled at suspiciously by the wolfhound Necker, Leo's friend. His failure to make any real contact throws H. H. into a condition which, in earlier years, had brought him time and time again to the brink of a Kleinian suicide: "to let oneself fall from the edge of the world into the void, into death" (VI, 52). But times have changed; death now is not nothing but has some content (a maternal content?) and utter despair can now be endured like a severe physical pain. In this moment of present meaninglessness, of envious, remorseful longing for times long past, H. H.'s account of the Journey to the East seems to lose all value in itself; it may only be a purifying task which *might* give him back some contact with his own experiences and thus with the Order. A confused letter to Leo, in which he confesses his despair, brings a response the next day; Leo reappears, now formally an emissary of the Order, and leads H. H. through the streets of the city to headquarters.

The way back, even at this advanced stage, proves devious and slow: H. H. is irritated and utterly confused by the delays and by the "detours, circular routes, and zigzags" (VI, 55) by which he is led. This is yet another test which H. H. fails (for impatience in an initiate is a cardinal offense); Leo's behavior reflects the *pietas* of the superior "aimless ones" who yet have a secret aim, that reverence also of the present in the past and the past in the present as it was practiced on the Journey itself, in pauses at the shrines and monuments of mankind. H. H. feels prepared to be judged by the Order, to demonstrate—as he is still persuaded is true—that he has not been unfaithful, for, as in the case of Harry Haller, self-justification is of the essence of his being. In the chancellery of the Order an extraordinary assemblage sits in judgment, in a boundless dream-hall—among these Albertus Magnus, Vasudeva the ferryman, and Klingsor the painter. H. H., of course, is a "self-accuser" (VI, 58). He finds himself assenting to all sorts of accusations, including the central indictment—that he deserted [14] the Order shortly after Morbio Inferiore. He confesses that he had been in the act of writing a history of the Journey, whereupon his judges to his bewilderment relieve him of his troublesome oath of secrecy about the inner essentials and open up the entirety of the infinite archives to his labors.

In these archives he finds his own narrative filed away (of course only the first completed chapters); a copy of this book within a book is also kept in another place under the heading of "Morbio Inferiore," alongside the attempt of two other historians to relate the self-same set of "facts." Flicking over the cards in this limitless index to the collective unconscious, H. H. not unnaturally flinches at pursuing the references to his own name; similarly Leo's card, which bears the warning "*Cave!*" frightens him off. He does find the place where Fatme's medallion is preserved and soon becomes lost in his passionate memories again: "But how sweet, how innocent, how holy had been that dream which my youth had pursued, and which had made of me a reader of *Märchen*, a musician, a novice, and had led me to Morbio!" (VI, 62). Now at long last H. H. discovers the absurdity of his undertaking; his is the ironic situation of the charlatan initiate who has always played with "secrets" and who then finds that the real secrets need not be kept because they cannot be disclosed: "I had been so simple-minded as to want to write the history of this league, I who could not decipher

---

[14] "Fahnenflucht." It is curious and significant that the same word is used to describe Knecht's defection in *The Glass Bead Game*.

or understand a thousandth of these millions of documents, books, pictures, symbols in the archive" (VI, 62). The final mystery, the "league charter," is filed under the sign of the artist, Goldmund,[15] but even this H. H. cannot read. It is ultimately appropriate that Leo, "Leo arrayed in gold" (VI, 65), that servant who is in reality the Superior of the Order, should now appear in his regalia to pronounce a judgment which is preceded by H. H.'s revolutionary constatation that he himself had indeed been a deserter, a doubter, that his separation from the Order had resulted entirely from his own loss of faith. As sentence is pronounced, we are bound to recall the arraignment of Harry Haller before the court of the Immortals; as his punishment Harry was laughed at, and in the same way H. H. receives the chastisement of a smile. It is, however, very curious that it is precisely those errors which he himself regards as the worst—"the worst of my sins" (VI, 65)—which are dealt with in this lenient fashion; we remember, in the case of Goldmund, that it was by no means those sins which worried the penitent which were of concern to Narziss. These, as H. H. thinks, grave sins— loss of faith in the Order, attribution to the Order of his own guilt and folly, doubt in the Order's continued existence, and the artistic vanity involved in even attempting to portray such things in words —all this turns out to be "comprehensible and very excusable . . . the blunders of a novice" (VI, 65). To regard such behavior as sinful is to regard the world as sinful, or even as avoidable, and over this belief the river in *Siddhartha* laughs; to consider the world, the inevitable, the natural as sinful is indeed a laughable error. Goldmund's life in the world is not sinful, because it is the inevitable manifestation of himself; the life of the Prodigal is itself subsumed in the all-comprehensiveness of the Father.[16] Such a life is sinful only in the eyes of the Pietist who lives in Harry Haller and has to be laughed out of court (this Pietist lives too, it would appear, in Goldmund and in H. H.). Really serious, however, are certain sins of omission, Goldmund's failure to confess and communicate regularly, H. H.'s impatience before the doors of the cathedral while Leo is inside, and, in the next novel, Plinio Desig-

[15] "Drawer Chrysostomos, Cycle V, verse 39, 8." An allusion of some kind? The numbers may possibly be pure mystification, or an entirely private joke.

[16] Cf. Gide, *op. cit.*, p. 481: "Ceci aussi que tu vas supprimer, vient du Père."

nori's neglect of the techniques of meditation; for all these are sins of *formlessness;* they show that lack of fundamental reverence for the Spirit which must at all costs be retained as an element of form in the inevitable chaos of the illusory world. To use "Mozart's metaphor": through the distortion of the radio transmission one must always seek for, and indeed hear, the true music. H. H.'s worst sin of all, perhaps, was the sale of his violin, that instrument of form; this error compounded, if it did not lead to, "Your desperate, stupid, narrow-minded, suicidal life, which you have been leading for years" (VI, 67). This was, of course, Harry Haller's real sin, the failure to live out the world with sense of form, his riddling the world and neutralizing form with morbid introspection, hyperreflection, and the moralizing will.

In this issue lies, perhaps, the spiritual core of *The Journey to the East.* It is an insight which in retrospect further illuminates both *The Steppenwolf* and *Narziss and Goldmund.* The fate of H. H., Leo tells the judges, is in itself not a very uncommon one: the accused has only just understood that his defection and abberations were a test; eventually the condition of exile became unbearable, "his suffering became too great, and you know that as soon as suffering is great enough there is progress" (VI, 68). Despair is the ineluctable consequence of any attempt to master life with the aid of virtue, reason, and sense of justice: "This side of this despair the children live, on the other side those who are awakened" (VI, 68). Leo delivers himself of this explanation and judgment in a voice "as cool and as penetrating as the voice of the Commendatore when he appears at Don Juan's door in the last act" (VI, 68)—and it is rather remarkable that in the rarified, all but sexless atmosphere of *The Journey to the East* this old motif of Hesse's should occur; it reinforces the connection, to which a number of features in the story point, between H. H. and Harry Haller. H. H. then receives the return of his ring,[17] lost long before and preserved for him by

[17] The motif of the ring is of great importance and shows us a good deal about Hesse's symbolic methods. The "ring words" (VI, 14) which are pronounced when the novice first receives his ring have been traced to Christoph Martin Wieland's *Oberon.* Wrase, to whom we owe this identification, quotes further from *Oberon (op. cit.,* p. 11):

"Auch kann durch keine Macht im Himmel wie auf Erden

Leo; he also recalls the spiritual exercises connected with it which he had forgotten for years. His task being now self-knowledge, he is confronted with the necessity of opening the archive upon himself, only thus can he complete his development and himself become one of the Supreme Ones. What he finds under his name in the archive is a strange double figurine, "an old and worn looking sculpture of wood or wax, pale in color, some kind of graven image or barbarian idol" (VI, 75). The two back-to-back figures are H. H. himself, feeble and decrepit in appearance, and a flourishing, healthy-looking Leo; the surface of these joined figures is at one point transparent, and H. H. notices that there is some sort of movement within:

Something like a very slow, soft but unbroken flowing or melting, and indeed there was a melting or running from my image over into Leo's, and I recognized that my image was in the process of surrendering more and more to Leo and streaming into him, feeding and sustaining him. With time, it seemed, all the substance of the one image would run over into the other and only one would remain: Leo. He had to increase, I had to decrease [VI, 75-76].

The biblical allusion is clear enough—it is to the relationship of Christ with John the Baptist: "He must increase, but I must decrease." [18] The pupil, once baptized, will soon become the master; the character will become more real than his author or, on the level of hermetic philosophy, the small self must die so that the great self may be born.[19]

The purely "aesthetic" interpretation of *The Journey to the East* has always had its exponents,[20] but it is—as almost always in Hesse's works—much too restricted. Critics who do take such a view have merely fallen into a carefully laid snare, have been deceived by the convolutions of the story's irony. The final reflective observation

---

Dem, der ihn nicht geraubt, der Ring entrissen werden."
The ring saves its bearers from drowning:
    "Doch, sorget nicht, der Ring lässt sie nicht untergehen."
In this oblique fashion the motif of death by water, that peril always lurking along the Spiritual Way, is alluded to afresh.
[18] John 3:30.
[19] Cf. also Jung, *Symbols of Transformation*, p. 196: "This relation applies equally to Jesus and John the Baptist, and Jesus and Peter."
[20] Cf., e.g., R. B. Matzig, *Hermann Hesse in Montagnola*, pp. 96-97.

of the narrative, before the exhausted—but now apparently peaceful—H. H. seeks out a place to sleep, is in fact the observation that a writer's characters may truly be more real than he is himself. But this remark is not the real end of *The Journey to the East*, which oddly enough, is to be found in the first words of Chapter 4: "Now everything looks different again, and I still don't know whether my cause has really been advanced by this or not." [21] In any case we have already noted in *Narziss and Goldmund* the intimate analogy between the work of art and the perfected self; to divide the former from the latter is—in the context of Hesse's later books—to make an illegitimate distinction. H. H.—as his real last words tell us—remains at the end uncertain as to what, if anything, he has actually achieved.

Certainly *The Journey to the East* has a positive message: essentially the requirement of service and the real possibility of grace; it thus sums up the experience of a whole decade, extracts its wisdom, and points toward the great novel of Hesse's old age. It reopens the crisis of *The Steppenwolf* on a higher level of insight and comments upon the nature of that spiritual resignation with which *Narziss and Goldmund* was also concerned. But it sounds a new—if tremulous—note of hope. In fact, the mystery of the double figurine is profounder than emerges from Leo's conventional analysis of H. H.'s passage through the gate of hell (Morbio Inferiore); for the double figurine really signifies that failure on the Way is in the last resort impossible, since each relapse, each aberration is itself but a part of the Way; the Journey, once started, never ends, nor can the Traveler become lost; errors and detours are, unknown to him, the high road all the time. Thus all the agonies and hopes of the Hallers and Goldmunds are so much foam upon the wave; through all and in all and indeed by means of all the process of transfusion within, of hermetic gestation of the

---

[21] "It is the crowning irony of *Die Morgenlandfahrt* that its last words are here hidden at the beginning of the penultimate chapter" (Middleton, *op. cit.*, p. 304). Wrase's view that this "contradiction" of the content of Chapter 5 cannot have been intended and must have been an error of the storyteller (who failed to see that his time schedule for the last two chapters forces this remark to apply inappropriately to Chapter 5 as well as to Chapter 4) is almost inconceivable in the context of such a carefully constructed work as *The Journey to the East*.

self, goes on for evermore. This is perhaps the deepest idea Hesse's works have yet expressed, indeed it is "beyond belief"; hence it is encased in irony. Perhaps the miracle is real, perhaps no—"I don't know yet."

The Journey to the East is not a *Märchen*. It is written as if all takes place upon the same level of reality, and there is this time no opium-shroud between the relative realism of the first four chapters and the translucent fantasy of the last one. A first-person narrative, the first since *Demian*, it may be argued that the story is pure monologue, addressed to no one but the author; although the deeper irony is of course that this is not really so at all. Sometimes it has the precision of allegory, and the treatment of the incident with Leo's baggage bears some resemblance to the methods of Kafka. In struggling to reconstruct his memories, the narrator comes up against the problem of the "thing in itself": it is impossible to penetrate the morass of subjective visions; all is reflected in the ego, which is itself "a nothingness, the topmost layer of a surface of glass" (VI, 35). The narrative is so constructed that the reader is at first enmeshed with the narrator in his own web of false judgments, which have all the appearance of the wisdom of hindsight; but what in the days of *Peter Camenzind* was a self-insight which could be relied upon is now held to be delusion. The reader is confused by the time shifts with which the work is riddled; and he is confronted—almost as much as with narrative itself—with expostulation upon the impossibility of narrative: "But how, by what device could it be made possible, how could the story of our Journey to the East somehow be rendered tellable? I do not know" (VI, 34). Purely personal confession—and we recall the contrast between Rousseau and Augustine—may very well end in pure "ornament," in "fine style." Truth is perhaps in any case unattainable; the historian is obliged to invent entities which do not really exist and then to describe the impact of events upon such entities. The three historians of the affair at Morbio Inferiore give wholly disparate accounts: "What was truth still, what was credible still?" (VI, 74). Narrators are distorting mirrors. To try to write such a narrative at all is in any case an act of egoism *par excellence*, an attempt like that of Lukas "to rescue life for myself by giving it a meaning again" (VI, 43). It is H. H.'s selfish pride which is the real reason for his forgetting; his memory is confused and dread-fully fragmentary, as it must be in one who has imagined himself isolated and thus cut himself off from the truth about the past. He is deluded, he faces the wrong way round; hence his struggles to escape from the darkness of forgetting only plunge him more deeply into it. Thus in *The Journey to the East* there is in one sense less detachment than in previous works, in that the protago-nist's travails are not described from without or at least (as Emil Sinclair's were) with a hindsight that can be trusted; on the contrary, the ruminations, reflections, the hesitant stops and starts of this story are the Way itself. Narrator and hero have all but totally coalesced; living out the *vita* is synonymous with the act of writing or, more precisely, writing is the *via purgativa*; the *via illuminativa* begins at the point where the futility and the super-erogatory nature of the activity of writing is perceived.

The Journey to the East is elaborately furnished with "ornamentations," with superficial ironies, essentially decorative games. There are puns—for instance that on *"Unerfahrenheit"* [22] and that on *"Tor"*; there are wry political jokes; and there are un-expected absurdities, even within the context of such a fantasy, for instance Hans C.[23] steering his Noah's ark through the shallow culture of his day, "between the tram lines and banks of Zurich" (VI, 24). There is comic hyperbole—"the transit, resolute unto death, across Upper Swabia" (VI, 38)—and even inversion of figures used in previous novels—"Mozart disguised as Pablo" (VI, 63). The book-within-a-book device suggests that Romantic mode of composition to which the work is so obviously indebted. Finally, one might hazard a surmise: we know now (as will be indicated in further detail below) that *The Journey to the East* was written at a time when the first idea of that work which was to become *The Glass Bead Game* had already germinated. Hesse was feeling his way toward a magnum opus which could express

[22] Cf. VI, 11–12. The pun is all but explained in the text. The passage of verse ("Er weit gereist . . .") comes from Canto 7 of the *Orlando Furioso* and there are several references to Ariosto in the tale.

[23] H. C. Bodmer, whose Zurich house was called "Zur Arch." Bodmer was Hesse's patron. Hesse connects him with Noah, thus alluding also to Johann Jakob Bodmer and his *Noachide* (cf. Wrase, *op. cit.*, p. 35).

the transtemporal unity of the ideal vision, but doubted his capacity to produce it. Perhaps, then, *The Journey to the East* should ultimately be regarded as a commentary upon the impossibility of composing itself.

The poem "Besinnung" (roughly: "Reflection") is of significance for the approach to *The Glass Bead Game*. Goethean in style, it opens with a hymn to the Spirit:

> Göttlich ist und ewig der Geist.
> Ihm entgegen, dessen wir Bild und Werkzeug sind,
> Führt unser Weg . . .[24]

> (Divine is the Spirit and eternal.
> Toward it, whose image and implement we are,
> Our path leads . . .)

The development of the poem's thought, however, is distinctly Christian,[25] and its conclusion a message of love:

> Und nicht Richten und Hass,
> Sondern geduldige Liebe,
> Liebendes Dulden führt
> Uns dem heiligen Ziele näher.

> (And not judging and hatred,
> But patient love,
> Loving patience leads
> Us closer to the sacred goal.)

A rather irritated letter,[26] dated August 1934, shows Hesse defending this poem against the criticism of a young detractor: "Of course, you can make fun of the poem "Besinnung" to your heart's content, but how you can conceive of it as an attempt to absolve Man of his responsibility I cannot understand." "Spirit" is here defined as "the divine substance," not synonymous therefore with God. Existence is said to be both tragic and sacred, and

---

[24] V, 740–741.

[25] "I never belonged to any community, church, or sect, but nowadays I more or less consider myself a Christian. The poem 'Besinnung' is a confession in which I tried to express the foundations of my current belief as precisely as I could" (*Letters;* VII, 588).

[26] *Letters* (VII, 572).

it is claimed that there is no contradiction between this view of man and that expressed for instance in *Crisis:* "And faith in the Spirit and the spiritual destiny of man by no means excludes the misery and despair of physical existence (which is the subject of *Crisis*). If ideas nowadays were not so completely confused and if practice did not every day derive devilish and fatal conclusions from this confusion I would perhaps never have felt the impulse to formulate my faith as that poem formulates it." The allusion, in these remarks, to the uncomfortable political developments of the day is transparent, and Hesse is in fact speaking of that immediate motivation as a result of which not only "Besinnung" but also *The Glass Bead Game* finally took form. In fact, the novel begins with a commentary upon "confusion of ideas," transcends this in the formulation of a pattern of devotion to "pure spirit," and apparently concludes with an act of "Christian" love.

The problem of the genesis of *The Glass Bead Game* is a complex one, not fully resolvable in the absence of the manuscripts, and yet cardinal to any even partially satisfactory understanding of this, the most massive and most ambiguous of Hesse's novels. On the basis of recently published letters and other material it does, however, now seem possible to establish a more comprehensive genesis than has hitherto been done.

The Glass Bead Game (1943) appears to be a not entirely successful marriage of two initially totally distinct elements. There is evidence that the conception of the book dates back as far as the late nineteen twenties, and that what was seminal was "the vision of an individual but transtemporal biography," [27] a novel which was to portray "several biographies of the same man, who lived on earth at different periods or at least imagined he had had such existences." [28] In a letter to Thomas Mann ("end of 1933") the second chief element is mentioned: "The visualization of the plan I have had for two years (the mathematical-musical mental game) is

---

[27] *Briefe (Erweiterte Ausgabe,* 1964), p. 436, letter to Rudolf Pannwitz. For a more detailed discussion of the problem of genesis, as well as of the relevance in this matter of the recently published "Fourth Autobiography," see my article, "*Der vierte Lebenslauf* as a Key to *Das Glasperlenspiel,*" *Modern Language Review,* LXI (1966), 635–646.

[28] Letter to Hesse's sister, Adele (1934), in *Prosa aus dem Nachlass,* p. 604.

growing into the visualization of a work of several volumes, in fact a library." [29] We may therefore date what appears to be the first clear idea of the Game itself at least to the end of 1931; by 1933 the notion of the "library" had taken shape, that is, the plan for a series of biographies or autobiographies, as alluded to again in the important letter to Rudolf Pannwitz (1955): "One day, many years before I started writing it down, there came to me the vision of an individual but transtemporal biography." If "many years" can be relied on at all, this must put the vision of the "transtemporal biography" back well beyond 1931. Hesse observes that the years "between the first conception and the real commencement of work" were years in which he was concerned with "two other tasks," which fixes the date again, for these can only be *Narziss and Goldmund* and *The Journey to the East*.

This was a period in which his ideas for the novel fluctuated between the grave and the more playful. The first plan for the book involved a series of reincarnations in the past only, and it was not until the early 1930's, when he began to take the Nazi movement seriously, that Hesse felt compelled to summon up all his energies to confront the deplorable present with a utopian "kingdom of the spirit and the soul as existent and unconquerably visible,"[30] at the same time relegating this present (in the introduction) to a triumphantly surmounted past. This introduction also went through a number of versions: a letter to Gottfried Bermann (January 1933) tells us that by then some kind of preface was already in being, perhaps that version which Hesse told Mann was written in the early part of 1932;[31] to Bermann, Hess imparts something of the "utopian" conception of the novel and an indication of its major theme:

I simply intend to write the story of a Glass Bead Game master, his name is Knecht and he lives roughly at the time at which the preface ends. More than this I do not know. The creation of a purified atmosphere was necessary for me, this time I didn't turn to the past or the timeless fairy tale, but constructed the fiction of a dated future. The secular culture of that period will be the same as today, but on the other hand

[29] *Letters* (VII, 562). [30] Letter to Pannwitz, *op. cit.*
[31] *Letters* (VII, 556).

there will exist a spiritual culture, and it will be worth-while to live in this and to serve it.[32]

The last observation affords us the insight that Hesse's view of Castalia, at this time, was wholly positive and not fraught with doubts. However, the introduction he sent to Bermann was evidently very different from the version we know, since he feels obliged to add these explanations; moreover the phrase "lives roughly at the time at which the preface ends" makes it quite clear that this early draft was not retrospective in its view of Knecht's life, a fact which suggests rather strongly that the fiction of the Castalian narrator (complete with his hindsight) had not yet been conceived by Hesse. The original introduction (possibly this particular manuscript) contained—as Hesse tells Pannwitz—specific strictures on dictatorship and such evils, and these were subsequently struck out altogether. Within a year this introduction itself had been dispensed with as useless, although the replacement for it was not yet finished;[33] the introduction we have was in fact completed in the summer of 1934, "in a very much changed version."[34]

Perhaps the most striking thing about the letter to Bermann is that it makes no reference to the so-called "autobiographies" in which the motif of reincarnation eventually took form and three of which are appended to the main narrative in the published novel. The letter to Mann, at the end of this same year (1933), implies the idea of them, and that to Adele in 1934 speaks of these tales as an integral part of the book's plan, remarking that the first, "The Rainmaker," is already written.[35] Thus, although Hesse had had the idea of the "transtemporal biography" several years before, there is no positive evidence available that he finally juxtaposed it—as a compositional principle—to the theme of the Game and of the Castalian utopia until 1933, and there is some negative evidence which may suggest that he did not do so. Furthermore, the "transtemporal biography" may well have been linked initially with a quite different notion, as may be deduced from the letter to Pannwitz: "I conceived of a man who lived through the great epochs of human history in several reincarnations."[36] This reference to the great epochs of

[32] *Letters* (VII, 540–541). [33] Letter to Adele, *op. cit.*
[34] *Letters* (VII, 575). [35] *Prosa aus dem Nachlass*, p. 604.
[36] *Briefe (Erweiterte Ausgabe)*, p. 436.

human history puts the stress quite otherwise than does the finished novel; it would be stretching terminology greatly to apply such a description to any of the existing "autobiographies" (except, possibly, the incomplete fourth); but this idea had left some sediment which we can still detect in the final work, in its inadequately integrated historical problematics, the puzzling quasi-Hegelian perspectives of the book.

The fact that the motif of Joseph Knecht's defection from Castalia, so central to the main novel, does not appear in any of the three completed autobiographies has been used to substantiate the argument that Hesse's conception of the novel changed fundamentally in the course of composition "from detached aestheticism to engagement." [37] It seems doubtful, however, whether such a view of *The Glass Bead Game* as far as its totality—or even perhaps its essential tenor—is concerned does full justice to the complexity and proliferated ambiguities of the novel. Hesse confesses in a letter to Siegfried Unseld (1949 or 1950) that a book such as his, compiled over as long a period as eleven years, may well have certain structural defects; he continues:

Perhaps in the course, maybe, of the first three years my perspective changed slightly several times. In the beginning I was above all, indeed almost exclusively concerned with making Castalia visible, the scholars' state, the ideal secular monastery. . . . Then it became clear to me that the inner reality of Castalia could only be made convincingly visible in a dominant figure, a spiritual hero and sufferer, and thus Knecht moved to the center of the tale, prototypical and unique not so much as an ideal and perfect Castalian, for there are many of these, as rather in the fact that he cannot be satisfied with Castalia and its unworldly perfection long-term.[38]

Allowing for the possibility that Hesse's memory, in 1949, should not be fully relied upon on a point like this, nonetheless if "three years" is anything like accurate it severely limits the period of shifts of focus in the author's view of his book. Since we know that Hesse was specifically preoccupied with the Castalian-utopian theme from some time in 1931 (not to speak of the "transtemporal

[37] Ziolkowski, *The Novels of Hermann Hesse*, p. 334.
[38] *Letters* (VII, 701–702).

biography"), we may reasonably conclude that the motif of Knecht's defection must have been in his mind as early as 1935 or even 1934 (the year of "The Rainmaker"). Here again the existing introduction, largely composed in parallel with the writing of "The Rainmaker," may seem to imply, at least, that Hesse conceived of Knecht as a great reformer in the history of Castalia,[39] and it is rather plausible that his inspiration of introducing a Castalian narrator and investing him with hindsight (a step we have dated tentatively to 1933–1934) went hand in hand with the change in the conception of the novel—and of Knecht's role—described in the letter to Unseld. This would indicate that Hesse's view of his work was fully formed by about the time the introduction was finally completed.

Such a deduction would be of immense significance for the interpretation of *The Glass Bead Game;* if correct, it makes it extremely unlikely that the three completed autobiographies, "The Rainmaker," "The Father Confessor," and "Indian Autobiography" [40] belong to an early, "aesthetic" conception of the novel subsequently transcended [41] and consequently forces us to regard them as relevant to the substantial final vision of the whole book. Furthermore, it throws doubt on the ultimate validity of any understanding of the novel based primarily on a progression from aesthetic

---

[39] The narrator points out that it is in individuals that we can best see historical evolution mirrored. This has been so in the history of the Glass Bead Game: every vital development "reveals itself most clearly precisely in the character of the one who introduced the change, who became the instrument of reform and perfection" (VI, 81). While not conclusive, it is at least arguable that this passage shows foreknowledge of Knecht the rebel.

[40] "The Rainmaker" was published in *Neue Rundschau,* XLV (1934), 476–512. Here also appeared the poem "The Glass Bead Game" (p. 637) and the completed introduction (pp. 638–665). The second autobiography, "The Father Confessor," was published in 1936 (*Neue Rundschau,* XLVII, 673–701), as also was the poem "A Dream of Joseph Knecht's" (pp. 1009–1012). In 1937 the *Neue Rundschau* published two further "poems of Knecht" (XLVIII, i, 190) and the third autobiography, "Indian Autobiography" (ii, pp. 7–40). The poem "The Last Bead Game Player" appeared in 1938 (*Neue Rundschau,* XLIX, i, 105). In 1940 a section of the main novel, "The Mission," came out (*Neue Rundschau,* LI, 317–329).

[41] As has been impressively argued by T. J. Ziolkowski, but without access to the letters to Adele and to Pannwitz, and to the "Fourth Autobiography," which together shed new light on the matter.

dream to existential choice. However, these important conclusions are not themselves totally dependent on the accuracy of this tentative genesis. *The Glass Bead Game* is a very elusive work indeed; originally bifocal, it remained internally inconsistent; a study of its imagery in the light of earlier works of its author and especially in the light of the fragmentary "Fourth Autobiography" leads to the view that on its deepest level this book, struggling manfully as it does to come to terms with a new and terrible world —Nazi Germany and the Second World War—remains primarily a subtle reweaving, in a luminous revisualization, of the patterns of a lifetime's dreams.

The Glass Bead Game was finally published *in toto* in 1943, after eleven years of effort; in the Germany of the immediate postwar era it had an enormous impact, for conspicuous reasons, and the critical literature which rapidly grew around it is far more massive than is the case with any other of Hesse's works.[42] Its dedication—"To the Travelers to the East"—suggests that the author regarded it as an esoteric book. This, in many ways, it is. The subtitle—"Attempt at a Biography of the Magister Ludi Joseph Knecht together with Knecht's Literary Remains"—is ironically tentative, while the title of the preface—"The Glass Bead Game: Attempt at a Generally Comprehensible Introduction to Its History"—is doubly ironic. For the meaning of the Game will disclose itself only to the initiate, and popularization is a perilous, self-vitiating act. The task of the historian in this book is at least as difficult as that of his predecessor in *The Journey to the East;* he is faced with the necessity of portraying the improbable and unprovable as though it existed, so that it may, like Rilke's unicorn, "be brought one step nearer existence and the possibility of being born" (VI, 79).

Castalia, a scholars' utopia, exists incapsulated within a world of the future which is essentially unchanged from that of today; great wars have led to a long period of apparent stability but have failed to purify the worldly sphere; this failure fits the Castalian view, which, with its disguised Schopenhauerian premises, regards mundane progress as an illusion, although historical fluctuations may

---

[42] Waibler alone lists 136 items up to 1961.

indeed occur. The name of the province signifies, no doubt—and in view of Castalia's official attitude to art this is very odd—"fountain of the Muses." The date of the narrative is fixed at about 2400 A.D.,[43] at which time Castalia has been in existence for several centuries and the life of Joseph Knecht lies then already a considerable time in the past. The province is conceived as one of several such which arose upon the wreckage of twentieth-century civilization, constituted by the political authorities of the world as vehicles for the recovery, purification, and uncontaminated transmission of the ideals of the Spirit, above all the astringent service of truth, the loss of which is said to have been a major cause of the decline of the West. The pedagogical provinces are also utilitarian in their training of teachers to man the educational establishments of the outside world. Within its own borders Castalia functions through the monkish Order to which its dedicated scholars and teachers belong, and through its representative ritual, the sublime cult of the Glass Bead Game.

Joseph Knecht's biographer is himself a Castalian of the elite; his preface serves to evoke the pedagogical province in its outlines by contrasting it and its purposes with the so-called "age of the feuilleton," the twentieth century. This first attempt since *The Steppenwolf* at a critique of contemporary civilization is couched in a mildly ironic, quasiacademic, and hyperreflective style. (We know from Hesse's remarks to Pannwitz that the point of the satire had been deliberately blunted somewhat.) Central to the critique is the constatation that intellectual honesty has decayed, devotion to the absolute of scientific truth has been undermined by an obscene political and social pragmatism, learning and the arts have been prostituted. The narrator quotes from a specialist in the study of this period, one Plinius Ziegenhalss, who characterizes the "age of the feuilleton" as a fundamentally bourgeois era, obsessed with individualism; the bane of the twentieth century had been the excessive indiscipline, flippancy, and irresponsibility of intellectual life. This dissolute condition was exemplified by such phenomena as the cult of the crossword puzzle, and of course supremely by the proliferation of the "feuilleton"—digests, weeklies, the "intellec-

---

[43] Hesse's footnote to the introduction in the *Neue Rundschau*.

tual" pages of the newspapers. The feuilletons, the historian constates with some astonishment, were both written and read without irony. Titles of dilettantist essays are cited, the fashion of public lectures also made its contribution to "that terrible devaluation of language" (VI, 93), leading in the end of course to a great reaction and reversal, a reformation of intellectual life in the spirit of a heroic asceticism. Political and material catastrophe in the twentieth century was accelerated and compounded by the mind's loss of confidence in itself. It was an age of mechanization, of immorality, of unbelief, of charlatanry in the arts—"just as in that wonderful Chinese fairy tale, the 'music of doom' had sounded" (VI, 94).

It was in the very rush of this decline, this inflation of ideas, that there began that process characterized as *Besinnung* (VI, 95), a rediscovery of obligation toward the achievements of the human mind, a return to standards of scholarly precision and honesty exemplified first in the rise of a new musicology, as well as the survival, in spite of everything, of the Order of the Travelers to the East. If the former required the restoration of the astringent exercises of logical thinking and scientific method, the latter had preserved an unbroken tradition of contemplation. On the subject of this resurrection the Castalian narrator hazards one of his rare similes: "One could compare the intellectual life of the feuilleton era to a degenerate plant dissipating itself in hypertrophic luxuriance, and the subsequent remedy to a cutting back of the plant to its roots" (VI, 105). As devotion to truth returns, *res publica* itself is restored. The thought behind this nexus is perhaps not so much Greek as Chinese.

The dream of Castalia is born from the experience of *Besinnung*, its manifest form is that of a secularized City of God: "In *The Glass Bead Game* I have portrayed the world of humanistic spirituality, which respects the religions but exists outside of them." [44] Mathematics and music (the latter, potentially one of the least personal of all the arts) are now regarded as the supreme achievements of the postmediaeval epoch, and are the foundations of the Castalian structure. In the career of the mind the rule is now

[44] *Letters* (VII, 685).

a severe asceticism; education, both within and without the walls of the province, is ultimately in the hands of the rigorous Order, in so far as it is not still under the sway of that sole alternative vehicle of the humane tradition, the Roman church. Pointers are given in the preface, but the detailed portrayal of Castalia remains the function of the body of the novel.

The Castalian narrator is confronted with one especially arduous task: the introduction of the reader to the Glass Bead Game itself. His success in giving the layman an impression of the "game of games" is inevitably rather limited. The Game is "a kind of highly developed secret language . . . in which several sciences and arts, in particular mathematics and music (or musicology) play their part and which has the capacity to express the content and results of almost all disciplines and to relate them to one another. The Glass Bead Game, therefore, is a game with all the contents and all the values of our culture" (VI, 84). In a sense the Game is no new invention; the idea of its possibility, the dream of it may be found among the Pythagoreans,[45] the ancient Chinese, the Gnostics, and the great Islamic thinkers. The Game, like Castalia itself, has some of the characteristics of a timeless ideal. Yet it also possesses, for the semiinitiated at all events, something like a fragmentary history, passing from Pythagoreans and Gnostics through the Scholastics and the Humanists to the mathematical academies of the seventeenth century and thus to Novalis,[46] Hegel, and beyond. In a sense

---

[45] One may compare the numerological conceptions of a modern "Pythogorean," Hans Kayser. See his *Akroasis: Die Lehre von der Harmonik der Welt* (Basel, 1946). Hesse was himself troubled by inventors who tried in vain to interest him in their glass bead games. He writes thus to a certain Alfred Henning in Weimar: "I have, however, to disappoint you in your expectation that I shall devote the rest of my life and strength just to the study of your work" (*Letters;* VII, 683).

[46] Hesse was certainly familiar with the relevant Novalis aphorisms, e.g.: "Do not God and Nature play too? Theory of play, sacred games. Pure game science—*common*—and higher. Applied game science" (*Schriften*, III, 127). Novalis writes on language and music: "Language is a musical instrument. The poet, rhetorician, and philosopher play and compose grammatically. A fugue is completely logical or scientific. It can also be treated poetically" (III, 205). He comments on language and mathematics: "The numbers system is the model of a genuine system of linguistic signs. Our letters should become numbers, our language arithmetic" (III, 18). Besides Novalis, probably Schiller influenced Hesse's conception of the Game. In his letters Hesse calls it "a

the reconciliation of art and knowledge, and a *Universitas Littera-rum*, it has as its progenitors Abelard, Nicolaus Cusanus, and Albertus Secundus (a pseudonym for Hesse himself). Although the Tarot is rather surprisingly not mentioned here, the connection with chess is.[47] The Glass Bead Game proper was invented simultaneously in Germany and England (the thought here, evidently, is of the calculus), in the former country by a certain Bastain Perrott of Calw,[48] who used a method rapidly outmoded, glass beads moving on wires, the abacus, in order to assemble, contrast, develop, and transpose musical phrases and themes. The intimate relationship between the evolution of the Game and the rise of the new musicology is persistently stressed. Composers of the sixteenth, seventeenth, and eighteenth centuries—"who based their musical compositions upon mathematical speculations" (VI, 86) —may have conceived of the Game. The Castalian narrator quotes in detail from Ziegenhalss and Cusanus, but the scholarly apparatus is hinted at rather than ostentatiously displayed, for of course the preface is a game too.

Practiced by each specialized discipline in turn as the Castalian ideal evolved, the Glass Bead Game ultimately acquired what became its essential characteristic: "the capacity for universality, hovering above the disciplines" (VI, 107). The new, stringent idealism had begun by discounting universality as an aspiration, fearful with good reason of dilettantism; the Game, in providing the separate disciplines with the possibility of interconnection, elevated the Castalian Renaissance to its apogee, but simultaneously put the entire achievement at risk by hazarding a relapse into feuilleton. A certain ambiguity, then, lies in the fact that the various

---

language, a complete system" (VII, 640) and remarks that it is something most people instinctively understand. His father, Johannes Hesse, was a keen inventor of games and even published a book on the subject (see "The Beggar," IV, 657).

[47] And Novalis wrote: "Perhaps by means of a game similar to chess, structures of thought could be created.—The old logical disputation game was exactly like a board game" (III, 255). We recall the "chess player" in *The Steppenwolf* and note the "Magic Theater" is said to have been one of the early "synonyms" for the Game (VI, 109).

[48] Perrot was the name of the machine shop in Calw where Hesse once worked.

pedagogical provinces found their supreme self-revelation—and self-contemplation—in this art. The fact that it could be seen as an "art" at all had, indeed, to throw doubt upon its justification, as the novel works out in detail. The responsibility for recognizing the Game's synthetic possibilities is laid at the door of one Lusor (or Joculator) Basiliensis, a Swiss musicologist and mathematician; a Parisian sinologist had already drawn attention to the need for a new sign language, like the Chinese ideograms, capable of rendering universally and impartially the totality of knowledge in its logical and analogical connections. Achieving such a conjunction in the restricted sphere of music and mathematics, the Basel scholar provided the impetus for the ultimate florescence of the Game, its development "into the epitome of the spiritual and the artistic (*Musischen*), into the sublime cult, the *unio mystica* of all the separate members of the *universitas litterarum*" (VI, 109).

An ironical institution, the Glass Bead Game has an ironical history. Such definitions as the above indicate something of its horizons, the extent of its playful reality, in Hesse's world. Blending the reflective and the anoetic-poetic, it is the sanctification of the secular, the objective correlative of that arcane conjunction in the soul which is the recurrent motif of Hesse's works. Furthermore, it is evidently the simulacrum of both the world of letters as a whole and of the individual *Sprachkunstwerk*. There are those who wish to see in these last the primary meanings of this elaborate metaphor.[49] In Castalia each discipline has its master, the Magister Ludi being the supreme custodian of the Game. That the elegant Thomas von der Trave (a transparent pseudonym for Thomas Mann)[50] is Joseph Knecht's precursor in office might seem to support the "literary" interpretation, as might the insistence that the Game is a form of art ("an art form *sui generis*"), also the comparison of particular compositions in the genre with dramas, as well as the pointed allusions to Romantic theory of literature,

---

[49] Cf. e.g., Hans Mayer, "Hermann Hesse und das 'Feuilletonistische Zeitalter,'" in *Studien zur deutschen Literatur* (Berlin, 1954), p. 237.

[50] "A great worker, which people who only saw him from his representative side did not suspect" (VI, 219)—the representative function of the writer in respect to his nation preoccupies Hesse, for obvious reasons, in these years and in this novel.

"universal poetry" and the rest: "every active Glass Bead player
dreams in fact of a perpetual expansion of the areas of the Game,
until they encompass the whole world" (VI, 220). We know from
certain passages in *The Journey to the East* that Hesse was now
once again taking stock of his literary past, especially his Neo-
Romantic beginnings with their highly ornamented language; and
it is evident that the periodic stylistic mutations of the Game are a
metaphor for literature. The musical paradigm, of course, is never
far away, and the aesthetic aspect is continually stressed.

"The entirety of life," the young Joseph Knecht notes, "physical and mental, is a dynamic phenomenon of which the Glass
Bead Game encompasses basically only the aesthetic side" (VI,
186). A substitute for art in a province of the mind where the arts
are in fact taboo, the Glass Bead Game is art raised to a sacred,
cultic function among those who have no religion: the solemn,
public Games are conducted according to inviolable formal rules,
the participants themselves are subjected to a stern ἄσκησις. The
hall in which the Game is played is the sacred, separated place of
which Johann Huizinga speaks in *Homo Ludens* (1938); an influence of some of Huizinga's ideas cannot be ruled out.[51] Castalia,
as the Benedictine Pater Jakobus observes with irony, has sought
to make a sacrament out of the Glass Bead Game; for the true
Castalian it is confessedly "almost synonymous with divine worship" (VI, 113); Knecht in one of his courses on the Game refers
to the place of the "Game Village," the Vicus Lusorum, in Castalia,
and of the function of the Republic itself as a vehicle for the
artistic and the holy. This aspect is disclosed most clearly by a
remark about the annual Ludus Sollemnis: "It possessed for the
believers the sacramental power of genuine sacred festivity, and
for the unbelievers it was at least a substitute for religion and for
both it meant bathing in the pure spring of the beautiful" (VI,
292). This curious distinction—in the context of this humanistic
province—between believers and unbelievers shows up the sham
secularism of the utopian metaphor. The nexus of the sacred and
the beautiful goes back to *Hermann Lauscher;* while the imagery

[51] Huizinga points to the analogy (even identity) of sacred ritual and
game; both subserve rigid rules, and both are performed in a specialized, enclosed place. Cf. J. Huizinga, *Homo Ludens* (Basel, 1949), pp. 32-33.

of bathing is most striking, recalling as it does Goldmund's penance and indirectly even Siddhartha's moment of enlightenment. Like Goldmund's meticulous repetition of prayers, the cryptographic gymnastics of the Glass Bead Game are a spiritual exercise, a posturing dance around a holy center, the hollow center of the megalo- and the microcosmos, of the work of art itself:

> Sternbildern gleich ertönen sie kristallen,
> In ihrem Dienst ward unserm Leben Sinn,
> Und keiner kann aus ihren Kreisen fallen,
> Als nach der heiligen Mitte hin.[52]

> (Like constellations they sound crystalline,
> Their service has brought meaning to our lives,
> And from their orbits none can fall
> But toward the holy center.)

As in *The Steppenwolf* and *Narziss and Goldmund*, the integration of form and content is on one level a metaphor for the structural unity of the spiritual life. To its exoteric devotees, the Game is essentially, "an ingenious kind of stenography" (VI, 202), to the esoteric initiate, however, it is a *lingua sacra* (VI, 197), each ideogram the threshold of a meditation. The "psychological method of play" is distinguished from the "formal method"; the latter concerned itself with achieving unity and harmony in the interaction of the material entities, mathematical, linguistic, musical, and so on, composing the individual game; the former pursued "cosmic roundness and perfection not so much in the selection, arrangement, intermingling, interlocking, and confrontation of the contents as in the meditation which followed on each stage of the game, on which it put the whole emphasis" (VI, 284). This means that the "formal method" was concerned with the Game itself as surface, the "psychological method" with the psyche of the player as content. We recall Hesse's remark as to the purpose of meditation: "a shifting of the state of consciousness, a technique the highest goal of which is a pure harmony, a simultaneous and uniform functioning together of logical and intuitive thinking." In the preface we find some account of the introduction into the develop-

---

[52] "The Glass Bead Game," final poem of "The Poems of the Pupil and Student" (VI, 556).

ing Glass Bead Game of the techniques of meditation employed
for so long by the Travelers to the East, as a corrective to the
tendency of all ritual functions to degenerate into mere virtu-
osity. Yogic methods have become, indeed, a vital constituent of
the Castalian way of life, lending it inwardness. So also, meditation
points the Game itself not only toward external and formal but also
toward inner and psychic harmony; as a model of the cosmos, "the
starry world of the Glass Bead Game" (VI, 182) is hollow with
the divine. This ancient symbol,[53] modified by the modern space-
time symbolism of *The Steppenwolf*, undergoes a further mutation
when the Magister Ludi, Joseph Knecht, takes his friend Plinio
to the window and points to the stars. Symbols of clarity and order,
the stars themselves are also "deep": "The deep of the world and
its mysteries is not to be found where the clouds are and the blackness, the deep is in the clarity and the brightness" (VI, 417). But as
depth is a function of clarity, so meaning is dependent on form.
The Old Music Master writes to Knecht one day of the dangers of
unbridled esotericism (here in the sense of "psychologizing," the
pursuit of psychological methods without adequate formal discipline, content without surface); he warns that such a tendency is
especially perilous for a teacher. The notion that meaning is
primary to form leads to gross error, to philosophy of history and
other characteristic misdemeanors of intellectual life; music, to take
an example, never begins with meaning. An aphorism formulates
this fundamental issue in its pedagogical aspect: "Whether you become a teacher, a scholar, or a musician, respect 'meaning,' but do
not imagine it can be taught" (VI, 200).

The Glass Bead Game, like the Journey to the East, is essentially
indescribable. Part of the quality of this elusive novel lies in the
delicate balance which is maintained between form and meaning.
One might say that the book itself is composed according to the
"psychological method of play," but even this method must, by
definition, begin with form, with the surface cryptography of the
Game. Form, in the "psychological method," remains the starting
point, but is significant not for itself alone but for that which it

---

[53] Much star imagery has some oblique biblical connection. Its importance in
modern German writing may be underlined if we recall, for instance, its use by
Hermann Broch.

implies, that to which it constantly leads, the threshold it provides. In *The Glass Bead Game* the reflective analyses and conversations (of which there are many) are—much like those in *Narziss and Goldmund*—exoteric and "formal"; the numinous depth, as in music,[54] is immanent in the surface pattern. We may even go back as far as *Hermann Lauscher* and remember the formulation: "to reserve for oneself all the unspoken things with sophisticated awareness as a mystery revealed." To object that *The Glass Bead Game* has no dimension of depth [55] is perhaps to overlook this point, even to commit the very error which the Old Music Master's aphorism warns specifically against. We may note, on the other hand, that Knecht—an exponent of the "psychological method of play"—preferred to call this method "pedagogical." *The Glass Bead Game* is indeed formal, psychological, *and* pedagogical, itself a kind of Glass Bead Game. Too little attention, it would seem, has been paid to Hesse's observation that the figure of Knecht was secondary to the initial intention of the work; that many critics have concentrated their attention upon Knecht alone, or upon the educational or social issues apparently raised by the book, is nonetheless comprehensible, though it is a pity that some have done so with such disregard for the novel as a work of language. *The Glass Bead Game* is a work of poetry *and* didacticism, which is not at all the same thing as a work of didactic poetry.

The mock biographer [56] of this framework novel apparently venerates Knecht and will not judge him, nor even his extraordinary end. He writes a serenely confident and on the whole eulogizing account which is essentially and intentionally depersonalized; the cult of personality, we are told, was a vice characteristic of twentieth-century biographers, while the Castalian

[54] Cf. here Hans Kayser (*op. cit.*, pp. 66–67): "in the forms of the note-numbers logical and psychic values are a priori united in a precise fashion."

[55] Cf. Oskar Seidlin, "Hermann Hesses Glasperlenspiel," *Die Wandlung*, III, pt. 1 (1948), 307.

[56] The analogy, both formal and to some extent psychological, with Mann's Serenus Zeitblom suggests itself. But it does not take us very far; unlike Mann's narrator, Hesse's lacks self-pity as he lacks self-criticism. It has been argued that there is more than one Castalian narrator (Ziolkowski, *The Novels of Hermann Hesse*, p. 301 ff.). The evidence for this in the text, however, is not very substantial, and if the genesis offered above be accepted the necessity for such a view disappears.

ideal discounts individuality and sustains "as complete an integration as is possible of oneself into the communal, as perfect a service
as is possible of the superpersonal" (VI, 81). The biography of a
Castalian by a Castalian for Castalians should by definition be but a
history of function, in a sense an exemplary, skeletal *vita*, without,
however (a surprising proviso!), a complete loss of "the strong,
fresh, wonderful stimulus . . . which constitutes the aroma and the
worth of the individual" (VI, 82). In this respect the account of
Knecht's life might be called secularized hagiography, in which the
traditional framework of the saintly *vita* is adapted to the pattern
of the hierarchy; but in practice, of course, a strongly personalized
impression of Joseph Knecht is conveyed, all the same. The
apparent avoidance of personal detail applies only to trivialities;
at each vital point the function has personality, the skeleton has
flesh; there is therefore an inward *vita*, a second, parallel line, presumably the outsiderdom of the true saint, and this line swerves
violently away tangentially at the end. One must, however, go
further: a more satisfactory interpretation of *The Glass Bead Game*
as a whole will be shown to require what may, for convenience, be
called the *third* line of Knecht's *vita*, much more deeply hidden in
the text.

Disregarding this last point for a moment, we may note that form
and content, hierarchy and person, externally and internally
patterned *vitae* of Joseph Knecht are linked together, and
ultimately rent asunder, by the phenomenon which he himself
designates by the term "call" (*Berufung*). The story of Knecht's
life begins, in fact, with his first experience of "call"; we learn
nothing else about his childhood, except that there was no conflict
between home and school. The Swabian note, then, is sounded
early, and with some irony. Then comes the visit of the Castalian
Music Master to Knecht's school in the outside world and his test-
ing of Joseph; the experience is a sacramental one: "He had experienced the process of call, which can properly be characterized
as a sacrament; the revelation and inviting opening up of the ideal
world" (VI, 126–127). The boy's soul is opened to the vision of
harmony in music, his heart to the emotion of veneration. The
Music Master (like Demian) is a hierophant (*Zaubermann*) (VI,
129); the call itself, which may take many forms, has always the

same (using a favorite phrase) "kernel and sense" (VI, 129): "The soul is awakened by it, transformed or intensified, so that instead of dreams and presentiments from within suddenly a summons from without, a fragment of reality is there and intervenes" (VI, 129). "Call" and "awakening" are perhaps two aspects of the same experience; the latter refers to a change of consciousness, of state of being, the former to a response to destiny, a bending of the will. Both, as the Master of the Order, Alexander, is one day compelled to think in connection with Knecht, may be of the Devil.

At the first moment of *Berufung*, the detection in the examinee of the merest grain of personal purpose, of careerism, would have caused the Music Master to exclude the boy from the pedagogical province altogether. As it is, his name is inscribed in the register of the Castalians-elect, "the golden book" as the preparatory school boys call it, or, less respectfully, "the place-hunters' list" (VI, 128); Joseph Knecht has passed his provincial examination. Now that the magician's hand has touched him, he begins to grow within, like a plant which "suddenly in an hour of miracle has become conscious of its form" (VI, 130), the secret of its seed; the Within and the Without evolve toward each other in harmonious balance. The Castalian narrator, giving an account of this period, slips inadvertently into poetry, and we suddenly have Goldmund-Giebenrath before us again: "and he could at other times forget everything and go off into dreams with a softness and submission which was new to him, listen to the wind or the rain, stare into the flowing water of the river" (VI, 130). Like Goldmund, indeed, the adolescent Knecht has forgotten his childhood, and the Castalian archives are silent upon this period of his life, as silent as they are upon the legend in which his life terminates. We will not be mistaken if we guess at a connection between these two periods.

Eschholz, the junior of the Elite Schools, which Joseph Knecht now begins to attend, is the Castalian variant of Maulbronn; "Hellas House," which the newcomer joins, is the old name from *Beneath the Wheel* (and from real life). Knecht's gradual absorption by the Castalian educational system proceeds smoothly and without incident; the narrator interpolates an account of the Elite School system, "a wise and elastic selective system" (VI, 134), with which is integrated the Order, whose members, even when they leave the province to teach in the outside world (as the majority do), remain bound by its rules, including poverty and celibacy: "half in mockery, half in respect, the people call them 'mandarins' " (VI, 136). Those who remain behind to live and work in the province itself are provided with ideal conditions for scholarly research, freed of material wants and of the need to consider material purposes, but deprived also of any kind of luxury. The antithesis between the ideal pattern of the hierarchy and the inner life of Joseph Knecht is pointed out even at the time when "the second degree of call" (VI, 158) is due to make of him a consummate Castalian. He is, for instance, disturbed when the Educational Authority dismisses a boy from Eschholz and sends him back into the world; he entertains impermissible thoughts, for example the idea "that the 'world' outside, from which we Electi all once came, had not ceased to exist in the degree in which it appeared to me to have done so, that for many it was rather an immense reality full of drawing power which lured them and ultimately recalled them. And perhaps it was this not only for individuals but for all of us . . . perhaps the apparent relapse which they suffered was not a relapse at all and they did not suffer it, but it was rather a leap [*Sprung*] and a deed, and maybe we who stayed well behaved in Eschholz were precisely the weaklings and the cowards" (VI, 144–145). This thought, in its original form, no doubt proved comforting to Hermann Heilner; it was a critical matter on any estimate, debated further in Joseph's conversation with one of his comrades, on their way to visit the Music Master in Monteport, when the significant word "*springen*" recurs. The leap which Joseph Knecht already dreams of making is, however, "not back into the lesser, but onward and into the higher" (VI, 150), that is, in the terms of "A Bit of Theology," the qualitative leap to the third stage, no sick reversion à la Giebenrath but a Heilneresque break with the institution; but for this would-be saint the model of Hermann Heilner conceals a profound irony.

In Monteport, the Music Master introduces Joseph to the technique of meditation (with a musical theme as starting point), in preparation for the yogic practices which he will learn in the higher schools. The relationship between the master and his pupil here sheds light upon a peculiar feature of *The Glass Bead Game* in its capacity as a *Bildungsroman:* the Music Master is Joseph's guru, who, although himself in high office in the Castalian hierarchy, here in effect bypasses the official educational system. It is indeed a curious and notable fact that we learn little or nothing of Knecht's work within the framework of the schools, but much about his evolution under the hands of his several personal teachers. This aversion to school as a system is not only particularly ironical in this novel and not only characteristic of Hesse, but typical perhaps of the whole tradition of the German *Bildungsroman.* Neither Wilhelm Meister, nor Heinrich von Ofterdingen, nor Stifter's Heinrich Drendorf, nor Keller's Heinrich Lee learn anything worth knowing in schools. In *The Glass Bead Game,* this feature, in pointing back toward the school novel, discloses not only the movement along the second line of the *vita* but even perhaps a glimpse of the hidden third line.

The Music Master, of course, is the vehicle for the supreme single educative factor in the young initiate's life, music itself. In this novel Hesse's worship of classical and preclassical music reaches its expressive climax. Castalia, despite its name, is by inclination and by decree a province which produces no art, "but we believe," says the narrator, with his mandarin self-assurance, "that we have grasped, in what we today call classical music, the secret, the spirit, the virtue and the piety of those generations" (VI, 98). "Those generations"—that is, the fifteenth to the eighteenth centuries—were, as *The Steppenwolf* noted, the great era of religious music. Chinese music also has its lofty place in the pantheon of the pedagogical province; perhaps the Chinese conception of the relationship between the condition of music and the stability of the state supremely exemplifies the *moral* function of this magic art. In classical European music, Knecht remarks himself: "We possess . . . the inheritance of the ancient world and of Christianity, a spirit of serene and valiant piety, an unsurpassable chivalrous morality" (VI, 116).[57]

---

[57] Cf. also: "My theoretical interest in music is very limited. . . . I am interested in counterpoint, the fugue, the change of harmonic modes, but behind these purely aesthetic questions there are others alive for me, the true spirit of genuine music, its morality" (*Letters;* VII, 570–571).

Music is form in time; its "shapes" are an object of meditation; at the same time it is an art that may be learned as a craft (VI, 163). For a while, indeed, Knecht's preoccupation with the technical and sensuous side of music holds him back from the extremer distillations of the Glass Bead Game—"and he who may be able to read scores but cannot play any instrument perfectly should have nothing to say about music" (VI, 164). Somewhere in between form and meaning is the sphere which is entered in meditation; the Music Master, in meditating, descends into his thoughts "like a weary man into a foot bath" (VI, 152), and the bathing symbolism occurs yet again: "From a private music lesson with him one emerged as though from a bath and a massage" (VI, 145). For he is a vehicle of the holy, and religious figures are constantly applied to him: his very first appearance is like "an archangel from the supreme Heaven" (VI, 129), and Knecht has been duly "blessed." The Music Master speaks of the mandatory passion of the seeker after being, in language which, reversing the equation of Goldmund's lovemaking, is at once sacred and profane: "but I tell you, he must glow (*glühen*) and burn" (VI, 157). His is again the message of Siddhartha, that truth indeed exists, but that there is no valid teaching, his the insight that meaning cannot be transmitted from teacher to pupil, all that can be conveyed (and all that needs to be), is skill and discipline, the mastery of form.

Knecht's invitation to Monteport is an event which itself implies "the second degree of call"; he is now the Music Master's "personal" pupil, indeed his spiritual child ("It is as though I had a son . . ." [VI, 223]); when he all but loses the Way, it is the Music Master who leads him back to it by means of a story from his own youth which emphasizes that the source of all error lies in loss of form, the omission—in this case—of the meditative exercises. Much later in the novel, the central issue of the relationship of teacher and pupil attains symbolic expression when Joseph Knecht, confronted with his imminent nomination as Magister Ludi, withdraws into a meditation which commences with the memory of his first encounter with his master, more than thirty years before, and which continues thus: "the scene in the classroom, the entry of the old man to the boy, repeated itself again and again, an infinite number of times . . . so that soon it was no longer possible to tell who was coming and who going, who was leading and who following" (VI, 310). The interdependence, indeed interchangeability, of teacher and pupil is a great secret; it is "the symbol of Castalia, indeed the game of life itself, which flows on endlessly divided into old and young, day and night, yang and yin" (VI, 311).

The decline and death of the Old Music Master is a process of depersonalization, his "perfection" is manifest in a radiant serenity unaccompanied by speech. The musicologist Carlo Ferromonte,[58] on his own confession no lover of the mystical, represents in his reserved skepticism an ironical counterweight to the effect produced on Knecht by the apparent transfiguration of the Old Master; he tells Knecht dryly: "You will scarcely be intending to introduce a canonization process in favor of the Old Master, there would not be a competent authority for such a thing in our Order" (VI, 352). However impersonal the prototypical *vita* of the saint may be, it seems in the end always to involve individuality, which transcends the sameness of the hierarchical; the problem of the artist-saint has therefore not been exhausted in the antithesis between Augustine and Rousseau. It is noteworthy that Ferromonte's position is in the last resort overridden—there is no question where Knecht's feelings lie. Just before his end the Old Music Master is transformed into an unmistakable figure, "hidden and sheltered behind his golden mask" (VI, 351), from whose surface the world runs off "like rain from a stone." When the mask is removed by death, Gotama-Demian's last human features are "shrunk and sunken into a silent rune and arabesque, a magic figure, no longer legible and yet as though speaking of smiling and of perfected happiness" (VI, 377–378). This transfiguration became the stuff of numerous Castalian legends, which is not surprising, for we know since *Siddhartha* that legend is the ultimate refuge of that utter paradox, the supreme "impersonal individual," the artist-saint.[59]

---

[58] Carlo Isenberg, Hesse's nephew—according to the author the most direct portrait in the book. See *Letters* (VII, 666).

[59] *Roman à clef* though *The Glass Bead Game* partly is, the Old Music Master resists identification with any model from life. For one suggestion see I. Halpert, "The Alt-Musikmeister and Goethe," *Monatshefte für deutschen Unterricht*, LII (1960), 19–24.

"*Gignit autem artificiosam lusorum gentem Cella Silvestris*"—this is the motto of Waldzell, senior Elite School, which specializes in the education of future Glass Bead players; of all schools, it is "the most artistic" (*musisch;* VI, 160). Its enemies in Castalia find that it produces by and large "conceited aesthetes and spoiled princes" (VI, 161). Topographically much like Tübingen (where Hesse arrived in 1895), with touches still of Maulbronn, the little town of Waldzell contains school and Game Village, which both turn out to contain their aesthetically minded eccentrics and *poètes maudits,* just as the Tübinger Stift had its Waiblingers and Tübingen itself its Hermann Lauschers. There are ultimate analogies not only between the life of the student in Castalia and that of the German student of popular repute but also between the latter and the life of the Castalian in itself; Castalia is *mutatis mutandis* the world of the "eternal student" hypostasized as an institution; and the thought is not without its relevance that since the "eternal student" also tends to be the "wandering scholar," the stability of this hypostasization is therefore questionable.

At Waldzell the ultimate molding of that representative Castalian, Joseph Knecht, takes place; but the reader scarcely meets the Button Molders themselves; of the Waldzell teachers only the school principal, Zbinden, is referred to, and even he never appears in person. The bias, again, is unmistakable, if perhaps unconscious; it is the "individuals," that is, the critic of Castalia, Plinio Designori, and the outsider within the walls, the "Elder Brother," who now hold the stage. Plinio comes of a distinguished aristocratic family (hence "De-Signori"); he is a *Hospitant,* that is, a student at Waldzell by ancient birthright, who is from the outset destined on the completion of his education to return to a worldly career. He is, moreover, an eloquent opponent of the Castalian way of life, and he disputes publicly and in part formally with Joseph Knecht, who is encouraged by the authorities to champion the province in these displays of dialectic.

In the debates, in fact, there emerges something of that Hegelian dialectic which is one of the structural features of the book; it is indeed no coincidence that Knecht, during his first terms at Waldzell, is drawn toward German philosophy, "Leibniz, Kant, and the Romantics, of whom Hegel was by far the one who most strongly

attracted him" (VI, 165). Indeed, the controversy between Narziss
and Goldmund has here been transferred on to the sociohistorical
plane. Narziss and Goldmund were both exceptional people; so
also Joseph and Plinio are at one in their patrician quality, but, like
Narziss and Goldmund, different from each other in every other
respect. Plinio decries the masters of Castalia as a priestly caste, their
pupils are a "hobbled and castrated herd" (VI, 171); he sneers
at the "resigned infertility" (VI, 172) of the pedagogical province,
the sophisticated musicology of a place and time in which no new
music is ever composed;—sharply pointed criticisms, these, which
disturb his adversary. In these dialectical arguments between the
two friends, both sides of the coin are displayed impartially; for
Knecht the debates are pivotal, and in finally molding him into a
fully representative figure they ironically water the seeds of his
later act of desertion. The true irony, of course, lies deeper still;
for these debates are not composed as an exhaustive philosophical
probing of the ultimate intellectual issues upon which the novel
depends or may seem to depend; they are in fact largely formal.
Novalis wrote of "the old logical disputation game" and compared
it with chess; the public disputes of Plinio Designori and Joseph
Knecht are indeed themselves a kind of game. In unwittingly playing this game, the protagonist of *The Glass Bead Game* comes
now to examine his conscience and to find that the "outside" world,
Plinio's world, must always be reckoned with; furthermore there is
a Trojan horse within the Castalian gates:

And this primitive world was innate in everyone, you felt something of
it in your own heart, some curiosity for it, homesickness for it, pity for
it. To be just toward it, to preserve for it a certain right to live in your
own heart, but yet not to relapse into it, this was the task. For alongside
it and above it was the second world, the Castalian, the spiritual, an
artificial, an ordered, a protected world which nevertheless needs
constant supervision and exercise, the hierarchy [VI, 176].

We recall the light and dark worlds of Emil Sinclair, we equate—
as we surely may—"hierarchy" with "father." The psychoanalytic
analogue is transparent: crudely stated, the world without is the id,
Castalia the superego.

Knecht's own adjustment to Waldzell and to his representative future does not proceed wholly without friction. "Some of the traits in this picture of a youth," the almost expressionless narrator observes, "are no doubt signs of puberty" (VI, 165)—but sex is too personal a matter to be of much interest in Castalia, where only celibacy has the desirable impersonal sameness.[60] Knecht devotes himself onesidedly to musical studies, an imbalance which requires the intervention of the Music Master to correct it. Years of financially emancipated free study would be disastrous without the gentle control of the Educational Authority and the spiritual hygiene of the yogic exercises—as indeed such freedom used to be for the students of the twentieth century and earlier, who frequently fell victim to a catastrophic Faustian dilettantism.

Neither the "citizens' daughters," however, nor yoga prevent Joseph Knecht from writing poems, poems which only appear as an appendix to *The Glass Bead Game* and which, whatever their literary merit,[61] are in themselves "a certain concession to the world of Plinio, a degree of rebellion against certain Castalian house rules" (VI, 182). Here we move along that line which will in the end project right out of Castalia, and on which the second and third levels of the *vita* temporarily coalesce. The peculiar custom by which the Educational Authority requires each student, during his long period of free study, to compose annually an account of his inner development and problems in the garb of a fictitious autobiography (*Lebenslauf*) set in another historical era is partly intended to provide a safetyvalve for repressed artistic impulses. To project one's ego in this fashion, into other skins and eras—this empathy has a good deal in common with the exercises Siddhartha learned from the Samanas; it is also the procedure of the novelist, and *The Glass Bead Game* is indeed not so much one novel and three autobiographies but more exactly *four* autobiographies in this sense, the fourth being a self-projection, by the author of all four, into the future, the contemplation in the guise of the future of the decisive moments of his own past. Writing the autobiographies, however, evidently did not suffice as a sublimation for Knecht's artistic

---

[60] The information is casually proffered that the daughters of the local citizenry marry late and meanwhile offer solace to the elite students.

[61] Often thought to be slight. See, e.g., W. Kohlschmidt, "Meditationen über Hermann Hesses *Glasperlenspiel*," *Zeitwende*, XIX (1947–1948), 274.

drives. Castalia has been regarded as tending toward "Alexandrinism," [62] a term which at once recalls Nietzsche and the polemics of *The Birth of Tragedy;* Nietzsche would have attacked the pedagogical province as Socratism gone mad, as the total demythologization of culture; yet he would have constated that Castalia too had its symbol of the dead end of intellect and maybe the coming rebirth of art, its "musical Socrates," [63] namely Joseph Knecht himself. On the way back to Eschholz from his first visit to Monteport, Knecht rests with his companion in the Oberland landscape (which, in this novel, is so rarely described), they take from their pockets their wooden flutes and play a duet. Flute playing had been a feature of the Travelers' festival at Bremgarten, with Pablo the principal performer. Later the flute is to become the secret figure for the triumph of the third, the innermost, stream of life.

The *chinoiserie* which enriches Joseph Knecht's personality at this time might well be regarded as little more than a further ironic and graceful adornment of the whole fanciful edifice of *The Glass Bead Game.* Certainly, it is a Chinese mask; but many of the features of this most Chinese novel are those of a mask; and the episode of the Elder Brother is in fact central to an understanding of the book. The Chinese themes of the work derive from a long-standing preoccupation with that ancient civilization. It was Johannes Hesse who first introduced his son to the thought of Lao-tzŭ: [64] "The doctrine of Jesus and the doctrine of Lao-tzŭ, the doctrine of the Vedas and the doctrine of Goethe are, where they touch upon the eternally human, the same. There is but *one* doctrine. There is but *one* religion. . . . It is the doctrine of the 'Kingdom of Heaven' which we carry 'within us.' " [65] In 1916, once more, Indian and Chinese mysticism are mentioned in the same breath,

---

[62] H. H. Groothoff, "Versuch einer Interpretation des Glasperlenspieles," *Hamburger Akademische Rundschau,* II (1947–1948), 274.

[63] Nietzsche, *Werke,* I, 87.

[64] Apparently in Grill's translation. Cf. "A Library of World Literature" (VII, 339). Johannes Hesse published a short study on the subject (*Lao-Tse: Ein vorchristlicher Wahrheitszeuge* [1914]). Hesse got to know the Chinese thinkers well, of course, in Richard Wilhelm's translations.

[65] "Christmas" (1917; VII, 94–95).

and reference is made to a tradition which extends from Lao-tzǔ
to Jesus.[66] "Chinese Consideration" (1921) comments upon the
spread of interest in classical Chinese philosophy during the previous decade; early Taoist thought is found to be a particularly fruitful source of help for the modern European. The essential
pragmatism, the apparent proximity to everyday life of the Chinese
recipe—"astonishingly homely and close to the people and everyday life" [67]—pleased Hesse; this was the quality the Indian mystics
most lacked. So China became for him "a spiritual refuge and
second home," Chinese thinking "a confirmation of my own
instincts." [68] Like the Greeks, but unlike the Indians, the Chinese
grasped the necessity for balance and proportion, in the concern
for which alone true humanism may be grounded.[69] Hesse noted
the close analogy between the rationalism of Confucius and that of
Socrates,[70] though it was to Lao-tzǔ and the *Tao Te Ching* that he
himself became most devoted. The Castalians are "mandarins," they
are Confucians as well as Socratics; much light is shed upon the
pedagogical province and also upon its theories of culture and the
state if their Confucian origin is realized.

Lao-tzǔ, of course, is another thing again; the mystical stream in
Chinese thought (from which, in the last resort, all the rest
emerged) led Hesse inevitably to *The Book of Changes*, the *I
Ching*, first made available in an acceptable translation by Richard
Wilhelm in 1924. Hesse appears to have acquired this volume at
once; in an article on his recent reading, published in 1925,[71] he
refers to it, explains briefly what it is and remarks that it (like,
indeed, the *Tao Te Ching*) is one of those books which cannot be
"read" in the normal sense. There is another reference to the *I
Ching* in "A Short Autobiography" (1925), and yet another in
"Library of World Literature" (1929). Nearly thirty years later
Hesse speaks of an occasion when, faced with a decision, he did

[66] "Recollections of India" (III, 852).
[67] "Favorite Reading" (VII, 420).
[68] *Ibid.*
[69] Cf. *Letters* (VII, 571).
[70] "My Faith" (VII, 373).
[71] "Erinnerung an Lektüre," *Neue Rundschau*, XXXVI, ii, (1925), 964–972.

what he had not done for a very long time, he actually consulted the oracle: "I submitted the decision to the Chinese oracle, *I Ching*, received an unambiguous reply and followed this." [72]

For the motif of the Elder Brother we may also adduce two references in the letters. No poet, we are told, has the right or duty to take the stance of a priest; the real leaders of humanity, if there be any, are the great sages of India and China: "My role cannot be that of the priest . . . and if I nonetheless have attempted to advise thousands of people in letters and indications, I never did it as a leader, always only as a companion in suffering, a somewhat older brother." [73] "Elder Brother," Hesse knows, is a Chinese form of polite address,[74] but he uses it, one may suspect, as a sign for a hidden relationship, a discreet but burning sympathy behind the mannered serenity of the outsider's old age. For Joseph Knecht and the Elder Brother of *The Glass Bead Game*—that scarcely tolerated Castalian eccentric who mimes the life of a Taoist mystic in his bamboo grove—are pupil and master, are brothers, are "friends"; they conceal—to apply the phrase once more—"the secret of their identity." It is when he immerses himself in his first Chinese studies that Knecht is directed by Castalia's East Asian Institute, albeit somewhat unwillingly, to the hermitage of the Elder Brother, who alone can give instruction in the functioning of that dubious philosophical machine and oracle, the *I Ching*. As it is the Confucian strain of Chinese thought—"the rationalistic and broadly antimystical" (VI, 206)—which is admired in Castalia (along with Chinese music), the *I Ching* is practically taboo. Even the Tao is a dangerous philosophy which will lead in the end to individualism and worse.[75] In the very heart, then, of the sphere of the intellect, of order and causality, is to be found the bamboo grove, a circle of freedom, a locale of the irrational, where the hexagrams of the

---

[72] "Circular Letter from Sils-Maria" (1954; VII, 912).

[73] *Letters* (VII, 534).

[74] *Ibid* (VII, 604). It is also, according to Jung, one of the forms in which the "shadow," the neglected self, may manifest. Cf. J. Jacobi, *The Psychology of C. G. Jung*, p. 145.

[75] Cf. *Letters* (VII, 721). In some respects one may indeed compare the Tao with the philosophy of Ivan Karamazov and the doctrine that "all is permitted" as adumbrated in *In Sight of Chaos*, though the comparison—as invariably when one is concerned with Lao-tzŭ—is misleading. Ivan was scarcely a Taoist.

I Ching reign; here what is worshiped is not the logical and the causal but the patterns of the adventitious, the "laws" of chance and synchronicity. The Elder Brother—who acquired his sobriquet by his obstinate employment of this form of address to all and sundry —is described as an "Outsider" and "legendary" (VI, 205).

In part a self-portrait of his author,[76] the Elder Brother has a meticulously kept Chinese garden, with a fountain in which goldfish swim. Waiting, just like Goldmund with Meister Niklaus, for the master's decision, Knecht copies Goldmund again and comes to sit beside this pool and stare down into it: "into the small, cool world of darkness and light and magically playing colors, where the bodies of the golden fish rocked in the dark greeny-blue and inky blackness and now and then dispatched flashes of crystal and gold through the sleeping darkness" (VI, 208). It is perhaps not necessary to spell out more exactly the parallels with *Narziss and Goldmund*, with *The Journey to the East,* and indeed with *Beneath the Wheel* that there are in this passage, not the fish alone for instance, but also the flickering gold in the cool crystal depths; but it is important to observe that such colorful, figurative language as this is rare in *The Glass Bead Game,* is a watery hollow in the crystal surface of the game. The contrast is a linguistic one, not merely an antithesis of symbol like the gargoyles and chestnut of Mariabronn. From the Elder Brother, Knecht learns the operation of the oracle, using the ancient method of yarrow stalks. The question as to Joseph's future is put to it; the answer is: "the sign of Mong. . . . This sign is called 'folly of youth.' Above, the mountain; below, the water; above, Gen, below Kan, at the bottom of the mountain the spring rises, symbol of youth" (VI, 210).[77] In its judgment, the *I Ching* praises persistence but warns that it will answer a question but once. Of extreme interest for the interpretation of *The Glass Bead Game* is the symbol of the mountain and water as used here; it may be seen to presage the

---

[76] "A slightly-built man, dressed in a gray-yellow linen suit, with glasses over his blue, reserved eyes, rose from a flowerbed" (VI, 207).

[77] The standard English translation is *The I Ching, or Book of Changes,* from the Richard Wilhelm translation, rendered into English by Gary F. Baynes, with a foreword by C. G. Jung (Bollingen Series XIX; New York, 1950). "Folly of youth" is here used in the sense of the inexperience, the naïveté of the young man who still stands at the beginning of his Way (and Wilhelm's explanatory notes refer to Parsifal).

scene of Knecht's death.[78] A little weary and wary of such peculiar things, the Castalian narrator remarks: "Now let us return to our factual report" (VI, 210). But on leaving the Elder Brother behind us we are not permitted to forget about China; Chinese music becomes Knecht's intensive study; the "Chinese House" is the basic motif of his first Ludus Sollemnis as Magister Ludi; he reads the *I Ching* before setting out on his mission to Mariafels, and it answers with the sign of Lü, that of the "wanderer"; the *Book of Changes* goes with him to Mariafels, for it turns out that it is a particular love of the abbot there—the man whom the young ambassador, who carries his spiritual power within, "his property with him" (VI, 232), enchants and wins over.

Indeed, the play with the *I Ching* is one of the most recondite games in *The Glass Bead Game*; it is linked with the second line of Knecht's *vita*, which culminates in the ideal of service through humility—"success through smallness," "*durch Kleinheit Gelingen*" (VI, 232). Subsequently Knecht regards the months he spends in the bamboo grove as the "beginning of his awakening" (VI, 211), an experience which, by virtue of the very place at which it occurs, is bound to be antihierarchical; and indeed the narrator admits rather unwillingly that it meant not so much an increasing sense of valid functional situation in the order of Castalia and the world, as an experience of selfhood, of uniqueness, and of the relativity of all outside things. Yet Knecht supposes that, while retaining deep respect for the Elder Brother, he has come to be able to shake off his spell; the recalcitrant hermit's Way is seen as "a way out, a renunciation of universality possible and permissible only for a few, . . . a sublime kind of flight, and Knecht had soon felt that this was not his way. But what was his way? Besides his great gift for music and for the Glass Bead Game he knew he had other powers too, a certain inner independence, a lofty self-will which by no means forbade him to serve or made it difficult, but which demanded of him that he serve only the highest master" (VI, 214). These words, which seek to dispose of the Elder Brother, initiate more strongly than before the theme of service, linking it with inward independence, and indi-

---

[78] For this very persuasive notion, and its consequences for the interpretation of the novel, see J. C. Middleton, "An Enigma Transfigured," *German Life and Letters*, n.s., X (1956–1957), 298–302.

cating the possibility of a loftier ideal than Castalia can provide.
They point again to the pivotal issue of leap forward or regression.
Much later, just before his breakout, Knecht's thoughts are more
nostalgic and even somber: "How this intrepid, whimsical hermit
had understood how to withdraw and keep himself free. . . . With
a sigh Knecht threw off this thought. He had gone—or rather had
been led—another way, and all that mattered was to go the way
shown him directly and faithfully, not to compare it with the ways
of others" (VI, 341). Knecht goes that Way his master did not wish
to go, possibly could not go. But perhaps the way up and the way
down are not so totally antithetical after all. When we recall who the
Elder Brother really is (or *almost* is), the irony suddenly becomes
bottomless. Did the author himself fully plumb it? And are we
meant to see, when Knecht plunges to his death, the vindication of
the Elder Brother's smile?

The matter of Pater Jakobus and Mariafels is somewhat less
elusive; it, indeed, provides a foreground, rather than an inconspicuous but ubiquitous background, to the action. It provides the smoke
screen of the book's historical perspective, which probably derives
in part from the initial notion of "great epochs." The fact that
Knecht is singled out for this mission by the then Magister Ludi,
Thomas von der Trave, clearly destines him for great things. In
theory he is to conduct a course at the monastery, for those monks
who are interested in the Glass Bead Game; in practice there is behind the feint a diplomatic purpose, of which even the emissary at
first guesses nothing. The long residence at Mariafels develops into
a successful attempt to win over Pater Jakobus, the influential Benedictine historian, to support for the establishment of relations between Castalia and the Holy See.

Jakob Burckhardt, to whom tribute is paid in the figure of the
Pater,[79] was referred to by Hesse as early as 1901, in connection
with his first Italian journey, in the same breath as Lorenzo Magnifico
and Arnold Böcklin.[80] (The influence of Burckhardt had in fact set in

[79] There is at least one direct borrowing from Burckhardt. Cf. Paul Böckmann, "Die Welt des Geistes in Hermann Hesses Dichten," *Sammlung*, II
(1948), 229. Hesse tells us that Burckhardt was the model for Jakobus in a
letter (VII, 702).
[80] "Italy" (1901; III, 761).

in Basel in 1899.) Hesse once declared that the three influences which had combined to inculcate in him a resistance to the forces of mass psychosis together with an instinctive moral judgment in political matters were the Christian tradition of his family, the Chinese sages, and "the influence of the only historian toward whom I ever felt trust, respect, and grateful discipleship, Jakob Burckhardt." [81] Hesse admired Burckhardt as a thinker; the illusionless realism of the *Weltgeschichtliche Betrachtungen* seemed to him to show history as it really is, not as a meaningful metaphysical pattern, but as a dark chaos of egoism, violence, and will-to-power. "World history" (and we remember how this critic of the Sedan myth disliked the word) is spoken of several times in *The Glass Bead Game*, but now with a ring of Burckhardt rather than of the chauvinistic Swabian schoolmasters. Burckhardt, Hesse notes, had himself been influenced by Schopenhauer: in this negative sense his view of historical reality and that of the Castalians meet.

But Pater Jakobus' function in the novel is that he forces Joseph Knecht, the representative of a province which practically knows no history, to confront historical reality. Castalia cultivates only the history of ideas and styles and not the history of man. Hesse, as Romantic individualist, was rather nervous of history; to think "historically" was for him to think inhumanely.[82] In *The Glass Bead Game*, under the sign of Hegel, this matter comes to the fore; if the movement of history which creates and destroys such provinces as Castalia can be said to be Hegelian.[83] We have, however, to recall Burckhardt's sarcasms about Hegel and "philosophy of history"; and of course Hegel and Lao-tzŭ contrast absolutely; in the work of art, indeed, Hegelianism and the thought of the Tao are little more than vague terms for motifs in which the unresolved dualism of the novel can be expressed. Mariafels is the antithesis of the bamboo grove, and exactly so, for it is the island of discipline in the sea of chaos; and yet in a sense Burckhardt's "world history" and the Tao are really the same, for in both "all is permitted." The monastery and the bamboo grove are perhaps both reconciled in the supreme syn-

---

[81] "Preface to the Edition 'War and Peace'" (1946; VII, 435).

[82] Cf. "The Way of Love" (VII, 132).

[83] Cf., e.g., T. Litt, "Die Geschichte und das Übergeschichtliche," *Sammlung*, V (1950), 6–19.

thesis of Knecht's death at Belpunt, the "beautiful bridge," though this event has many possible meanings.

Knecht's mission to Mariafels is an approach to Rome, and *The Glass Bead Game* in general shows Hesse's deep preoccupation with the Roman church. His sympathy toward this institution had grown with the years; the interest in hagiography and the early cult of St. Francis pointed the way, while the influence of Dr. Lang and above all of Hugo Ball accelerated the process of approximation in the decade after 1916.[84] Ball's *Byzantinisches Christentum* (1922) seemed to Hesse symptomatic of a genuine regeneration of the Christian tradition. In the later 1920's we find an expression of keen interest in "the secret life of the Christian Middle Ages," [85] especially in monasterial literature and art. A letter (March 3, 1935) returns to the interpretation of the poem "Besinnung": "You are correct to presume that this poem is founded on a change in me, in fact the beginnings of recalling and reflecting upon my origins, which are Christian." [86] Hesse proceeds to dispute the suggestion that a Protestant "church" really exists; there is but one church, and yet conversion would be weakness. Again we note the analogy with the attitude of Gide.[87] The Catholic church is "this greatest cultural edifice of the West," however much its political manifestations may repel. Furthermore, Catholics have something infinitely valuable, an altar to pray before and a confessional (and unlike Goldmund's, theirs is complete with priest) in which to confess; they are not obligated to subordinate this confession "simply to the irony of lonely self-criticism." [88] And the great dangers in self-absolution had been made clear to Hesse by his mentor, Dr. Lang, who had had a Benedictine education. Above all, the Roman church represents form, tradition, and history. But the Castalian narrator is rather shy of the direct question of Joseph Knecht's religious experiences (if any) at Maria-

---

[84] What impressed Hesse about his friend Ball, though he had little sympathy for his strict Catholicism, was this Dadaist's willingness to make the *sacrificium intellectus*. See *Letters* (VII, 569).

[85] "A Library of World Literature" (VII, 342).

[86] *Letters* (VII, 589).

[87] Gide wrote to Jammes, who had hoped he was about to be converted, that he recoiled from such a step as "dishonesty." See *Correspondance: Francis Jammes et André Gide* (Paris, 1948), p. 238.

[88] "My Faith" (VII, 374).

fels; he hints only at Knecht's conclusion that "piety, that is, believing service and fidelity unto the surrender of life" (VI, 258) is possible in every confession and upon all levels, while conversion for him would be "a not wholly worthy form of flight." Catholic church and pedagogical province are in a sense comparable institutions; the parallelism, constantly drawn, is an illuminating one; Leo, in *The Journey to the East*, himself appeared as a pope, so also the Magister Ludi is "a prince or high priest, almost a divinity" (VI, 115).

For Castalia, seen in the context of Hesse's work as a whole, may be regarded as a secularized church ("the ideal secular monastery"); the Game itself has its Scholastic aspect while the Vicus Lusorum is reminiscent of the Tübinger Stift. Thus when Joseph Knecht goes as ambassador to Mariafels he, so-to-say, steps out of the mirror, goes from art to life, to the real object from the mere image or replica. He goes, in the words of the *I Ching*, "his property with him," not therefore as the penitent, but as the reverent free spirit and committed artist that Hesse always remained. When he goes, he is already mature and has a long development behind him. His period of "free study" was his essential preparation; it began with his withdrawal from the public eye: "The famed pupil Knecht vanished and was to be found no more" (VI, 194). Like Narziss he disappears to undertake, in effect, his "great exercise"; for it is precisely during this period, away from the rituals and the formalized instruction of the Vicus Lusorum, that Knecht penetrates the surface of the Game and begins to gravitate toward its mystical center. An experience while still at Waldzell had pointed the way, the realization "that in the language or at any rate in the spirit of the Glass Bead Game . . . every symbol and every combination of symbols . . . led to the center, the mystery of the world and its innermost part, the primal wisdom" (VI, 196–197). Knecht makes use of his years of free study in a novel way, he walks alone, an "Outsider" (VI, 202), trying to evade the destiny of responsibility, leadership, and "representation" which he instinctively expects. He turns only to his real teachers, his transinstitutional teachers, the Music Master and the Elder Brother. Like Narziss he vanishes for a time from the hierarchy, to prepare for his "priesthood." And his very isolation, which he thinks is close to freedom, is therefore but a stage in a hierarchical pattern of duty, a link in a chain. When he begins to find his own pupils, it is clear that his time has come. Magister Thomas von der Trave summons him, answers with mild irony his desperate request for a little longer freedom, prescribes his entry into the Order, and commissions him to Mariafels. Here of course also Knecht finds pupils, monks, the doting boy Anton, and even Pater Jakobus.

In his friendship with Pater Jakobus is drawn the ironical balance between the Castalian and the Benedictine orders; but only later, in his days as Magister Ludi, does Knecht fully grasp "the function—as secret as it is powerful—of the Order, . . . the living soul of the Castalian state" (VI, 332–333). The Order gives Castalia its "piety," makes possible an equilibrium between the active and the contemplative life. Such a balance has also been achieved by Jakobus, whose manner—highly ironically in view of the structure of the novel—is almost Chinese, a mixture of superiority, mockery, wisdom, and ceremony. Symbolic, also, is the Pater's competent though unprofessional playing of old keyboard music, and Joseph listens entranced to Purcell outside the Benedictine's door; this gesture has importance, for similarly Emil Sinclair listened to Pistorius. Jakobus is skeptical about Castalia as a new-fangled institution which impermissibly apes the religious forms, is suspicious of its scholarly activities and of its cult, the Glass Bead Game. The long self-doubt of the man of letters finds disguised expression in the Pater's comment that the Game, sublime though it may be, remains but a game after all. The hostility of Jakobus is gradually modified by the impression Knecht makes on him; the representative Benedictine and the representative Castalian reach an accord; the man of God who hides the politician and the man of the mind who conceals the artist agree to teach one another. Teacher and pupil is seen to be a synonym for pupil and teacher. Both find common ground in admiration for Johann Albrecht Bengel, whose exegetical and encyclopedic activities seem to Knecht to presage the Glass Bead Game. While Knecht explains to Jakobus the structure and *raison d'être* of the pedagogical province, the Pater in return imparts the history of the Benedictines and beyond this "world history," now seen through the eyes of the supreme historian of Basel; between them the two play a formal game, a "competition in the exercise of patience" (VI, 239). Both are patricians, both come of an aristocratic tradition, and aristocracy is style, and style, of course, is game.

The tremendous event in which *The Glass Bead Game* culminates —the moment at which Joseph Knecht lays down his office of Magister Ludi and leaves Castalia to become a teacher in the world outside—is the point of divergence between the hierarchical *vita* and that of the individual. Knecht's recognition of the demands of history and of the dialectic forms only the pretext for his action. In his letter to the Educational Authority, the Magister Ludi refers to the justified Castalian suspicion of Hegel and of philosophy of history, but in his arguments there still remain traces of the Hegelian view. To Magister Alexander, however, in greater candor, he explains that his motive is to be found not in sense of history so much as in the will to serve only the highest gods. Meanwhile Hesse has striven to make the whole event credible through the carefully laid traces of Knecht's anti-Castalian individualism and his artistic personality. And yet all this—and even the symbolism of the *I Ching* —belongs only to the second level of the *vita* and scarcely discloses the even more hermetic third line. When Knecht returns to Waldzell from Mariafels, he has, to be sure, history in his soul; almost at once Thomas von der Trave dies and he is elected Magister Ludi; young —at nearly forty—for the office, he accepts it as fate, as sacrifice. Fighting for and compelling—as every new Magister must do—the admiration and subservience of the elite of the Glass Bead players, he goes on to carry his new function to success. Outwardly apparently incapsulated wholly in his function, a mere tool of the system, inwardly the depersonalization process has failed to penetrate far in him. Almost from the outset he is intimate with the idea of his unheard of future act. At the time of his composition of his first Ludus Sollemnis, the "Chinese House" game, he recalls the Elder Brother, and with this thought comes "recollection at the same time of freedom, leisure, student days and the colorful paradise of youthful dreams" (VI, 341). The Castalian narrator feels obliged to point out the polarity of Knecht's being: the golden ceremonial [89] of this first public game is more than just surface style but distinctly less

[89] Cf. VI, 357.

than the psychological totality: "The two basic tendencies or poles of this life, its yin and yang, were the tendency to conservation, to loyalty, to selfless service of the hierarchy, and on the other hand the tendency to "awakening," to pressing forward, to laying hold on reality and grasping it" (VI, 371).

The narrative approach to the "exemplary event" of Knecht's desertion leads between two friendships, that with Plinio and that with Fritz Tegularius. Tegularius is a brilliant intellect and supreme "player," but a badly integrated personality; as a foil to Knecht, he certainly brings out the Magister's poise and rounded selfhood. His passionate friendship for Knecht has many precedents in Hesse's works. Knecht's own notes upon his character sound much like a synopsis of Harry Haller's traits. The visit Tegularius makes to Mariafels accidentally all but undoes Knecht's work with the Benedictines. A "lone individualist and enemy of all normative standards" (VI, 438), he has, however, no point of contact with the Elder Brother, on whom he pays an unsuccessful call. He represents the decadent consequences of Castalian extremism and is, banefully enough, the probable Castalian type of the future. Plinio Designori, on the other hand, exemplifies another kind of decadence, that of the outside world; half a Castalian, he can therefore never be wholly a "worldly person," a "child-person" indeed (for the words used remind us strongly of *Siddhartha*): "I wanted to be nothing else but one of them, I wanted no other life but theirs, their passionate, childlike, cruel, uncontrolled life flickering between happiness and fear" (VI, 415).

The working out of the Designori motif is full of interest. At a moment when Joseph is approaching the end of his years of free study, Plinio returns to Castalia for a summer school, and the two meet; the impression Plinio makes is—as Knecht admits years later —wholly negative and disagreeable; this erstwhile elite schoolboy, already a promising politician, is entirely a dilettante in his pursuit of the Game. This ephemeral contact—which may be compared structurally with the encounter between Siddhartha and Govinda on the riverbank—is illuminated many years later in long discussions between Plinio and Joseph. Plinio now provides his friend with the material opportunity for flight over the Castalian wall; and at the same time he needs—and obtains from the Magister Ludi—therapy for his sick worldly soul. Plinio has tried and failed to synthesize in his life the pedagogical province and the political world, a synthesis which Knecht, from his quite different standpoint, has also in mind to assay. On his earlier return to Castalia, Plinio had been ashamed to discover how unlike he was to the representative man of the Order, Joseph-Narziss; but Plinio is no Goldmund, although—and this is very significant—he finds in himself and then fulfills a need to *confess* to his friend. And like Goldmund he is disappointed to discover how unmoved the Magister Ludi is by what seems to him the most important part of his confession—the details of his unhappy worldly existence. Knecht censures the penitent (as does Leo and as does Narziss) for something quite different. Indeed, change a few words and it might even seem to be Hermine talking to *her* penitent prodigal, Harry. Knecht tells him: "You have divided your own soul into Castalian and secular and you torment yourself excessively about things for which you bear no responsibility. Possibly, however, you take other things too lightly the responsibility for which does lie with you. I presume that for a long time now you haven't practiced any exercises of meditation. Isn't that so?" (VI, 414–415). Of course it is so. Plinio has to be taught the spiritual exercises again; he has to be led back toward form.

It is part of the ironic structure of *The Glass Bead Game* that Joseph Knecht, on the point of abandoning Castalia, defends it before Plinio as resolutely as ever before: the Castalian life is no mere flight into a world of play, though there might be individual Castalians with whom such a rebuke should properly lie—"this detracts not at all from the genuine serenity of the heavens and of the spirit" (VI, 418). The attainment of this serenity, as the Old Music Master attained it, as music above all incarnates it, is the highest of goals; a drop of it is frequently the loftiest distillation of the most tormented art. The Indian doctrine of the Four Ages bears witness to this; through all the characteristic misery of "world history" certain lines of form may be discerned; each age is trampled to pieces by the dancing Shiva and recreated by the smiling Vishnu out of his golden dreams.

The scene with Plinio which culminates in the vision of the starry heavens, and in Knecht's playing a movement from the Purcell sonata which Pater Jakobus especially loved, burns with sincerity and indeed with poetic force, wholly bursting the shell of the Castalian narrator's bureaucratic prose: "Like drops of golden light the notes fell upon the silence, so softly that the song of the old flowing fountain in the court could be heard in between" (VI, 421)—the music of a living Romantic past. The link here with the imagery of *The Steppenwolf* (and of "Old Music") is equally unmistakable: "Softly and severely, sparingly and sweetly the voices of the lovely music met and entwined, valiantly and serenely they danced their fervent roundelay through the nothingness of time and transience, for the short spell that they endured they made the room and the nighttime hour wide and vast as the world" (VI, 421).

To say that, generally speaking, the language of *The Glass Bead Game* lacks the poetic nuance might be regarded as an understatement. The "parodistically flavoured chronicle style" [90] of the narrator has often found little favor with critics of the novel,[91] but due allowance must always be made for the fact that this style is especially designed to appear both professorial and self-ironizing—though a consistent illusion is not maintained. The reflective posture is, in fact, itself directly ironized, a thing which has not occurred in any preceding novel except *The Journey to the East*; the author's relationship to his style or styles is quite other than that which subsists, for instance, in *Demian*. There, there is no conscious detachment from reflection; here (as already in *The Journey to the East*) such detachment is of the essence. Mann's term *"verkleidete Essayistik"* might be justifiably applied, at least up to a point, and a comparison with the method of the *Joseph* novels (rather than with *Dr. Faustus*) drawn. There is poise and sensitive contemplation in this finely involuted style; at least one great writer, protected by his own creative insight from the errors of academic criticism, praises the style of Hesse's old age highly; in his preface to the French translation of *The Journey to the East* (Paris, 1948) André Gide writes: "Chez Hesse, l'expression seule est tempérée, non point l'émotion ni la pensée; et ce qui tempère l'expression de celles-ci, c'est le senti-

---

[90] Kohlschmidt, *op. cit.*, p. 164.

[91] Though, for instance, Kohlschmidt singles out as the target of his particular animadversions not the narrative style so much as the conversations (as being commonplace) and also Knecht's poems. The poem "Steps" is called "little more than an arabesque around a platitude" (*ibid.*, p. 218).

ment exquis des convenances, de la réserve, de l'harmonie, et, par
rapport au cosmos, de l'interdépendance des choses; c'est aussi je ne
sais quelle latente ironie, dont bien peu d'Allemands me semblent
capables."

In *The Glass Bead Game* the parodistic technique is supported by
all the obvious methods: commentary on the problem of sources,
the pretense of authentic documentation, reflections about the difficulties of the biographer. *Some* of the thumping clichés, at least,
may justly be attributed to the Castalian narrator and his limited
vision. But the fiction of this narrator is certainly lost from time
to time, as when the standpoint switches suddenly to within the
Music Master's mind: "He sighed. That there was no ultimate order,
no elimination of recognized mistakes!" (VI, 153). A game ceases
to exist if its rules are willfully broken, and Hesse made his best
efforts to avoid inconsistencies in the structure of *The Glass Bead
Game*.[92] Transcending the framework itself are the author's own
games—for instance the name-play, Chattus for Hesse, Ludwig
Wassermaler for Louis Moilliet, Veraguth—now transformed into a
tribune of the people. Many of the allegorical devices are not at all
transparent—for instance the employment of the motifs from the
I Ching, and notably the whole curious episode of Bertram, the
deputy to Thomas von der Trave, in which episode the "shadow"
motif finds its ultimate restatement.

When Magister Thomas falls sick at the time of the annual Ludus
Sollemnis, the deputy Bertram is obliged by precedent to preside
over the grand public game. This unfortunate man, however, does
not enjoy the confidence of the elite of the Vicus Lusorum. His
position is weak, in any case, because of the tradition that no deputy,
or "shadow" (as he is called—VI, 298) may succeed his master.
Supported by the elite—only for the sake of the institution—with
but the most frigid formality, Bertram struggles to the end of the
unhappy ceremonial game, then takes leave of absence and falls to
his death in the mountains. In the serene context of Castalia this
event seems to the reader remarkably shocking, indeed all but

---

[92] As he tells us in a letter. Hesse also points out that the Castalian biographer
has at his disposal Castalia's oral and written traditions, its archives, "and
naturally also his own capacity for imagination and empathy" (*Letters;* VII,
702).

inexplicable. Many questions arise; for instance, what is a master's "shadow"?: "the borderline between master and deputy is like a symbol for the border line between office and person" (VI, 297). We recall the dual meaning of "Magister," a level in the hierarchy and a level on the Spiritual Way (for what is the hierarchy but a projection of the inner stairway into the forms of the external world?). Jung's doctrine of the "shadow" is also surely relevant.[93] The meaning, then, at least in part, is that all masters must have their "shadow" and that in fact the "shadow" can never come to be the master. But the Castalian narrator strives to defend Bertram—"He was much more victim than culprit" (VI, 299)—and this defense perhaps points elsewhere again. A strange rumor—specifically designated a "legend"—is spread about the dying Magister Thomas and his "shadow": namely, that the Magister permitted his deputy to take his place against his better judgment and then, in the face of catastrophe, himself accepted the responsibility for this and consciously paid with his life.

What can this curious (and in the context of the narrative wholly unlikely) story be meant to signify? That the condition of saintliness is very hard to maintain and, further, that in weakness to fulfill sacred functions with the organs of the lower self (the shadow, the unconscious Adam) is the gravest of sins? And Bertram's appallingly un-Castalian end—is this the self-immolation of the sinner who has seen the unforgivable nature of his sin (for the elite are described as being "inexorable"; VI, 305)? Or is the whole odd episode best understood as the tragedy of the writer who overreaches his talent, whose public image is out of consonance with his real gifts, and who loses the respect and recognition of his erstwhile peers?

The significant point is of course not that these questions can be answered (for they hardly can), but that they can be sensibly posed at all. *The Glass Bead Game* has, evidently, many recondities which have often been overlooked. The allegorical nuance is discernible in

[93] If the "shadow" is supposed to represent the personal unconscious, Jung finds that the collective unconscious may be personified by the "Wise Old Man." Cf. the treatment in *Mysterium Coniunctionis* (1954). There are, of course, several "wise old men" in Castalia. The "shadow" (Bertram) might conceivably be regarded as the inferior, personal self which no one in Castalia is prepared to confront honestly.

unexpected places and its presence can never be entirely discounted. Parody, contrapuntal persiflage, what Thomas Mann called *"sprach- liche Humorigkeiten"* [94] are of the essence of the Game. In this framework novel, with its elaborate montage technique, the tract element of *The Steppenwolf* is now paramount again: witness the endless citations, the long-winded letter which Magister Knecht ad- dresses to the Educational Authority and the response to it. The use of conversation as an interpretative device, pronounced in *Demian* and *Narziss and Goldmund*, finds its significant place in this work too. These conversations are essentially formal, an intellectualization of structural relationships; the contrast between Knecht and Plinio is "musical," their disputes are philosophically all but nominal, are reflections of the dialectic of their lives. Even in their last conversa- tion this is so, when Plinio recounts his side of an experience we have previously seen only through Knecht's eyes; he doubts whether two such contrapuntal voices as he and Joseph will ever really understand one another. The irony of the relationship between Joseph and Plinio is remarked on by Plinio himself, after the Magister's death: "He was a much greater rogue than his people suspected, full of play, full of wit, full of artfulness" (VI, 428); Plinio sees that Joseph cunningly enticed him back to the Castalian ideal at the very moment he was himself struggling desperately to surmount it. And the game which Knecht plays is similar to that game played by the author of the novel: "to make Castalia visible," to evoke for the reader an ideal dream, this is achieved precisely by demonstrating how the central figure in that dream, heroic and suffering, breaks out of it. But the dream itself is not thereby destroyed forever.

Neither Knecht nor Hesse reject Castalia; both seek a marriage of Castalia with the world. There is, however, more than one dialectical movement in this novel, since there are at least three parallel lines of development. It is certainly true that over few episodes within the corpus of modern German literature has there been so much contro- versy—some of it passionate and a good deal of it superficial and ill founded—as there has been over the ending of *The Glass Bead Game*. Whatever view may be taken of the significance of Knecht's departure from Castalia, and of the manner and meaning of his death,

[94] *Neue Rundschau*, LVIII (1947), 247.

it must inevitably influence decisively the interpretation of the novel as a whole and of its supposed "message." If the problem is approached—as Kohlschmidt approaches it [95]—as essentially one of logic, it remains bewildering. Some critics have regarded Knecht's death as a symptom of his failure. His act—when he dives into the mountain lake to vie in physical prowess with his pupil, Tito—has been frequently regarded as rash and foolish. It does perhaps seem that he promptly succumbs to that external world which it is his hope to transform, and moreover succumbs by pure mischance. As troublesome as the issues of logic and of ethical judgment has been the aesthetic flaw frequently constated in the novel's unexpected and somewhat precipitate end.

Hesse expounded his own view of it thus: "Knecht's death can naturally have many interpretations. For me the central one is that of sacrifice, which he valiantly and joyfully fulfills. The way I intend it he has not thereby broken off his task of educating the youth, he has fulfilled it." [96] This practically gives carte blanche to the interpreters, which is just as well, since Hesse's own view is clearly very partial and even scarcely consonant with all the facts: on the evidence of the text, Knecht's sacrifice, if it is a sacrifice at all, cannot feasibly be regarded as a conscious one. It is usually supposed that Hesse meant the reader to understand this "sacrifice" as having a traumatic effect upon Tito, turning this unruly youth inward, accomplishing in an instant what more orthodox educational methods would have needed years to achieve.

Not many critics, however, have given the last chapter of the novel that close reading which such an ambiguous, pivotal section requires. A necessary prolegomenon to a study of this issue is a comparison between Hesse's work and Goethe's *Wilhelm Meister*. The name "Knecht" probably had its origins here, and Hesse openly borrows the term "Pedagogical Province" from Goethe; nonetheless it has been shown conclusively that the differences between *The Glass*

---

[95] Castalia must be either "conditionally right," "unconditionally wrong," or else "unconditionally right" (*op. cit.*, p. 165). The application of such terms is deplorable here. Hesse observes: "The book is in no sense a treatise, still less a philosophy, it is a story and a confession, and structure, cadence, and coloring are just as significant as the ideas" (*Letters;* VII, 641).

[96] *Letters* (VII, 640).

Bead Game and *Wilhelm Meister* are more striking than the similarities. In contrast to Goethe with his pedagogical province, Hesse requires of his reader "a double vision which would recognize both his positive and his critical message." [97] In Castalia there is little interest in *"das Nützliche"*; the social and utilitarian ethic of the *Wanderjahre*, at least, is practically the antithesis of the Castalian outlook. It is a shrewd observation that the Castalian hierarchy brings individuals together not primarily because they seek to form a true community with an ideal of social service but because each wishes to serve Spirit and, moreover, each for himself.[98] The conclusion that the novel has more in common with the ethical humanism of the *Lehrjahre* than with the humanitarian "socialism" of the *Wanderjahre* [99] is superficially valid; but there is a sense in which *The Glass Bead Game* forms common cause with Novalis and the Romantic hostility to the *Lehrjahre* itself; for in the ultimate analysis *The Glass Bead Game* cannot be regarded as a *de facto* rejection of the aesthetic existence. For even if the Apolline, or Alexandrine, culture of Castalia is finally spurned and transcended, perhaps it is only Dionysos who triumphs.

The conversations between the Master of the Order, Alexander, and Joseph Knecht in Hirsland, where the latter travels one September morning to lay down his office, are the nodal point at which the personal *vita* finally diverges from the line prescribed by the hierarchy. The dialectic of their conversation discloses the dialectic of history. In his celebrated letter to the Educational Authority, the Magister Ludi has already made known his conviction that time is running out for Castalia, that a new era of troubles in the outside world will swallow up the province and others like it, save for decisive action on the part of Castalians. He requests them therefore to release him from his office and allow him to supervise an ordinary school in the outside world, as the beginning of a fresh expansion of Castalia's practical educational mission. It is a request which he knows will and must be refused, and—significantly enough—he has no real wish that it be acceded to.

His reading of the historical situation, deriving from his studies

[97] I. Halpert, "Hermann Hesse and Goethe" (diss., Columbia University, 1957), p. 119.
[98] *Ibid*, p. 141.   [99] *Ibid*, p. 144.

with Pater Jakobus, differs entirely from that of Meister Alexander. Alexander's outlook is not only much more anti-Hegelian than is Knecht's, it is conspicuously Schopenhauerian, just as the Glass Bead Game itself has been regarded as the blending, after the theories of Schopenhauer, of the three spheres of liberation of the mind: art, religion, and philosophy.[100] On balance, however, it might well seem that Alexander has the better of the argument with the deserter, who is constantly reduced to the appeal to subjective principles. There is, furthermore, the interesting consideration that Knecht's predictions are actually proved false, by the very fact that the Castalian narrator can write as he does generations after the death of the Magister Ludi Josephus III! In the day of the narrator, the Order is still "unshaken" (VI, 106); there have, it is true, been certain adaptations, but not at all those which Joseph Knecht recommended: "a tendency toward the removal of many specializations in the business of scholarship which were felt to be overcultivated, and that in favor of an intensification of the practice of meditation" (VI, 374).

To be sure, the Castalian narrator praises Knecht for having seen so early the necessity for therapy and innovation, but if Knecht's deed is to be construed as a *coup de main* in favor of ethical action, a sanctification by sacrificial example of the *vita activa*, then it can have little enough to do with the actual Castalian development, in which it is precisely the *vita contemplativa*, upon which the emphasis has been laid. The outside world in fact has *not* engulfed Castalia, and it is not Knecht's performance which has saved the day. The Educational Authority's reply to Knecht's letter—itself a banal document about which the only sensational thing is that a Magister Ludi could write it!—has subsequently been justified by history; the Knechtian view of things has indeed turned out to be "exaggeratedly pessimistic" (VI, 475–476).

These considerations serve principally to show the relative uselessness of the dialectical process as a philosophical key to the novel; to understand Knecht's breakout as essentially a flight from the unhistorical and in a sense a return to Hegel is not even to take the surface meaning of the book at its face value. Alexander does not believe in the historical pretext, and Knecht himself scarcely does.

[100] Litt, *op. cit.,* p. 15.

We may compare Hesse's rebuke to Faesi for overestimating the importance of the quasihistorical context.[101] Hesse did not intend to pass a judgment, historical or ethical, upon Castalia; he was concerned with quite different issues.

The "historical" synthesis, the attempted marriage of Castalia and the external world, is an open symbol for a psychological process. Knecht, Hesse wrote, is to be conceived of not so much as "a brother of Christ" but rather as "a brother of the saints," and in the same place he defines the saints: "They are distinguished from "ordinary" men by their integration into and submission to the superpersonal not on the basis of lack of personality and individuality but through a plus in this respect." [102] In these terms, also, Hesse had described geniuses. And it is just this "plus" which carries Knecht right out of Castalia toward the fulfillment of his personal *vita* as he and Hesse both conceive of it. We recall Harry Haller, and even Peter Camenzind: "These are they who truly love, the saints . . . in them the whole problem of the individualist, the overgifted, the difficult, and often desperate personality is fulfilled and justified. For genius is capacity for love, is longing for surrender, and it achieves total fulfillment only in the full and final sacrifice." [103] The artist, in and through his love of mankind, becomes the saint.

Behind the smoke screen of history, the conclusion of *The Glass Bead Game* must therefore be regarded, on one of its levels, as the allegory for an attempted solution to the problem of the outsider, as this is adumbrated in Hesse's works. Through *Besinnung*, through service, the extraordinary personality breaks away from the limitations of the hierarchical *vita* and finds fulfillment and integration in a positive ideal. So spoke, also, *The Journey to the East*, although H. H. found fulfillment only by return to the hierarchy where, in his case, the ideal of service was still enshrined. And the self-realization of the individualist in service is a principal thought of the three completed autobiographies which are appended to the main body of the book. Even the Castalian narrator regards these autobiographies, which of course *he* did not write, as "perhaps the most valuable part of our book" (VI, 192). His opinion is by no means

[101] *Letters* (VII, 636).
[102] "Notes at Easter" (VII, 906).
[103] *Letters* (VII, 719).

absurd. Unconvincing as these stories are in their forced connection with Knecht, they are certainly vividly told, their rich, colorful texture, their conventional but lively exoticism contrast sharply with the main section of the novel. In some degree they restate the central theme of service. Knecht's action in abandoning Castalia in order to become private tutor to Plinio Designori's son Tito is not reflected directly in any of the three tales (though the motif *is* strongly suggested in the—until recently unpublished—"Fourth Autobiography"). In all three, however, there is present the idea of *imitatio;* all are situated in an essentially timeless, unhistorical world and all deal with some species of sainthood. The autobiographies are not *Märchen,* but legends.

It is in the first, "The Rainmaker," that the theme of service is sounded most clearly; at the heart of this legend is the teacher-pupil relationship; the rainmaker gives his presumptive successor a "wordless" education, epitomized one moment when the moon rises and the master speaks of his death and his union with the moon.[104] Turu dies and Knecht becomes rainmaker to this primitive gynocracy; then the latter himself finds a pupil, which means "the return and reversal of the great experience of his youth" (VI, 584). The activities of master and pupil are here bound to and wholly encompassed by the natural world; they play not with the mind but with the things of nature. And yet for them also their real aim, "the game for which he and his master lay in wait was . . . the Spirit, the whole, the meaning, the interconnection" (VI, 574), a goal moreover which can only be attained through self-development, the cultivation of "what was already within him" (VI, 574). Colorful and fabulous though "The Rainmaker" is, it bears little resemblance to such works as *Pictor's Transformations* and "Iris." The reflective element is pronounced; the ironical legerdemain of certain passages resembles that of the parent novel. Knecht's rituals are to be compared with those of the Glass Bead Game and thus with the methods of the artist; artist and rainmaker require a similar intuitive touch. The theme and culmination of "The Rainmaker" is, however, the self-immolation of the individual for the good of

[104] The analogy between this scene and that at Belpunt has been pointed out by H. D. Cohn, "The Symbolic End of Hermann Hesse's *Glasperlenspiel*," *Modern Language Quarterly,* XI (1950), 354.

the community, the total absorption and sublimation of the personal in the function of the servant.

"The Father Confessor" also stresses service and sacrifice; it is a hagiographical legend in which Josephus Famulus and Dion Pugil, two hermit confessors with wholly disparate styles, come eventually to confess to one another and become linked in the reversible interaction of teacher and pupil. They assume the roles of father and son; Dion leaves behind him "a tree and . . . you, you are my son" (VI, 638). Josephus, by his technique (like Vasudeva's) of utterly passive listening, gives form to confessions: "to listen patiently and lovingly, and thereby to give complete form to confessions which were not yet fully formed" (VI, 608), while Dion, for his part, knows what Narziss, Joseph Knecht, and Leo know, that worldly sin—the offenses of those outside the wall—is not really sin at all, but a kind of innocence, "innocent just in the way children are" (VI, 635).

The reverberation of themes from the parent novel continues also in what might be held to be the most important of the autobiographies, "Indian Autobiography." The core of this story is the dream of a life which Dasa (Sanskrit—"Knecht") dreams at the edge of a spring, peering into a pool. Having requested the yogi to show him Maya, Dasa now dreams a life of power, violence, and suffering. Suicide seems attractive but a delusion, better than this is to do whatever service may be laid upon one—for instance to bear the bowl of water from the spring to his new master's hands.

Only one of the autobiographies, "The Rainmaker," specifically introduces society, a restraint which confirms the view that service to society was never the primary ethos of The Glass Bead Game. "The Father Confessor," indeed, separates the sphere of teacher and pupil sharply off from the world of the "child-people" and shows a preoccupation with sin which is uncharacteristic of the parent novel. "Indian Autobiography" not only makes this separation, but presents the whole of existence as illusion, Maya, agonized blind will, and ends with a gesture of total withdrawal: "He never left the forest again" (VI, 685). It is the Schopenhauerian undertone of the main novel which is here suddenly orchestrated in full. Therefore to use the autobiographies as a key for the elucidation of The Glass Bead Game is fraught with difficulties. It cannot be successfully maintained that these "interpretations," taken as a group, clarify the whole book; they do no more than summarize the enigmas. Only the unfinished "Fourth Autobiography" is startlingly illuminating in this respect, and this precisely because it was not used in the published book. The three autobiographies which were used, composed as they were in the early stages of the entire undertaking, reflect—as they might well be expected to do—the ironies, uncertainties, and idiosyncrasies with which *The Glass Bead Game* is instinct. In the last analysis the theme which the three completed and utilized stories do have in common is not so much service as the transmission of the spiritual seed—the essential function of Knecht's contact with Tito.

We cannot, however, be satisfied with this interpretation of the novel; beneath this entire action, another current flows. As Hesse has admitted, the intentions of an author, while interesting, are certainly no ultimate criterion in such matters. To uncover the concealed stratum, it is necessary to look closely at the last section of the "Castalian autobiography"—the novel proper. This section is called "The Legend." Earlier in the book there is a passage which suggests that Joseph Knecht is perhaps more inclined than is his biographer to use poetic diction; he recounts: "So we went out, and it must have been a particularly beautiful day in the world or in my feelings. . . . The land was damp but free of snow, and there were already bright green hues along the streams, in the bare bushes buds and the first emergent catkins gave a breath of color, and the air was full of odors, an odor full of life and full of contradiction, there was an aroma of damp earth, decaying leaves, and young plant shoots, every minute you expected to smell the first violet, though as yet there were none" (VI, 142). This passage is, indeed, still reflective enough; it goes on to give an account of a synaesthetic memory and to discourage the use of such highly personal experience in the Game. The memory in question here is first of all one of odor, the odor of the sap of the elder branch. In *Beneath the Wheel* the scent of the cider press brought back to memory the whole past course of the year. But *Beneath the Wheel* is a book in which the senses and nature have quite a big part to play. It has been noted, on the other hand, that the descriptions of nature in *The Glass Bead Game* are rare. On Knecht's journey to Monteport there is a cursory sketch of the landscape of the Oberland; on his way to the bamboo grove—pointedly enough—there is an evocation of the countryside of Tessin. Then, in the last pages of the novel, the Magister Ludi abandons his official car and leaves Castalia on foot; it is a long time since he has enjoyed the delights of walking, apparently not since his second— and final—journey back from Mariafels (which was not in fact described):

At other moments if he thought back to those times and particularly to his student years and the bamboo grove it had always been as though he were gazing out of a prosaic, cool chamber into spacious regions full of cheerful sunshine, into the irrecoverable, what had become a paradise of memory. . . . Now, however, in this serene light September afternoon with the vivid colors close around and the softly hazed, dream-fragile shades of the distance, verging from blue toward violet, with this agreeable hiking and idle contemplating, that journey on foot of so long ago did not gaze into a resigned present like something afar off and paradisiacal, but today's trip was fraternally similar to that one, today's Joseph Knecht to the one of long ago, everything was once more new, mysterious, full of promise, all that had been could come again and much that was fresh besides. It was a long time since the day and the world had looked at him thus, so unburdened, beautiful, and innocent. The bliss of freedom and independence flooded through him like a strong drink; how long it was since he had experienced this feeling, this lovely and delicious illusion! [VI, 521].

This rather reminds us of Siddhartha outside the grove of Jetavana, but in fact a still more striking analogy may be found:

The big limes on the church hill shone dully in the hot sunlight of the late afternoon, on the market place both large fountains splashed and sparkled, the close blue-black pine hills gazed in over the line of the roofs. The boy felt as though he hadn't seen all this for a long time, and it all seemed unusually lovely and enticing [I, 380].

This passage is from *Beneath the Wheel*. Joseph Knecht and Hans Giebenrath, indeed, sense the same seductive force in nature, which brings them through similar linguistic gestures to recall the forgotten and so distant past: "how long it was . . ." For both it is the same nostalgia: "how long it was since he had seen all this" (*Beneath the Wheel*, I, 403). With the provincial examination behind him, Hans Giebenrath escapes to his fishing, whistling a melody: "The others were sitting in school and had a geography lesson, only he was free and released" (I, 406). Joseph Knecht, who is shortly to find his way to water too, "was completely open to the sense of relaxation and freedom which filled him as a peasant after his labors is filled by a sense of the end of the working day, he knew he was secure and had no obligations. . . . He had no duty to work, no duty to think" (VI, 522). And Hans Giebenrath, leaving the Rector's house just before the examination may still have a headache (like Goldmund, who sought relief from this by going "into the village"), "but today he did not have to learn anything more" (I, 380). Joseph Knecht does not whistle a melody, but he hums a march from his schooldays at Waldzell and then, in this fruitful, colorful landscape, this "musical Socrates" takes out his flute, sits and plays it under a cherry tree: "He put his hand in his breast pocket and took out something which Master Alexander would not have expected him to have, a small wooden flute which he regarded with a certain tenderness. He had not possessed this naïve and childish-looking instrument for very long (VI, 522). . . . With pleasure, he felt the smooth round wood between his fingers and thought of the fact that with the exception of the suit on his back this little flute was the only piece of property he had permitted himself to take with him from Waldzell" (VI, 524). The analogies between these passages from *The Glass Bead Game* and those from the early chapters of *Beneath the Wheel* seem rather persuasive. Furthermore, Knecht now stands, as did Siddhartha when the landscape lit up for him, on the brink of his plunge into the outside, that is, the erotic world; this is the manner, as Hesse has declared, in which poets and "seers" see, and those who have been touched by Eros (cf. Chapter 4, page 139). The flute, moreover, is a well-established erotic symbol, and it cannot be overlooked that this passage is rich in sexual undertones. There is, to sum up, a convincing analogy between the incipient puberty of Hans Giebenrath and the "recurrent puberty" of Joseph Knecht.

It is remarkable that critics have not concerned themselves seriously also with the evident repetition in the context of the "Castalian autobiography" of the "exemplary event" which Hermann Heilner initiated—perhaps this is because the similarity has been felt to be both obvious and unimportant. However, in the light of the recurrence of the motif through so many of Hesse's works such a disregard is clearly impermissible. To establish this pattern, as fundamental to the conclusion of *The Glass Bead Game*, is in itself, however, only the first step. For a subtler insight into "The Legend" we must refer to the fragmentary "Fourth Autobiography," a study of a reincarnation of Joseph Knecht in the world of early eighteenth-century Württemberg which never found its way into the finished book. Two versions of this fragment exist. It was not completed, as Hesse tells us, because "the all too precisely known and all too richly documented world of this century resisted incorporation into the more legendary sphere of the other lives of Knecht." [105] The story of the "Fourth Autobiography" concerns the education of a youth, Joseph, and his subsequent choice and pursuit of a career. In its narration of crucial episodes from his childhood and his student years it moves characteristically upon a double plane of pedagogical form and subjective experience, it expounds upon the pivotal importance of a moment of revelation or "call" at the end of childhood and it plays in counterpoint the motifs of pious duty and artistic vocation. Joseph's father is a "simple and childlike character," [106] a well-maker; his mother, in a reversal of the usual situation in Hesse's novels, is the one who is devout, bigoted, and sectarian-minded, and it is she who dominates the household. A rudimentary artist, father Knecht plays the flute—"a slim little wooden flute without a stop." [107] He plays it alone in the woods to his children Joseph and Benigna, and for preference not the chorales which they sing at home with mother, but folksongs; his marriage to his strong-minded and pious spouse "spiritualizes" (*vergeistigt*) him in some degree, but flute playing and folksong singing are some of the ways (drunkenness is another) in which he finds a "safetyvalve" for his repressed and partially truncated nature. As for Joseph, he is the boy who—ironically enough under the influence of his mother—actually completes his theological education and enters the church (as Hesse's notes tell us), only to abandon it later for his own real

[105] Letter to Pannwitz, *op. cit.*, p. 436.
[106] *Prosa aus dem Nachlass*, p. 468.
[107] *Ibid.*, p. 448.

love, music. Like Hans Giebenrath, he recalls his childhood as paradise,[108] expecially those last moments before he is taken to his first teacher, Preceptor Roos.

In his religious education he encounters two forms of piety, the official and the private, the ecclesiastical and the personal, "the call from the pulpit and prayer in one's small chamber."[109] His teacher Bengel instructs him in this regard that pulpit and chamber, outer and inner, hierarchical and individual worlds are complementary and must never be confounded, and when the boy happens to see that pillar of the hierarchy, Spezial Bilfinger, at his troubled private prayers, his eyes are suddenly opened to the presence behind form of substance, behind the representational of the personal, behind *Ecclesia* of *Deus*. Joseph has three dreams of a career: first, to be what his father is, a wellmaker, second, to enter the church and emulate the Spezial, and third and hopelessly, to find his home in music; the first of these, we are told, was the "most innocent" dream, and it scarcely seems farfetched to recall here once again the structure of the spiritual life in "A Bit of Theology." If the first stage corresponds to Knecht's naïve wish to become a wellmaker, then the inevitability of ultimate despair in the second stage, the breaking of the will, is seen to be related to the frustrations of the ecclesiastical career with its personal and representational demands, and the transition—through grace—to the third stage, the Third Kingdom, must then correspond to the escape into art, into music, which Joseph eventually achieves. Joseph is fearful of entering the church, and when he tells his friend and teacher Oetinger of his hesitations, he receives a reply: "You know that you have the possibility of being given leave of absence by our Authority, if you accept a place somewhere as a private tutor."[110] This reply is quite fascinating, in view of the "real" Joseph Knecht's eventual application for leave of absence to become private tutor to Plinio's son, Tito.

It is overwhelmingly clear that in composing "The Legend," the last section of the "Castalian autobiography," Hesse fell back in various respects upon the "Fourth Autobiography," on which he had worked intensively in 1934. Not only the reference to leave

---

[108] *Ibid.,* p. 470.   [109] *Ibid.,* p. 500.   [110] *Ibid.,* p. 531.

of absence and not only the motif of the flute show this. Magister
Knecht has practiced on his wooden instrument "a number of those
chorales and lieder" which were to be found in "a book of old
melodies which Ferromonte had edited for beginners" (VI, 523);
now he recalls one—an old hymn of resurrection, "well suited to
the hour" (VI, 523). Similarly, in the "Fourth Autobiography" a
number of such lieder are quoted, and in the absence of confirmation on the point we may suppose that this one also is to be found in
the *Geistliche Seelen-Harpffe oder Württembergisches Gesang-
büchlein*, a hymnbook dated 1700, which we know Hesse possessed.
In the first version of the autobiography there also occurs a description of Joseph's taking leave of Tübingen (with its ironically
hidden memory of Hesse's own youth), which is rather like the
account of the Magister Ludi's departure from Castalia:

A goal had been attained which had seemed difficult of attainment. . . .
But there was no joy in it. Only with the breaking through of the sun
and the beginning song of the birds did his youth and love of life wake
up in him, and when he reached the deeper part of the wood he began to
sing. . . . He sang chorales and arias, and then folksongs, and as he
thought of his father and the flute he had once given him he first became
conscious of how much he was looking forward to seeing his father.[111]

Since the "Fourth Autobiography" inverts the usual relationship of
father and mother in Hesse's writings, it is an easy matter to decode
this passage. The nature of the "Fourth Autobiography" and the
presence of its material beneath the surface of much of "The
Legend" implies a good deal. It confirms the conclusion tentatively
reached through the study of the novel's genesis, namely, that
Knecht's defection was indeed already in Hesse's mind in 1934, for
the autobiography, had it been finished, was to have dealt with
Joseph's abandonment of the church for music. It suggests strongly
that this defection (however much it may be argued—as Joseph
himself argues before Master Alexander—that it is an act of devotion to a higher duty) had originally to do with the issue of the
self-realization of the artist *not* by the canalization of his drives
into ethical action and service, but by his eventual discovery of and
participation in a fully satisfactory form of *aesthetic* activity (for

[111] *Ibid.,* p. 534.

the Württemberg Joseph, work as a simple church organist, studying and playing the new music, that of Bach).

In fact, the "Fourth Autobiography" sheds a still stronger light than this: it is constructed upon Hesse's understanding of the inherent polarity in the Pietistic tradition, in which he was widely read. The Tübingen Pietists, with Zinzendorf and his Moravians in the background, represent the pith of this experience, the passion of the religious enthusiast. The theologian Bengel, on the other hand, stands for the purity of the written word, for textual (Castalian) rigor, essentially for verbalism and orthodoxy, that representational self-discipline which is the shell of the Pietistic life.

This issue is then reflected in the treatment of music: the "Fourth Autobiography" finds in the contrast of chorale and folksong something of the antithesis of pious and impious—yet both are after all music, and in their love of music Joseph's father and mother are for once united; music is the "guardian angel of the home." [112] It would appear then that Hesse saw in the old polyphonic music of the sixteenth century and then in the later work of Bach and his contemporaries the suggestion of a possibility, to put it no higher, of harmony, of the eventual reconciliation of pious discipline with artistic freedom, of the shell with the pith, of the hieratic and the representational with the secret ardor of the heart.

At the core of *The Glass Bead Game*, the "Fourth Autobiography" suggests, lies the conflict between the ecclesiastical and the artistic, between two poles which are themselves internally bipolar, between discipline and freedom, form and inspiration, surface and center; and the true source of Magister Joseph's flight lies in this direction, the pursuit of a reconciliation in life like that to be found only in Goldmund's "realized" work of art (but *not* in his life), and in the music of J. S. Bach. This is the hermetic goal of the third line of the Knechtian *vita*.

With this material before us, certain elements in the multivalent "Legend"—and even perhaps the bewildering death itself—are somewhat less perplexing. In returning his insignia of office to Alexander, Joseph Knecht disposes of his allegiance to Castalia

[112] *Ibid.*, p. 482.

(just as the young Hesse had once freed himself from the alien disciplines of Pietistic and institutionalized Christianity). And Knecht "confesses" to Alexander, his superior, his "father," [113] that traditional confession which ironically he, the forthcoming Prodigal, this time offers *before* a flight from which (as once before—for Friedrich Klein) there will be no return. Sad but patient, Alexander speaks: he asks Knecht to explain; he will listen "whether it be confession, justification, or renunciation." And Knecht replies: "The one who is running amuck expresses his thanks and his pleasure. I have no denunciation to make. What I would like to say has for me the sense of a justification, for you it may have that of a confession" (VI, 504). "The one who is running amuck"—the Magister Ludi even now surveys his own act with a certain ironic detachment. And confession has now ceased to be confession, except in the eyes of the confessor; for the Prodigal himself it has at long last become unrepentant self-justification, unmollified allegiance to "self-will" (VI, 497). Thus Siddhartha abandoned the Samanas, then Buddha, turned his back forever upon his father and went his way. Later, however, even Siddhartha came to confession, to Vasudeva, Sri Krishna, God. But Alexander is not God, unluckily; indeed: "If the earth were an elite school, and if the Order were the community of all men and the president of the Order God, how complete then would be those principles and the entire rule!" (VI, 488). Knecht's absolution, if he finds one, is not in Castalia, but in the blaze of the rising sun god at Belpunt. Now as he bursts out of Castalia, the depersonalized, skeletal *vita* of the institutionalized saint yields sudden place to the legendary *vita* of the highly personalized individual, the artist, *l'enfant prodigue*.

Knecht's last talk with Tegularius stands at the opening of "The Legend." In the peace of the magisterial garden, the subconscious stirs, and a moment of memory comes to the Magister Ludi. He recalls a line of a poem written in his youth, which he had then entitled "Transzendieren." [114] Tegularius remembers it well, but dislikes it—it is too moralizing and didactic; but he finds that if

[113] Alexander functioned as Knecht's private guru during the first hard months of his magisterial office.
[114] In the appendix entitled "Steps" (VI, 555–556).

these elements are stripped away the poem reveals itelf in essence as "a meditation on the nature of music, or if you like a eulogy of music, its permanent presence, its serenity and resolve, its nobility and restless resolve and readiness to hasten on, to leave behind the space or fragment of space it has just entered" (VI, 484). Knecht argues that the source of the poem did indeed lie in the experience of music, as a model for the endless transitions of life, but that the work deals in fact with the moral aspect of that experience, communicating an "admonition . . . to myself" (VI, 485), a moment of awakening with an ethical imperative. But Knecht has two judges, Alexander *and* Tegularius. And Tegularius formulates a damning verdict most succinctly: "In short, in this poem a vision, something unique, beautiful, and splendid is falsified and exploited for pedagogical ends" (VI, 484). This would do rather well as a critical judgment upon the novel itself, and there is a real sense in which it may be so regarded.[115] More than any earlier novel of Hesse's, *The Glass Bead Game* is impaled upon the duality of didacticism and poetry. And in that he speaks for poetry and against teaching, Tegularius is here the spokesman of the hidden third line. Knecht's will to transcend Castalia is the will to convert the energy of the artistic personality into the service of men and in this way to realize the integrated self, while Tegularius doubts that such a thing is possible or even desirable. On the other hand, the experience of "awakening" is deplored by Alexander for its extreme self-centeredness; Knecht's explanations, he says, are all resonant with "an excess of concern for your own person" (VI, 510). One has no right, in Alexander's view, to change one's sworn master upon finding another who seems better—a point Knecht fails to answer. To Alexander, the goal for which Knecht aims seems wholly capricious and personal; to Knecht, who sees in it the canalization of his artistic drives into ethics, into practical sainthood, it is a new and richer subordination of the personal, it is the true vocation of a Magister Ludi, the very meaning of his Latin

---

[115] The issue is conspicuously present already in the "Fourth Autobiography": Joseph's mother holds the view "that music was fine . . . but ultimately it was not so much a question of singing as of what one sang" (*Prosa aus dem Nachlass*, p. 487). This displays the moralist's suspicion of the aesthetic life.

name ("schoolmaster"). The culminating episode of the novel is the transfiguration of teacher and teaching; it deals with this "perfected" schoolmaster's encounter with his pupil, Tito.

On the day after his breakout, Joseph follows his new pupil to Belpunt, to a chalet in the High Alps, where he is to make his first real effort to win the boy's confidence. The initial conversations at Belpunt give the teacher an opportunity to suggest that their pedagogical relationship will flourish best as a two-sided one, with each learning from the other. In these unaccustomed heights Knecht feels a curious weariness, dizziness, and unease. The next morning he watches Tito, carried away by the glory of the rising sun, perform an ecstatic pagan dance in its rays. Then Tito leaps into the mountain lake and races the sun to the far cliff: Joseph Knecht, trying to emulate his pupil (for *imitatio* is reversible on all its levels) overestimates his strength and dies of heart failure in the freezing water. A precipitate end, no doubt, but by no means an accidental one, as the Castalian narrator himself makes clear early on (cf. VI, 119). And yet a most ambiguous end. Hesse, it has been noted, claimed to regard Knecht's act as a sacrifice which, in its effect upon Tito, has its reward. The ingenious application of the hexagrams of the *I Ching* to the scene at Belpunt, which has been worked out,[116] seems to show a gradual identification of Knecht himself with the rising sun. Knecht's leap into the water, the sun upon the lake, is sacrifice, integration of opposites, "marriage of heaven and earth," and Tito is a "new man" born alchemically out of that process in which the "old man" is consumed. In picking up (and putting on?) his drowned master's bathing robe Tito accepts the discipleship. This interpretation, if valid, does indeed show how "the pattern of Knecht's destiny is not broken but fulfilled by his death," [117] and that the novel has a logical, coherent end in Knecht's simultaneous self-realization and self-propagation, the culmination of the second line of the *vita*. But another much more negative interpretation of the same symbols, albeit without allusion to the *I Ching*, finds that Knecht is identified not with the sun but with the ominous elements of the stark environment, that his initial un-

[116] Middleton, "An Enigma Transfigured," *op. cit.*
[117] *Ibid.*, p. 301.

ease is a symptom of his half-realization that he has now come into strange territory, that he is out of his depth before the heathen dance of Tito (the sun), and that "it is a strong possibility that a purposeful death is the most Knecht can hope for." [118] This latter critic finds Knecht's death deliberately highly ambiguous, ensconced in multivalent imagery.

And the end of *The Glass Bead Game* is indeed multivalent and phenomenally ambiguous. Self-realization is Janus-faced. Beneath the consciously and cunningly organized action in which the *vita* of the teacher, the canonized artist, apparently finds its fulfillment, there lies concealed yet another movement with a totally different implication. One commentator, Walter Kramer, has noted that Knecht's leap into the lake is a reawakening of his repressed vital urges.[119] This observation lacks substantiation from the text, but nonetheless it is a penetrating one. Indeed, concealed in the last chapters is a bland admission not only that the historicizing arguments are pretext, but that the motivation of the whole episode of the breakout from Castalia is the liberation of a repressed segment of the self. At this stage it is still the narrator who is speaking, not the "unknown" author(s) of the "Legend": "More and more during the period of this slow process of detachment and leave-taking did it become clear to him that the real reason for his becoming a stranger and wishing to go was probably not his knowledge of the dangers threatening Castalia and his concern for its future, but that it was simply an empty and unoccupied segment of himself, his heart and his soul which now demanded its rights and desired to fulfill itself" (VI, 448). Better one could not describe that force which propelled Heilner, Veraguth, Klein, and Goldmund over the wall. The "exemplary event" in *Beneath the Wheel* had seemed to be essentially a flight, a crying need for freedom. The same final insight into the errors of life within the wall had even been burlesqued in *Spa Visitor:* "I, who am a sinner, have once again made the mistake of trying the way of righteousness" (IV, 104).

---

[118] K. Negus, "On the Death of Josef Knecht in Hermann Hesse's *Glasperlenspiel*," *Monatshefte für deutschen Unterricht*, LIII (1961), 186.

[119] "Hermann Hesse's *Glasperlenspiel* und seine Stellung in der geistigen Situation unserer Zeit" (Schriftenreihe der nordwestdeutschen Universitätengesellschaft [Wilhelmshaven, 1949], pt. 2, p. 11).

The Way of the baths at Baden was the Castalian Way, the Way of righteousness.

Knecht's vain hope is that he may persuade Alexander that he is not in search of freedom, but of "new, unknown, and strange commitments," that he is "not a refugee but a man called, not self-willed but obedient, not a lord but a sacrifice" (VI, 490). Yet what he is obeying, on his own admission, is something within, "which now demanded its rights." For the philosopher of *amor fati,* supreme service and supreme freedom are one and the same, but service not of mankind primarily, but *of the self.* The distinction is crucial. It is a curious and significant fact that Knecht has no real desire to serve Castalia outside the wall in the most useful possible way—by employing his great talents and experience in some important worldly function, or at least by managing a school. What he desires and is resolved to get is something highly idiosyncratic and indeed Romantic—"a human being who needs me" (VI, 441). Steppenwolfian nuances may be discerned when Knecht declines Magister Alexander's reasonable offer of unlimited leave of absence: "On the contrary what I desire is risk, impediment, and danger, I hunger for reality" (VI, 504)—"What I seek is not so much the satisfaction of a curiosity or a lust after worldly life, but rather the unconditional" (VI, 503).[120]

Knecht, one critic has remarked, tries to go the diverging ways of Narziss and Goldmund one after another, and fails twice.[121] He is indeed Narziss leaving Mariabronn, in search—no doubt—of his mother. The leap upward, the breakout, is suddenly itself regression and fall. That perfect musical blending of discipline and freedom which is the goal of the third line of the *vita* is no more realizable for Knecht than it was in *Narziss and Goldmund.* What dominates at the end, in the death, is after all the pattern of the mother. And yet not totally. As always, two antithetical elements are present. There is the portentous drive up into the high mountains, into an air much thinner than Castalia's, the air of the Immortals; it is a drive into a raw and stony landscape which reminds us once more of "The Steep Road." The leap with which the protagonist of

[120] Cf. Ch. 5, p. 201.
[121] Hans Mayer, *op. cit.,* p. 231.

"The Steep Road" follows his guide into the void is paralleled by Knecht's leap, following his pupil-teacher Tito, into the icy lake. Tito leaps not wholly out of enthusiasm; his face—twice described as masklike, and also as ageless—suddenly becomes childish, "like that of someone suddenly woken from a deep sleep" (VI, 541), as he seeks to escape the embarrassing situation in which he finds himself at the end of his dance: he is being observed by a superior mind, and such observation and reflection are quite alien to his pagan nature. If Joseph Knecht, the impenitent individualist, finds his death by water, finds that mother he has always sought, and if thus his *vita* reaches its all but inevitable, passionate end, Tito's dive into the lake is an escape from observation, from the unaccustomed separation of the I's within him, a conversion of a moment of reflection into action, into rapid animal motion. That the *coda* of such a reflective and didactic novel as *The Glass Bead Game* should have such poetic grandeur, should offer such a blaze of color and of movement, is an entirely consistent piece of irony.

Selected Bibliography

This list is restricted, first to secondary literature on Hermann Hesse, and second to other authors who are significantly quoted or paraphrased.

Bachofen, Johann Jakob. *Mutterrecht und Urreligion: Eine Auswahl.* Stuttgart, 1954.

Ball, Hugo. *Hermann Hesse: Sein Leben und Werk.* Zurich, 1947.

Baumer, Franz. "Das magische Denken in der Dichtung Hermann Hesses." Diss., Munich, 1951.

Baynes, Gary F., ed. *The I Ching, or Book of Changes.* (Bollingen Series XIX.) New York, 1950.

Bernoulli, Carl Albrecht. *Johann Jakob Bachofen und das Natursymbol.* Basel, 1924.

Böckmann, Paul. "Die Welt des Geistes in Hermann Hesses Dichten," *Sammlung,* III (1948), 215–233.

Boulby, Mark. *"Der vierte Lebenslauf* as a Key to *Das Glasperlenspiel," Modern Language Review,* LXI (1966), 635–646.

Bürger, Heinz Otto. *Die Gedankenwelt der grossen Schwaben.* Tübingen and Stuttgart, 1951.

Cohn, Hilde D. "The Symbolic End of Hermann Hesse's *Glasperlenspiel," Modern Language Quarterly,* XI, (1950), 347–357.

Dahrendorff, Malte. "Hermann Hesses *Demian."* Staatsexamensarbeit, Hamburg, 1953.

Deschner, Karl-Heinz. *Kitsch, Konvention und Kunst: Eine literarische Streitschrift.* Munich, 1958.

Deussen, Paul. *Sechzig Upanishad's des Veda.* 4th ed.; Darmstadt, 1963.

Farquharson, Robert H. "The Identity and Significance of Leo in Hesse's *Morgenlandfahrt*," *Monatshefte für deutschen Unterricht*, LV (1963), 122–128.

Gide, André. *Romans, Récits, et Soties.* Paris, 1958

——. *Le Voyage en Orient.* Paris, 1948. Preface by André Gide.

Gontrum, Peter B. "Oracle and Shrine: Hesse's 'Lebensbaum,'" *Monatshefte für deutschen Unterricht*, LVI (1964), 183–190.

Groothoff, Hans H. "Versuch einer Interpretation des Glasperlenspiels," *Hamburger Akademische Rundschau*, II (1947–1948), 269–279.

Halpert, Inge D. "The Alt-Musikmeister and Goethe," *Monatshefte für deutschen Unterricht*, LII (1960), 19–24.

——. "Hermann Hesse and Goethe." Diss., Columbia University, 1957.

Hauptmann, Gerhart. *Das Abenteuer meiner Jugend.* Berlin, 1937.

Hoffmann, E. T. A. *Das Kreislerbuch.* Leipzig, 1903.

Huch, Friedrich. *Mao.* Berlin, 1907.

Huizinga, Johann. *Homo Ludens.* Basel, 1949.

Jacobi, Jolande. *The Psychology of C. G. Jung.* New Haven, 1951.

Jung, Carl Gustav. *Psychological Types.* New York, 1933.

——. *Symbols of Transformation.* (*Collected Works*, V; Bollingen Series XX.) New York, 1956.

Kayser, Hans. *Akroasis: Die Lehre von der Harmonik der Welt.* Basel, 1946.

Kliemann, Horst, and Karl H. Silomon. *Hermann Hesse: Eine bibliographische Studie zum 2. Juli 1947.* Frankfort, 1947.

Kohlschmidt, Werner. "Meditationen über Hermann Hesses *Glasperlenspiel*," *Zeitwende*, XIX (1947–1948), 154–170, 217–226.

Kramer, Walter. "Hermann Hesses *Glasperlenspiel* und seine Stellung in der geistigen Situation unserer Zeit." Schriftenreihe der nordwestdeutschen Universitätengesellschaft, Wilhelmshaven, 1949.

Litt, Theodor. "Die Geschichte und das Übergeschichtliche," *Sammlung*, V (1950), 6–19.

Maier, Emanuel. "The Psychology of C. G. Jung in the Works of Hermann Hesse." Diss., New York University, 1956.

Mann, Thomas. "Hermann Hesse: Einleitung zu einer amerikanischen *Demian*-Ausgabe," *Neue Rundschau*, LVIII (1947), 248.

Matthias, Klaus L. "Die Musik bei Thomas Mann und Hermann Hesse." Diss., Kiel, 1956.

Matzig, Richard B. *Hermann Hesse in Montagnola*. Basel, 1947.

Mauerhofer, Hugo. *Die Introversion: Mit spezieller Berücksichtigung des Dichters Hermann Hesse*. Bern and Leipzig, 1929.

Mayer, Gerhard. "Hermann Hesse: Mystische Religiosität und dichterische Form," *Jahrbuch der deutschen Schillergesellschaft*, IV (1960), 434–462.

Mayer, Hans. "Hermann Hesse und das 'Feuilletonistische Zeitalter,'" in *Studien zur deutschen Literatur*. Berlin, 1954.

Middleton, J. C. "An Enigma Transfigured in Hermann Hesse's *Glasperlenspiel*," *German Life and Letters*, n.s., X (1956–1957), 298–302.

——. "Hermann Hesse as Humanist." Diss., Oxford University, 1954.

——. "Hermann Hesse's *Morgenlandfahrt*," *Germanic Review*, XXXII (1957), 299–310.

Mileck, Joseph. *Hermann Hesse and His Critics*. Chapel Hill, N.C., 1958.

——. "Names and the Creative Process," *Monatshefte für deutschen Unterricht*, LIII (1961), 167–180.

Negus, Kenneth. "On the Death of Josef Knecht in Hermann Hesse's *Glasperlenspiel*," *Monatshefte für deutschen Unterricht*, LIII (1961), 181–189.

Nietzsche, Friedrich. *Werke*. Ed. Karl Schlechta. Munich, 1954–1956.

Novalis. *Schriften*. Ed. Paul Kluckhohn and Richard Samuel. Leipzig, 1929.

Prabhavananda, Swami, and Christopher Isherwood. *Bhagavad-Gita*. London, 1948.

Rose, Ernst. *Faith from the Abyss*. New York, 1965.

Schiefer, Peter. "Grundstrukturen des Erzählens bei Hermann Hesse." Diss., Münster, 1959.

Schmid, Hans Rudolf. *Hermann Hesse.* Leipzig, 1928.

Schmid, Max. *Hermann Hesse: Weg und Wandlung.* Zurich, 1947.

Schöne, Albrecht. *Säkularisation als sprachbildende Kraft.* (Palaestra, no. 226.) Göttingen, 1958.

v. Schröder, Leopold. *Indiens Literatur und Kultur in historischer Entwicklung.* Leipzig, 1887.

Schwarz, Egon. "Zur Erklärung von Hesses *Steppenwolf*," *Monatshefte für deutschen Unterricht,* LIII (1961), 191–198.

Seidlin, Oskar. "Hermann Hesses *Glasperlenspiel*," *Die Wandlung,* III, pt. 1 (1948), 298–308.

Stekel, Wilhelm. *Die Sprache des Traumes.* Wiesbaden, 1911.

Strauss, Emil. *Freund Hein.* 9th ed.; Berlin, 1905.

Wackenroder, Wilhelm H. *Herzensergiessungen eines kunstliebenden Klosterbruders.* Ed. Gillies. Oxford, 1948.

Waibler, Helmut. *Hermann Hesse: Eine Bibliographie.* Bern and Munich, 1962.

Wasserscheid, Rosemarie. "Die Gestaltung der Landschaft in Hermann Hesses Prosadichtung." Staatsexamensarbeit, Cologne, 1951.

Weibel, Kurt. *Hermann Hesse und die deutsche Romantik.* Diss., Bern; Winterthur, 1954.

Wrase, Siegfried. "Erläuterungen zu Hermann Hesses *Morgenlandfahrt*." Diss., Tübingen, 1959.

Ziolkowski, Theodore J. "Hermann Hesse and Novalis." Diss., Yale University, 1957.

——. "Hermann Hesse's *Steppenwolf:* A Sonata in Prose," *Modern Language Quarterly,* XIX (1958), 115–133.

——. *The Novels of Hermann Hesse.* Princeton, 1965.

General Index

Plato, 203, 239; academies, 151; Platonism in *The Steppenwolf*, 199, 203, 204; theory of art, 228
Political attitudes in Hesse, 82
Pool, motif of, 5, 7, 229, 289
Prabhavananda, Swami, 106
Pre-existence, 115, 126
Pre-Raphaelitism, 4, 19, 107
Preyer, Wilhelm, 40
Principium individuationis, 84, 131, 137
Prodigal Son, motif of, 69, 91-92, 103, 104, 141, 149, 168, 169, 187, 225, 235, 255, 316
Profligate: motif of, 103, 168, 201, 232; and Pietist, 164; and saint, 176, 186, 235
Prometheus, 104
Protestantism, 68, 122; churches, Hesse's attitude to, 67-68
Proust, Marcel, 209
Psalms, 110, 132
Psychoanalysis, 8, 76, 84-88, 208, 219; and dreamer, 98; effect on Hesse, 102, 112
Psychoanalytic criticism, 88, 102, 127; of *Demian*, 115
Purcell, Henry, 295, 298
Pythagoreans, the, 270

Rank, Otto, 87
Ratiocination, 51, 96, 118
Realism, 52, 134, 214-216; in school novel, 55
"Recurrent puberty," 191, 311
Reflective element: in character of Demian, 98; in Hesse, 2, 3, 7, 13, 18, 33, 36, 37, 43, 59, 98, 120, 124, 128, 150, 157, 163, 165, 203-204, 211, 242, 256, 268, 276, 299, 307, 309, 321; and memory, 88
Reincarnation, motif of, 264, 267, 312
Religious impulse in Hesse, 83, 156, 211
Rembrandt, 192
Repetition, 132, 133
Richter, J. P., 24, 52, 56, 72, 86, 87, 165, 172, 201, 204
Rig-Veda, 100
Rilke, R. M., 267
Rimbaud, Arthur, 49
River as symbol, 128, 142, 148, 150, 218
Rolland, Romain, 82, 132, 192
Romanticism, 4, 5, 207; aggression, 177; agony, 3, 49; allegiance in

Peter Camenzind, 34; atmosphere, 26; and *Beneath the Wheel*, 49; composers, 7, 160; cosmos-hatred, 25; emotion in *Peter Camenzind*, 33; epigone, 11, 18, 209, 249; experience, 72, 113; Germans, 8, 113, 283; in *The Glass Bead Game*, 299, 320; heritage in early Hesse, 79; imagery, 35, 218; imagination, 114; Indians, 122; individualism, 292; irony, 4, 201; language, 150, 185; late Romantics, 197, new, 210; mode of composition, 260; mysticism, 17; narrative art, 204; pastiche, 77, 127; pessimism, 231, 241; Peter Camenzind, 33; pilgrimage of H. H., 247; Pistorius, 114; poetic diction, 1; poetry, Hesse's attitude to, 57; pose, 11; prototype, 77; of style, 118; subjectivism, 17; theories of the self, 86; theory of literature, 272; tradition, 122, 133, 225, in *Peter Camenzind*, 34, and schools, 49; view of music, 161; writers, 5
Rose, Ernst, 107, 166
Rosicrucian symbolism, 250
Rousseau, J. J., 209, 212, 259, 282; Rousseauism, 11, 171
Ruskin, John, 12, 36

Sabatier, Paul, 35
Sainthood, 117, 216, 307; and Joseph Knecht, 317; and music, 164
Saints, 8, 78, 103, 131, 134, 136, 149, 164, 172, 180, 186, 187, 193, 201, 205, 209, 212, 233, 239, 241, 279, 282, 306, 316; and artist, 212, 306; and outsider, 171, 277; and profligate, 176, 235; and senses, 176
Samadhi, 205
Sankhya, the, 137
Satan, 105; *see also* Devil, the
Satire, 20, 30, 42, 45, 52, 178, 268; function, 66; novel, 44, 48
Scheffel, J. V. von, 89
Schiefer, Peter, 97, 164, 235, 242
Schiller, J. F. von, 21, 87, 270; aesthetics, 7; belief, 75
Schizoid personalities, 188
Schizophrenia, 54, 144, 167, 179, 196; projection, 56; and Romantic art, 56
Schlaf, Johannes, 152
Schlegel, Friedrich and A. W., 121, 161

Index of Hesse's Works